New SUPER MARIO BROS.®

The Official Nintendo Player's Guide

Table of Contents

Introduction

World 1

World 2

World 3

World 4

World 5

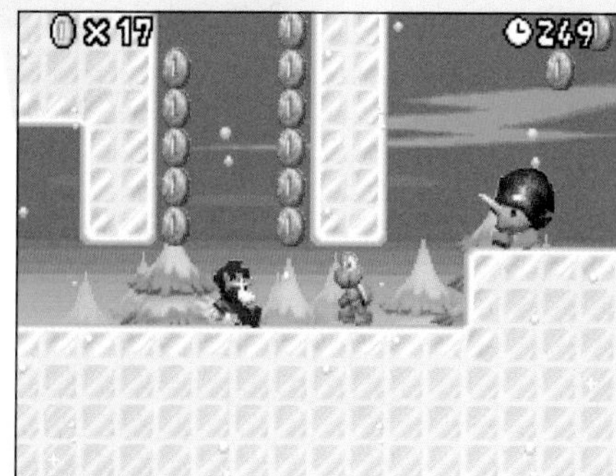

World 6

World 7

World 8

Multiplayer & Minigames

Plumber Power to the Rescue!

Princess Peach has been kidnapped (again!) and only Mario can save her (again)! To rescue the princess, the mustachioed plumber will need to traverse perilous plains, deadly deserts, slippery slopes, lethal lava, and much more. Many obstacles and enemies stand in Mario's way, but with this guide at your side, you'll be able to thwart Bowser, get the girl, and still be home in time for some piping-hot lasagna.

Controls

The basic controls of New Super Mario Bros. should be familiar to fans of the series, but the dual screens of the Nintendo DS add an interesting twist.

Top Screen

The top screen is where the majority of the action takes place. You'll also find a tally of Mario's collected coins and a clock displaying your remaining time in the upper corners of the screen. On the world map, the top screen also displays your current level, accumulated Star Coins, and reserve item.

Bottom Screen

The lower screen displays the score, your remaining lives, a diagram of your progress, and the Star Coins you've found in the current level. If you have an item in reserve, you can tap its icon to drop it at Mario's current position. When Mario is on the world map, the lower screen displays a route map of the current world and a diagram of all eight game worlds. Once you've visited a world, you can revisit it any time by tapping its icon.

Pipes to the Underworld

Whenever you enter a pipe that connects to an underground area, the action will shift to the lower screen. Since you can no longer touch your reserve item, you won't be able to use it in these areas.

Select Button

Select is not used in this game.

Start Button

Press the Start Button to pause or unpause the game. While it's paused, you can abandon your progress and return to the world map (if you've completed the level previously), access the options screen, or quit the game and return to the main menu. Once you've beaten the game, you'll be able to press Start to save on the world map.

L & R Buttons

The L and R Buttons scroll the game screen left and right, respectively, allowing you to see what you're getting into without making blind jumps. This is possible both in game levels and on the world map.

Control Pad

Press left or right on the Control Pad to move Mario in that direction or to modulate the distance of your jumps. Press up to open doors, enter overhead pipes, and climb vines or other objects. Press down to crouch, descend when climbing, or enter pipes underfoot.

Menu-Screen Options

When you start your game you'll find four options on the lower screen. Navigate the menu with the Control Pad and the A Button, or simply tap your desired selection with a finger or the stylus.

Mario Game

Select Mario Game to play the main single-player game. You'll go to the file-select screen where you can select, copy, or erase one of three saved game files.

Mario vs. Luigi (See pg. 120 for more information)

Compete wirelessly against a friend in a special multiplayer game in which Mario and Luigi race to see who can collect the most stars.

Minigames (See pg. 122 for more information)

Play one of 18 bonus minigames (divided into four categories) by yourself or via LAN with up to three other players.

Options

Change the sound settings to Stereo, Surround, or Headphones, and switch your button control style.

Button Control Styles

There are only two button functions during gameplay—jump and dash. Each is mapped to two buttons, and by switching the control style, you're sure to find a pairing that feels comfortable.

Control Style 1

X Button: Dash
Y Button: Dash
A Button: Jump
B Button: Jump

Control Style 2

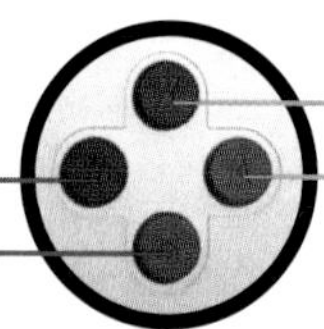

X Button: Jump
Y Button: Dash
A Button: Jump
B Button: Dash

Navigating Menu Screens

The A and B Buttons are also used to make selections on menu screens. Press the A Button to move forward through menus or confirm selections. Press the B Button to move backward through menus or to cancel selections.

Basic Moves

Like any skilled plumber, Mario has mastered the arts of Goomba-stomping, platform-hopping, and Koopa shell-kicking. Here's a quick refresher course for nontradesmen.

Jumping and Attacking

Despite his girth, Mario is quite nimble. You can leap wide gaps and land with precise accuracy by pressing left or right to vary the distance in midair. You can jump slightly farther and higher if you're dashing, or by pressing both the run and jump buttons together to do a long jump. But beware—the farther you jump, the farther you'll skid when you land.

Attack from Above

Jumping on top of certain enemies will damage or destroy them. You can chain a series of stomp attacks by bouncing from foe to foe, and you'll rack up points and earn extra lives for the trouble! However, some foes are invulnerable to stomp attacks and will damage you instead.

Attack from Below

When you jump into a block above you, you'll knock free any coins or items hidden within it, and also damage any foes standing on that block. If you're Super Mario or any other large version of Mario, your strength may shatter the block completely.

Dashing

To run faster, hold the dash button down while moving left or right. This will let you traverse long distances quickly and provide a running start for longer jumps.

Crouching

Press down on the Control Pad to crouch, allowing Super Mario (and other large versions) to duck under enemies and squeeze through tight spots.

Throwing Shells

Some foes can be used as weapons. For example, Koopas retreat into their shells when stomped, and you can pick them up by holding the dash button. Release the button to throw the shell at foes or kick it into items such as Star Coins to claim them from a distance.

Swimming

Mario can hold his breath indefinitely underwater, and is a more-than-capable swimmer. Dodge enemies and hit blocks by pressing the jump button to do a quick paddle that propels Mario upward. But beware: you can't damage foes underwater unless you're Fire Mario.

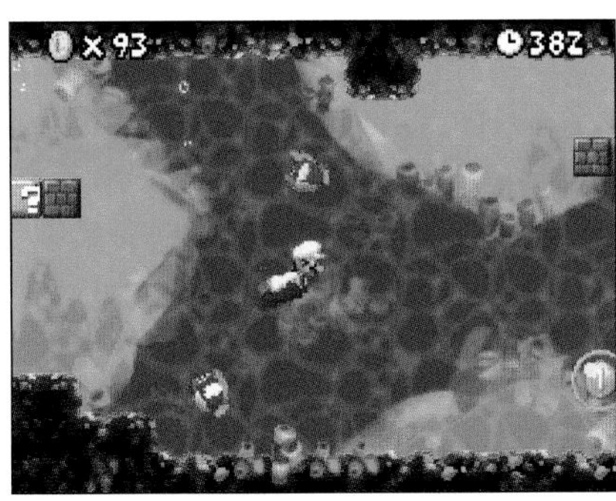

Climbing and Swinging

You can have Mario climb objects such as vines and fences by pressing up or down in front of them. You can leap onto loose-hanging ropes and poles in the same manner, and pressing left and right will then start them swinging. Jump at the apex of their arc to leap a great distance.

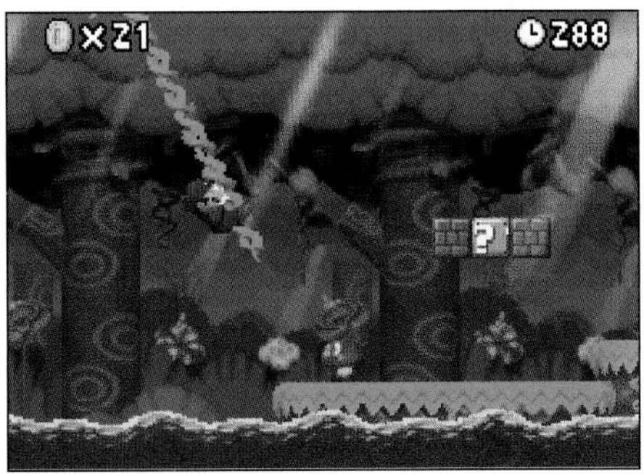

Advanced Moves

Mario has learned a lot of tricks in the last 25 years, and now has a wide repertoire of advanced moves to use in his quest to save Princess Peach from Bowser Jr.

Wall Jump

Mario can jump against a wall then rebound off of it when you press toward the wall with the Control Pad and jump again. Once you master the timing, you can use Wall Jumps to save yourself from falling, or Wall-Jump repeatedly to reach high areas.

Crouch Slide

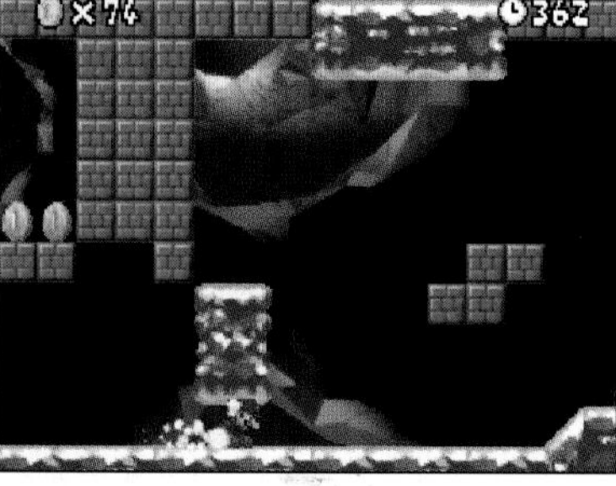

Super Mario is too big to fit into small gaps, so he'll need to use a crouch slide to squeeze through. Start a slide by either dashing then pressing down, or jumping when crouching and pressing down and toward the gap.

Triple Jump

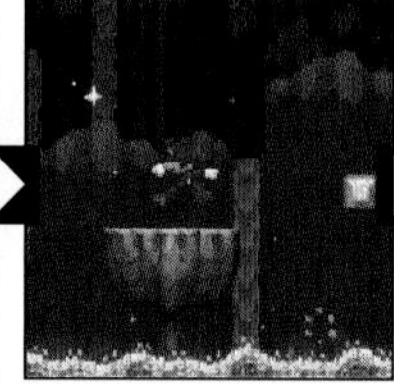

If you dash at maximum power and jump three consecutive times (starting each new jump the instant you land), you'll perform a special triple jump that culminates in a long-distance somersault.

Ground Pound

Jump up and press down to land hard on a block or enemy. This attack does double damage to enemies and can be used to break blocks below you and liberate their items. The Ground Pound will continue for as long as you hold the Control Pad down; you can smash through a column of blocks or knock all the loot from a Coin Block.

Incline Slide

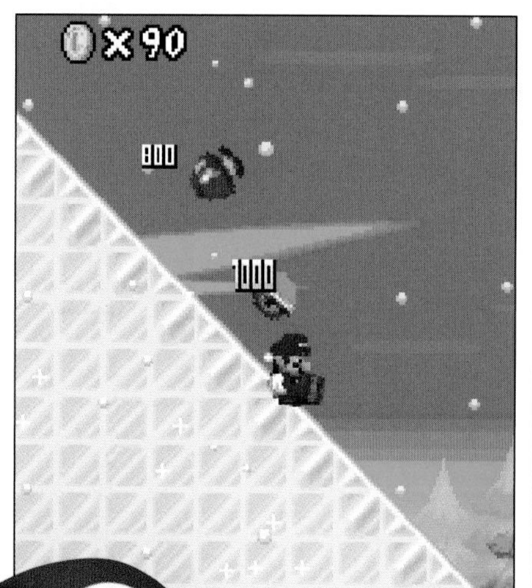

Crouch on an incline to perform a slide that damages all foes in your path (but some can still hurt you!). You can dash before you crouch to gather a little more speed, or jump at the end of your slide to perform a special high jump.

Wall Slide

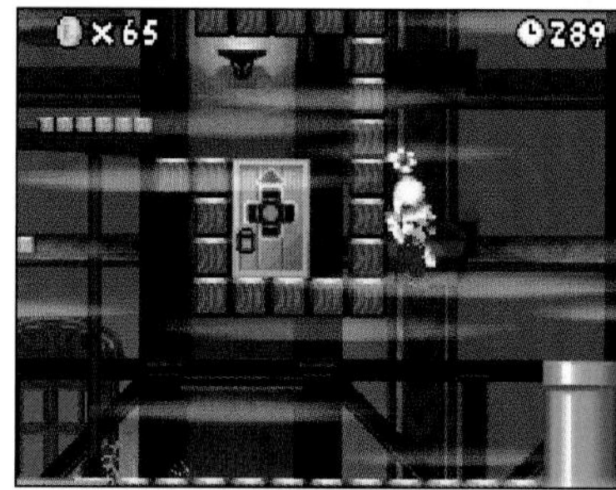

While falling, you can slow yourself by sliding along a wall and holding the Control Pad in the wall's direction. This will also leave you poised to perform a Wall Jump with a tap of the jump button.

Gap Dash

No need to jump across every little gap in the floor. As long as you're running, Mario will dash right over gaps that are one block's-width or less.

Mario's Suits

Grab power-ups to change Mario into different forms with different abilities. Being the right Mario at the right time is the key to unlocking many of the game's secrets.

Super Mario

When you grab a Super Mushroom, Mario will transform into Super Mario. Super Mario can smash blocks from above (with a Ground Pound), or below (with a fist), and reverts to standard Mario instead of dying when hit.

Mega Mario

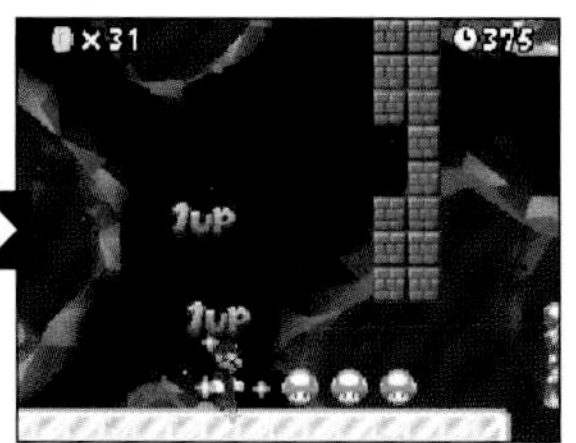

Rare Mega Mushrooms transform Mario into a giant who is nearly impervious to harm and capable of destroying nearly everything in his path. The more havoc you cause, the more points and 1-Ups you'll earn when the effect wears off. Sadly, Mario will revert to Super Mario after only a short time.

Fire Mario

Fire Flowers transform Mario into Fire Mario, who can throw bouncing fireballs across the screen with the dash button. When you're hit in this form, you'll revert to Super Mario.

Shell Mario

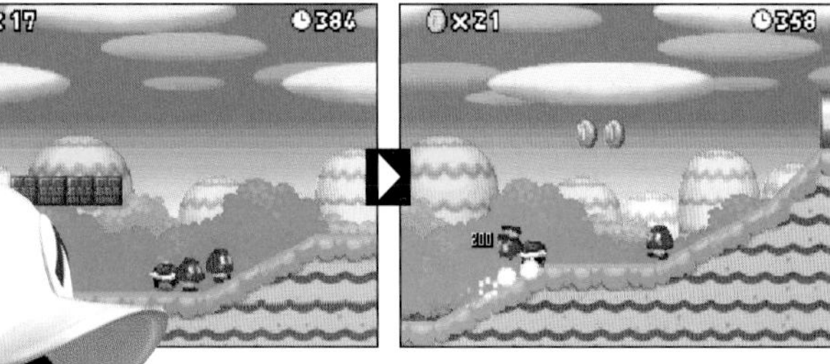

The blue Koopa shell puts a shell on Mario's back. You'll tuck into it whenever you reach a full dash, making you impervious to most enemies. But this suit isn't merely defensive—if you get a running start before you crouch, your spinning shell will destroy enemies and blocks just like a thrown Koopa shell!

Mini Mario

Grab the Mini Mushroom to shrink to a flea-sized Mini Mario who can fit into tight spaces, bounce on enemies' backs, dash across water, and glide for great distances after long jumps or Wall Jumps. Mini Mario's stomp attack doesn't hurt most enemies, but he can damage foes and blocks with the Ground Pound. You'll need to be Mini Mario to reach certain areas (including the entrances to Worlds 4 and 7), but move carefully—Mini Mario is very vulnerable and will perish after a single hit.

Items & Power-Ups

Every level of New Super Mario Bros. is packed with strange blocks, switches, and power-ups. Most will be familiar to fans, but a few are making their series debut.

Super Mushroom

Mario's most basic power-up doubles his size and grants him the strength to smash through blocks. It also allows him to survive a single enemy hit.

Starman

The Starman makes Mario invincible temporarily, allowing him to defeat foes by running right through them. Some Starmen come in "chains" in which certain ? Blocks will contain new Starmen if you already have one.

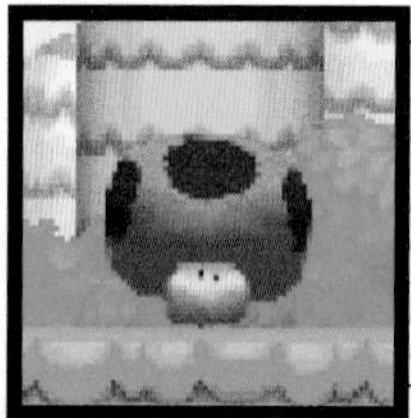

Mega Mushroom

This rare item swells Mario to enormous size. Use it to crush obstacles and enemies in your path, and earn 1-Up Mushrooms based on the amount of carnage you cause.

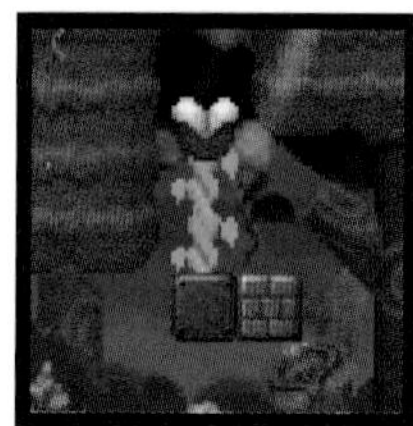

Vine

Some blocks conceal Vines that lead to hidden areas. A vine will grow away from where the block is hit, so you'll almost always want to hit Vine Blocks from below. Vines can't grow through other blocks—clear a path first!

Mini Mushroom

The Mini Mushroom shrinks Mario, granting him the ability to squeeze into tight places, hop on enemies, run and walk on water, and glide horizontally after jumps.

Gold and Blue Coins

Collect coins on your travels; you'll earn a 1-Up whenever you accumulate 100 of them. Some coins are out in the open, whereas others are concealed in blocks.

1-Up Mushroom

Green 1-Up Mushrooms grant Mario an extra life, and are often well-hidden in invisible or nondescript blocks. You can also earn them from Mega Mario rampages or red-coin rings.

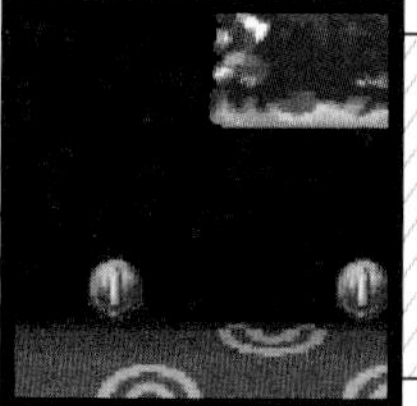

Red Coins

These are the red coins generated by the red-coin ring. Collect them within the time limit to earn a prize.

Blue Koopa Shell

The blue Koopa shell gives Mario a shell on his back, allowing him to dodge enemies by ducking into the shell to jump while running, and to smash through foes and blocks like a kicked Koopa shell.

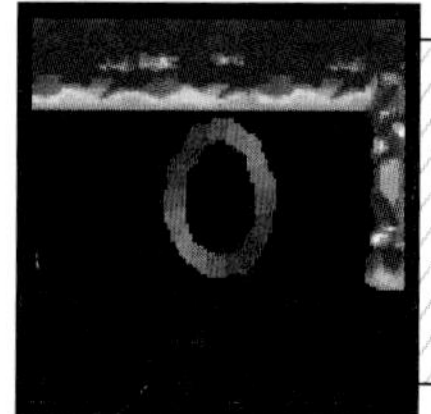

Red-Coin Ring

When you jump through a red-coin ring, eight red coins will appear. If you can collect all eight within the time limit, a power-up (or a 1-Up Mushroom if you're already maxed-out as Fire Mario) will drop from above you.

Fire Flower

The Fire Flower transforms Mario into Fire Mario, allowing him to throw fireballs that bounce along the ground and can damage or destroy most foes.

Star Coins

Three Star Coins are hidden within each level. Once found, they go into your inventory and can be used to buy passage through Star Coin signs, and to purchase wallpapers. Finding all of the Star Coins is the game's ultimate challenge.

? Block

These mystery blocks may contain coins or power-ups—usually the Super Mushroom or, if you're already Super Mario, the Fire Flower. ? Blocks with items inside are usually found at the beginning of levels and after checkpoints.

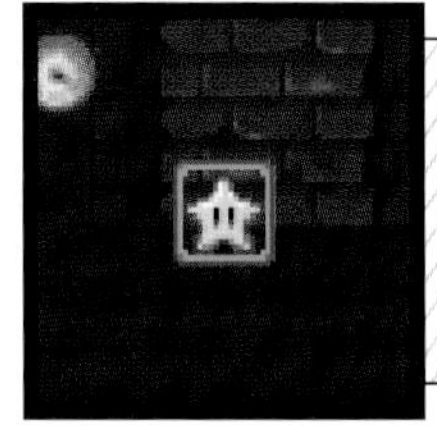

Roulette Block

These cycle between various items, such as a Super Mushroom, Fire Flower, blue Koopa shell, Mini Mushroom, and Starman. You'll get whatever item is displayed when you hit the block, so time your move carefully!

Invisible Block

Some blocks can't be seen, but will appear when Mario hits them from below. Some contain items (particularly 1-Up Mushrooms), and others serve as steps to reach higher areas.

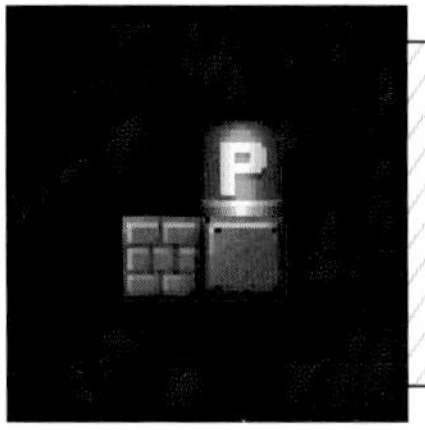

P Switch

P Switches transform coins into blocks, and blocks into coins, allowing you to earn lots of coins quickly and possibly reach new areas by traveling on platforms that used to be coins. The effect lasts for only a limited time, however.

Coin Block

Coin Blocks look like regular blocks, but contain multiple coins and possibly a Super Mushroom. Hit them with a Ground Pound and hold down on the Control Pad to drain their coins easily.

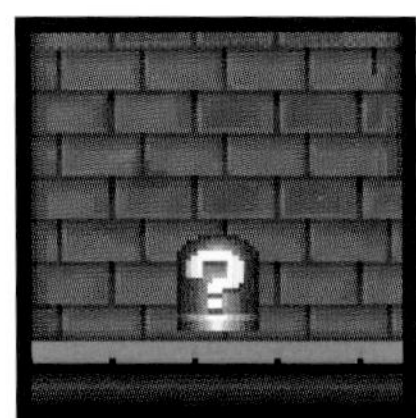

? Switch

You won't know what a ? Switch does until you hit it. It may raise the water level, transform the ground beneath you, or make platforms appear. Using ? Switches carefully is the key to beating many levels.

Winged ? Block

Yellow winged ? Blocks are a part of the level; red ones travel the world map to give you a boost at certain times. You can hit winged blocks for items, ride them to distant parts of a level, or use them as stepping-stones.

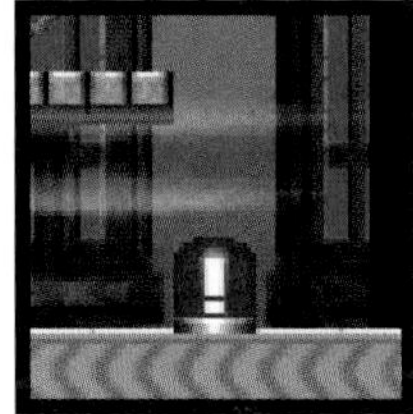

! Switch

Whenever you see white block outlines, you know there's an ! Switch nearby. Find and stomp it to make solid red blocks appear from the outlines.

Toad-House Items

In addition to finding items in levels, you can discover them in Toad houses on the world maps. Toad-house items go straight into your reserve slot if the item in reserve isn't as good as the new item. Once you've taken an item, the Toad house will disappear. But if you leap onto an end-of-level flagpole when the last two digits of the countdown timer are the same (like 22, 33, etc., but not 00), you'll see fireworks, and a new Toad house may appear! See page 128.

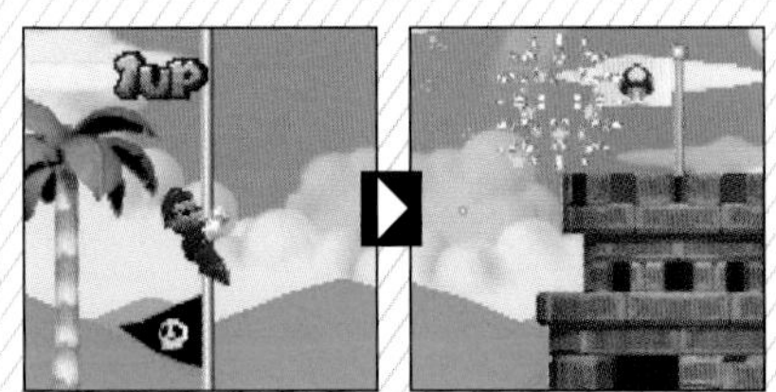

Reserve Items

When you take a power-up that's the same as or inferior to your current one (for example, you take a Super Mushroom as Fire Mario), it will automatically go to the reserve-item slot on the touch screen. Even if you die, you won't lose the item.

By using your reserve-item slot carefully, you can be Fire Mario for most of the game. Play an easy level to turn into Fire Mario, then put another Fire Flower in your reserve slot. Then, when you die and continue, use your reserve Fire Flower before you hit a ? Block that contains a power-up. Since you're already Fire Mario, it will give you a Fire Flower for your reserve slot instead of a Super Mushroom.

Enemies

The eight worlds of New Super Mario Bros. are crawling with vicious critters. Take the time to learn each creature's weaknesses before your journey begins.

The Goomba Gang

Goombas are some of Mario's most common foes, and are the easiest to defeat. You can stomp them, shoot them with fireballs, or do an incline slide into them. Paragoombas will take an extra stomp to defeat—the first hit merely knocks off their wings. Mini Goombas are among the few enemies that Mini Mario can kill with a stomp attack.

Goomba

Paragoomba

Mini Goomba

Koopa Troopers

Koopas may be Mario's most frequent adversaries, but they'll prove to be an asset nearly as often as they're a threat. One stomp will send a Koopa cowering into its shell, which you can then pick up (by holding the dash button) or throw (by releasing the dash button) to slide it at other foes, or into blocks or Star Coins. Koopa Paratroopas require an extra hit to destroy their wings, and can often be used to bounce onto otherwise-inaccessible platforms.

Green Koopa

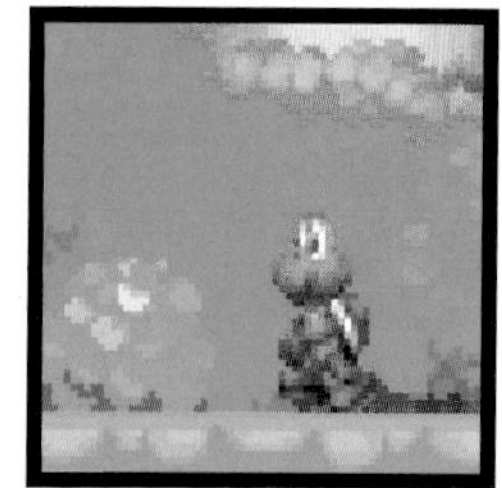

Green Koopa Paratroopa

Red Koopa

Red Koopa Paratroopa

Cadaverous Koopas

Even in death, Koopas cannot escape the urge to harass Mario. Dry Bones can be disabled with a stomp, and Super Dry Bones with a Ground Pound, but the effect is temporary—they'll return to life (or rather, undeath) a few seconds later. Only Mega Mario, Shell Mario, and the spiked balls in certain levels can destroy them permanently.

Dry Bones

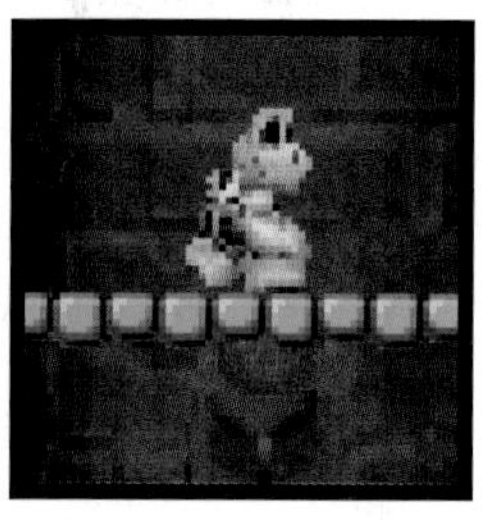

Super Dry Bones

Ballistic Ballistae

You can stomp individual Bullet Bills easily, but they rarely travel alone. Rather than trying to defeat the Bullet Bills, you should dash out of range, or seek safety by ducking under them or leaping atop the cannons that fire them. Larger Banzai Bills are harder to jump onto, but they, too, will collapse with a single stomp.

Bullet Bill (Cannon A)

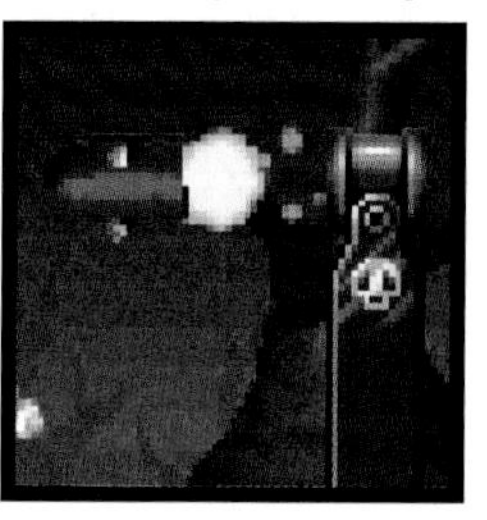

Bullet Bill (Cannon B)

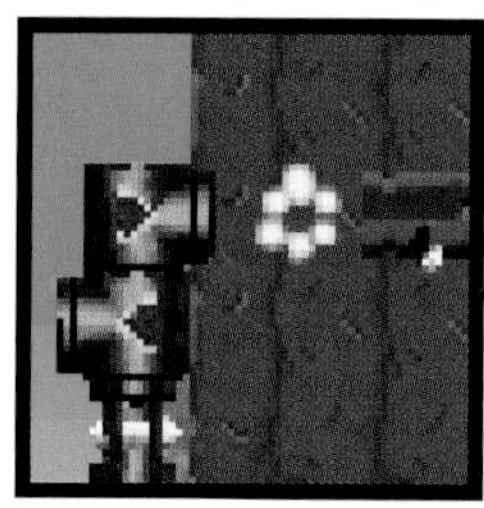

Banzai Bill

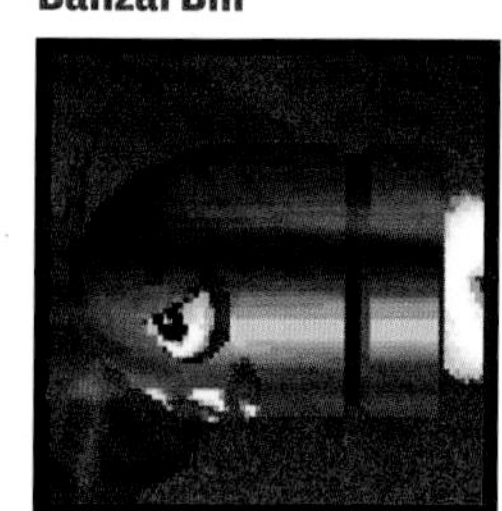

Tumbling Terrors

Thwomps of all sizes rise and fall in a perpetual attempt to crush Mario. They're clever, waiting until Mario is near before they fall. You'll usually have to time these foes' movements carefully to avoid them, but you can destroy them if you get your hands on a blue Koopa shell, a Mega Mushroom, or a Starman. Additionally, you can Ground-Pound Whomps to destroy them after they topple.

Thwomp Trap

Super Thwomp

Whomp

Aerial Irritants

These winged beasties don't appear often, but they can be a major pain when they do. Both Swoops and Crowbers wait until Mario approaches, then they swoop down to attack. (Additionally, Crowbers often circle above Mario before they strike.) They'll get in the way if you're trying to perform any tricky jumping maneuvers, so lure them out of hiding first and destroy them with stomp attacks or fireballs.

Swoop

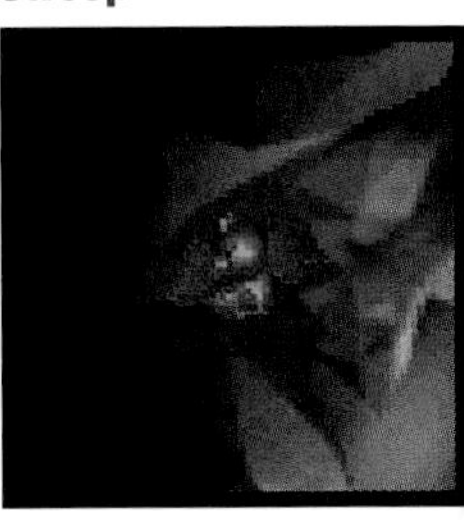

Crowber

Ghost-House Inhabitants

These enemies all haunt ghost houses, but they don't have much else in common. Boos and Balloon Boos are immune to nearly all attacks, but will freeze in their tracks when Mario looks their direction (Balloon Boos will hold their breath, swelling to massive size). Broozers are vulnerable to fireballs and stomp attacks, but don't be too eager to kill them—if you're clever, you can trick them into destroying all sorts of obstacles that block Mario's progress. Splunkins are similar to Goombas, but they take two hits to defeat.

Boo

Balloon Boo

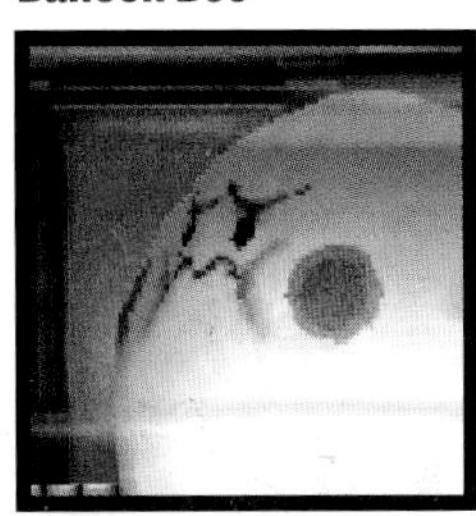

Broozer

Splunkin

Prickly Predator

You can blast away any segment of a Pokey by using a fireball, but only a shot to the head will defeat the creature.

Pokey

Critter Kabobs

Jumping on Wigglers will only make them angry, but they aren't aggressive and don't usually need to be defeated. When you do need to get one out of the way, hit it with a Koopa shell. Squigglers aren't so tough—a stomp or a fireball will do the trick.

Wiggler

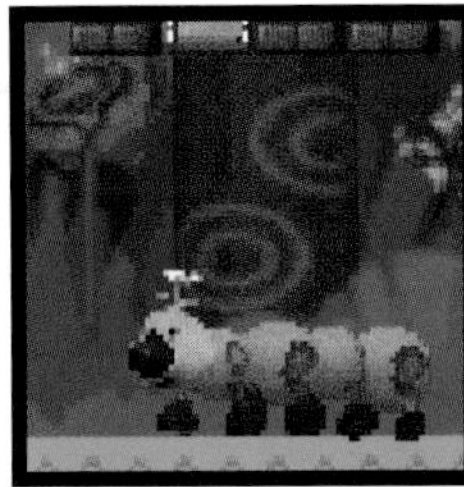

Squiggler

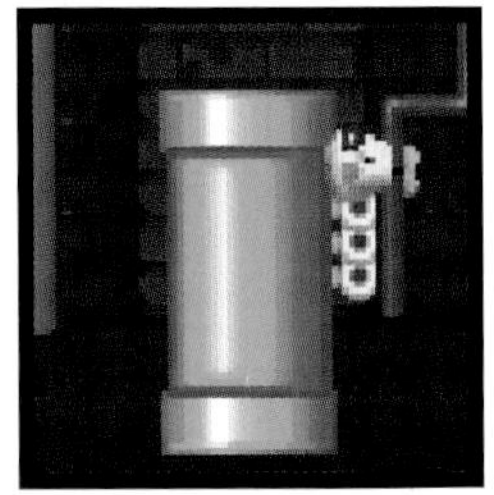

Short-Fused Shufflers

Damaging these foes will light their fuses, and the resulting explosions can destroy all sorts of obstacles. Bob-ombs are the more docile variety, and you can pick them up when their fuses are lit and throw them at foes or barriers. Kab-ombs can't be picked up, and they run around frantically before they explode.

Bob-omb

Kab-omb

Beastly Beetles

These sticky-footed critters can walk up vertical blocks and even upside down on ceilings. Buzzy Beetles can be beaten with stomp attacks, and their shells can be thrown like Koopas. We don't recommend stomping Spike Tops or Spinys—you'll need to hit the blocks they're walking on. Spinys curl into floating balls when they get wet, making them a threat in water as well as on land.

Buzzy Beetle

Spike Top

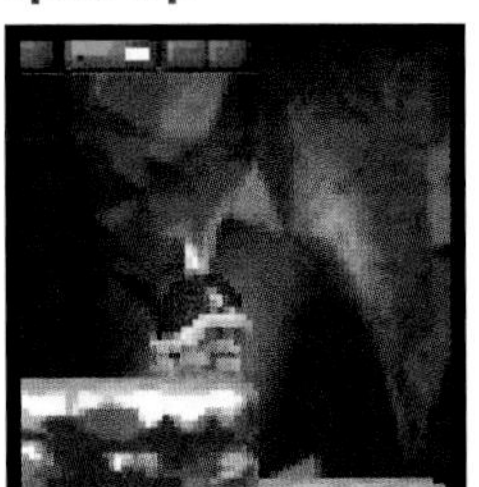

Spiny

Sizzling Serpent

Fire Snakes pursue Mario doggedly, and are immune to most of his attacks. You can destroy them with Shell Mario, a Starman, or a thrown Koopa shell, but it's usually easier simply to slip beneath them.

Fire Snake

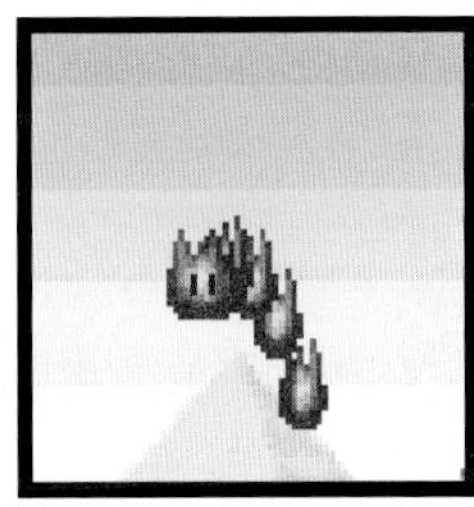

Scuttling Scofflaw

Scuttlebugs drop from the sky on thin webs. In early worlds they'll keep hanging, but in later worlds they may cut the strings to drop onto Mario. Any standard attack will destroy them, but if you let them live you may be able to use them as steps from which to bounce to higher areas.

Scuttlebug

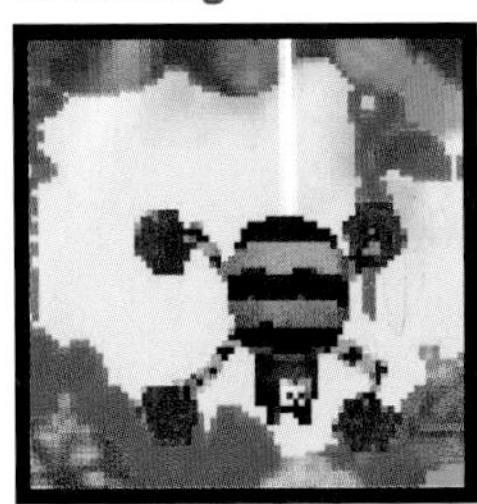

Piscine Perils

Mario is particularly vulnerable underwater, since he has limited mobility and can't stomp the foes beneath him. All of the foes in this section are vulnerable to Fire Mario's fireballs, but other Mario forms should focus on evasion. Cheep-Cheeps are easy to dodge, since they're oblivious to your presence, but Cheep-Chomps and Deep-Cheeps will actively pursue you. Only Cheep-Chomps can turn around, though; the others will give up the chase if you get behind them.

Cheep-Cheep

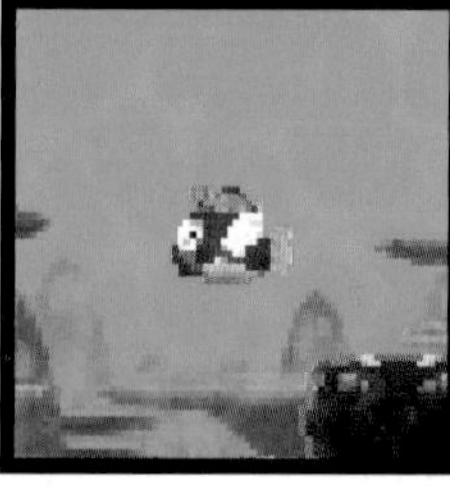

Mega Cheep-Cheep

Deep-Cheep

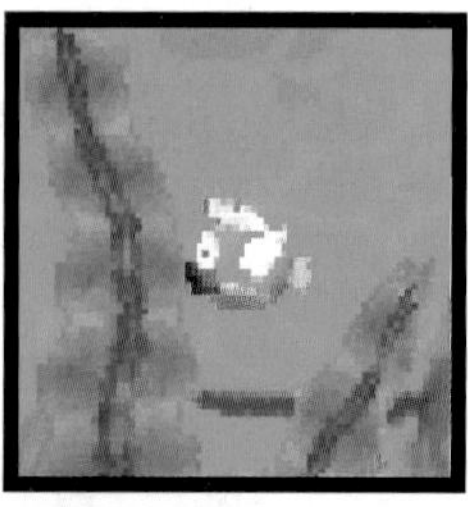

Mega Deep-Cheep

Cheep-Chomp

Blooper

Nautical Nightmares

Sushi swim straight ahead, and although they won't pursue you actively, it will take some nimble swimming to weave through their schools. Most Unagi can't leave their holes, but they'll snap at you if you get too close. If they're guarding an item, swim slightly above or below them to provoke a snap, then grab the item when they retract. Giant Unagi are indestructible and consume everything in their path, so the choices are simple: flee or die!

Sushi

Unagi

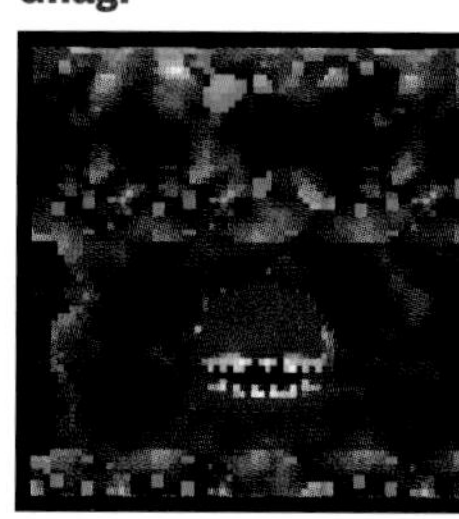

Mega Unagi

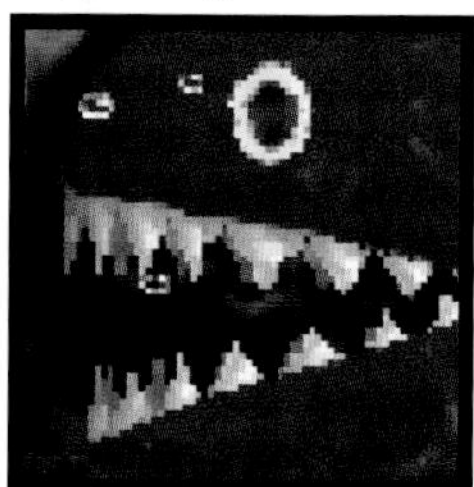

Brothers-at-Arms

You won't encounter Hammer Bros. and Boomerang Bros. often within levels, but the Hammer Bros. wander some world maps and will attack you if you enter the level they've wandered to. As with even rarer Fire Bros. and Sumo Bros., the easiest way to win is to let them throw their weapons, then jump on their heads or punch the block they're standing on from below. Sumo Bros. are the most dangerous of the bunch, because they have a Ground Pound-like attack that can stun Mario if he's nearby, and break the blocks beneath them.

Hammer Bro

Boomerang Bro

Fire Bro

Sumo Bro

Snow Foes

These two enemies appear exclusively in icy levels. Snow Spikes can be beaten with a stomp or a fireball, but Snailicorns are impervious to most attacks. Push them off a ledge or toss a Koopa shell to defeat them.

Snow Spike

Snailicorn

Amphibious Antagonists

These foes patrol the surface of the water. Skeeters will try to drop bombs on Mario as he swims beneath them, and Spike Bass will leap from the water to attack Mario when he's near the surface. Skeeters are quite vulnerable from above, and are easy to stomp, but you'll need a fireball or a Koopa shell to destroy a Spike Bass.

Skeeter

Spike Bass

Trundling Traps

These spiked balls have been placed throughout Bowser Jr.'s towers and castles. You can't damage them (unless you're Mega Mario, of course)—you'll need to rely on skilled jumping to survive. At times they may even come in handy, rolling over block obstacles and Dry Bones to clear the way for you.

Spiked Ball

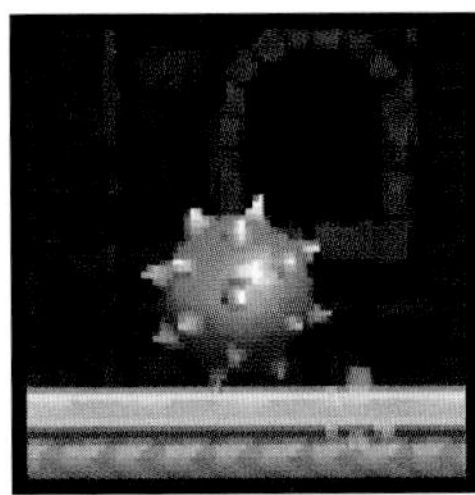

Giant Spiked Ball

Scourge of the Skies

Lakitus zip through the skies, tossing Spinys at Mario. If you can catch a Lakitu, you can stomp it from above. But if you hit it with a projectile instead (such as a fireball or thrown Spiny), it'll die and leave its cloud behind. You can then use the cloud to fly until it fades away.

Lakitu

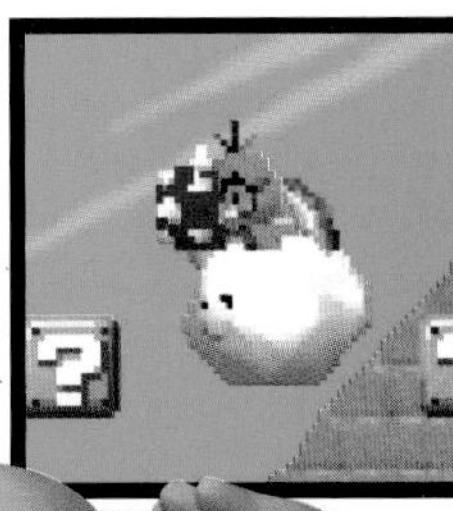

Bulbous Beasties

Chain Chomps and Amps are stuck in place and are best avoided. It's never necessary, but you can get rid of a Chain Chomp by Ground-Pounding its post three times after the Chomp lunges and misses. Distantly related Flame Chomps are vulnerable to fireballs and even stomp attacks (provided you don't touch the flames). Amps, however, are effectively indestructible.

Chain Chomp

Amp

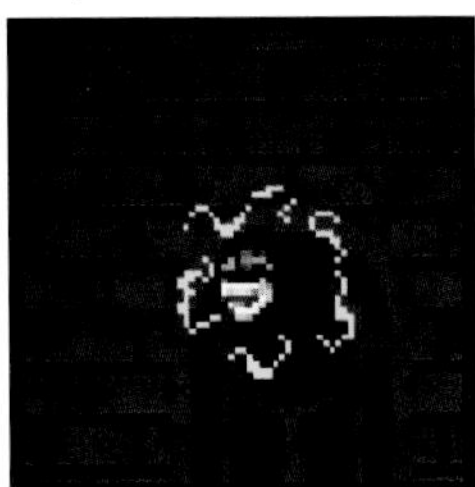

Flame Chomp

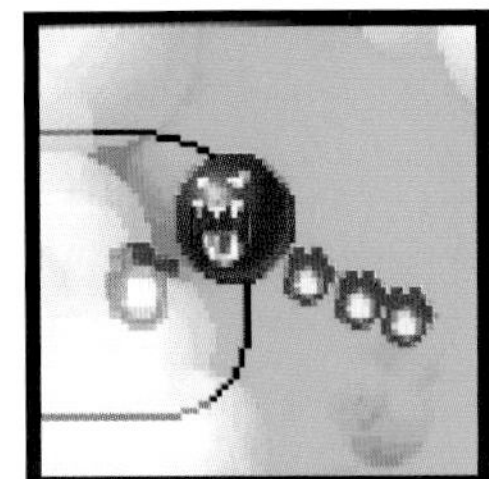

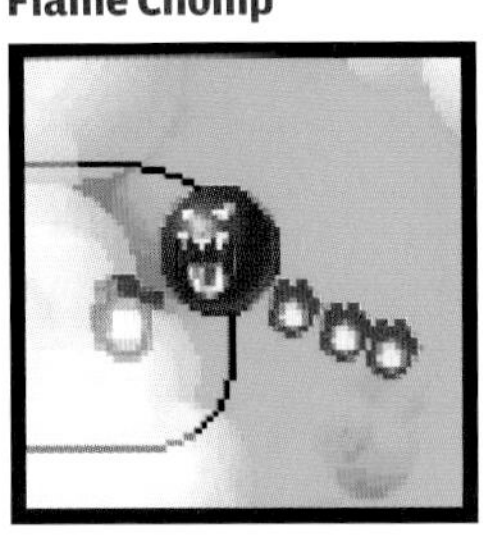

Floral Horrors

Most of the creatures in the Piranha Plant family live in pipes, from which they will pop out and retract at regular intervals if Mario is near. Some even shoot fireballs. You'll usually need to use carefully timed movements to get past them or into their pipes, but you can destroy them with projectiles like fireballs and Koopa shells.

Piranha Plant

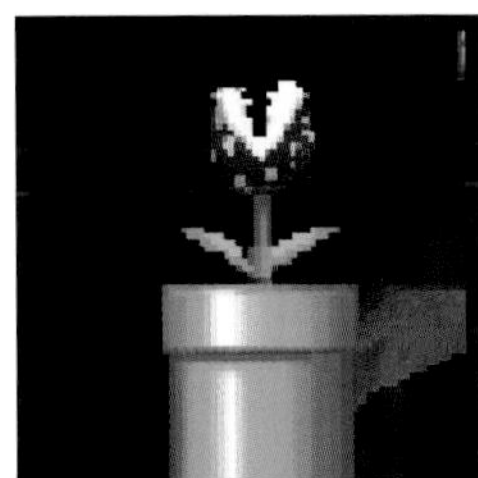

Venus Fire Trap

Super Piranha Plant

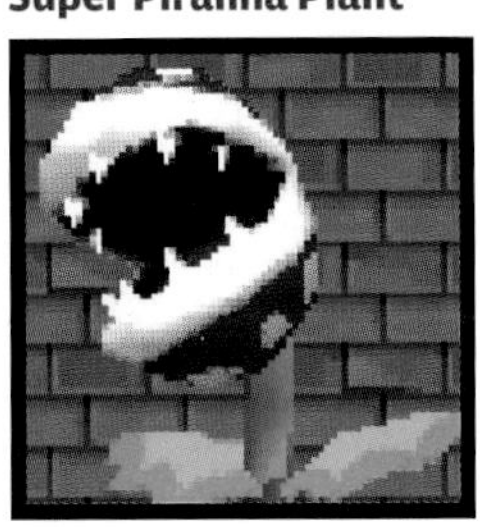

The Block Impostors

Blockhoppers pretend to be ? Blocks, usually at the bottom of a stack of regular blocks, but will leap at you when you approach them. You can stand safely on their heads and Ground-Pound them, or leap from their tops to higher platforms. They may be faking, but they hold coins at least, and some hold items like real ? Blocks do.

Blockhopper

Cowardly Coin Purse

Moneybags are rare but potentially lucrative enemies. They're vulnerable to most conventional attacks, but will try to flee by running through pit areas in hopes that you'll fall. Moneybags spit out a coin each time you hit them, and if you can hit them repeatedly, they'll drop a 1-Up Mushroom.

Moneybags

World Bosses

Each world ends at a castle that is guarded by Bowser or one of his minions. Typically, the bosses are superpowered versions of normal foes, and most take three direct stomp attacks to defeat.

Mummipokey

Most Pokeys are a little, well, pokey. But this mummified Pokey moves quickly, digging into the ground and popping out to attack from below. Get above him by using Wall Jumps, and stomp or Ground-Pound his head to inflict damage.

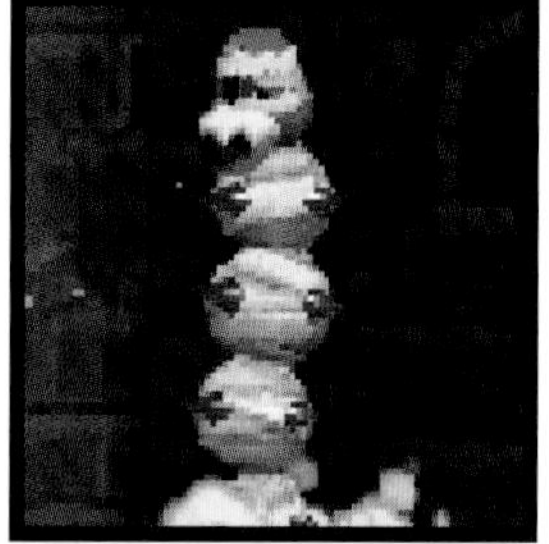

Cheepskipper

The Cheepskipper lets its Cheep-Cheep henchmen do much of the dirty work, but will eventually flop onto dry land and attempt to skid into Mario. You can then damage it with jumps or Ground Pounds.

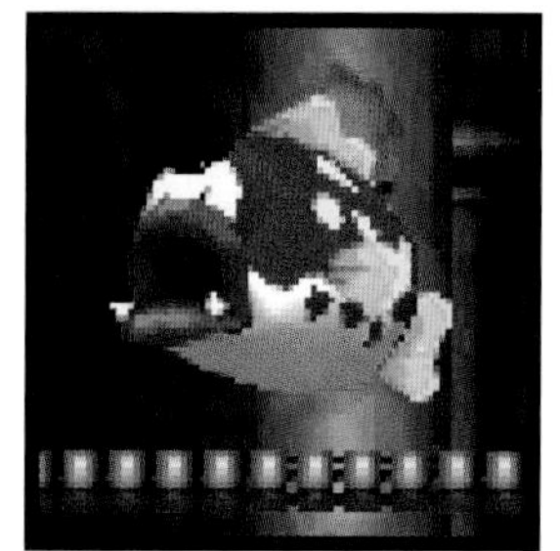

Mega Goomba

Looks like a Goomba got into the Mega Mushrooms! Regular stomps won't cut it this time, but you can Ground-Pound the Mega Goomba by leaping from rising platforms or using Wall Jumps.

Petey Piranha

Dash under Petey Piranha as he flies around the room, attempting to damage you with his own Ground Pounds. After Petey Ground-Pounds and misses, he'll fall on his back, giving you a chance to stomp or Ground-Pound his head or belly for damage.

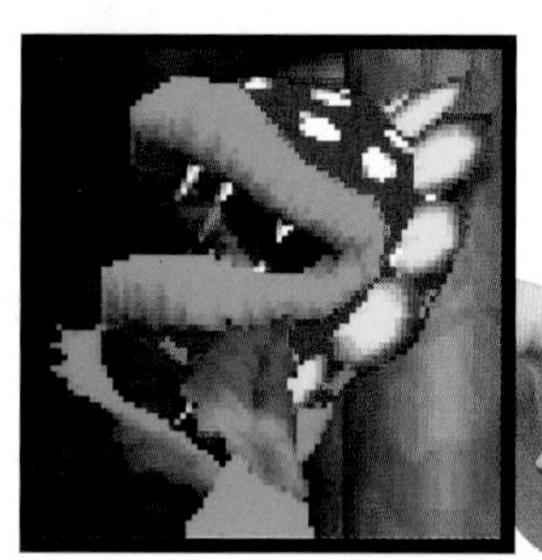

Monty Tank

Monty Tank's war machine grows an extra turret each time you hit him, allowing it to fire more Bullet Bills and putting Monty farther out of reach. Leap from the turrets to stomp him, or pick up Bob-ombs and throw them to cause damage.

Lakithunder

This Lakitu throws the usual Spinys, and can also blast Mario with lightning bolts from its special storm cloud. There's no way to get above it when it's high in the sky, but it will dive down at you from time to time, giving you a chance at a stomp attack.

Bowser Jr.

Bowser Jr. will appear to battle you at the end of every tower. Each fight is a little different, but he typically relies on two basic moves: tossing Koopa shells, and curling into his own spiky shell and sliding at Mario. To damage him, you'll usually need to stomp his head, or kick the Koopa shells back to knock him over and provide a chance to stomp his prone body.

Bowser

You'll always face down Bowser old-school-style. Instead of dealing damage, your goal is simply to get over or under the mighty Koopa and stomp the skull switch behind him. Doing so will destroy the bridge and end the fight.

The World Map

You can take many paths to reach the castle at the end of each world. Toad houses, extra levels, and hidden paths will allow you to make the routes your own.

Level Color-Coding

Each level is marked with a colored dot that shows its current status. Here's what the colors mean:

Locked Level

Black-dot levels are locked, either because you haven't beaten the levels before it, or you haven't yet found a route to it.

Unlocked Level

Red dots mean you've managed to reach the level, but haven't beaten it yet.

Completed Level

When you beat a level, its dot color will change to blue. Once that happens, you can proceed past the level, or reenter it at any time.

Star-Coin Count

This counter shows the number of Star Coins Mario holds. The number will decrease as you use them to clear Star Coin signs.

World Number

This area displays the name of the current world. If you've found every Star Coin in every level of the world, a Star Coin icon will appear next to the level name.

World Schematic

This is a simplified version of the current world map. It shows the entire world, not merely the part near Mario. You can use it to track the movement of Flying ? Blocks. It also provides clues as to which levels contain alternate routes; if there's no path connecting a distant level to the route map, you've missed an alternate exit.

Flying ? Block Location

Mario's Location

Tower Location

Castle Location

Level Information

Here you'll see the name of the current level and how many of its Star Coins you've collected. If a coin is flashing, it means you've reached a checkpoint but have not yet beaten the level to claim it.

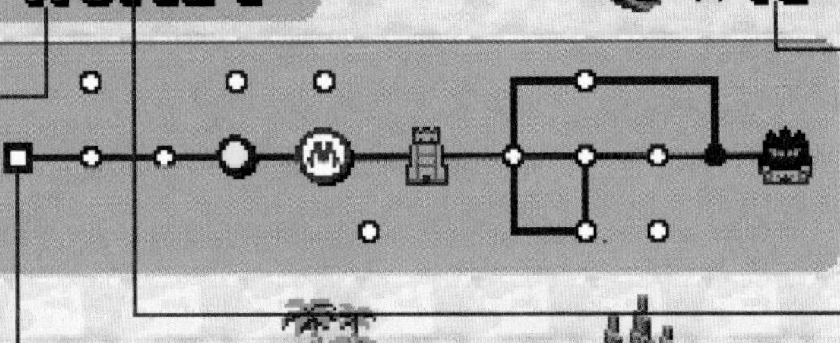

All Worlds Schematic

This diagram shows the game's eight worlds. You can return to any world you've visited by tapping its icon. To reach the lower-tier worlds (4 and 7) you'll need to beat the bosses of worlds 2 and 5, respectively, as Mini Mario. Worlds 4 and 7 are much tougher than upper-tier worlds!

Flying ? Blocks

Red Flying ? Blocks travel around the world, moving each time you beat a level, lose a life, or choose Return to Map from a previously defeated level. If you enter a level where a Flying ? Block is, you'll find the block waiting on the first screen. Hit it for a power-up to start the level off right.

Power-Up Reserve Slot

If you have a power-up in reserve, it will appear here. Touch it in a level to drop it onto Mario's position.

Remaining Lives

The upper-right corner of the touch screen shows the number of extra lives you have available. You can accumulate a maximum of 99 lives.

Hammer Bros.

Like the red Flying ? Blocks, Hammer Bros. roam some world maps. When you enter a level where they are, they'll challenge you to a fight, usually on the first screen of the level. Defeat them to earn a power-up.

Special Levels

In addition to the normal numbered levels and the hidden numbered-and-lettered levels, Mario will encounter three special level types on his journey.

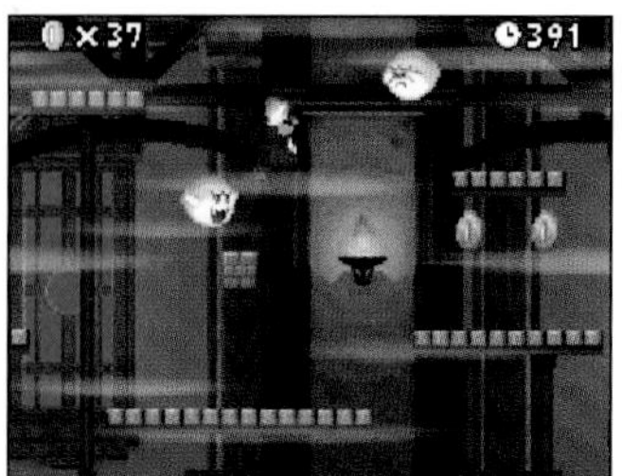

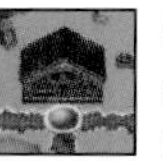

Ghost House

Ghost houses are strange mazes full of special enemies. Unlike other levels, they have no automap and no checkpoint from which to continue. Ghost houses often have well-hidden alternate exits that lead to warp cannons.

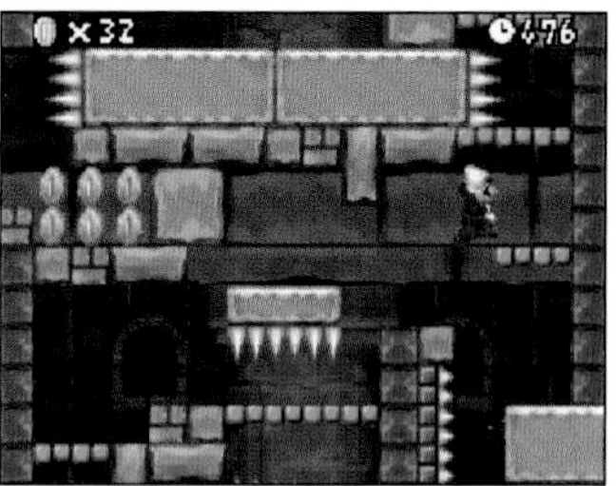

Tower

Bowser Jr. has established at least one tower in each world. These are typically vertically scrolling levels that are light on enemies but heavy on traps. At the end, you'll battle Bowser Jr. When you clear a tower, you'll have the opportunity to save your game.

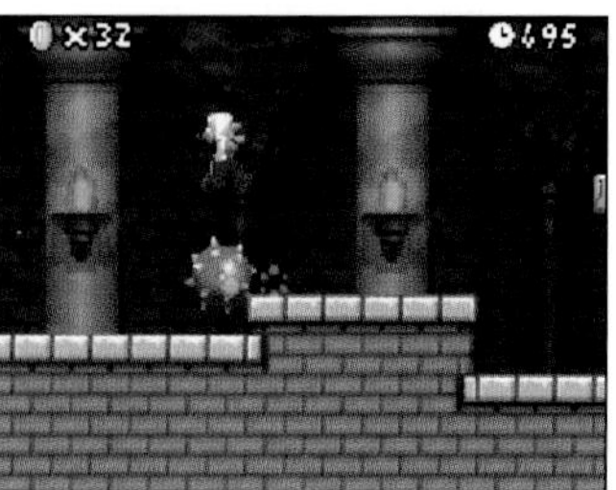

Castle

Castles are the trap-filled final levels of each world, and are often quite difficult to beat. At the end of each castle you'll fight a boss, and if you win you'll move on to the next world and have a chance to save your game.

Getting Around Quickly

Though you'll surely want to challenge every level eventually, no one will blame you for wanting to skip ahead and rescue Princess Peach as quickly as possible. By finding alternate exits in levels, you can zip through the game.

Pipes

Pipes are found in pairs, and allow you to move quickly from one part of a world to another, skipping over several levels.

Warp Cannons

Warp cannons allow you to skip entire worlds. For this reason, warp-cannon exits are among the game's best-hidden secrets.

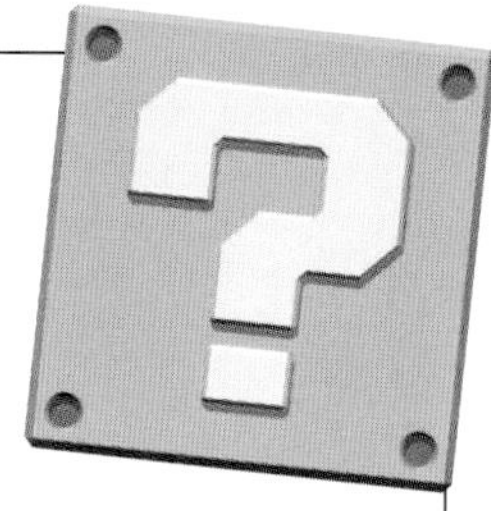

Toad Houses

Each world has several Toad houses you can visit to gain power-ups or earn 1-Up Mushrooms. To reach them, you'll usually need to find an alternate exit out of a level or pay Star Coins to clear a signpost. Each Toad house will disappear after you leave, so save them for when you need them. For more detail, see p. 128.

Red Toad House

In red Toad houses, you'll be given a chance to hit a giant Roulette Block that cycles between a Super Mushroom, a Fire Flower, a blue Koopa shell, and a Mini Mushroom. The item you win will go straight to your reserve slot.

Green Toad House

In green Toad houses, you play a game in which you hit blocks to reveal 1-Up Mushrooms. The game will end when you reveal the hidden Bowser card, and your accumulated prizes will fall to the floor. It's best to visit green Toad houses after you save your game so you can reset and try again if you get an unlucky break.

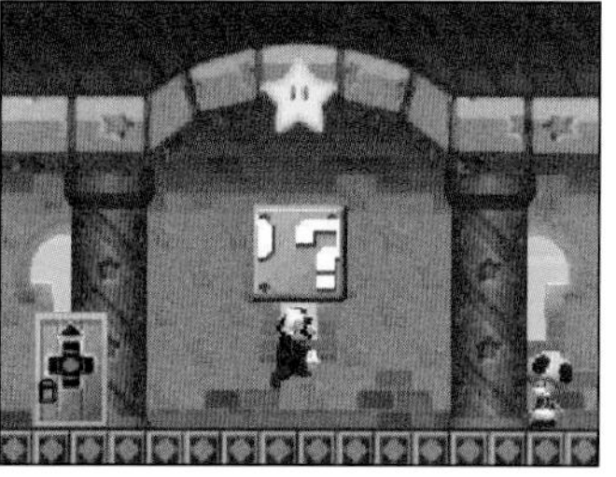

Orange Toad House

Orange Toad houses are like red Toad houses, but the prize is always the same: a Mega Mushroom. You can eat your Mega Mushroom in block- or pipe-filled levels to score 1-Ups, or save it to tear through a level that you're having trouble beating.

Saving Your Game

You can save your game only when you beat a tower or castle for the first time, or when you clear a Star Coin sign. Don't waste Star Coin signs by clearing them just because you have the coins—save a few for when you need to save your game. After you beat the game once, you'll earn the right to save at any time from the options menu.

Walk-through Map Key

The single-player walk-through maps are labeled with locations of useful items. Please note that we've assumed you'll be entering each level as standard Mario, so the first ? Block power-up is listed as a Super Mushroom, and later ones are shown as Fire Flowers. However, block contents will vary depending on your Mario version.

Super Mushroom	Mini Mushroom	Red Coin	Platform Switch
Fire Flower	Blue Koopa Shell	Star Coin	Vine
1-Up	Roulette Block	! Switch	Spring Block
Starman	Coin	P Switch	
Mega Mushroom	Coin Block	? Switch	

World 1

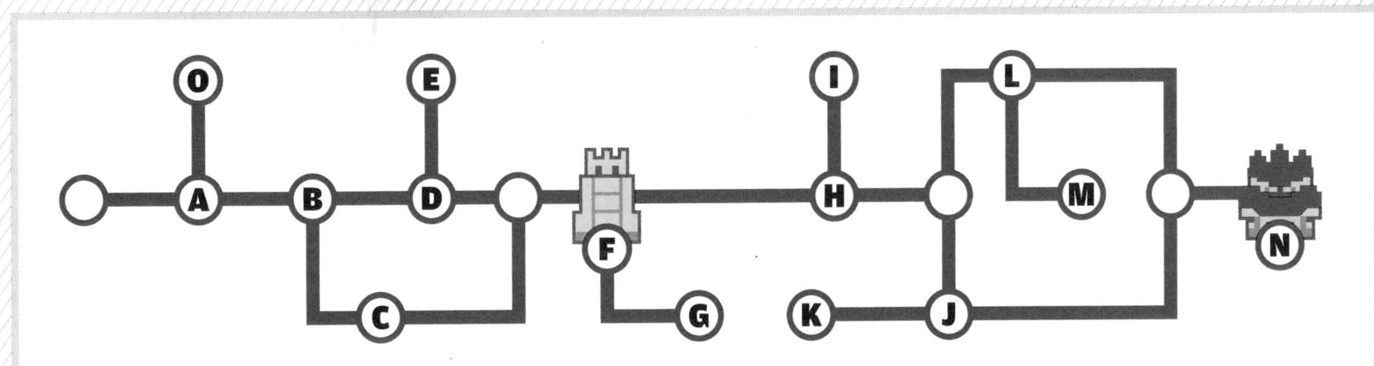

(A) World 1-1 (Page 18)
(Page 18)

(B) World 1-2 (Page 19)

(C) Red Toad House

(D) World 1-3 (Page 20)

(E) Green Toad House (5 Star Coins)

(F) World 1 Tower (Page 21)

(G) Warp Cannon (To World 5)

(H) World 1-4 (Page 22)

(I) Orange Toad House (5 Star Coins)

(J) World 1-A (5 Star Coins/Page 23)

(K) Red Toad House

(L) World 1-5 (Page 24)

(M) Green Toad House (5 Star Coins)

(N) World 1-Castle (Page 26)

(O) Blue Toad House (See Page 128)

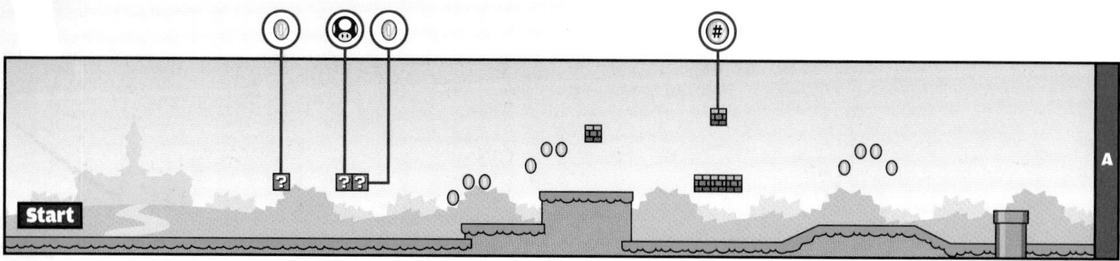

1 The Mega Mushroom transforms Mario into an impervious behemoth who obliterates every enemy or obstacle in his path. The damage you cause will earn you 1-Ups, but if you destroy everything you won't be able to climb the vines or enter the pipe at point B. You can always come back and do them next time.

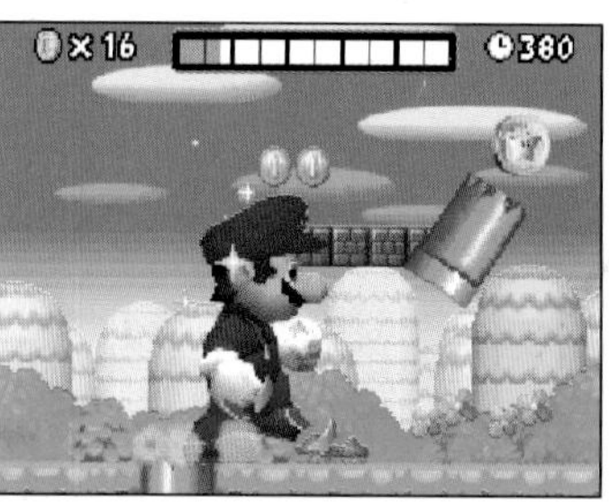

2 Red-Coin Heaven

Hit the Invisible Blocks from below, and jump from them to hit a block that sends a vine into the clouds. Climb to the heavens, where you can jump through a red-coin ring to reveal eight red coins—grab them all within a few seconds to earn an item.

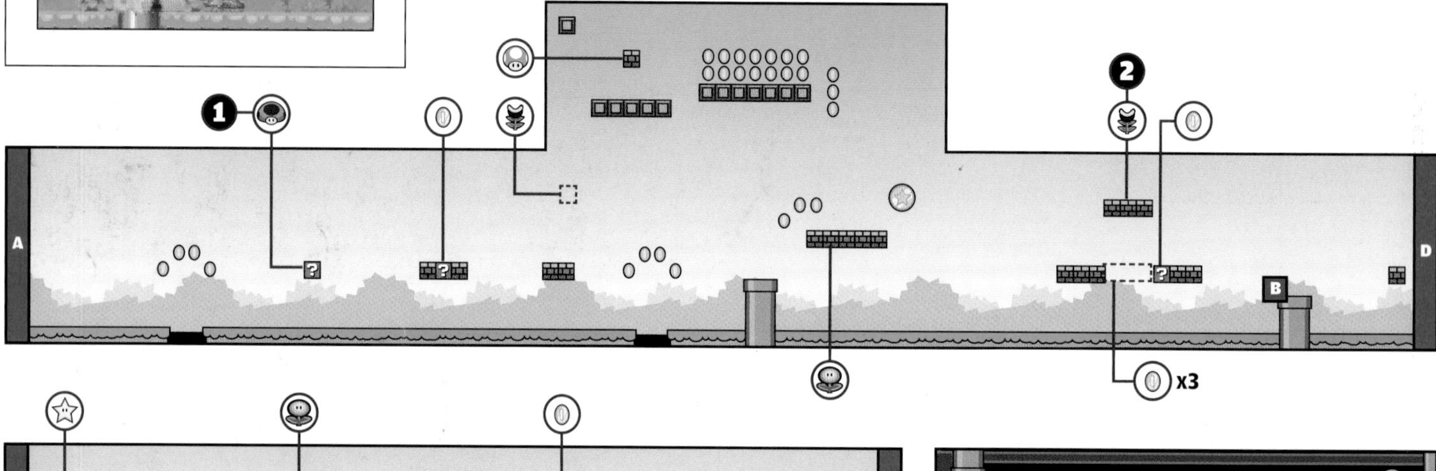

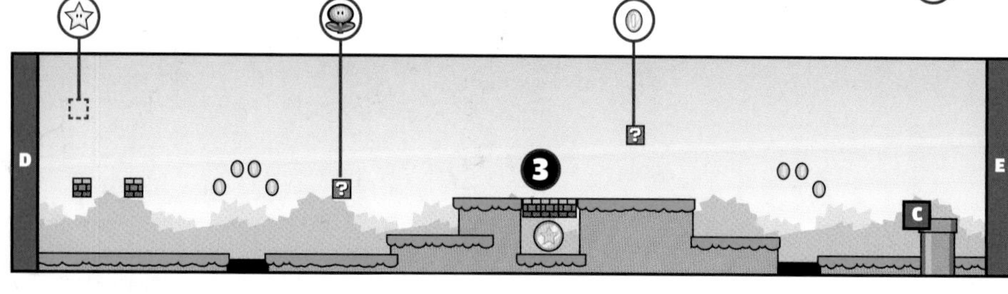

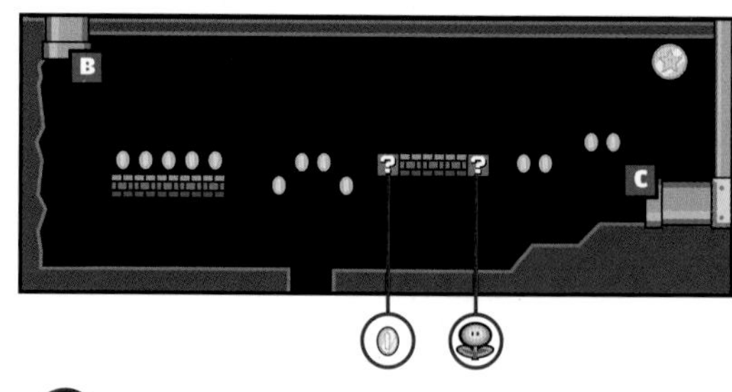

3 To get the final Star Coin, use a Ground Pound (jump and press down) as any large version of Mario. Mega Mario can smash through with a normal jump, but it will break your 1-Up-earnin' momentum.

World 1-2

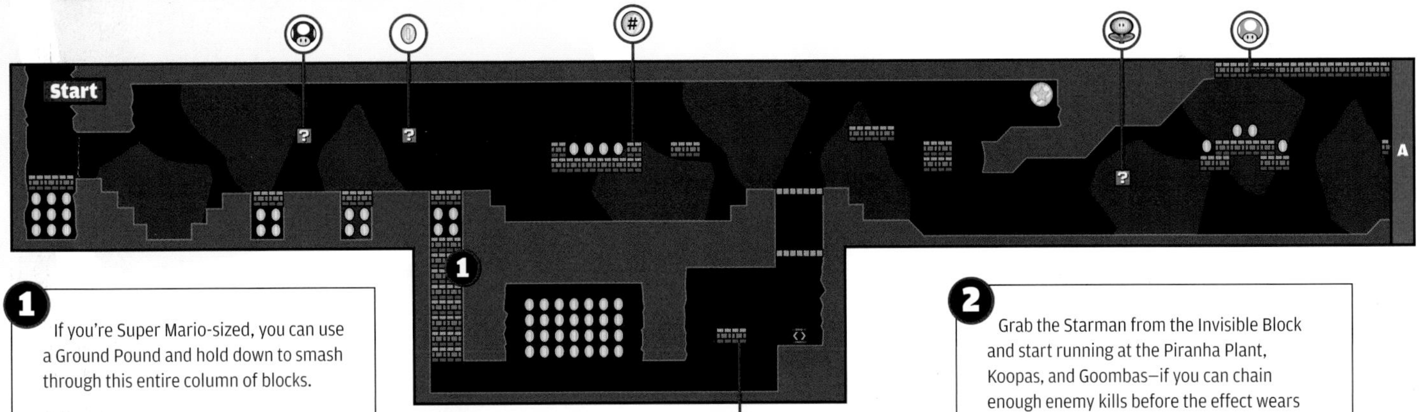

Start

1 If you're Super Mario-sized, you can use a Ground Pound and hold down to smash through this entire column of blocks.

2 Grab the Starman from the Invisible Block and start running at the Piranha Plant, Koopas, and Goombas—if you can chain enough enemy kills before the effect wears off, you'll earn a 1-Up.

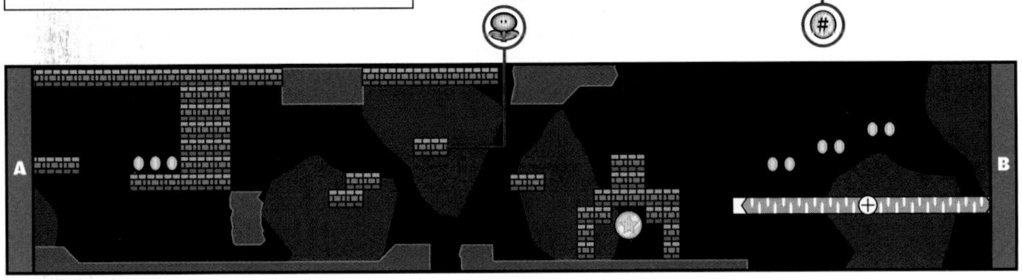

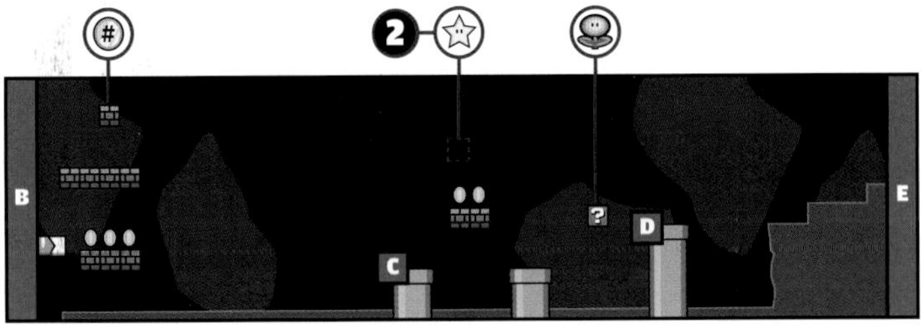

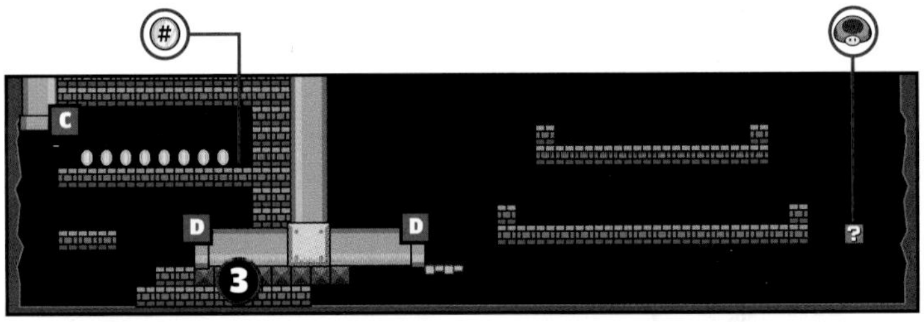

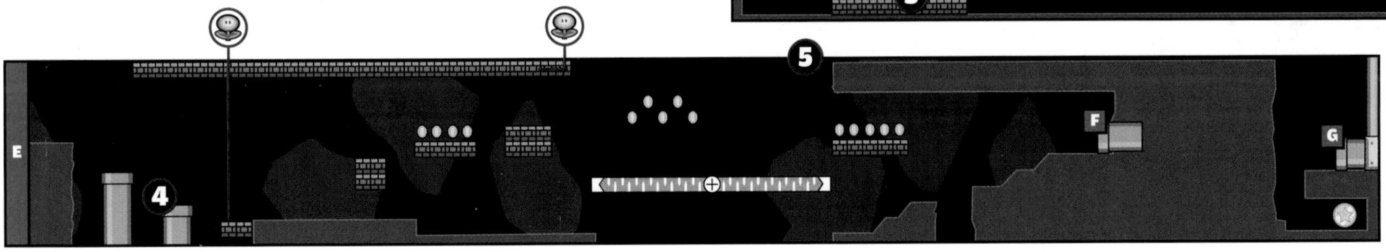

3 Knock over the Koopa and kick its shell to smash through the blocks along the floor. When the blocks are gone, do a dashing crouch to squeeze beneath the pipe to the other side, where a Mega Mushroom awaits. After Mega Mario destroys all the blocks and Goombas, repeatedly Ground-Pound the pipe for coins.

4 To get the nearby power-up, grab a Koopa shell by jumping onto a Koopa while holding the dash button, which allows you to pick up the shell automatically. Stand on the left side of the lower pipe, and kick the shell to the right to expose the item.

5 At the last teeter-totter, if you wait on the left side to raise the right side, you can jump from the right edge to the ceiling. Go right to find a second pipe out of the level, and the third Star Coin. This exit creates an alternate route on the world map, which leads to a red Toad house and provides a shortcut to the World 1 tower.

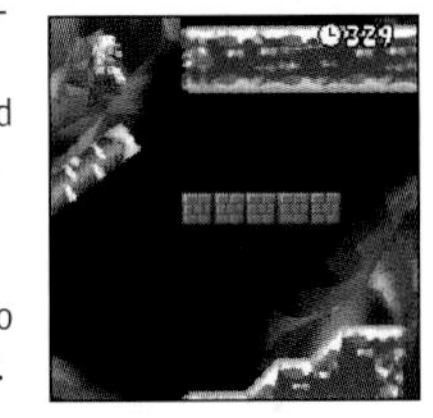

World 1-3

1 Jump on the Spin Block to propel yourself to the upper level, where a second Spin Block will send you soaring to a trampoline-like fuchsia mushroom. Bounce into a Star Coin, and glide down the path of coins to another.

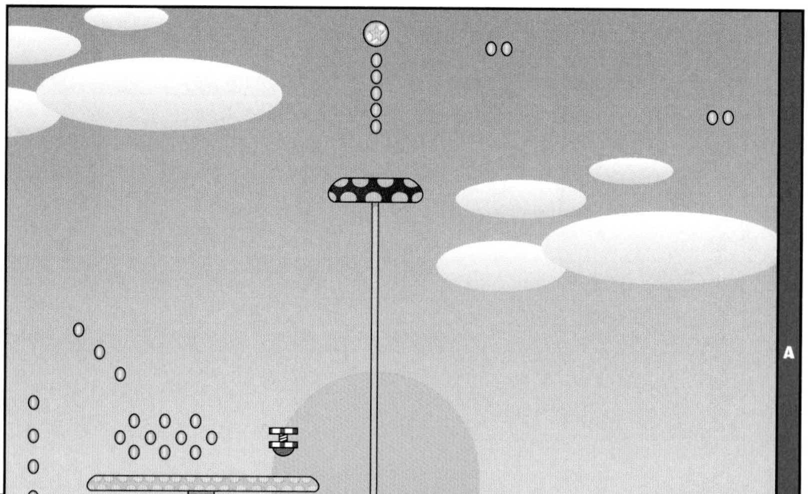

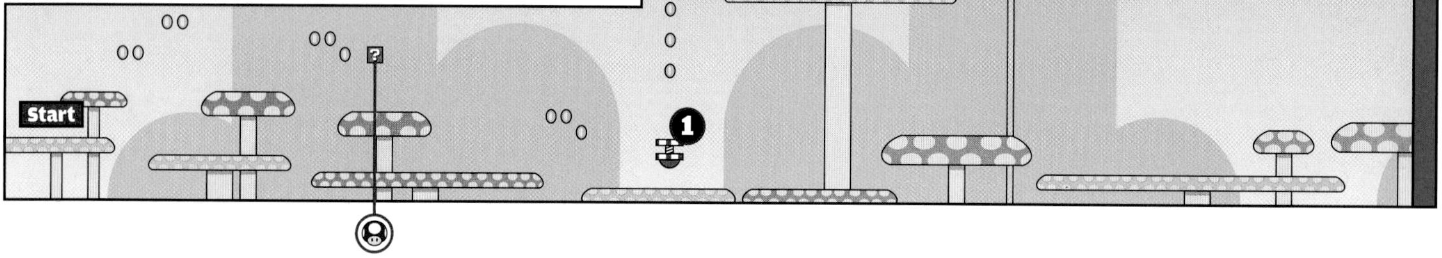

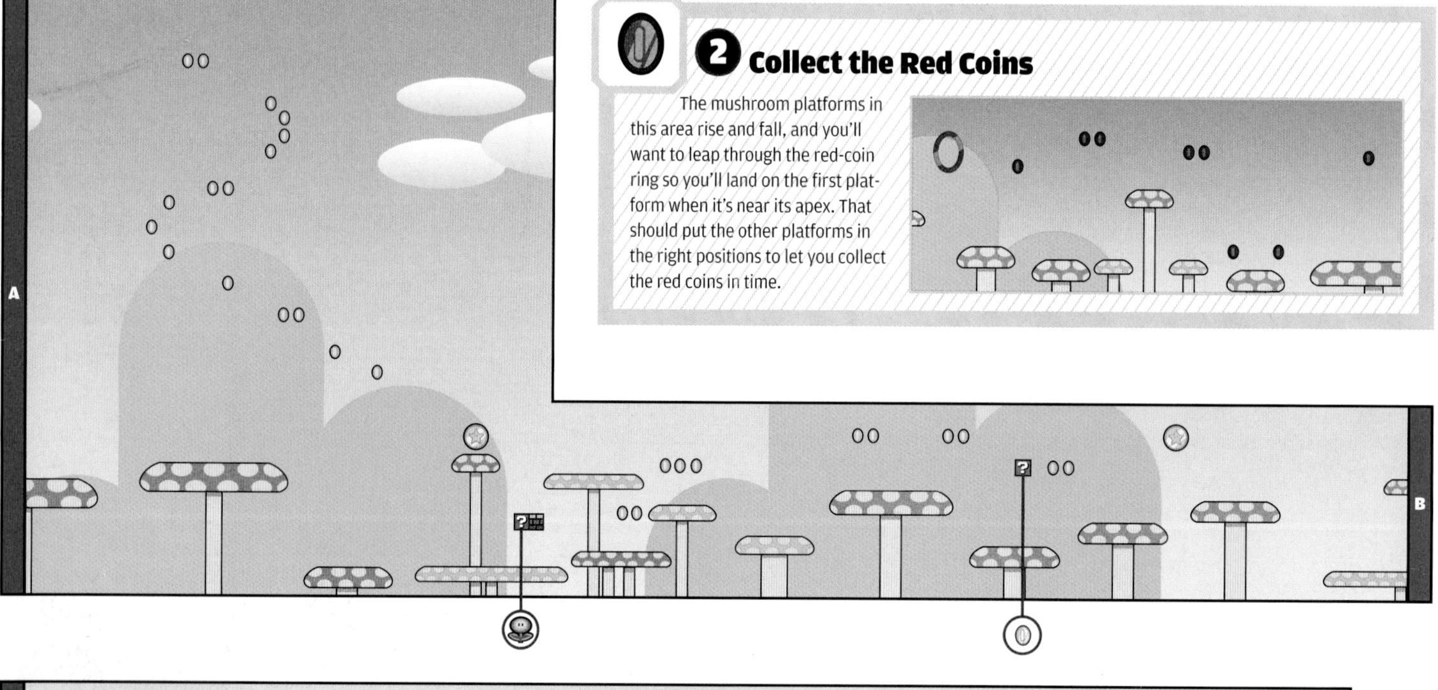

2 Collect the Red Coins

The mushroom platforms in this area rise and fall, and you'll want to leap through the red-coin ring so you'll land on the first platform when it's near its apex. That should put the other platforms in the right positions to let you collect the red coins in time.

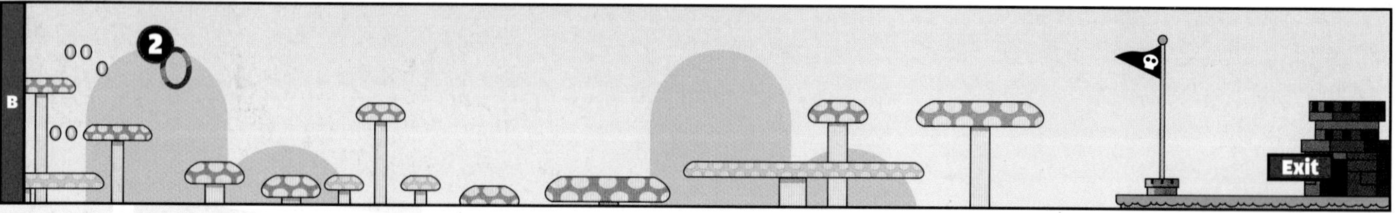

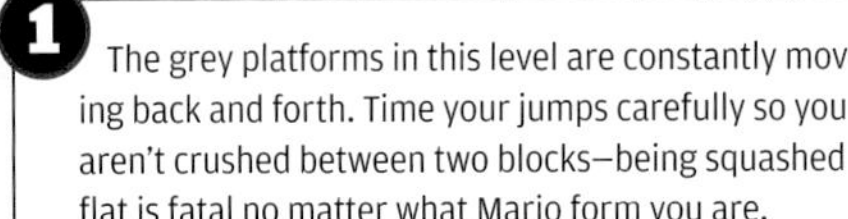

1 The grey platforms in this level are constantly moving back and forth. Time your jumps carefully so you aren't crushed between two blocks—being squashed flat is fatal no matter what Mario form you are.

2 Ignore the pipe for now and travel up the staircase of platforms on the right side of the screen to reach the Star Coin. Then drop through the line of outlined coins to make them appear, and squat into the pipe. It will rocket you up through the coins and up to door A.

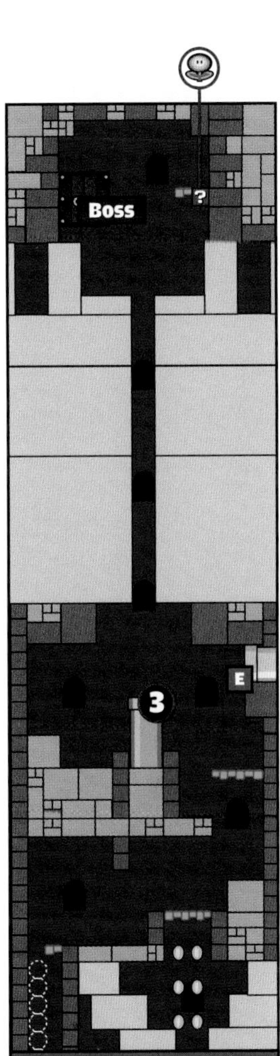

3 Stand atop the pipe at point 3 and watch for the platforms above you to meet. Wait one or two seconds, then squat into the pipe—it will blast you up as the platforms separate. Grab a power-up to the right before you open the door and challenge Bowser Jr.

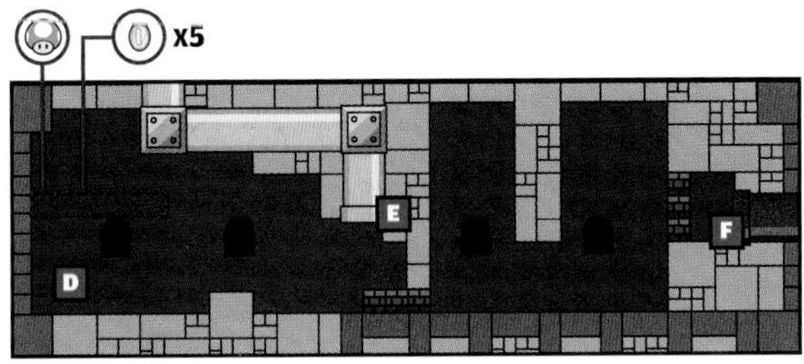

4 Step through the gap at the right side of the Star Coin room to enter a hidden area. Anyone can jump at the entrance to reveal a hidden 1-Up, but only Shell Mario can smash all the blocks with a dash-and-crouch and reach the pipe. This exit leads to a warp cannon that will blast you to World 5.

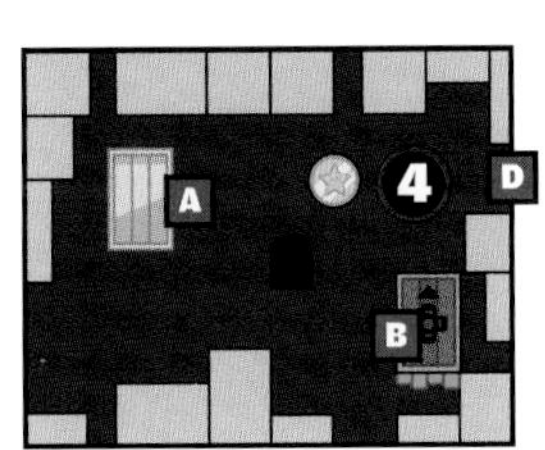

Boss

You'll need to stomp on Bowser Jr. three times to beat him, but be careful—after Bowser Jr. takes a hit, he curls into a spiked shell. If Mario is still hanging around nearby, he'll get poked.

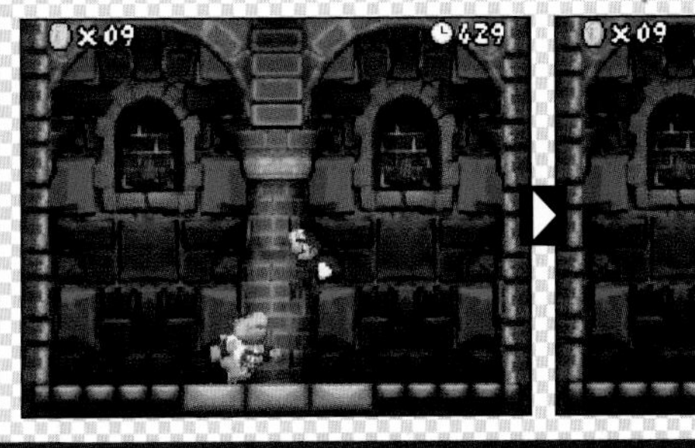

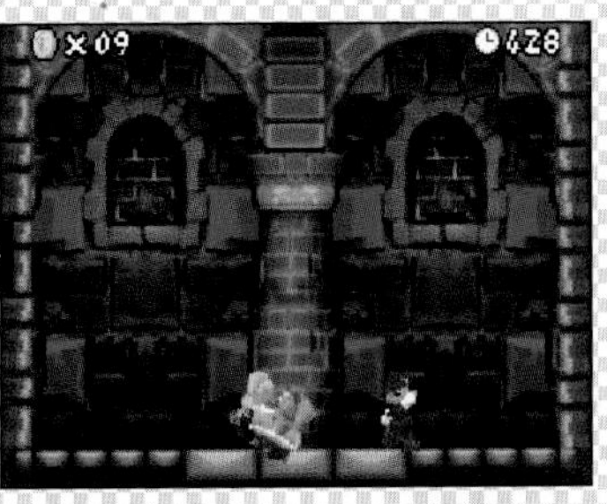

World 1-4

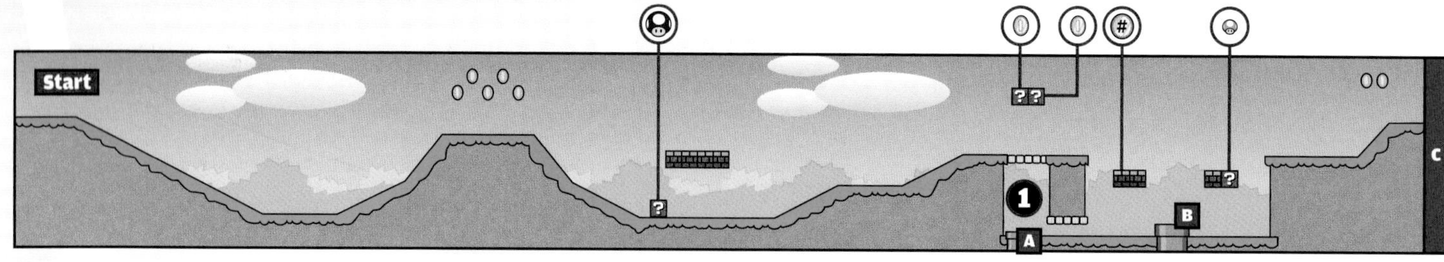

1 Grab the Mini Mushroom and run to the mini pipe as Mini Mario. The pipe leads to an area where you can Wall-Jump to the first Star Coin. If you can make it to the end of the stage as Mini Mario, you can dash off of the top of the pipe and do a long jump to the right. You'll soar above the flagpole and earn an easy 1-Up.

2 Stomp the Koopa at the top of this structure (Ground-Pound it as Mini Mario) and kick the shell to the right. It will smash through the blocks, exposing a 1-Up and the mouth of a pipe.

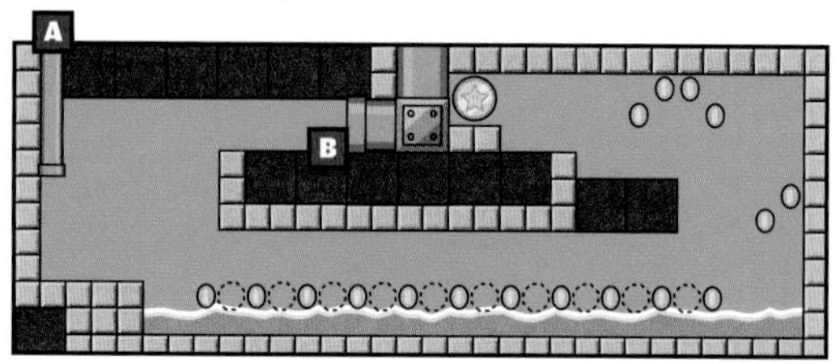

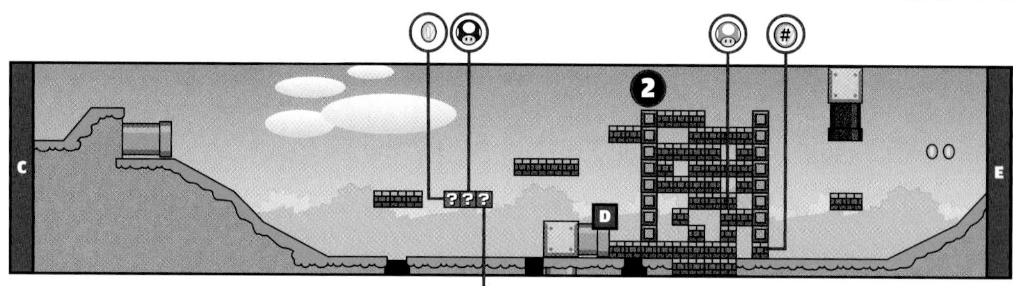

3 P Switch to the Star Coin

Don't touch the coins until you hit the block to reveal a P Switch. Stomp that to transform the coins into blocks that form a stairway to the second Star Coin. If you're quick you can scoop up several newly transformed coins near the entrance, too.

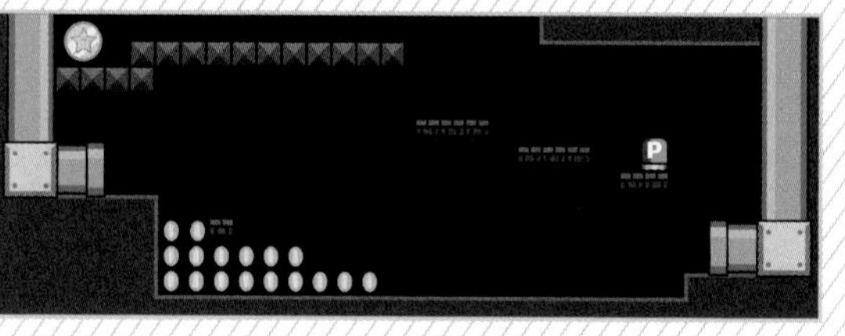

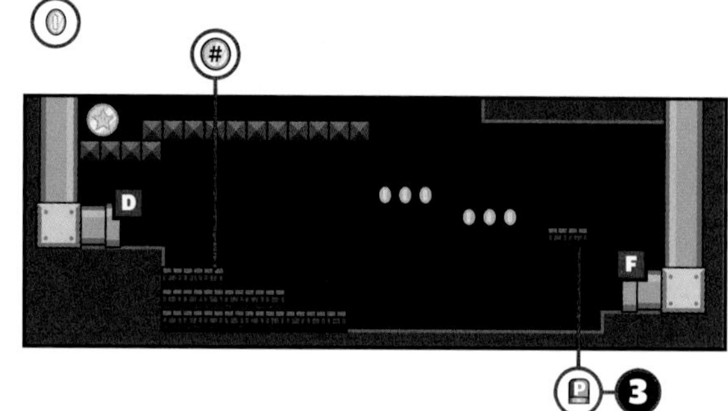

4 Standard or Mini Mario can simply dash over the gap to reach the star coin, but larger Marios will need to slide down the hill by running and crouching beneath the ? Block. Use the same slide technique to get back after claiming your prize.

5 To pull off a 1-Up loop, grab a Koopa shell from the block structure near point 2 and carry it to the end of the stage. Kick it in either direction from the sweet spot at point 5—it should bounce between the green and yellow pipes forever (if you're too far from point 5, it will disappear offscreen). Jump over the shell whenever it nears Mario to let it rack up 1-Ups by killing the Goombas generated by the pipe.

World 1-A

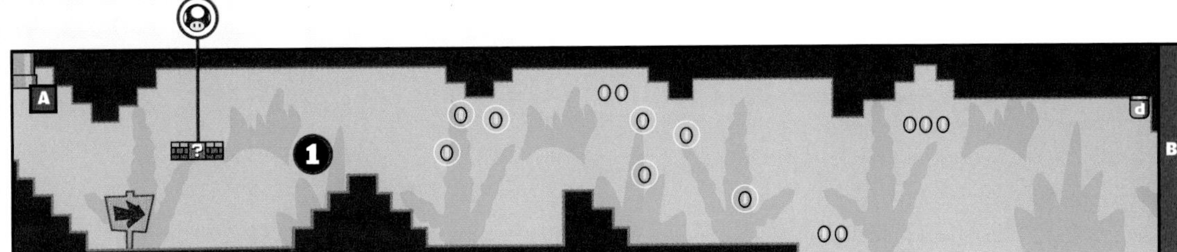

1 At this point the level will begin scrolling automatically. Don't get caught on the left side of a wall when the screen catches up with you, or you'll be crushed! Note that Shell Mario will have a bit more control when swimming.

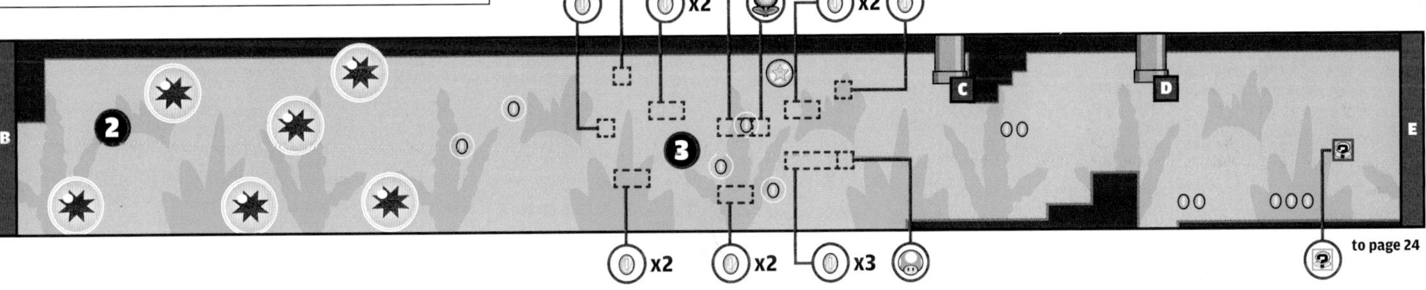

to page 24

2 P-Switch Coins

To maximize your earnings, don't hit the P Switch until it's toward the left side of the screen. But don't hit it too late, or you'll risk being crushed at the left side of the screen behind the wall.

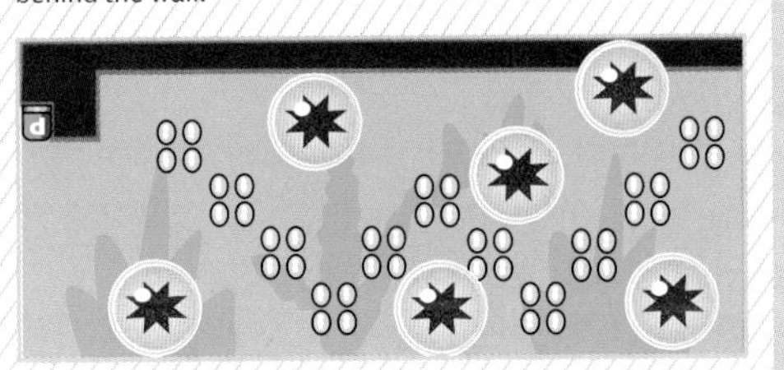

3 A maze of Invisible Blocks at point 3 conceals two 1-Ups, but the blocks will get in your way if you try to reach the Star Coin from below. So grab the first 1-Up and then swim along the ceiling to the Star Coin. Then let yourself sink to the level of the second 1-Up.

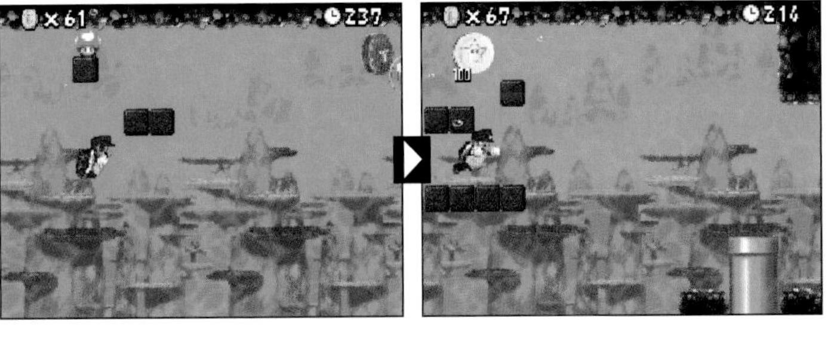

from page 23

4 Red-Coin Ring

Wait for the Sushi to pass (or blast them as Fire Mario), then swim after the red coins. Don't swim too close to the right side of the screen, or the Sushi could surprise you!

5 P-Switch Coins

The P Switch at point 5 will reveal scores of coins. Help yourself, but don't focus on filling your pockets so much as careful dodging—the air from the pipes will blow you into the Sushi if you aren't cautious.

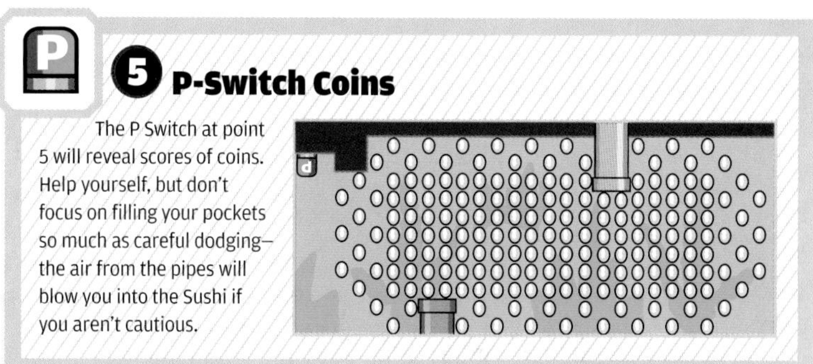

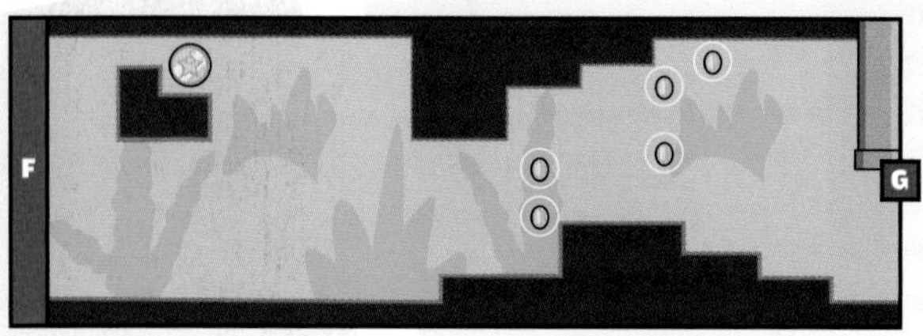

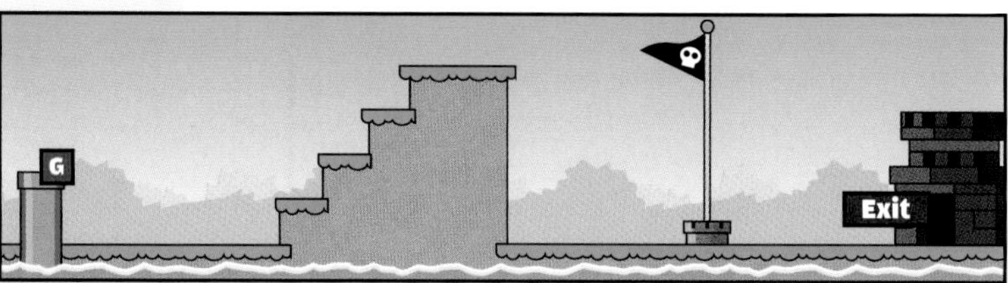

World 1-5

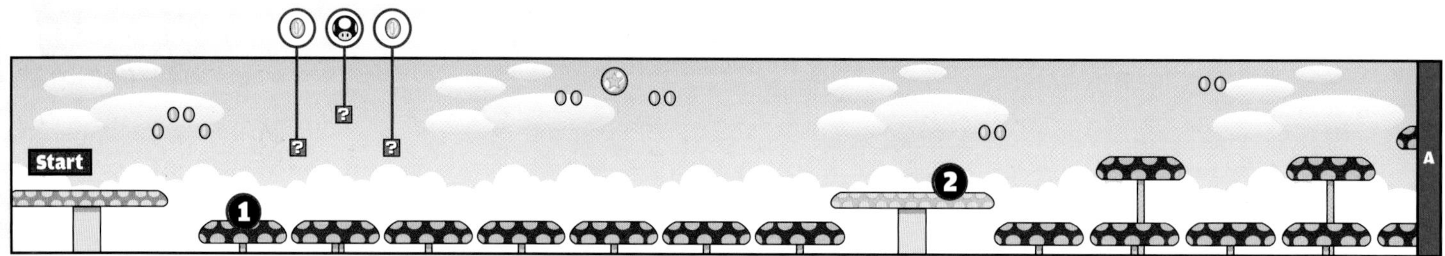

1 The mushroom platforms at point 1 will bounce you around the level whether you jump or not, but a well-timed leap will send you even higher, allowing you to dodge foes and grab items such as the first Star Coin.

2 Throw or kick a Koopa shell along the lower mushroom platforms. Then hold the dash button and run to dash-bounce along with it. The shell will rack up multipliers as it knocks off other Koopas, and you'll score a 1-Up if you can keep pace with it.

3 The wooden platforms at point 3 function as a pair: when you step on one it will fall while its counterpart rises. Avoid the impulse to jump off quickly, because you'll need the second platform to stop near the top—you won't be able to jump into the pipe (by pressing up and jumping beneath it) if the platform is too low.

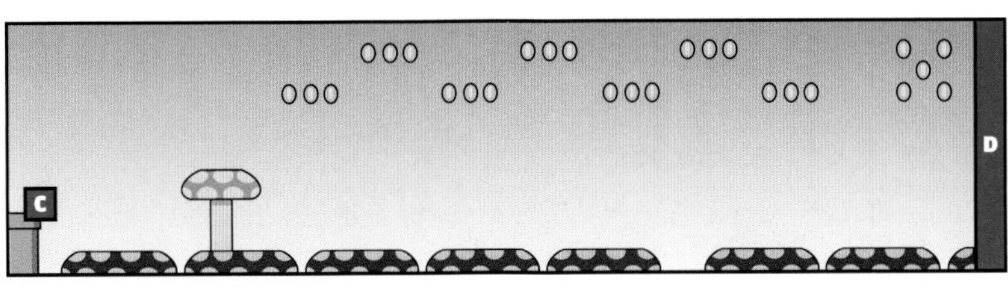

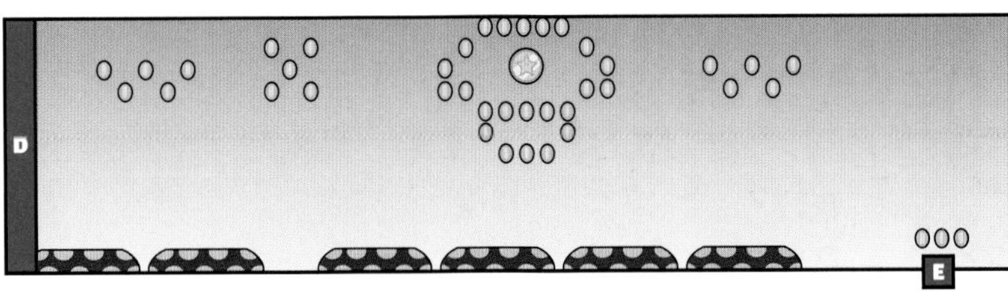

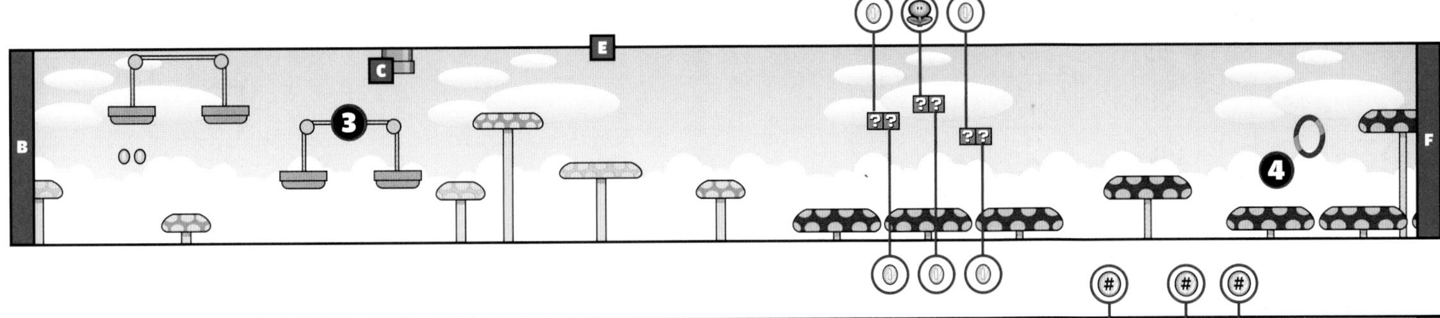

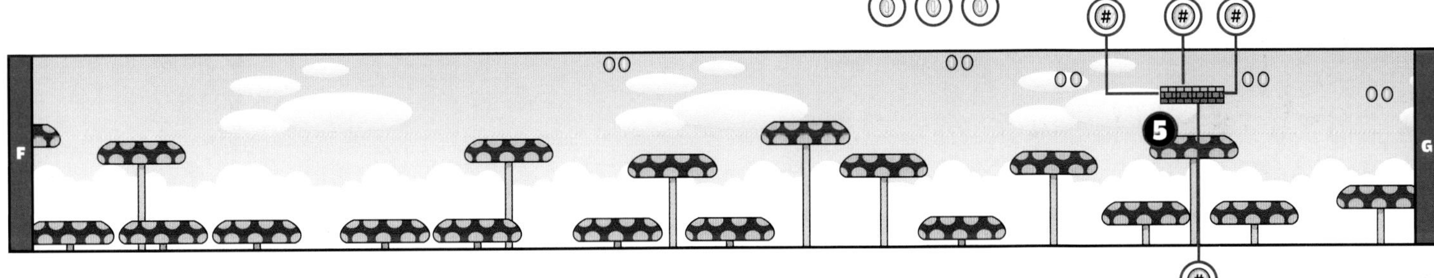

4 Red Coins and Trampolines

After you jump through the red-coin ring, grab the first coin, bounce off a mushroom platform and into the upper level of coins, then finally drop between the upper mushroom platforms to grab the lower coins. If you go for the lowest coins first, you'll bounce right into a Goomba.

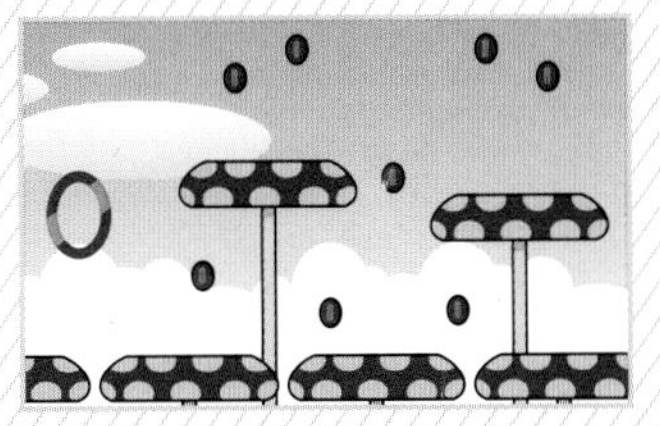

5 Jump from the lowest trampoline mushroom to hit a set of blocks from below. Then position yourself between the blocks and the upper mushroom platform so you'll ricochet between them continuously and collect all the coins.

World 1 Castle

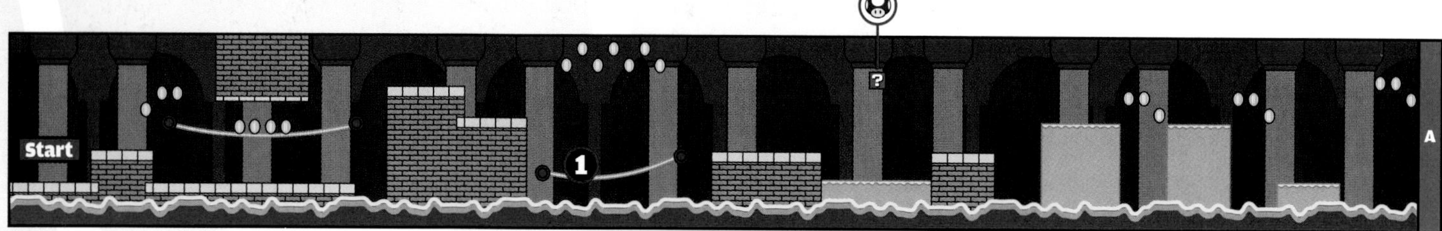

1 If you jump from the center of the rope bridges, they'll propel you high enough to grab the coins. Mario can't balance on the ropes for long, so don't dawdle!

2 Avoid contact with the descending spiked ceiling sections by dashing beneath them and pausing on the blue blocks, where you can safely wait for the spikes to rise again.

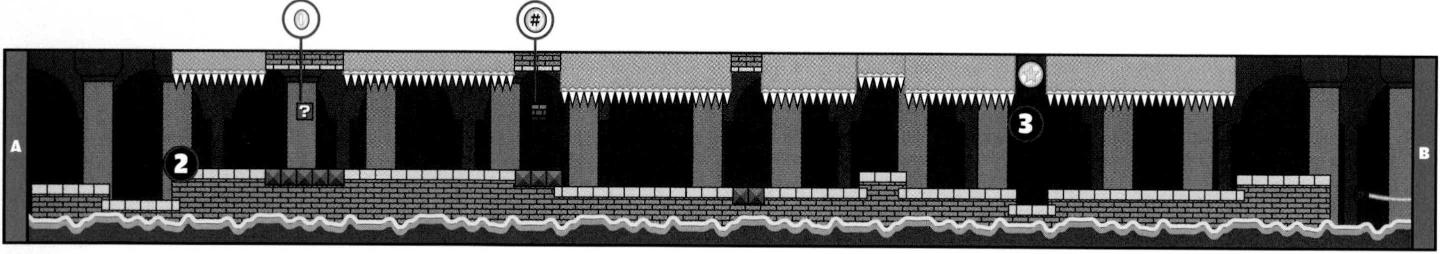

3 Wait at point 3 for the spiked ceiling sections to hit the floor, then do a pair of Wall Jumps off of the sides to reach the first Star Coin.

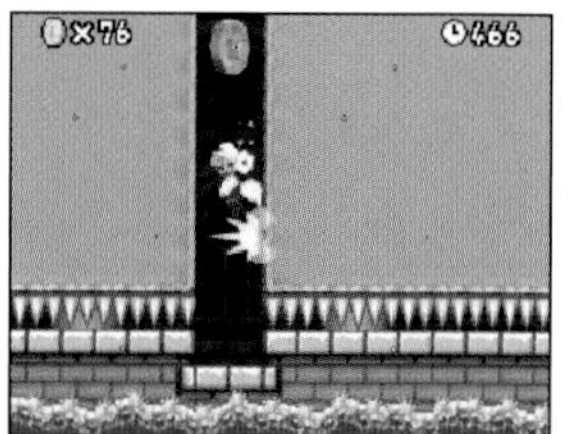

4 Stand near the center of the last long rope bridge and jump from the middle to reach the unseen pipe above (press up as you jump to pull yourself into it). The final Star Coin awaits inside.

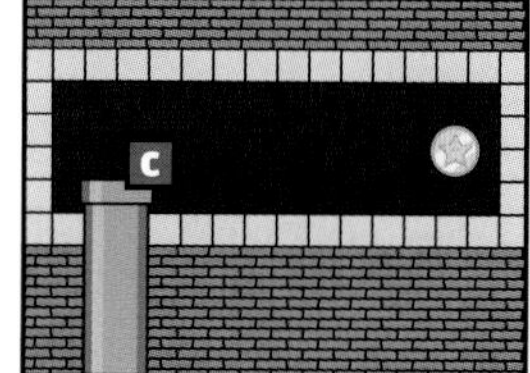

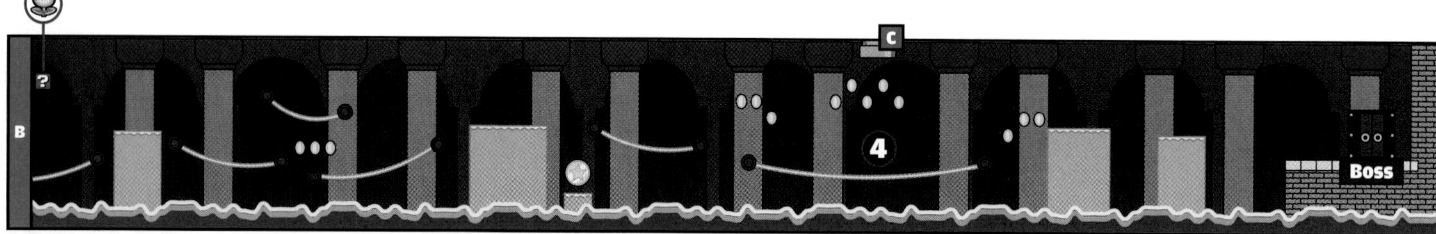

Boss

Your first encounter with Bowser is a cinch. When he appears, simply hop onto the platform, use a long jump to leap over him, and hit the bridge-retracting skull switch. If you jump when the rising platform is at its apex, you can land right on it.

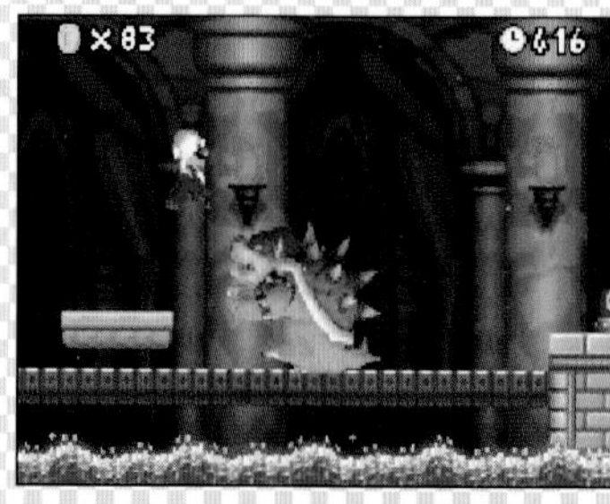

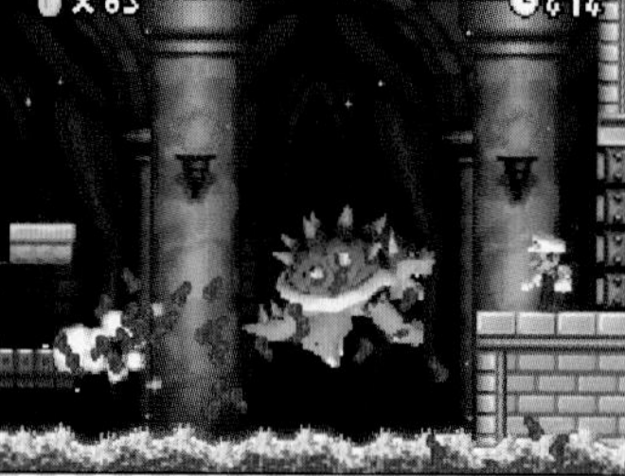

Bowser fires slow-moving fireballs that can hit you when the platform is at its nadir. Beat him quickly before he can pose a threat.

World 2

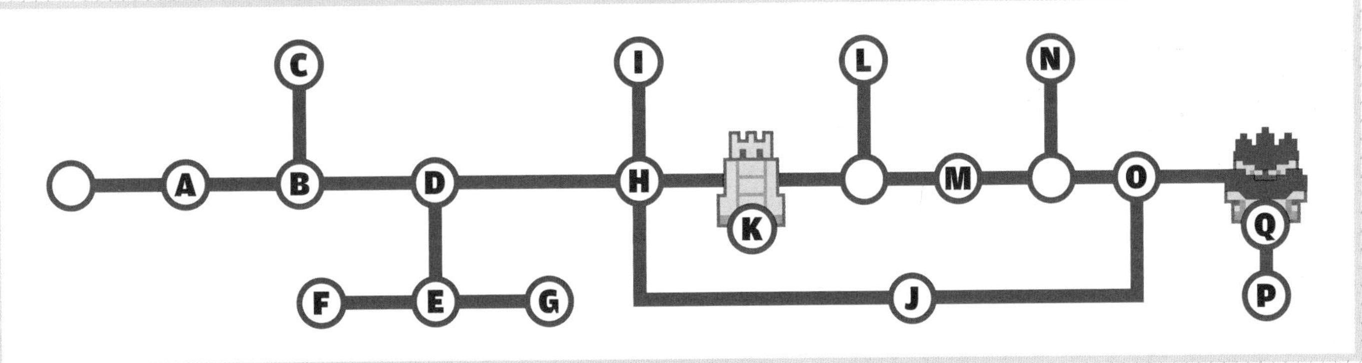

A **World 2-1** (Page 28)

B **World 2-2** (Page 29)

C **Red Toad House** (5 Star Coins)

D **World 2-3** (Page 30)

E **World 2-A** (Page 32)

F **Warp Cannon** (To World 5)

G **Warp Pipe** (Warp to P)

H **World 2-4** (Page 33)

I **Orange Toad House** (5 Star Coins)

J **Red Toad House**

K **World 2 Tower** (Page 34)

L **Green Toad House** (5 Star Coins)

M **World 2-5** (Page 36)

N **Red Toad House** (5 Star Coins)

O **World 2-6** (Page 37)

P **Warp Pipe** (Warp to G)

Q **World 2 Castle** (Page 38)

World 2-1

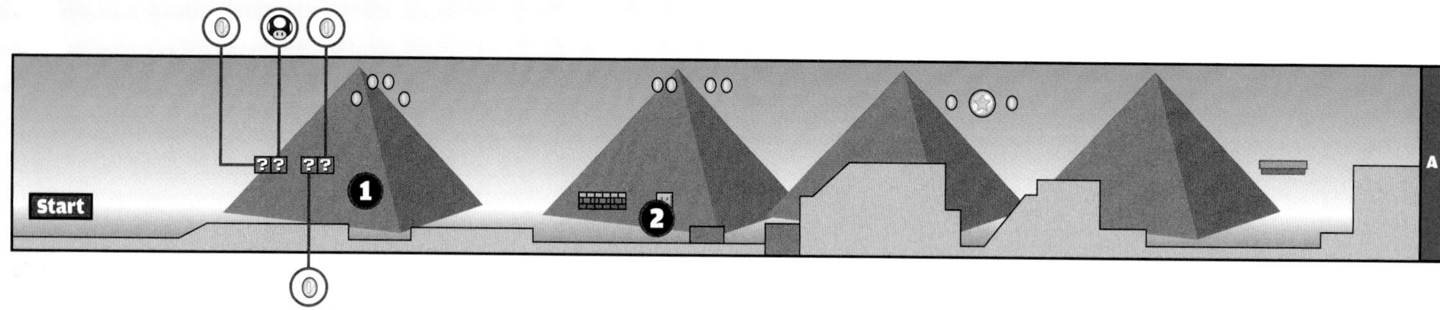

1 If you try to stomp or Ground-Pound the Pokeys, you'll end up with needle wounds in a sensitive area. But Fire Mario can destroy them easily—aim your fireballs at their heads for a quick kill, or score more points by shooting the lower segments first.

2 The blocks at point 2 will expand vertically when you hit them. Punch them three times to create a platform that's high enough to allow you to leap over the Pokey and reach the coins.

3 The quicksand will suck you under if you stand in it for too long. Jump continuously to fight its pull, or avoid it altogether.

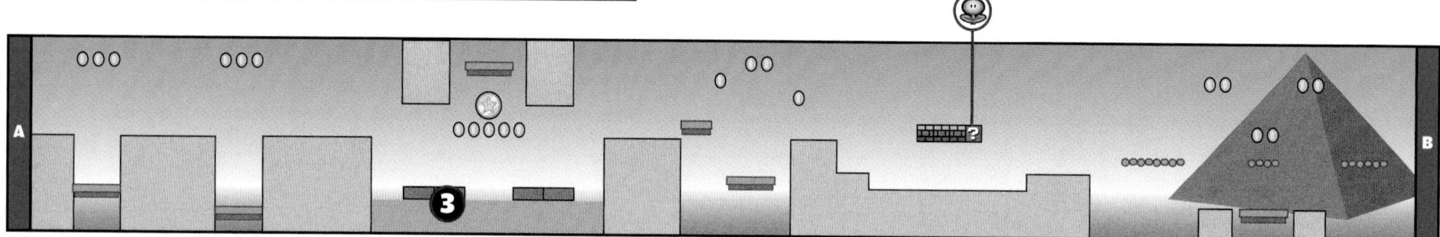

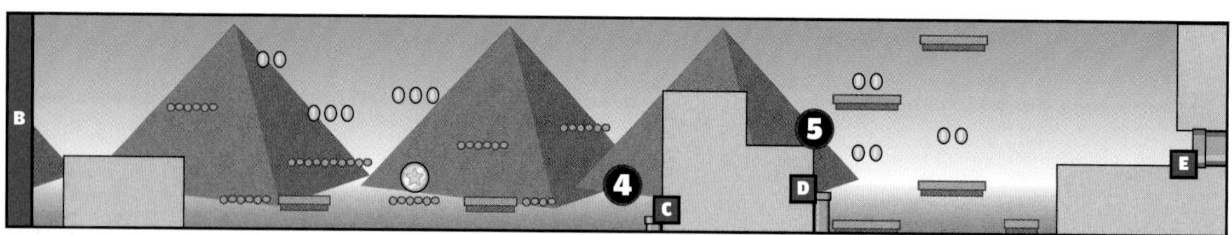

4 Only Mini Mario can enter the secret coin room beyond the pipe at point 4. There aren't any Mini Mushrooms on this level, so you'll need to get one elsewhere.

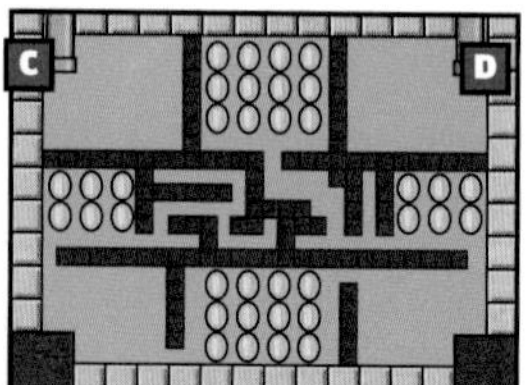

5 If you aren't Fire Mario, it will take some tricky jumping to get past the Pokey at point 5. Time your jump so that you land on the second moving platform just as it emerges from the top of the screen, then immediately long-jump over your foe.

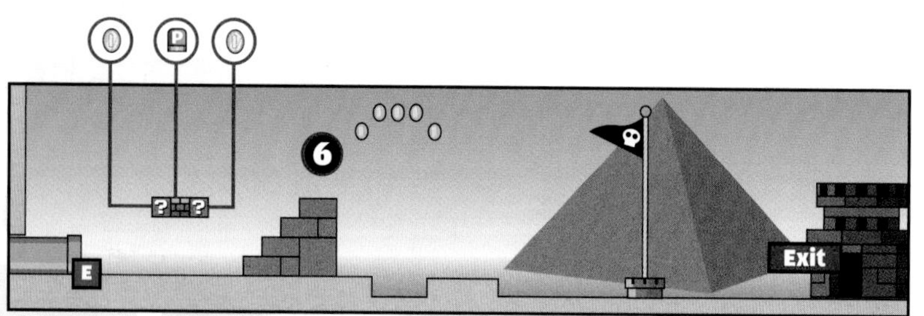

6 P Switch to the Exit

Hit the P Switch to change the coins to blocks, giving you a platform from which you can easily jump onto the flag. If you're still Mini Mario, you can soar right over it to earn a 1-Up.

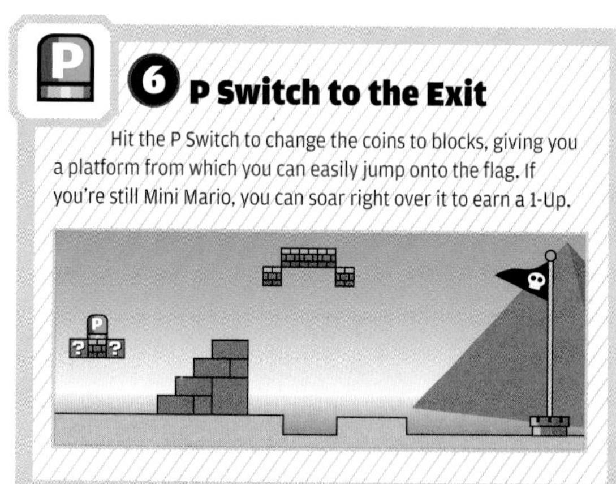

World 2-2

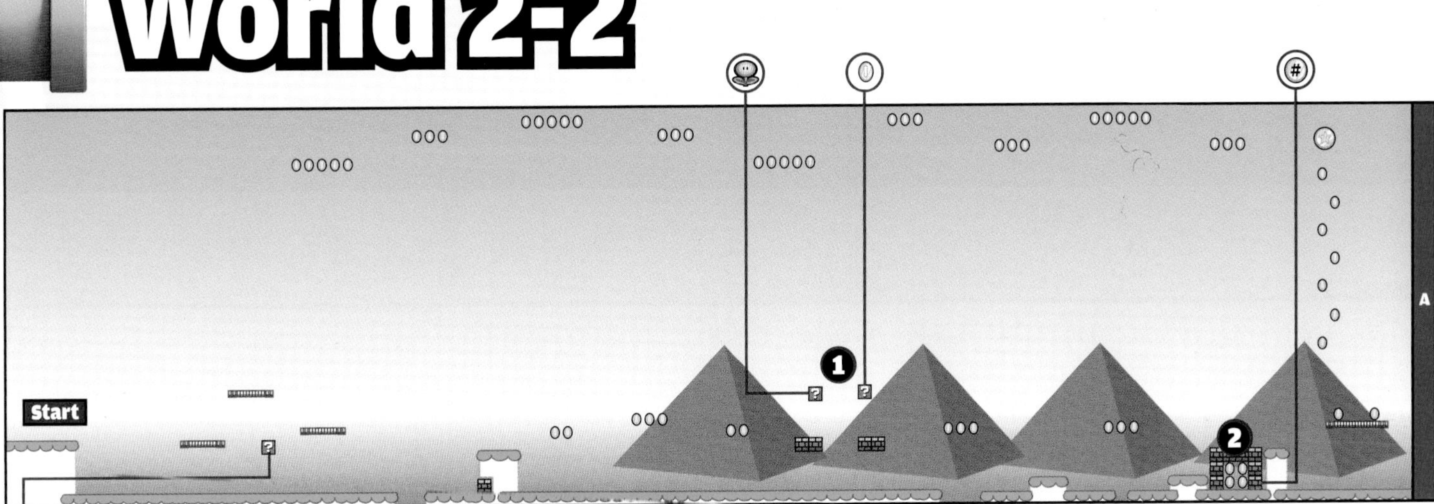

1 Hit Lakitu with a close-range fireball or a thrown Spiny to take it out without damaging the cloud. (To pick up the Spinys, you'll need to hit them from below while they're on a block.) You can then jump onto the cloud and soar into the sky, where a trail of coins will lead you to a Star Coin.

2 With a little work, you can create a Spiny deathtrap at point 2 that'll earn you infinite 1-Ups. Smash all of the blocks, then throw a Koopa shell into the gap. As the Lakitu tosses Spinys at you, jump back and forth to lure them into the Koopa shell.

3 Step into this pipe to be launched upward. Press up to pull yourself through the pipe in the sky and into a secret area that bears a Star Coin.

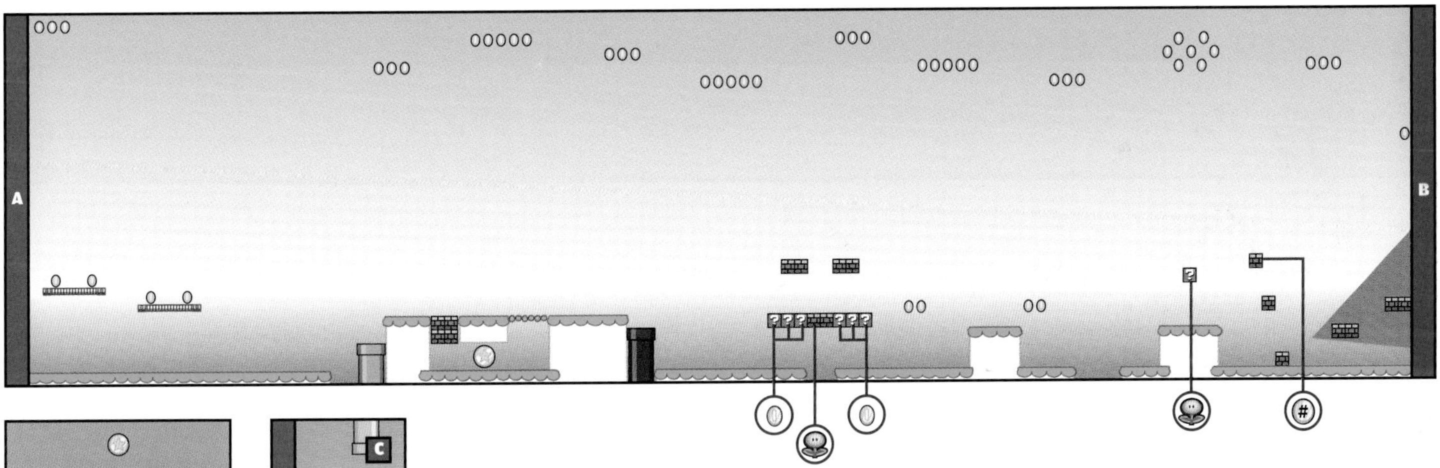

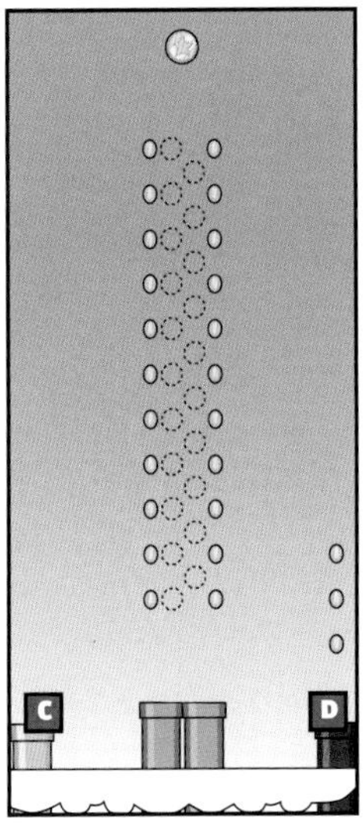

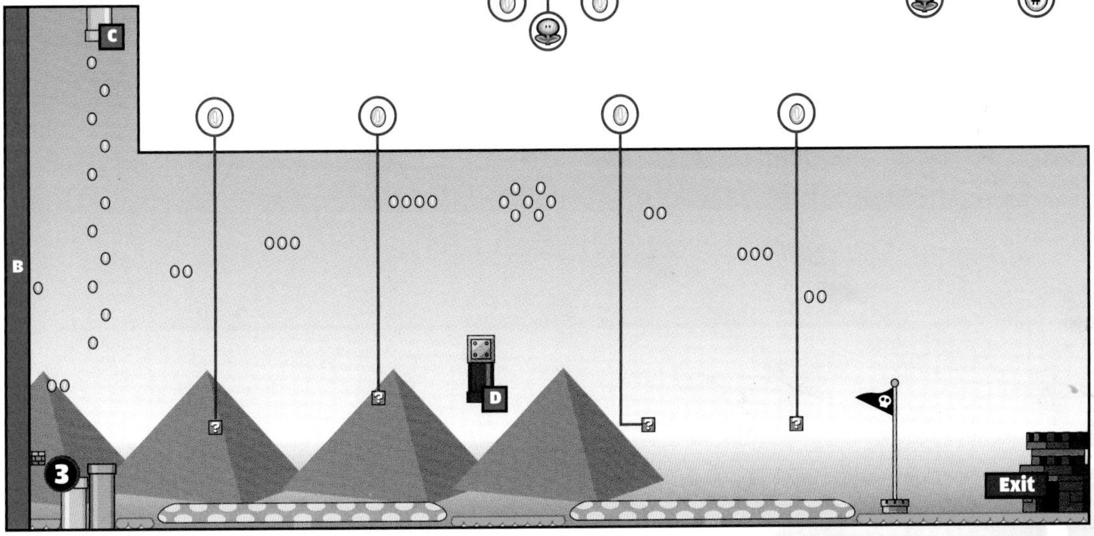

A B C D 3 Exit

World 2-3

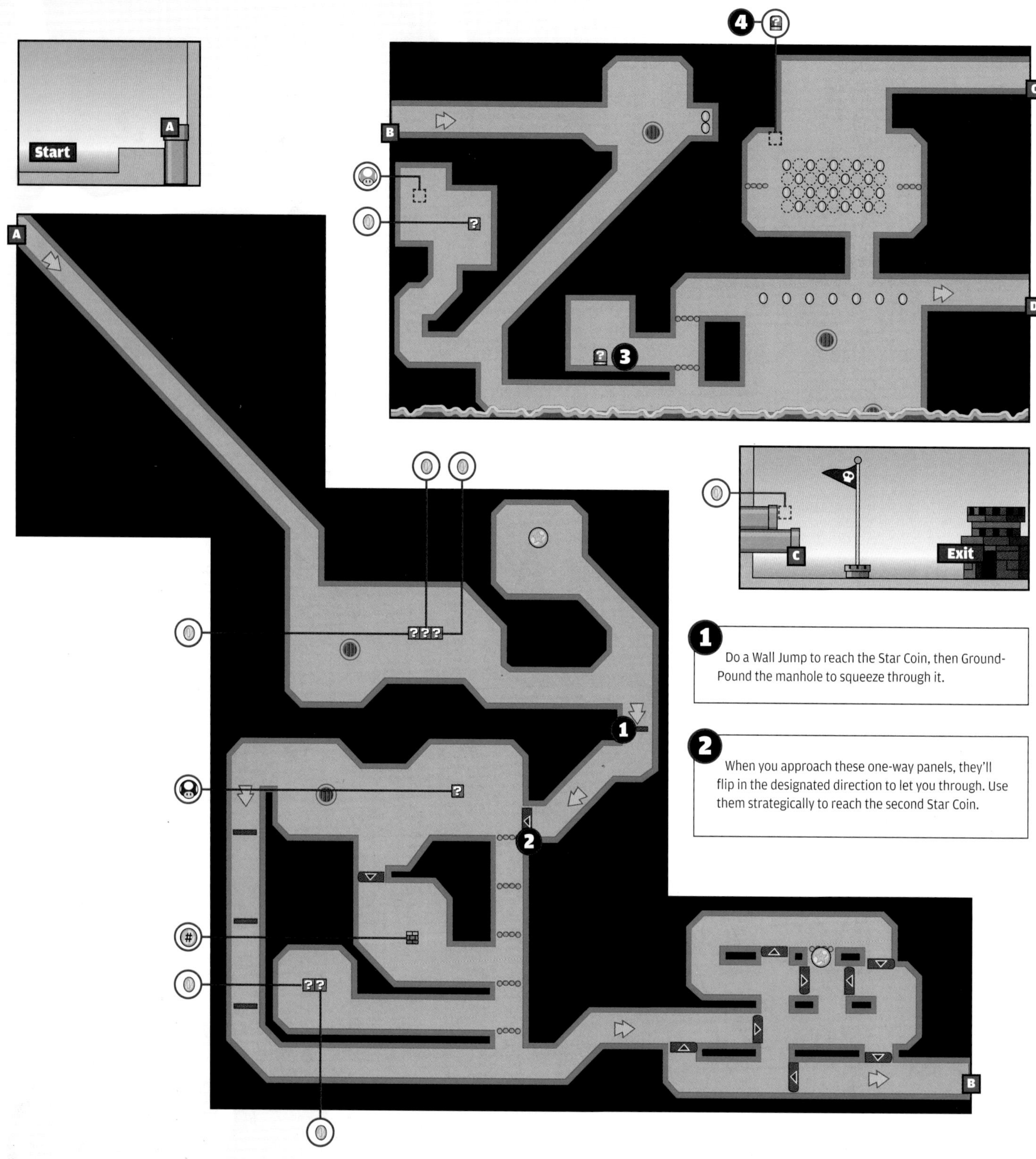

1 Do a Wall Jump to reach the Star Coin, then Ground-Pound the manhole to squeeze through it.

2 When you approach these one-way panels, they'll flip in the designated direction to let you through. Use them strategically to reach the second Star Coin.

3 Raise the Water

Hitting the orange ? Switch will raise the water level temporarily, allowing you to swim to the ledge to proceed, or to jump into the coin room above.

4 To the Alternate Exit!

If you're quick enough, you can find and hit a second ? Switch in the coin room, which will raise the water level even higher and allow you to swim to the red-flag exit to level 2-A. To give yourself a bit more time, hit the first ? Switch, wait for the water level to drop, and then hit the switch again as soon as it reappears. The water level won't start rising again until it stops falling—that means you'll have more time to swim through the hole in the ceiling, jump up to the ledge on the left, and hit the next ? Switch.

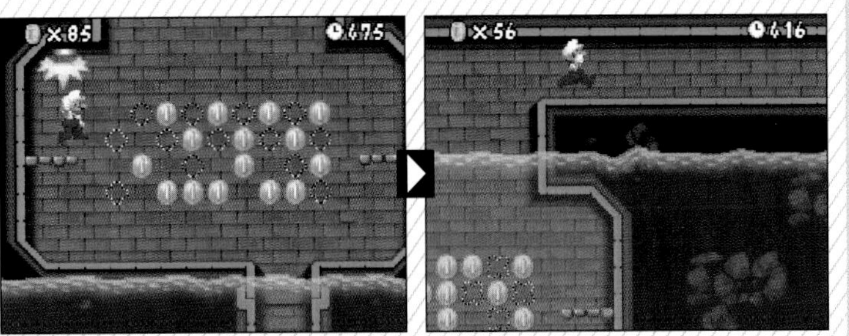

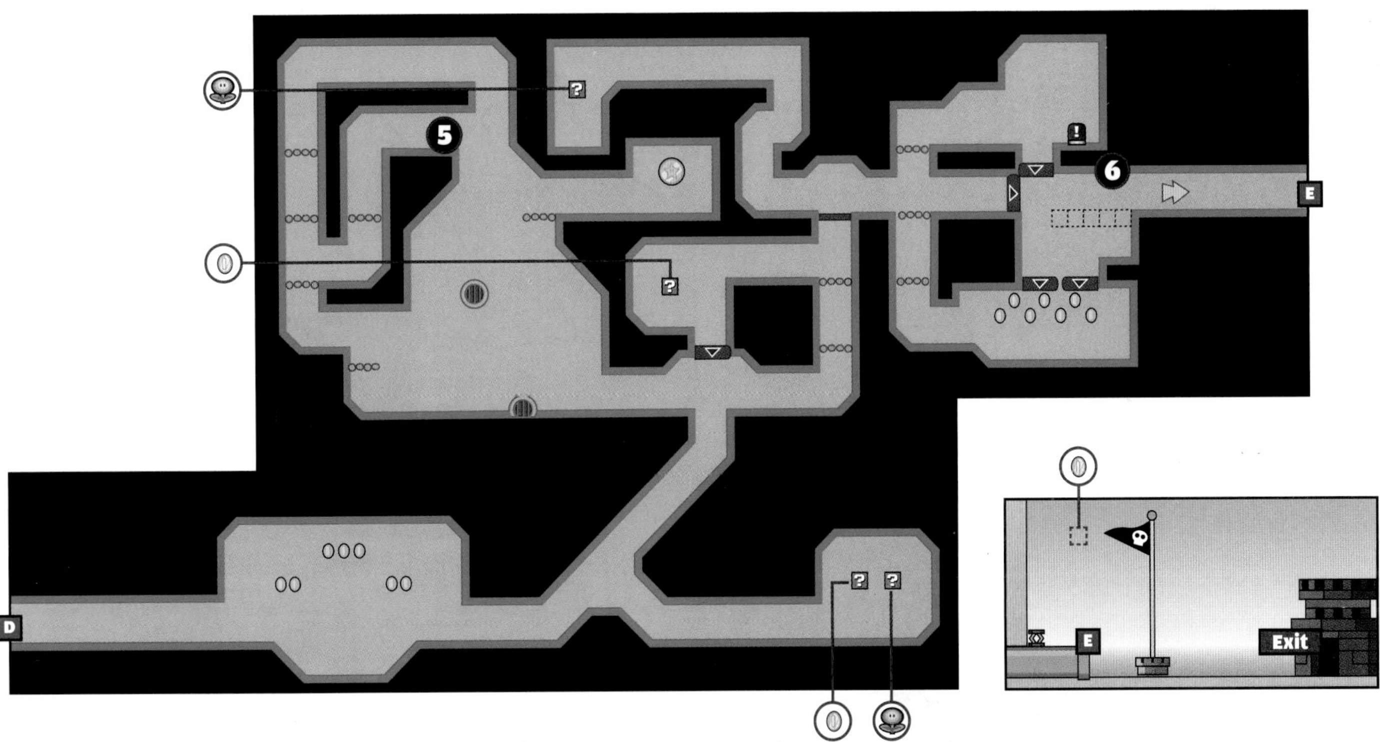

5 To get the final Star Coin, make your way up the ledges on the left side of the maze. From point 5, simply dash to the right; you'll land on the ledge near the Star Coin.

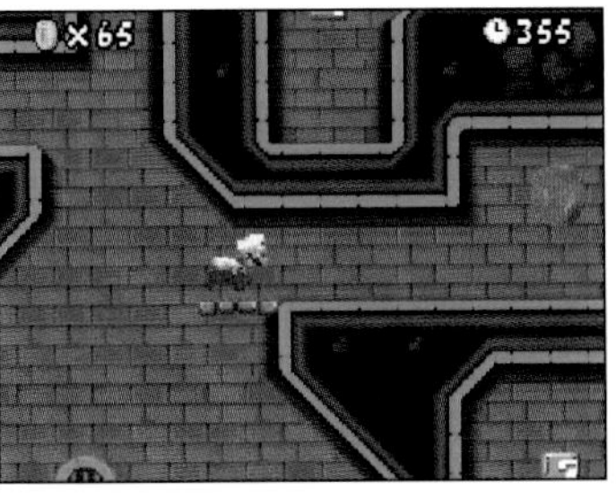

6 The ! Switch

Hit the ! Switch to make the outlined blocks appear. The flip panels will dump you to the bottom, from where you can then hop up the ledges to the left and push down the flip panel near the blocks. Be spry—those blocks won't last forever.

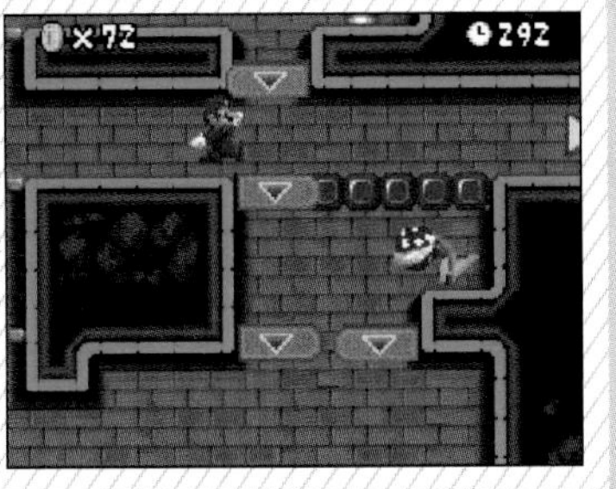

World 2-A

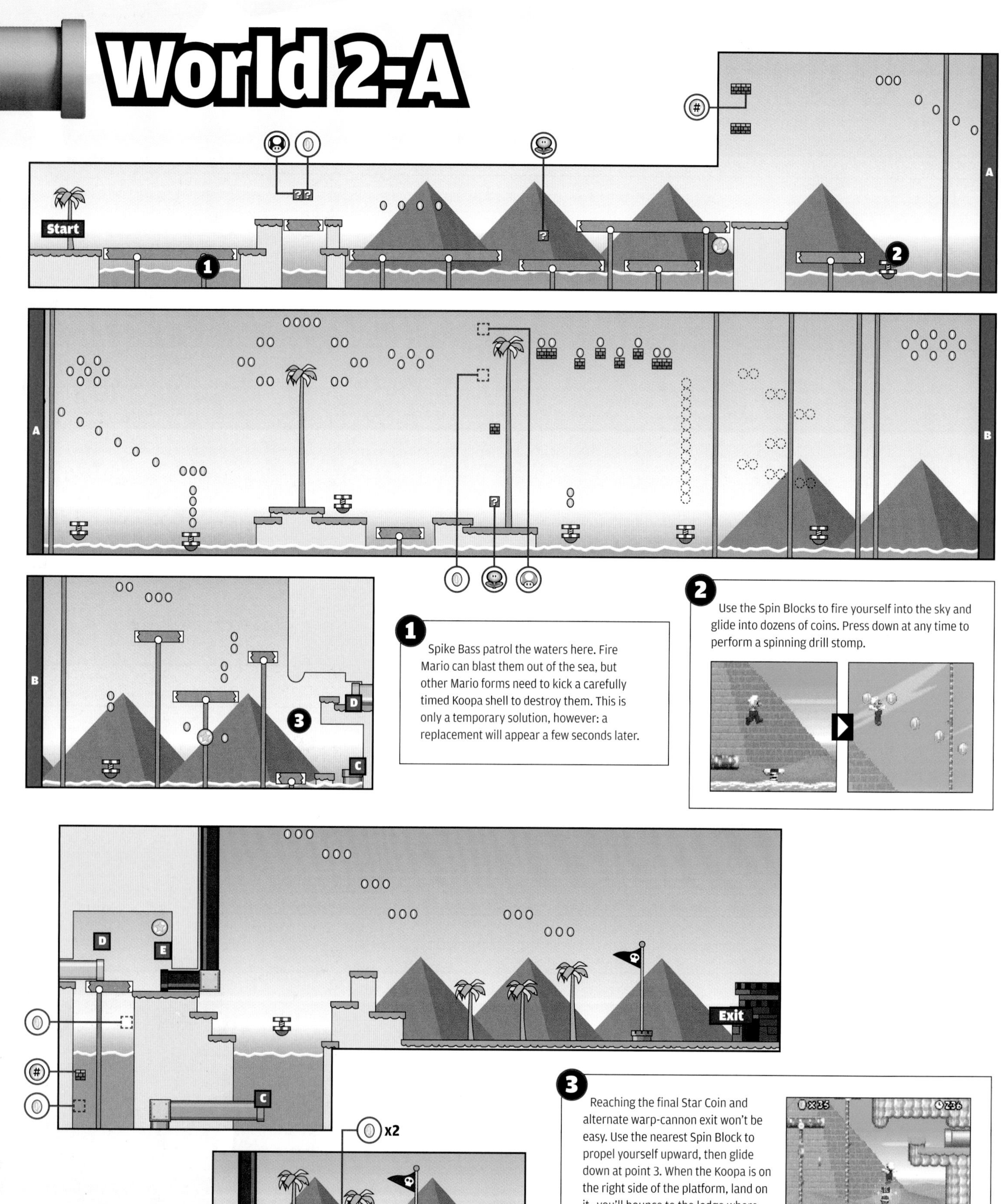

1 Spike Bass patrol the waters here. Fire Mario can blast them out of the sea, but other Mario forms need to kick a carefully timed Koopa shell to destroy them. This is only a temporary solution, however: a replacement will appear a few seconds later.

2 Use the Spin Blocks to fire yourself into the sky and glide into dozens of coins. Press down at any time to perform a spinning drill stomp.

3 Reaching the final Star Coin and alternate warp-cannon exit won't be easy. Use the nearest Spin Block to propel yourself upward, then glide down at point 3. When the Koopa is on the right side of the platform, land on it—you'll bounce to the ledge where the yellow pipe is.

World 2-4

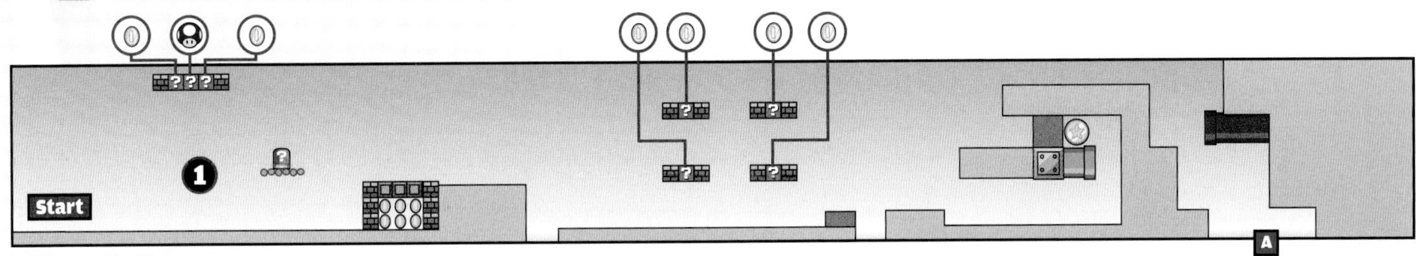

1 Making Molehills

The ? Switches in this level make flat earth swell into hills, giving you access to otherwise-unreachable spots.

2 Only Mini Mario can squeeze through this pipe to the alternate exit. You can't swim into it—you need to dash along the water's surface.

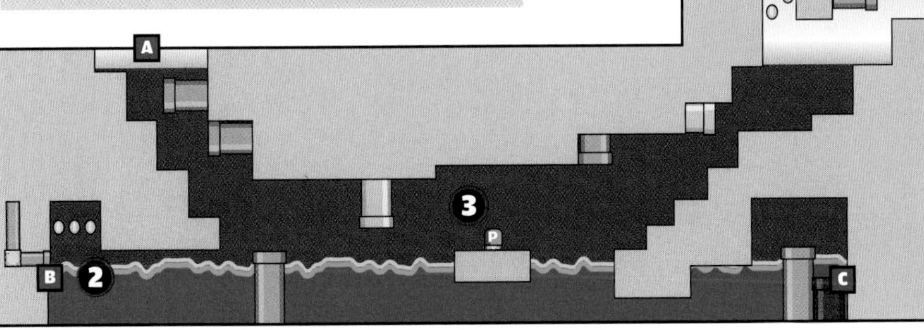

3 P-Switch Coins

This P Switch will make a number of coins appear. Since there's nothing to gain from the newly created blocks, you have time to grab them all.

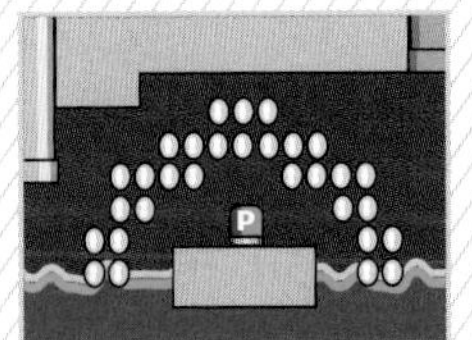

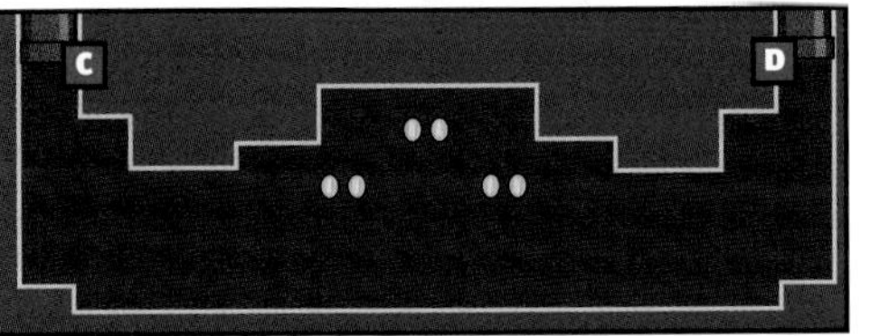

4 The red pipe will lead you to this area, where a ? Switch will create a hill to let you reach the exit. Grab the Star Coin before you hit the switch, or you won't be able to reach it. (The ? Switch's effect will fade after a few seconds.)

5 Hit the block at point 5 to reveal a ? Switch that raises two hills to the right. You'll need to jump from the second hill to get onto the ledge at the end, but the Piranha Plants will make it hard to proceed. If you have a Fire Flower in reserve, use it to clear a path.

6 Both Hammer Bros. guard the final Star Coin. Either jump onto the top row from the ledge, where you can Ground-Pound through the blocks to hit them from above. Alternatively, to whack them from below, you can hit the blocks they're standing on.

7 It's not easy, but if you can stomp the Koopa so its shell lands on the lip of a step, you can jump straight onto it and kick it repeatedly against the step for infinite 1-Ups. If you screw up, run left a bit to make the Koopa reappear.

World 2 Tower

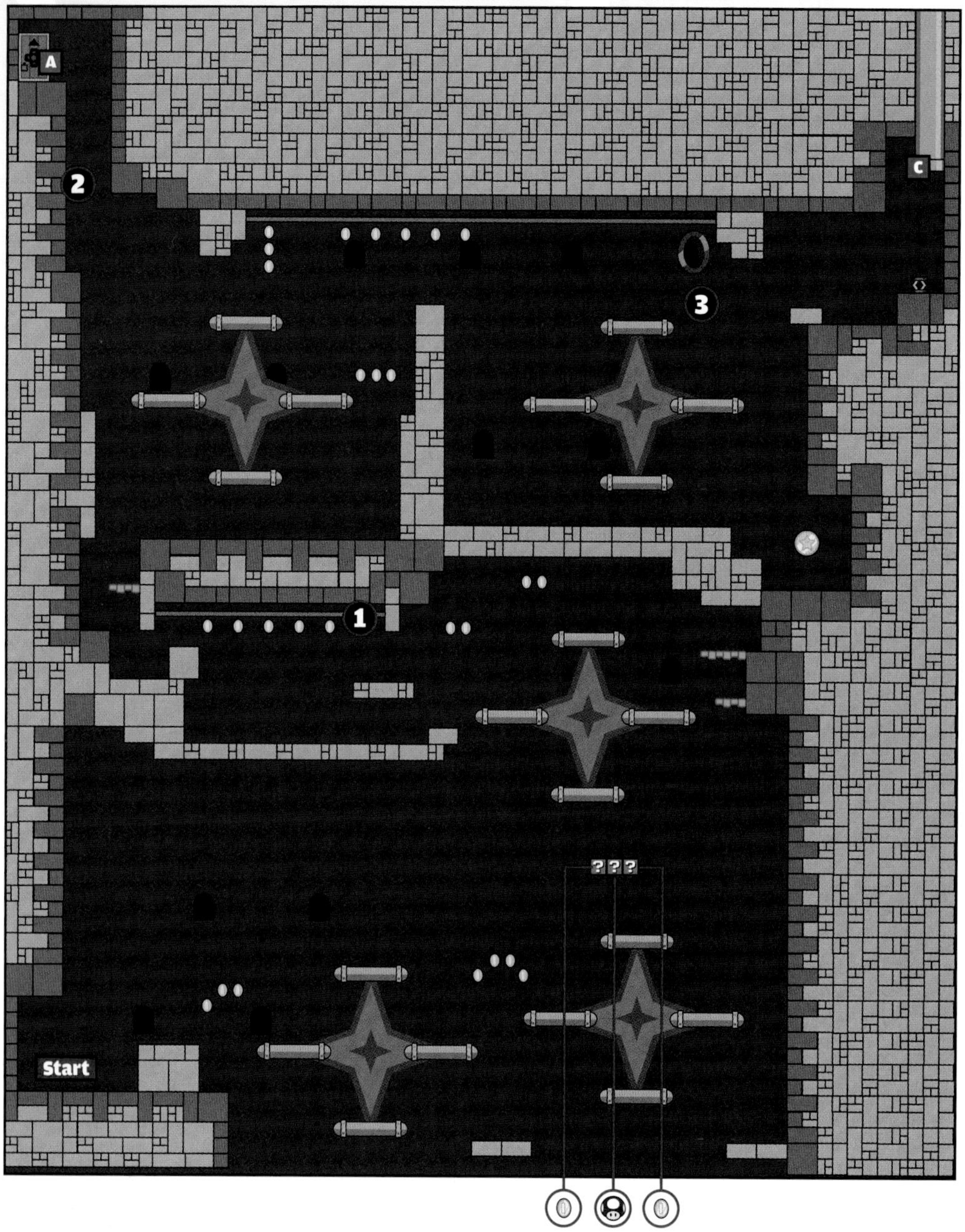

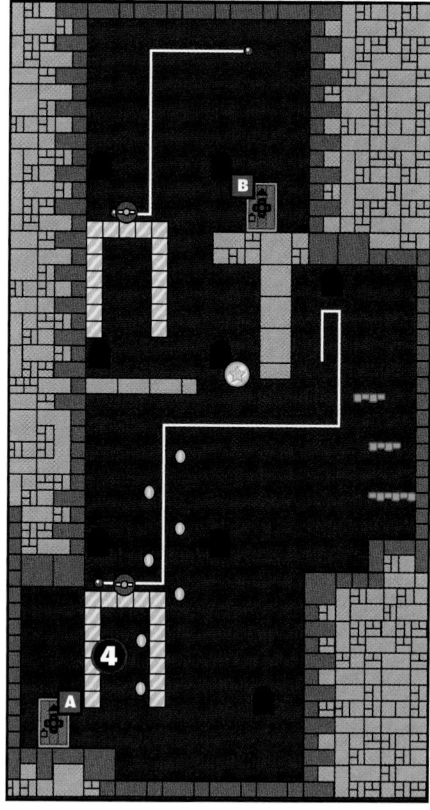

3 Red-Coin Loop

Pull yourself through the red-coin ring, then drop onto the first red coin and ride the platform in a full circle, grabbing each subsequent coin on the way.

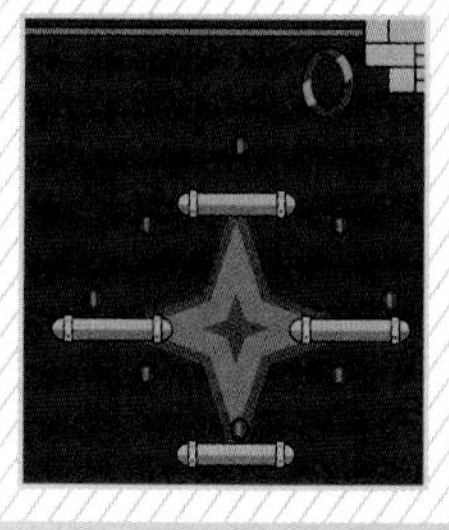

1 Jump and press up to grab the rope line at point 1, and pull yourself across.

2 If you're trying to get all the Star Coins in one playthrough, get the first one below point 3 before you head for the door at point 2. Then return to this area, do a long jump off of the rotating platform to the small ledge against the left wall, and Wall-Jump to the top.

4 You'll need to Wall-Jump continuously within this bell-shaped contraption to ride it to the upper part of the level. Drop out of it when you're above the ledge in the right wall, then jump on top of the bell to get to the Star Coin and the exit door.

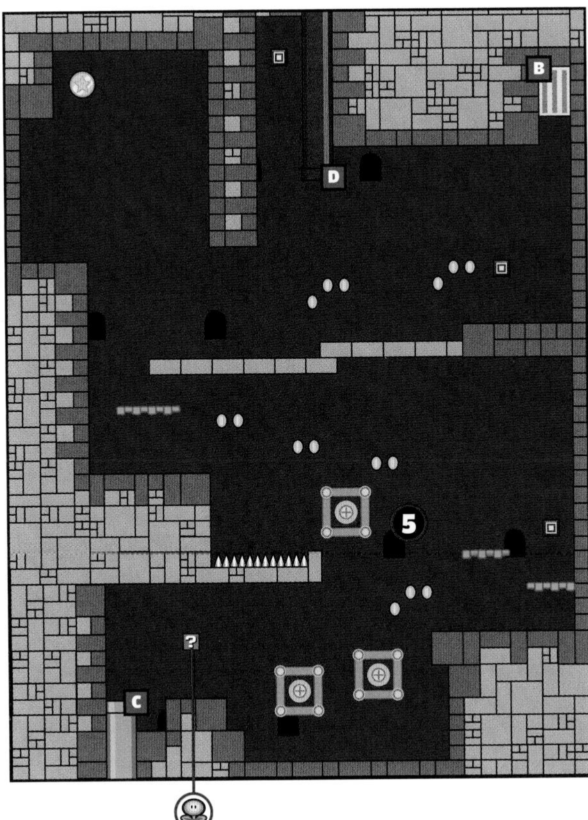

Boss

This battle begins just as it did in the World 1 tower, but Bowser Jr. will change his pattern and start jumping after you score the second hit. To finish him off, dash under his jumps and stomp him when he lands. If you fall into the quicksand, all is not lost—simply jump out and back to the battlefield.

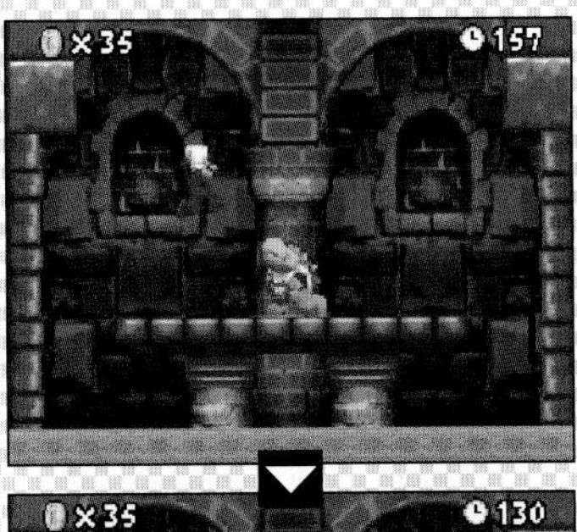

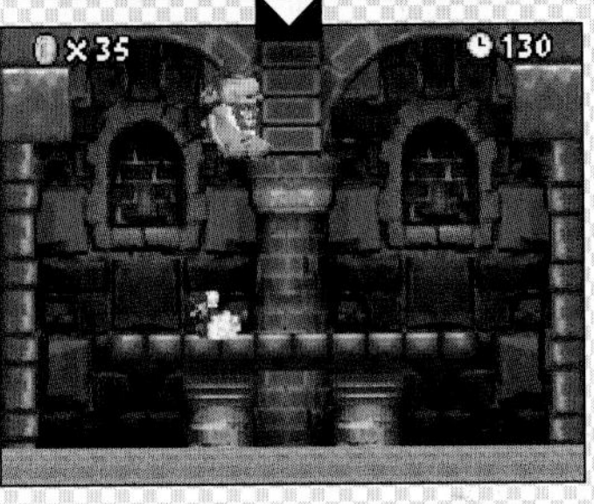

5 The Rotating Platforms

Hit the red-and-yellow blocks to generate a series of rotating platforms above the spike pit. In the upper level, a second switch will create a platform path to the red pipe, but to get to the final Star Coin you'll need to Wall-Jump between the pipe and the wall and hit one last switch.

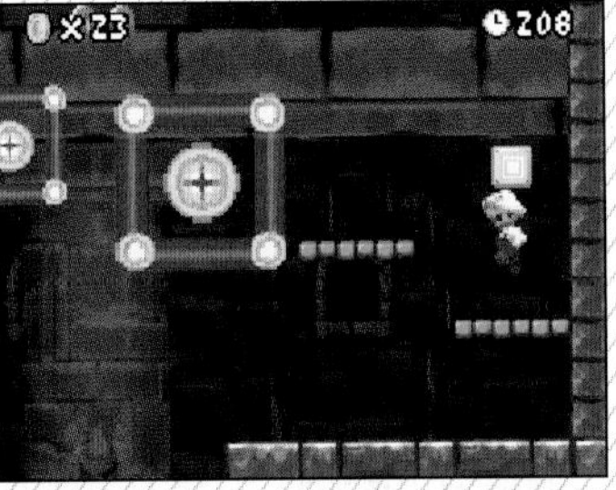

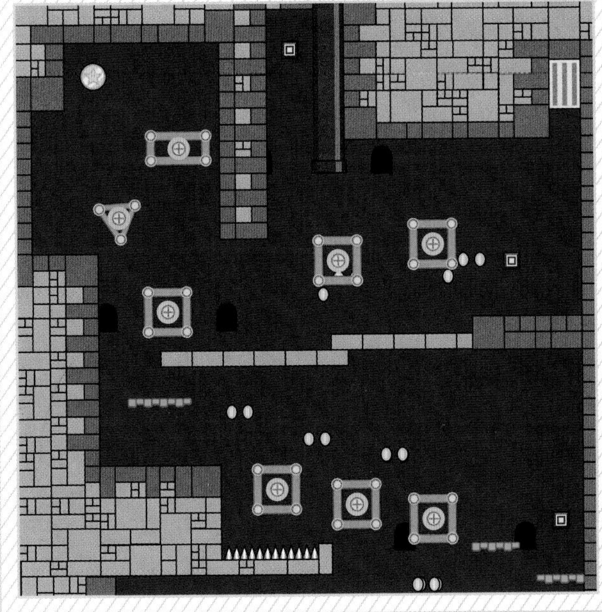

World 2-5

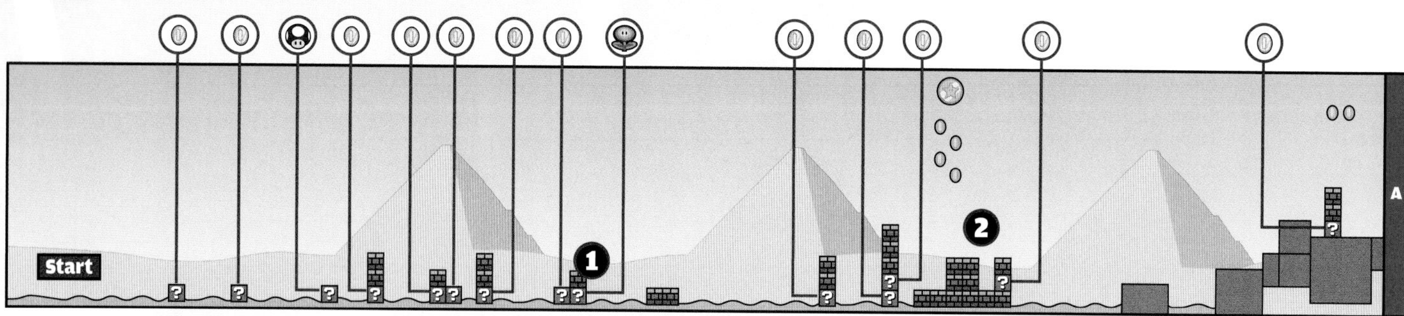

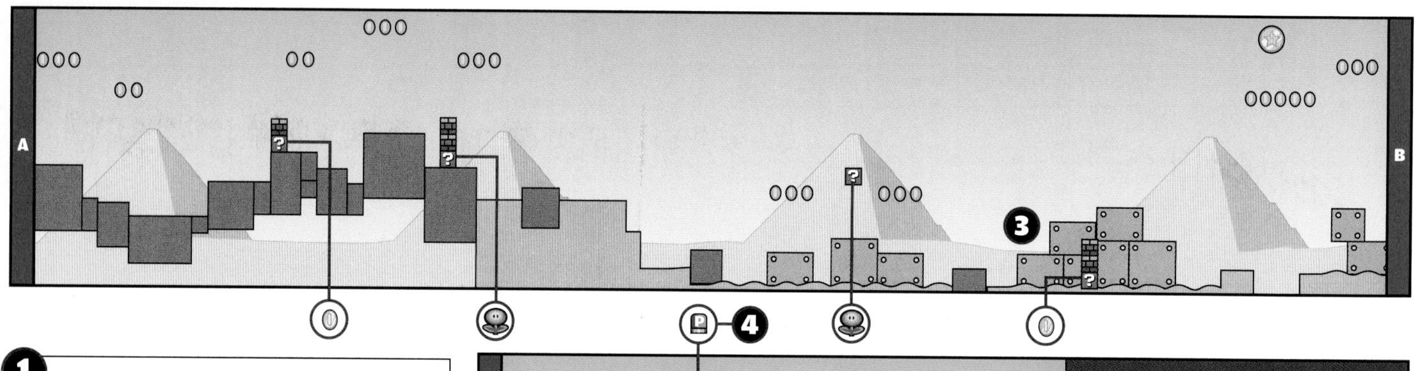

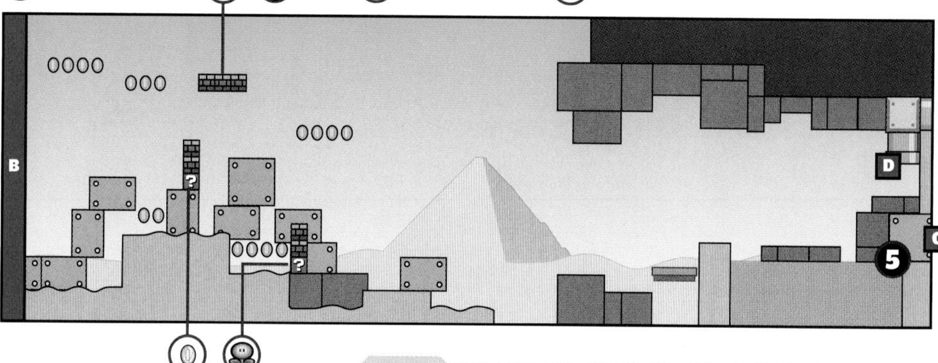

1 This stage seems to be full of ? Blocks, but many are enemies in disguise. You can Ground-Pound them for items, but if you stand too close, they might pound you.

2 Don't Ground-Pound the ? Block impostors at point 2, because you'll need to hop off of their tops to reach the first Star Coin.

3 The flaming snakes that prowl this area are vulnerable only to Mega Mario and Shell Mario. As other Mario forms, stay low to the ground and walk in front of the metal sheets to avoid the serpents.

4 The Golden Road in the Sky

Don't grab the floating coins after point 3—you can use them as platforms to reach the Star Coin once you find and activate the P Switch.

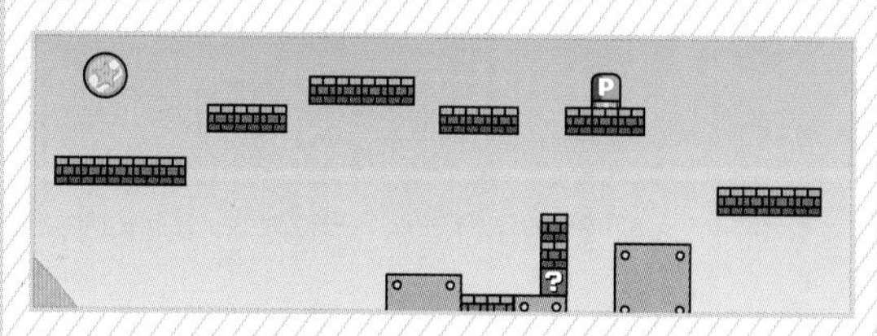

5 Leap over the bro's boomerangs (both when coming and going) and stomp his head. Or, if you're going for the final Star Coin, jump into the quicksand and let it suck you under the enemy's platform. Hit the jump button to swim through the muck, and emerge in the alcove that contains the metal sheet. Continue right to an area where you can jump off an impostor ? Block to reach the last Star Coin. Show your gratitude by Ground-Pounding the impostor for a 1-Up.

World 2-6

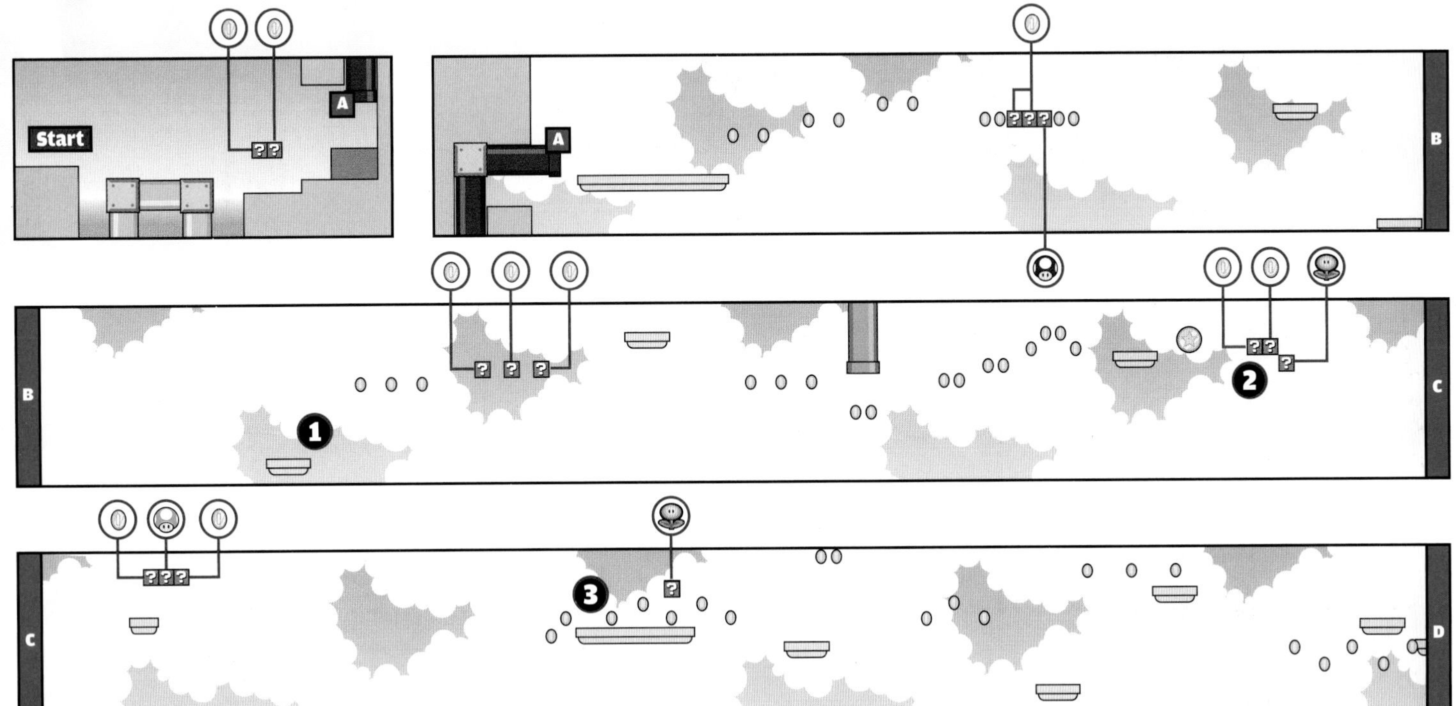

1. This stage is tough if you aren't Fire Mario. Not only will you need to dodge Piranha Plants from the pipe, but some may hitch a ride on your platform. Dodge them until you have a chance to grab a Fire Flower.

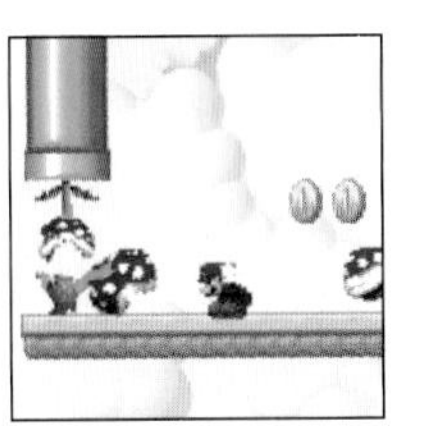

2. Study the map carefully, since it's difficult to hit every ? Block in the time allotted. If you know which ones hold the power-ups, you won't take unnecessary risks.

3. At point 3, jump on another platform to make it scroll along the map with you. Use it to reach coins and ? Blocks on the upper portion of the map, and to dodge hitchhiking Piranha Plants.

4. You've been through a lot together, but it's time to wipe away the tears and bid farewell to the platform that has carried you so far. Use the fixed platforms to jump through the remainder of the stage.

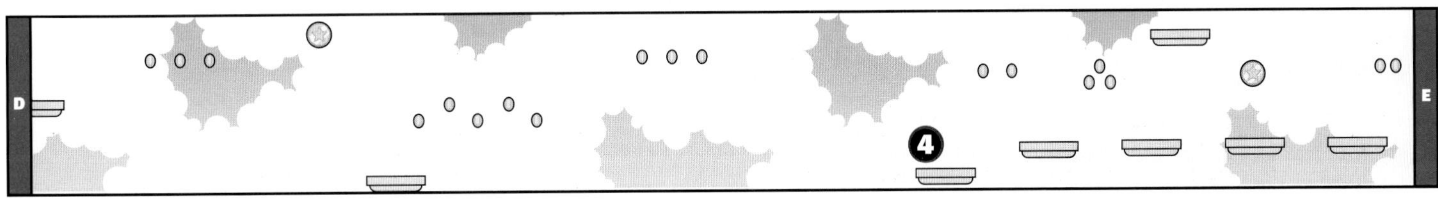

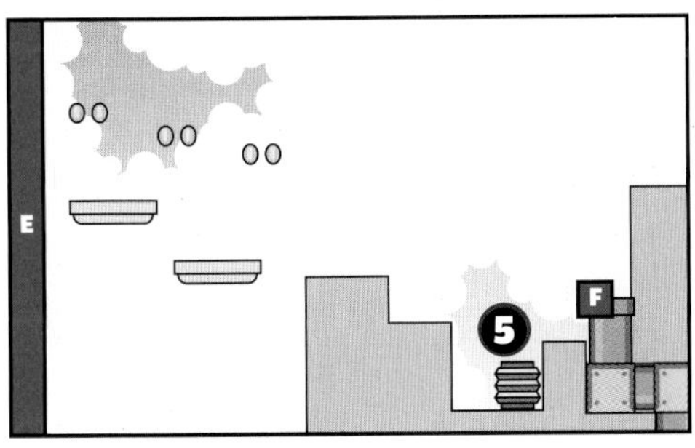

5. Jump on the accordion spring back on solid ground to launch the cork out of the pipe, and the Piranha Plant along with it.

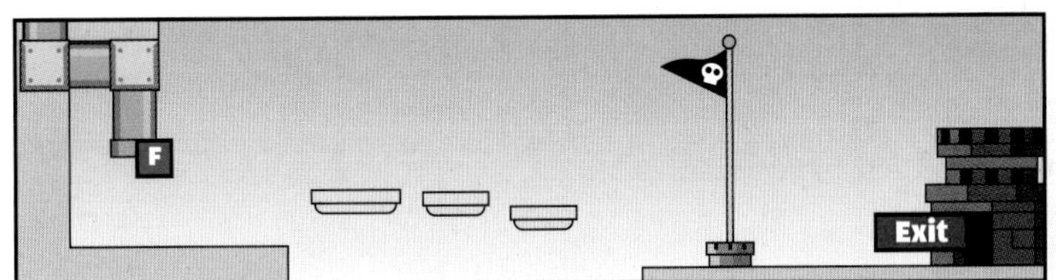

World 2 Castle

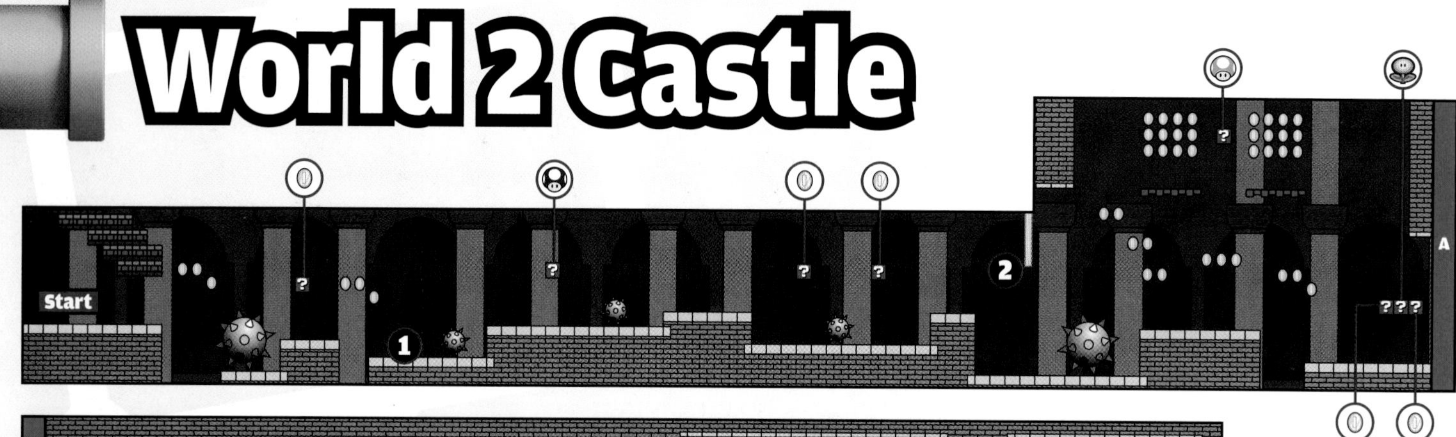

1 Wait for the massive spiked ball to roll into the pit, then leap over the smaller balls on the next few ledges. These heavy objects are impervious to everything except a kick from Mega Mario.

2 Long-jump onto the rope at point 2 and press left and right to get Mario swinging. When you're swinging so high that you're above the screen, leap onto a secret ledge. You'll hit the ground running, so be prepared to jump again to a second ledge, or you'll dash right off the edge! Your well-timed jump will also hit a block that holds a 1-Up Mushroom.

3 When you don't have room to jump the spiked balls, look for crevasses where you can crouch and let them roll safely overhead. Wall-Jump at the end of the tight passage to grab the first Star Coin.

4 You'll need to jump off of a Bullet Bill to reach the second Star Coin. Don't stress over the timing—if you hold down the jump button, you'll automatically hop off of your foe after you stomp it.

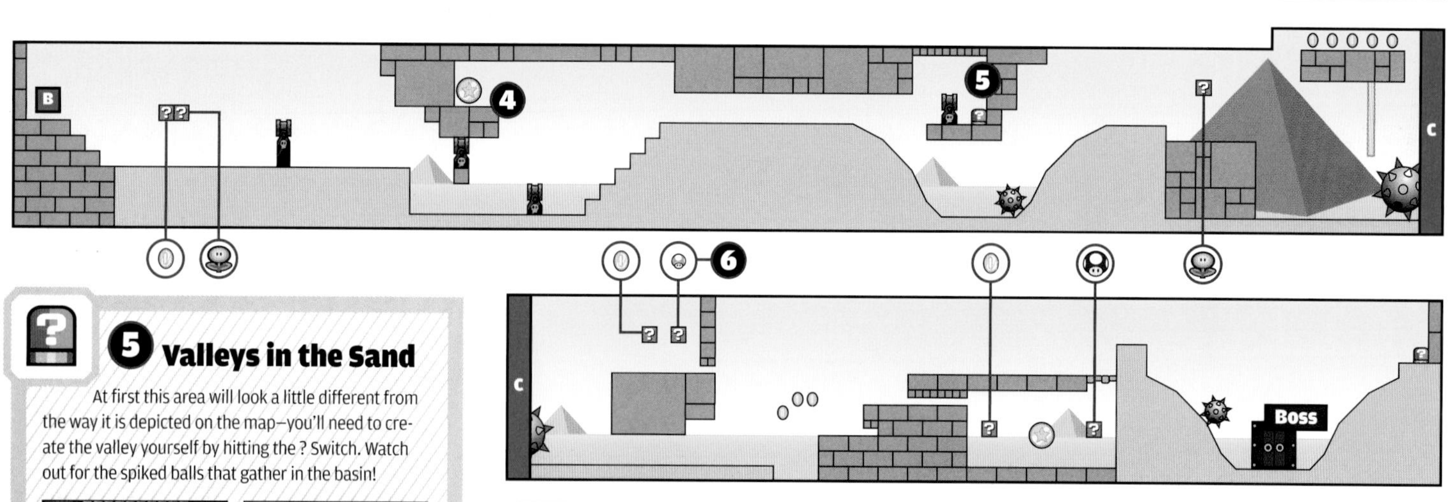

5 Valleys in the Sand

At first this area will look a little different from the way it is depicted on the map—you'll need to create the valley yourself by hitting the ? Switch. Watch out for the spiked balls that gather in the basin!

6 You'll need to use the Mini Mushroom at point 6 to get the final Star Coin, but think carefully before you trade it for a Super Mushroom afterward—beating the boss as Mini Mario is the only way to open the route to World 4.

Boss

You'll need to stomp Mummipokey's head to do damage, but at times its head will be higher than you can jump. To make things easier, hang out near the walls, and Wall-Jump off of them when the boss begins to emerge from the sand, then press down to do a Ground Pound when you pass overhead.

Most Mario versions can damage the boss with either stomps or Ground Pounds, but Mini Mario can deal damage only with the Ground Pound move.

World 3

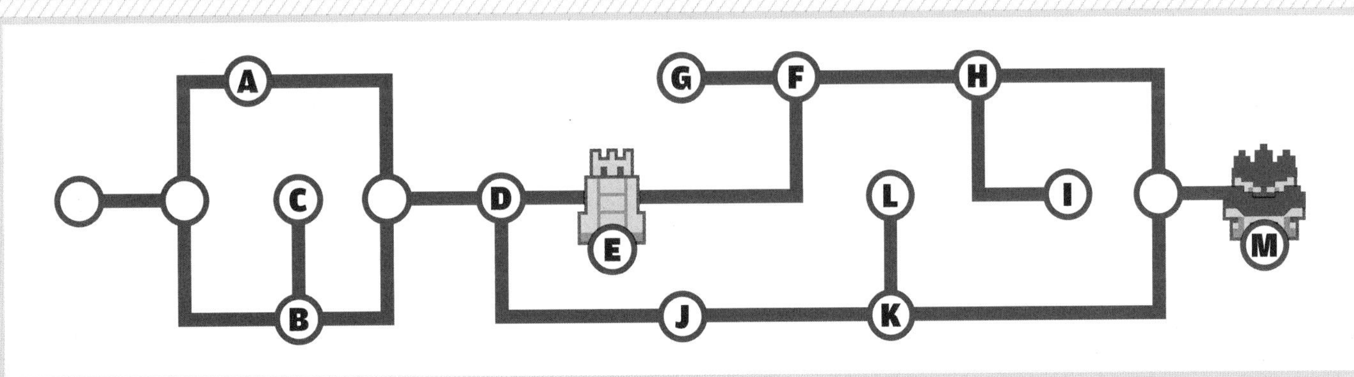

(A) World 3-1 (Page 40)

(B) World 3-A (Page 41)

(C) Red Toad House (5 Star Coins)

(D) World 3-2 (Page 42)

(E) World 3 Tower (Page 43)

(F) World 3-3 (Page 44)

(G) Orange Toad House (5 Star Coins)

(H) World 3 Ghost House (Page 45)

(I) Warp Cannon (To World 6)

(J) World 3-B (Page 46)

(K) World 3-C (Page 47)

(L) Green Toad House (5 Star Coins)

(M) World 3 Castle (Page 48)

World 3-1

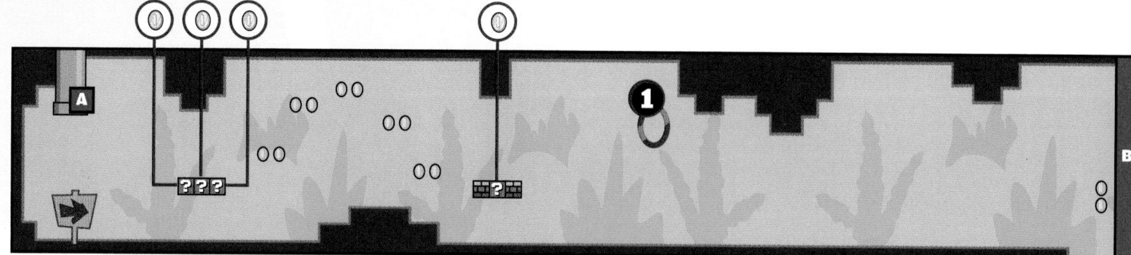

1 Red-Coin Ring

Weave between the schools of fish to collect the red coins generated by the ring at point 1.

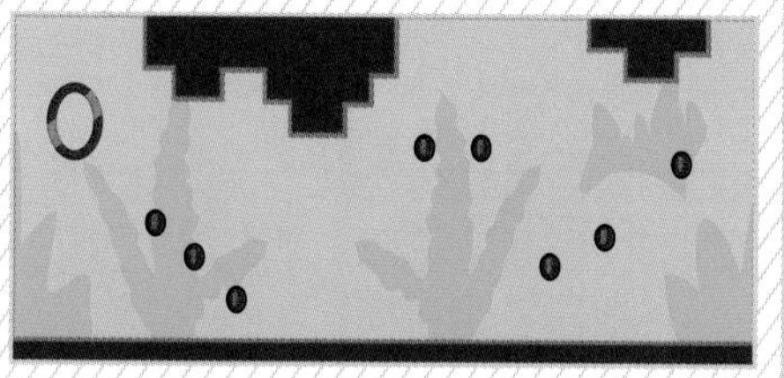

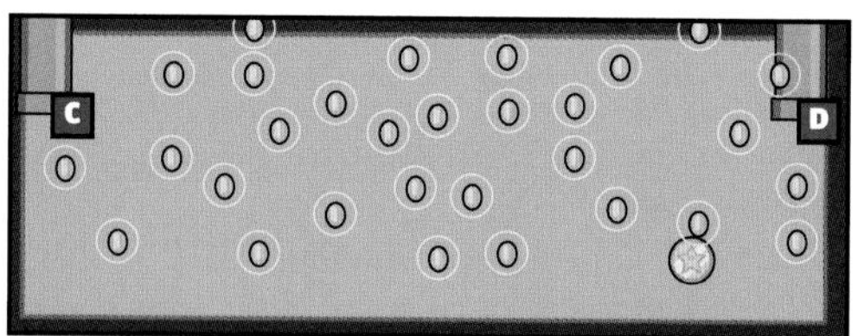

2

While the orange Cheep-Cheeps seem oblivious to your presence, the purple Cheep-Chomps will actively seek you out. If you can't blast a purple one with a fireball, lure it to the left of the screen so you can swim past it and reach the pipe (C) without risk of being blown into its maw by the air bubbles.

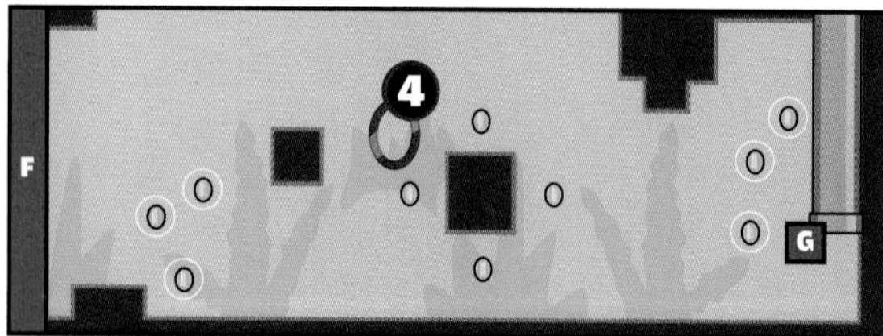

3 The P Switch and the Star Coin

If you're Super Mario, you don't need to worry about getting to the Star Coin before the P Switch effect fades, since you can punch right through the blocks. Smaller Marios, on the other hand, will need to hurry.

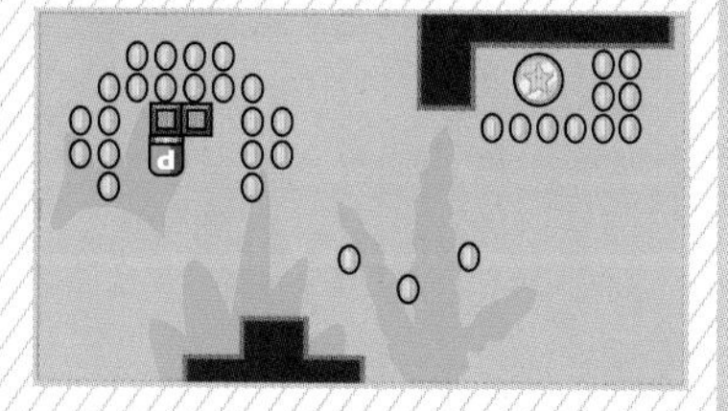

4 More Red Coins

The red coins generated by the red-coin ring can be tricky to get while the Cheep-cheep is chasing you. Stay one paddle ahead of your pursuer by grabbing the coin that's to the lower right of the loop and swimming in a figure-eight pattern from there.

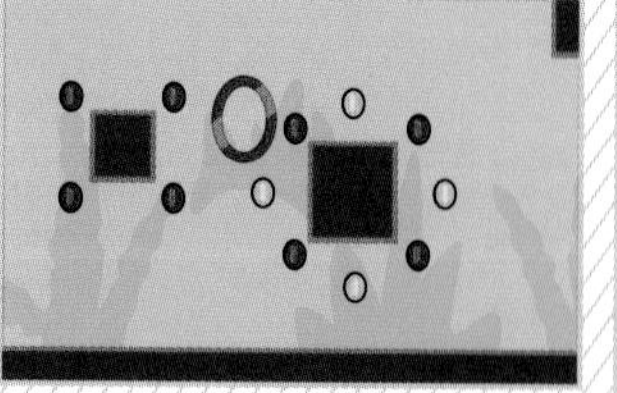

World 3-A

1 The floating Skeeters can be defeated with a good stomping, but at times they come in handy—the depth charge-like creatures they drop may destroy underwater obstacles.

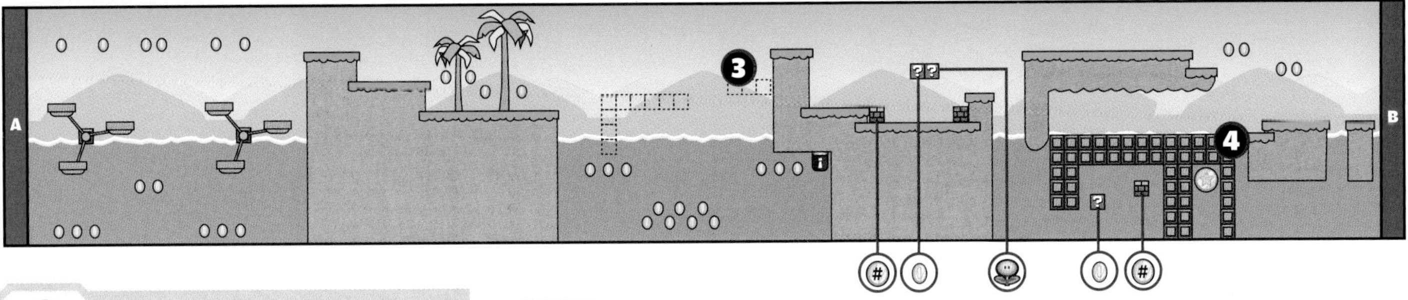

2 Red-Coin Ring

Defeat the Skeeter first, then collect the red coins in a clockwise motion, jumping up onto land and then off the right edge.

3 !-Switch Blocks

Use the ! Switch to generate a series of red blocks you can use to reach the ledge. Or for a challenge, jump off the Skeeter's back.

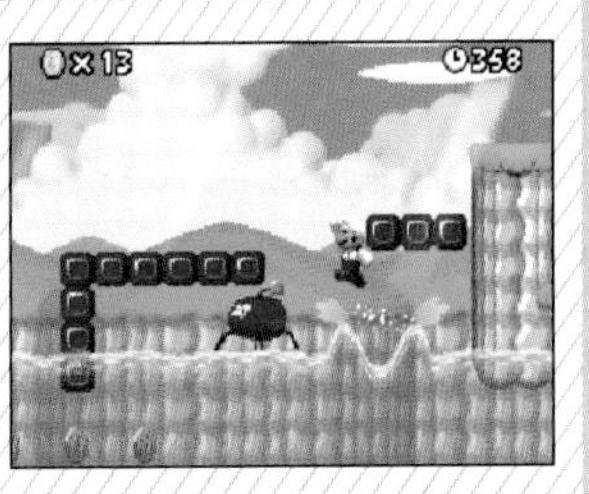

4 The Skeeter's bombs can destroy these otherwise-indestructible blocks, so trick it into creating a path to the Star Coin at point 4.

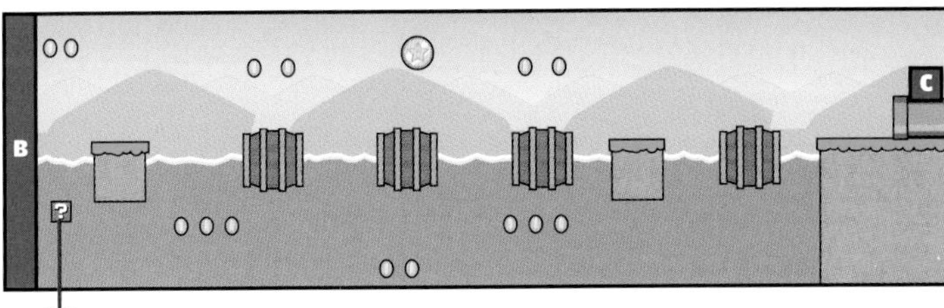

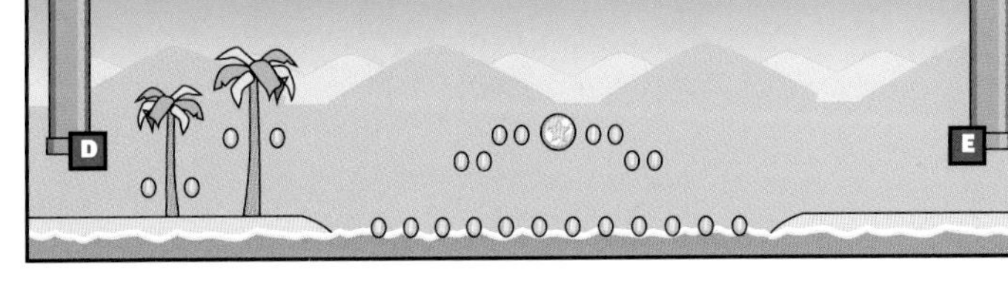

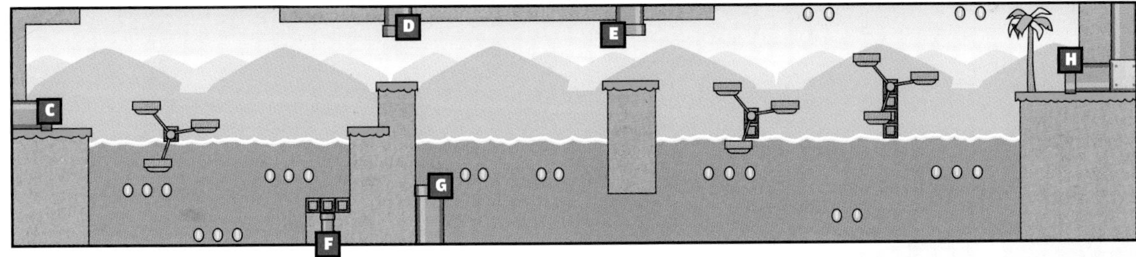

5 Eat the Mini Mushroom at point 5 and swim to pipe F, where a Skeeter will be happy to clear the blocks above it. When you emerge from pipe G, bounce off the Skeeter up to pipe D, which will take you to a beach area. As Mini Mario, you can dash along the water's surface to pick up the lesser coins, then jump into the final Star Coin. The Mini Mario form will also make it easy to hit the top of the flagpole.

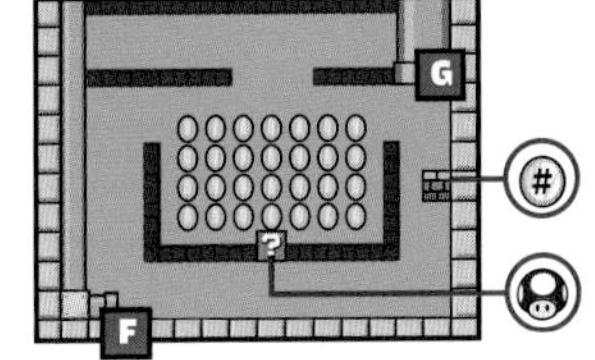

World 3-2

1 Stomp the Koopa and kick its shell to the right when the mushroom platform is tilting downward toward the block that holds the 1-Up. Grab the 1-Up Mushroom, then run left to make another Koopa appear, and carry its shell to the next mushroom platform. Kick it when the platforms right side is tilted upward, and run along with the shell to score two 1-Ups from the foes it hits. Watch out for the rebound when it hits the ledge!

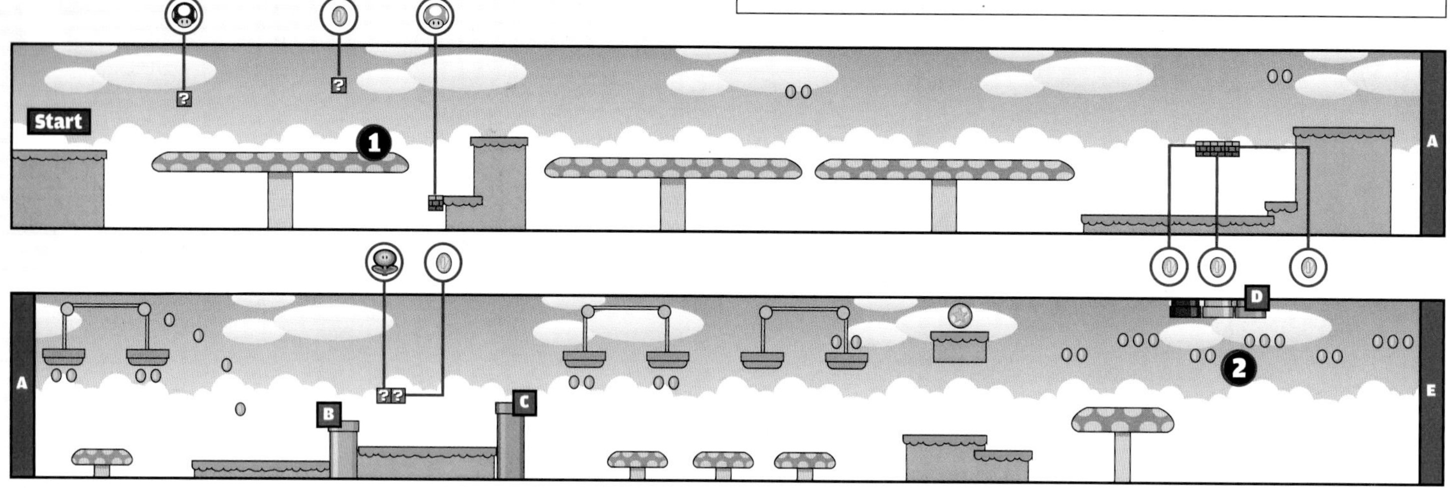

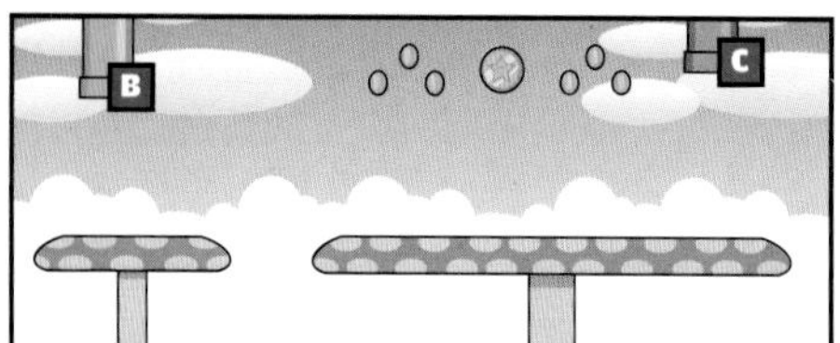

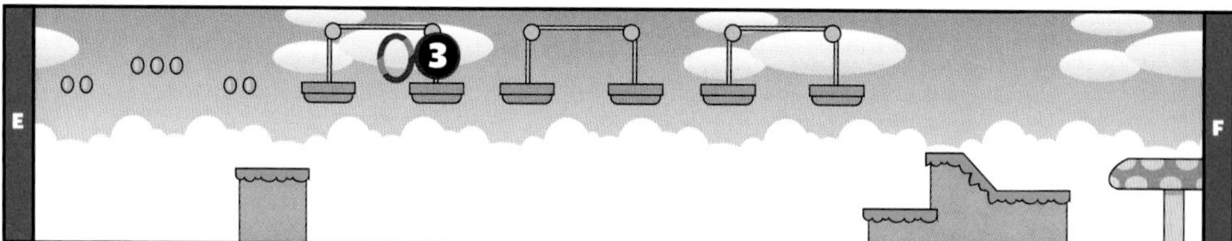

2 P Switch & Alternate Exit

Leap from the moving mushroom platform into the green pipe above, which connects to a cloud area with a P Switch that generates over 100 coins. The next pipe leads to a new area, where a dozen gyrating mushroom platforms stand between you and the red-flag exit.

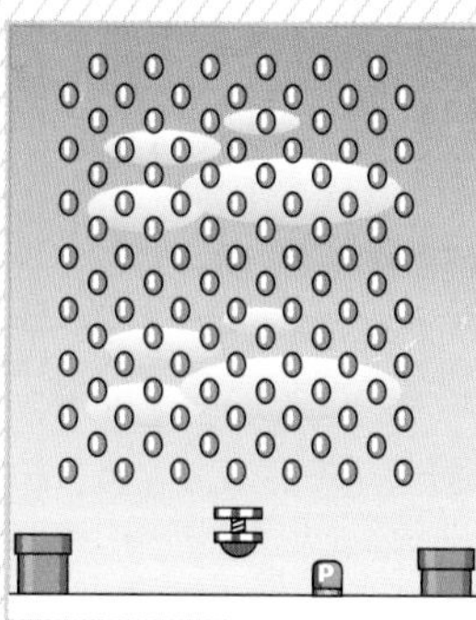

3 Red Coins on the Scales

This red-coin ring generates two coins at the bottom of the screen. Daring players can stand on the final platform until it falls into the coins, then leap to safety at the last possible minute.

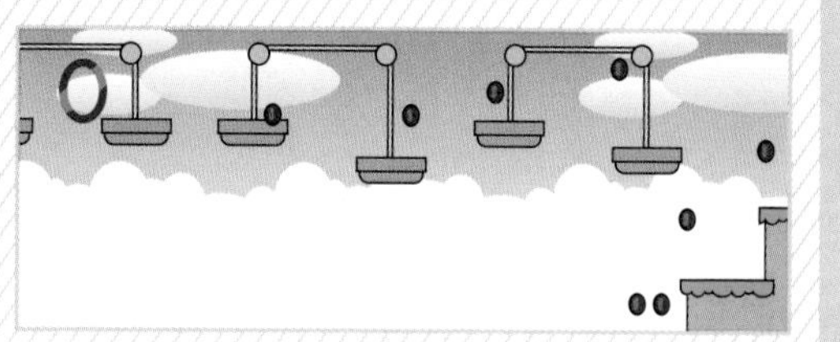

4 Stand at the right edge of the mushroom platform and jump to the Star Coin as the platform's right edge tilts upward. If you miss, you can get another chance by running to the left edge and jumping when that tilts upward. If you still can't get it, don't worry—the mushroom platform will travel back to the left eventually.

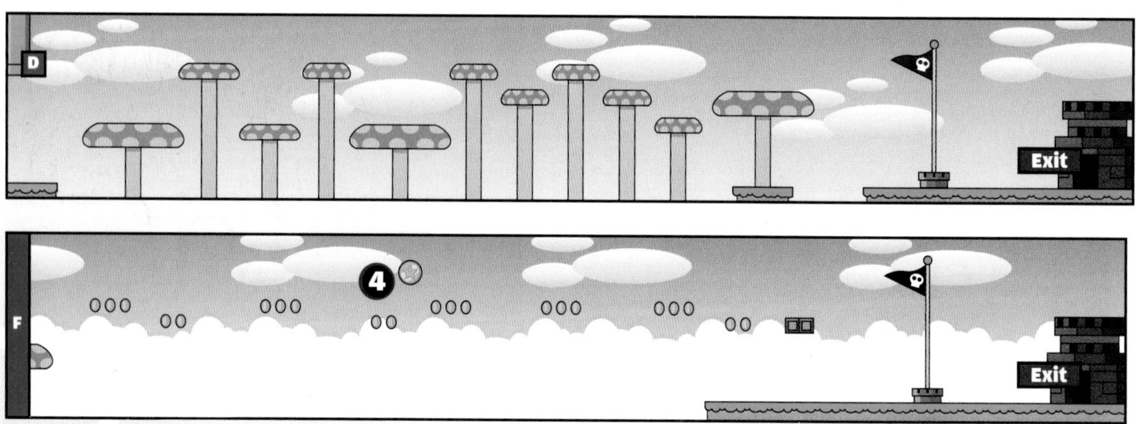

World 3 Tower

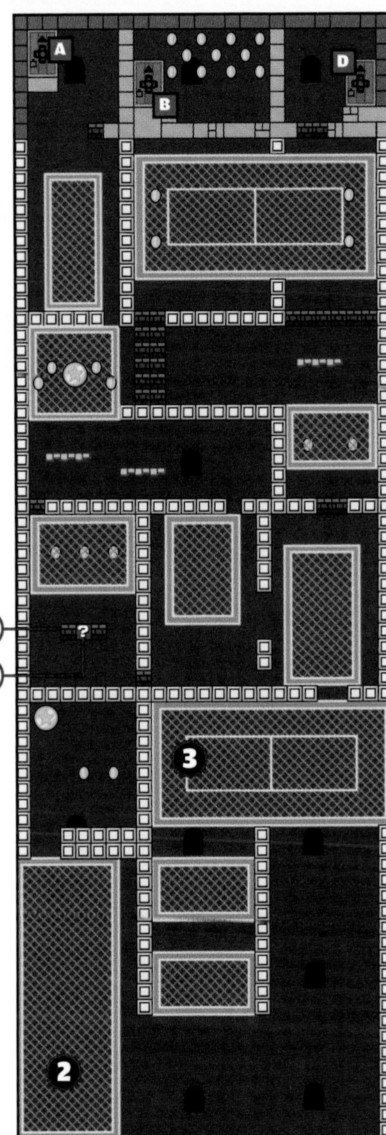

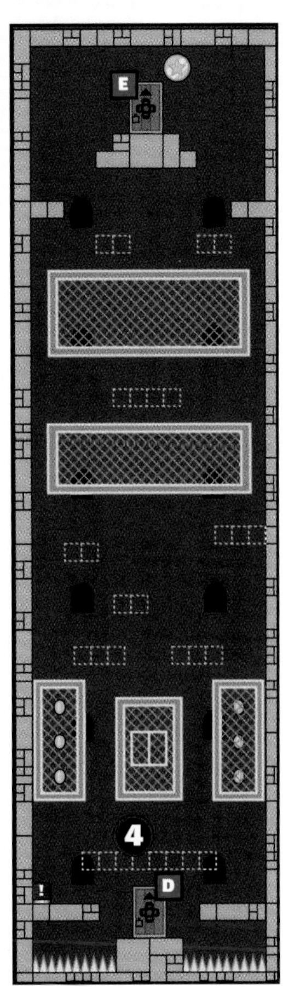

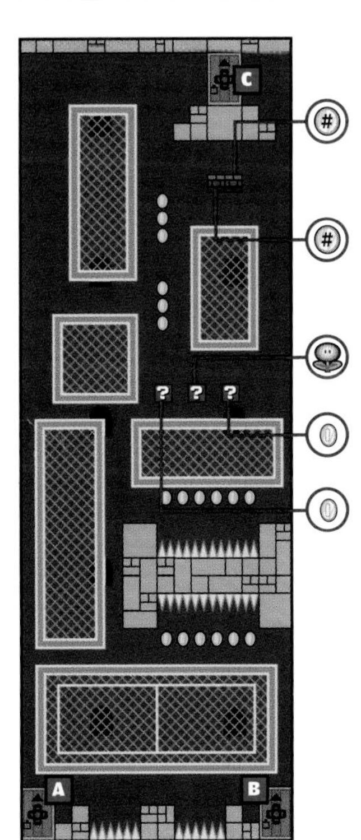

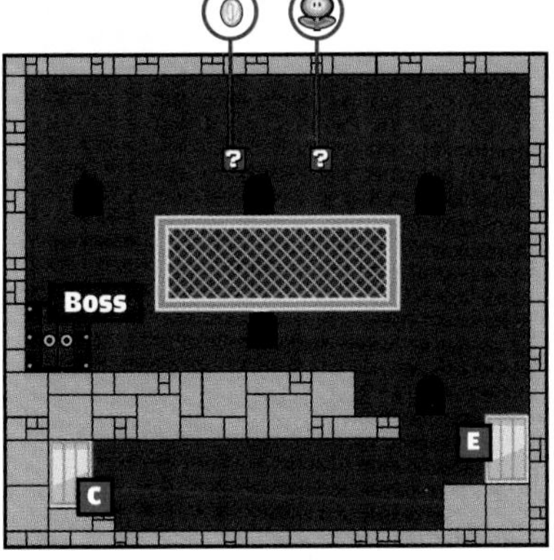

1 Launch yourself from the center pipe, pass the first fence, then grab it on your way down. You can climb that fence to the first Star Coin.

2 While you're clinging to fences, press the dash button to punch Koopas on the other side. If you're on the same side as a Koopa, you can stomp it from above.

3 When you punch the gates set in the fence, you'll flip the structure, putting Mario on the other side of the fence. You can proceed this way, but you'll need to loop around and reverse yourself again to get the second Star Coin.

4 The Red-Platform Climb

There are multiple paths to the boss door, but to get all three Star Coins you'll need to enter door D after claiming the first two coins. Inside door D's room, you'll find a ! Switch that generates a stairway of blocks you can climb to the top. If you run out of time, you can bounce off of the top Koopa to reach the final ledge.

Boss

As in World 2, Bowser Jr. will shake up his pattern by jumping after you score your second stomp. Be ready to duck the jump and retaliate!

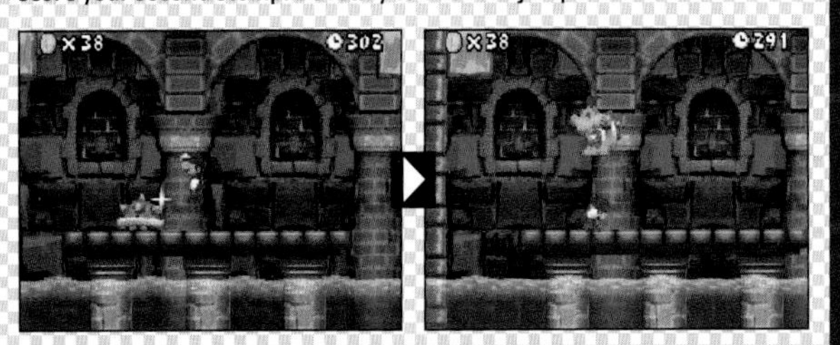

World 3-3

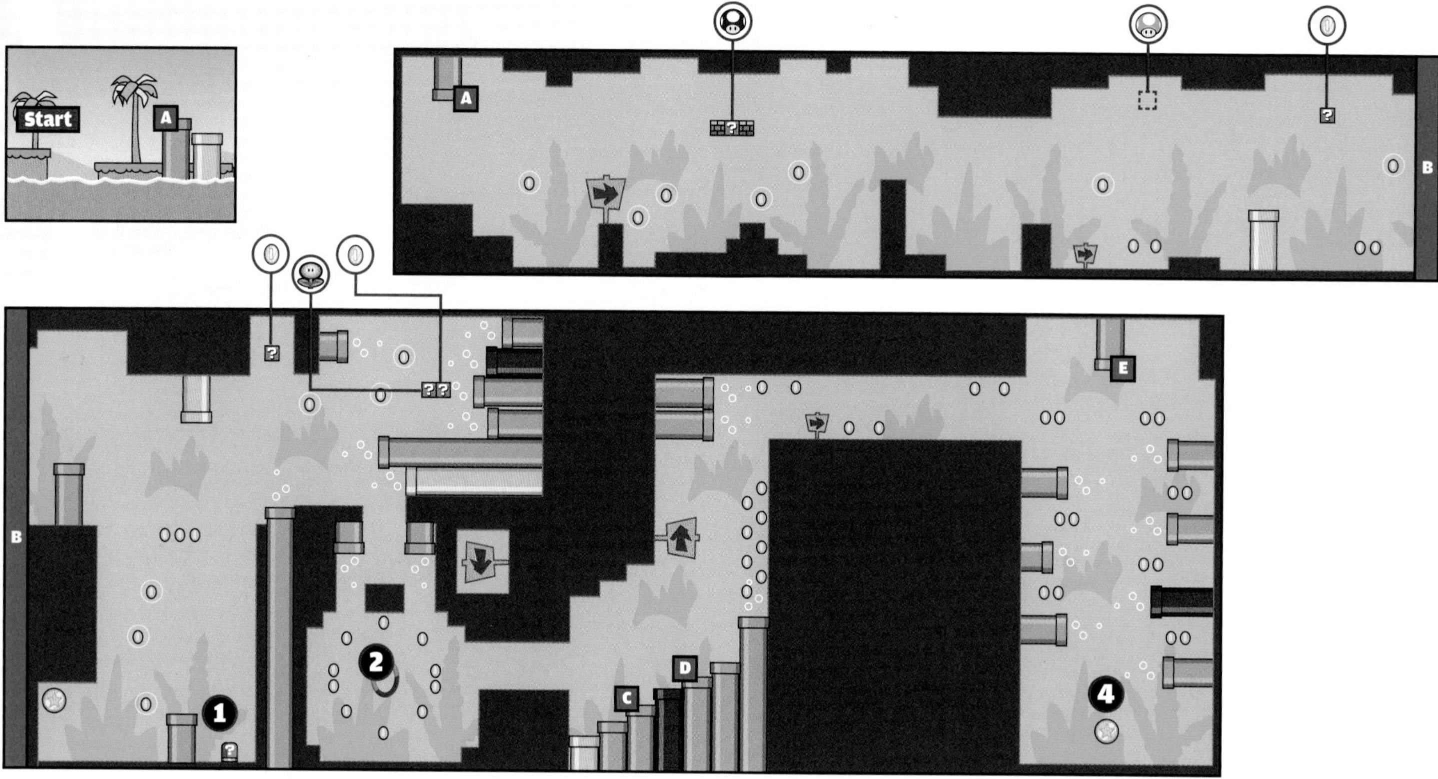

1 Hit the ? Switch at point 1 to stop the airflow from the pipes above, allowing you to slip through the gap beneath them. Don't worry if you run out of time by going for the power-up—the ? Switch will return.

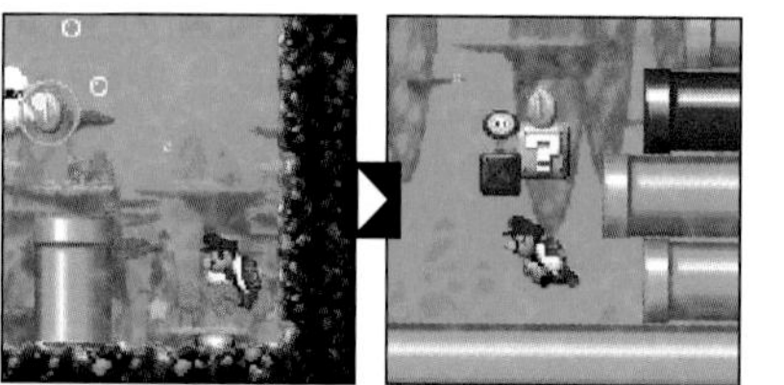

2 Red-Coin Ring

World 3-3's red-coin ring offers a simple test of your basic swimming skills. Take the four upper coins first and proceed clockwise or counterclockwise to pick up the rest.

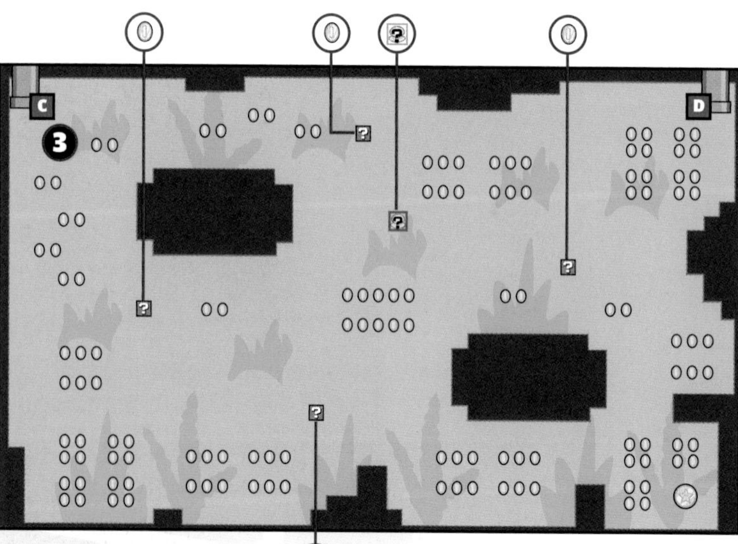

3 This vast area is filled with coins and ? Blocks, but guarded by a school of Bloopers. The Bloopers can generate smaller Bloopers and shoot them in all directions, so it's best not to engage them at all. Simply grab your Star Coin and swim to an exit.

4 When you take the Star Coin at point 4, four Bloopers will appear. Get the coin from below so you can sink to the exit without being blown into a Blooper.

World 3 Ghost House

1 Switches Reveal Steps

The ? Switches found throughout this level will make steps appear on the sharply inclined ramps. The steps will retract after only a few seconds, so don't dawdle!

2 Boos will freeze when you look their direction, but move closer when your back is turned. Lure them in by turning away, then leap over them when they get close.

3 The right-hand ? Block contains a Boo instead of an item. If you accidentally free it, at least it can't follow you out of the room.

4 Bounce off of a Splunkin to reach this Star Coin. Keep bouncing—if you can hit each Splunkin twice, you'll nab a 1-Up.

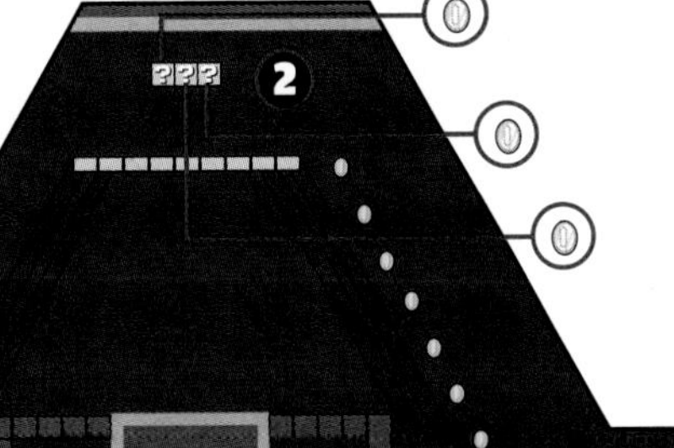

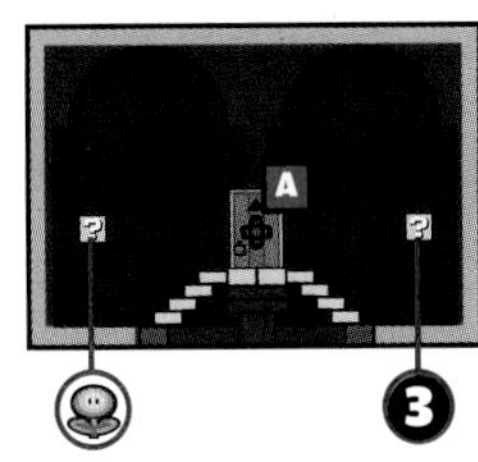

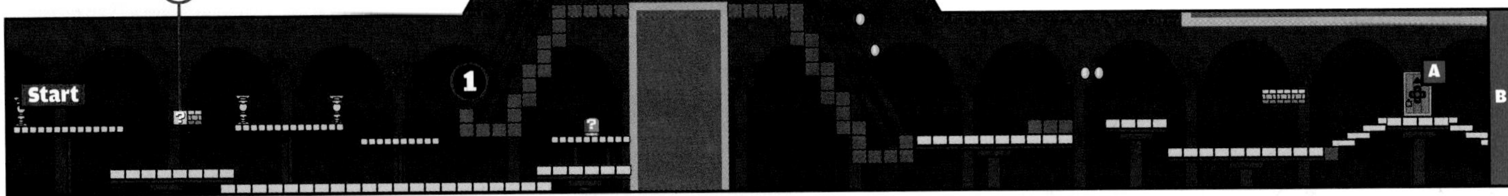

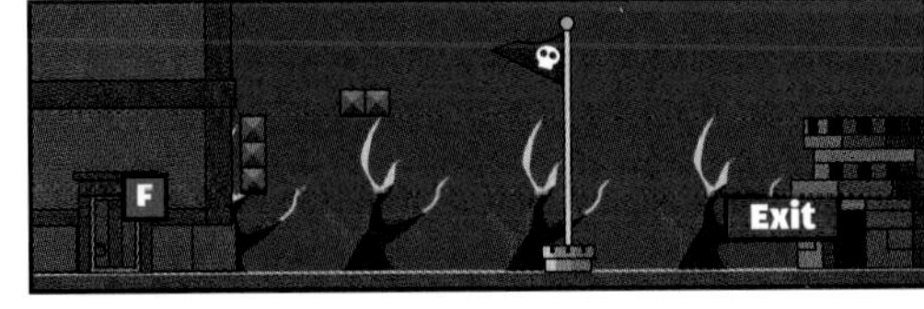

5 Race to the Alternate Exit

In addition to raising the stairs, the ? Switch at point 5 will make two doors appear on the map. Door D leads to the next area of the ghost house, but door G will take you straight to the warp-cannon exit. Reaching it in time won't be easy; stomp the block, dash to the right, Wall-Jump onto the staircase, long-jump from the platform at the end of the stairs, and leap down the stairs without touching them. Be ready to dash right to the door when you land—every millisecond counts!

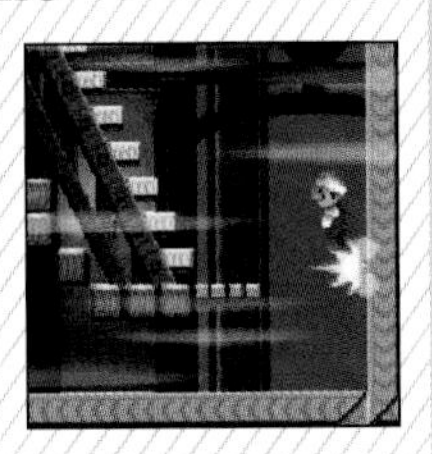

6 Use the Roulette Block to get a blue Koopa shell. Not only will it allow you to slide up the ramps without using a ? Switch, but it will also let you smash through the blocks that obstruct the final Star Coin.

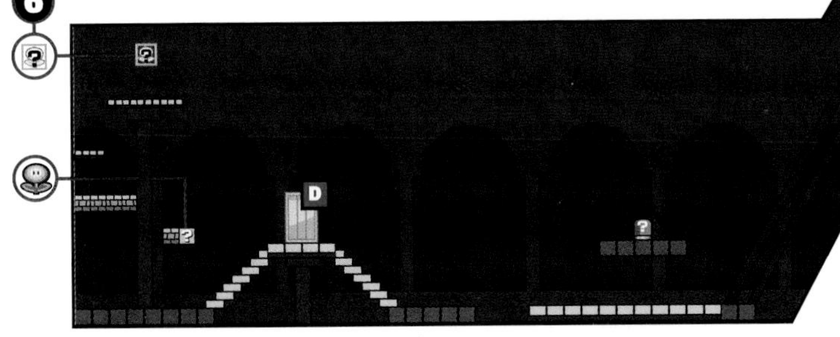

World 3-B

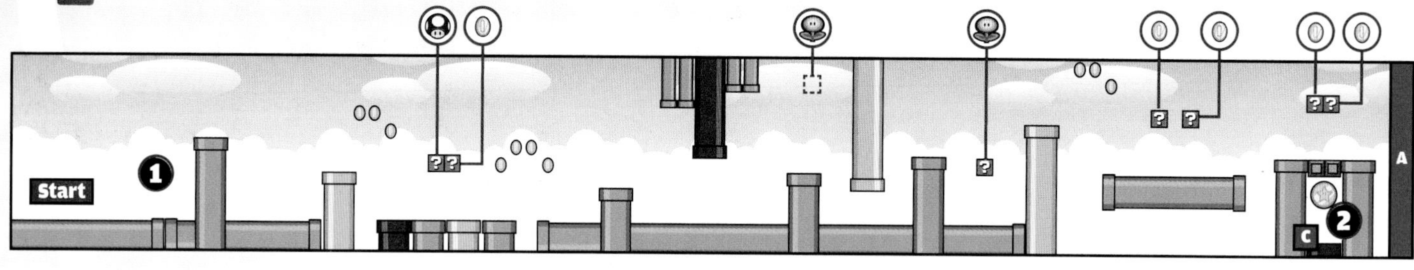

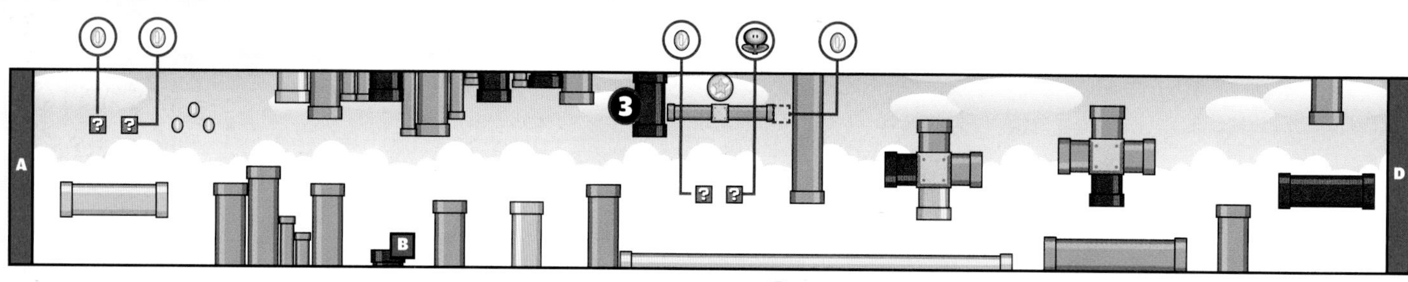

1 This is a great place to use a Mega Mushroom—smashing pipes fills up the carnage meter quickly and all but guarantees you all five 1-Ups.

2 Pass the first Star Coin, and continue until you see another red pipe set into the floor (B). That pipe will take you to a lower level with a Roulette Block and the red pipe that leads to the Star Coin. Beware of the Piranha Plants, which always return from the dead when you pass through a pipe.

3 A hidden block obstructs the direct route to the second Star Coin, but you can Wall-Jump between the red and green pipes to the left to reach it from above.

World 3-C

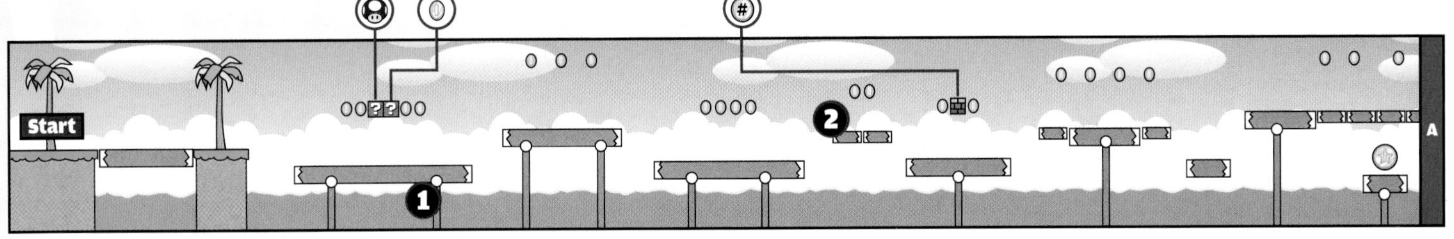

1 The Spike Bass in this stage are hungry for a Mario-flavored meal, and will leap out of the water to get it. Defend yourself with fireballs or Koopa shells.

2 If a platform isn't bolted to the ground, it will collapse when you step on it. Jump off quickly or you'll end up in the drink.

3 The small Cheep-Cheeps are fairly easy to dodge, but you can stomp them in midair if you're looking for some piscine payback.

4 The P-Switch Path to the Star Coin

You're going to need to get a lot of distance out of this P Switch, since the coins at the end of the stage form the only possible platform from which to jump into the red pipe (which will dump you onto the final Star Coin). You have only one shot at this, because the P Switch will not return when the effect fades. Take a second to grab the Starman from the ? Block on the way so you don't have to worry about dodging the Koopas.

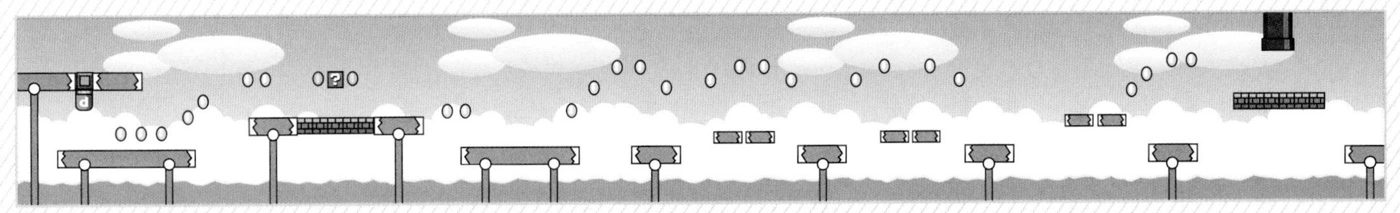

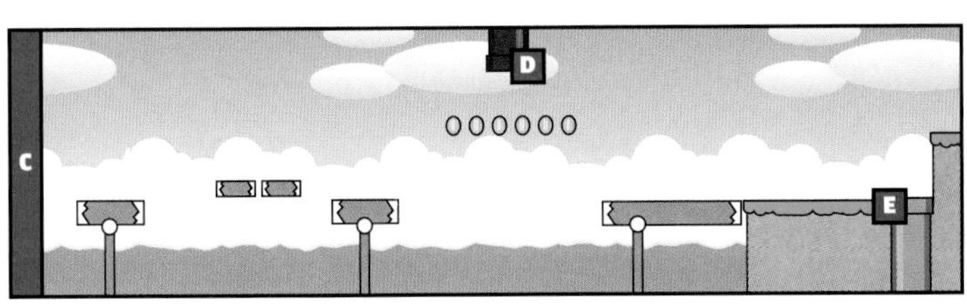

World 3 Castle

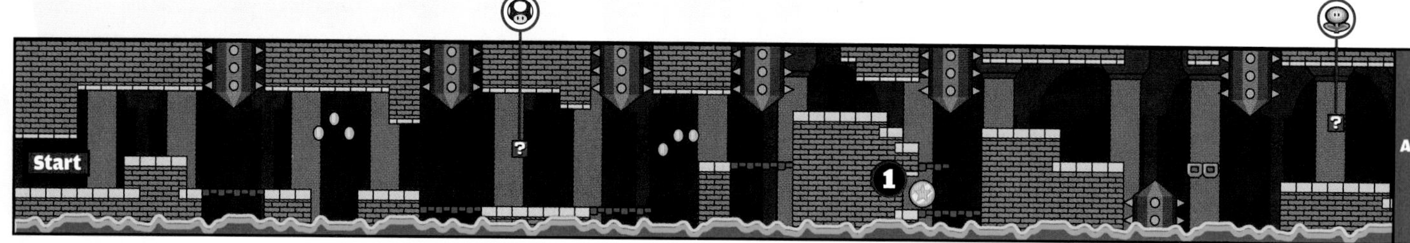

1 Grab the Star Coin and hide in the alcove while the spiked pillar smashes down. Hop back to ground level when it retracts.

2 You can pause near each Whomp, wait for it to fall, then jump on its back to proceed. Or you can zip through with flair by dashing through this area (the Whomps will fall behind you) and making a running leap to the pole. Either way, ignore the Star Coin for now; you can't get it from below.

3 Set the rope swinging, grab the tip, and jump left. Jump above the ceiling and continue left. When the Whomp falls, drop through the Star Coin and onto the Whomp's back.

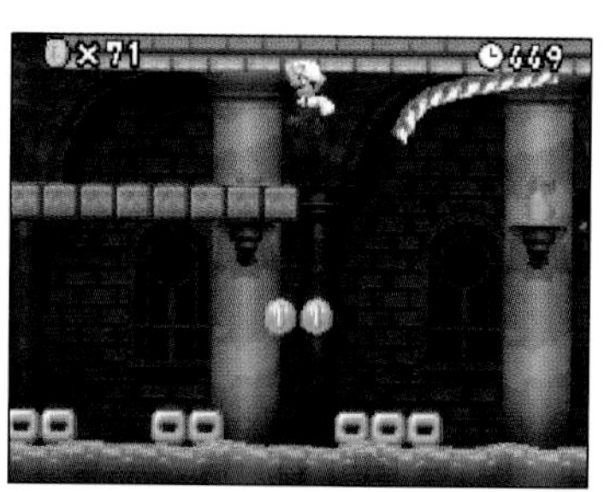

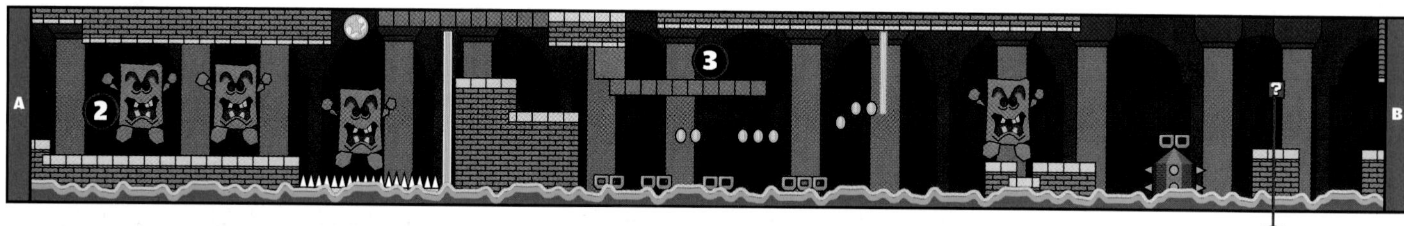

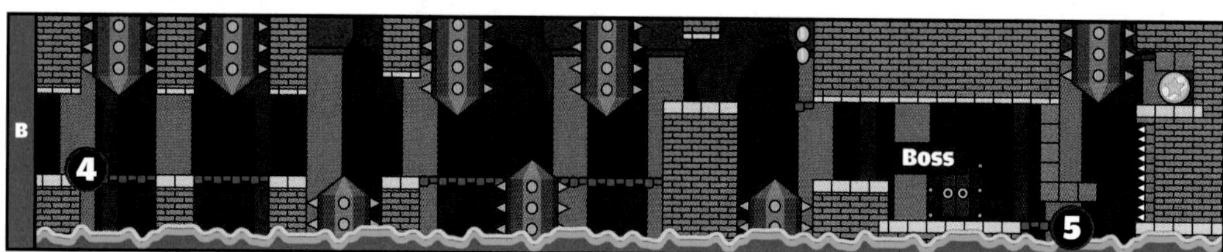

4 Once again, you have the choice of taking this leg slow and steady, or waiting for the first pillar to retract and zipping past the first six pillars with a single mad dash.

5 When the pillar retracts, do a dashing crouch to slip through the gap and into the water. Jump to the ledge and long-jump to the coin. Wait for the pillar to retract again before you head to the boss door.

Boss

Concentrate on dodging the smaller Cheep-Cheeps here—the Cheepskipper is such a huge target you're not likely to miss it when it does flop onto the bridge. Three normal stomps will destroy the boss and reveal the boss key.

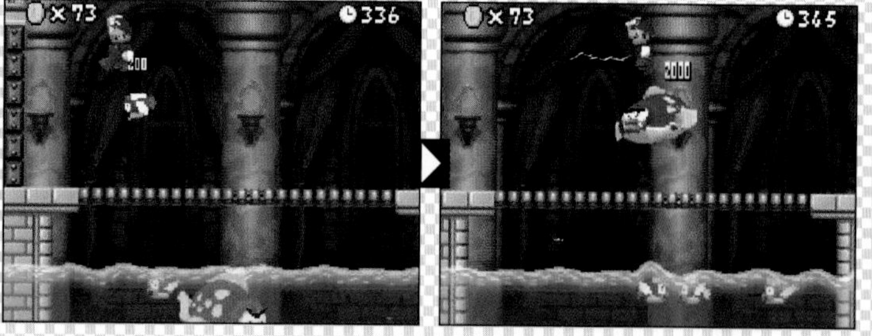

If you stay in the middle of the bridge and jump when the giant Cheep-Cheep does, you'll land on it when it hits the bridge, no matter which side it's jumping from.

World 4

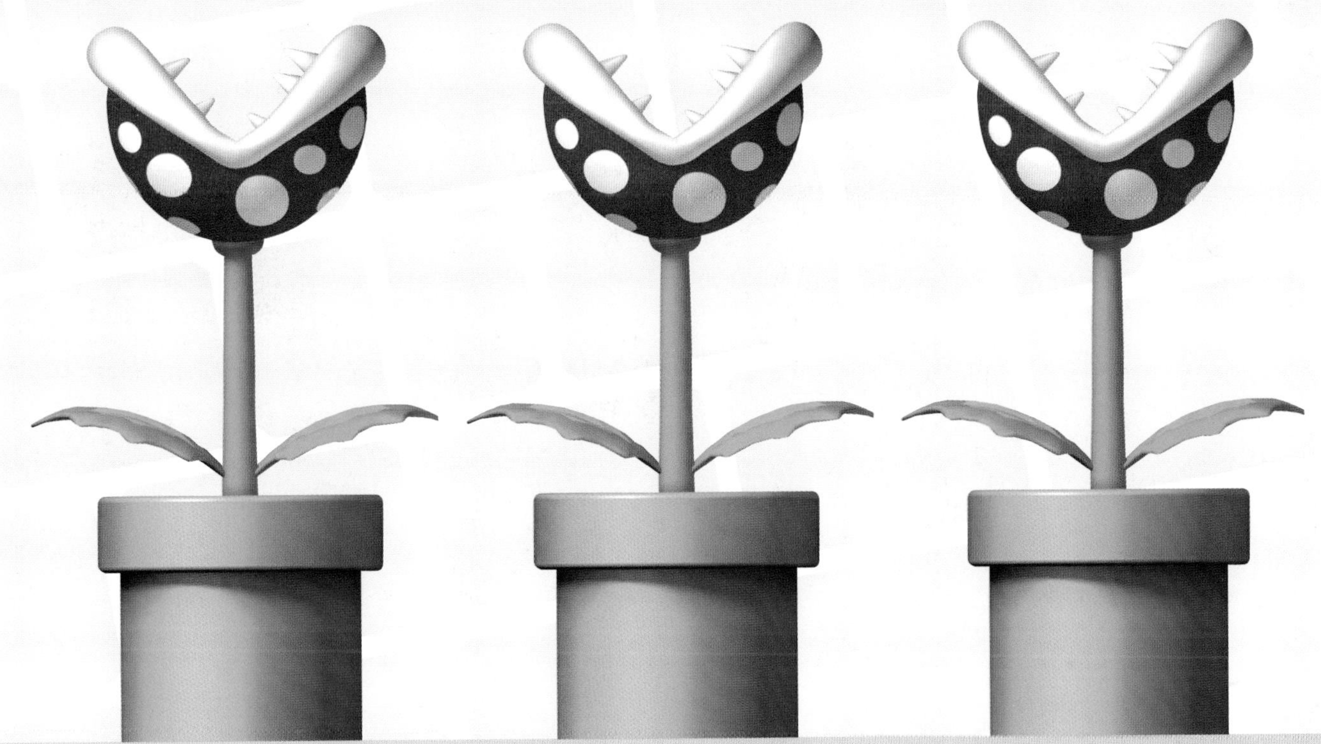

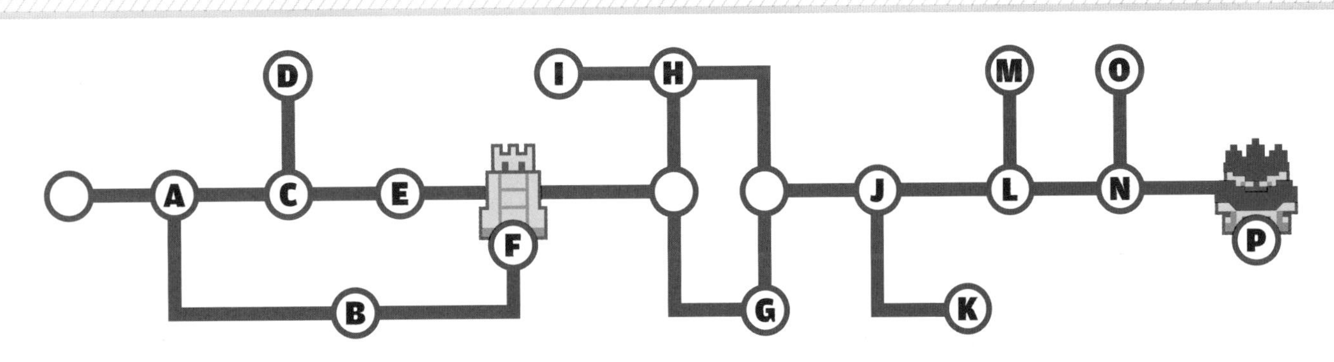

- **(A) World 4-1** (Page 50)
- **(B) Green Toad House**
- **(C) World 4-2** (Page 51)
- **(D) Red Toad House** (5 Star Coins)
- **(E) World 4-3** (Page 52)
- **(F) World 4 Tower** (Page 53)
- **(G) World 4-4** (Page 54)
- **(H) World 4-A** (5 Star Coins/Page 55)
- **(I) Orange Toad House** (5 Star Coins)
- **(J) World 4 Ghost House** (Page 56)
- **(K) Warp Cannon** (To World 7)
- **(L) World 4-5** (Page 58)
- **(M) Green Toad House** (5 Star Coins)
- **(N) World 4-6** (Page 59)
- **(O) Red Toad House** (5 Star Coins)
- **(P) World 4 Castle** (Page 60)

World 4-1

1 This world's purple water is toxic, and it will knock Mario dead if he so much as dips a toe in. The other new hazard is the giant Scuttlebugs that drop from the trees—jump off of their backs instead of trying to slip beneath them.

2 Beginners should focus on survival, but experts can try for 1-Ups by bouncing from enemy to enemy in a continuous chain. For best results, get a running start and hold down the jump button as you stomp them.

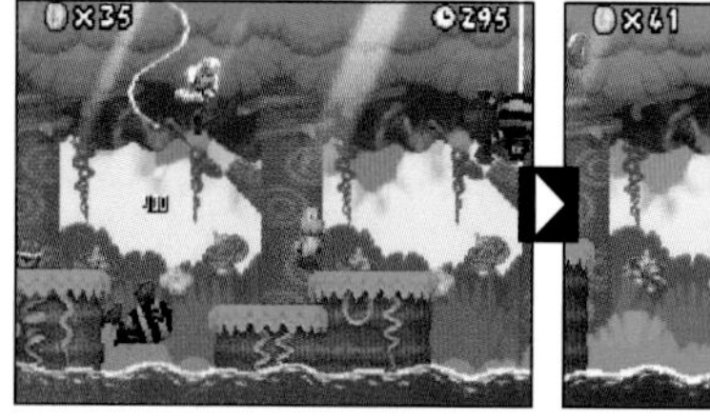

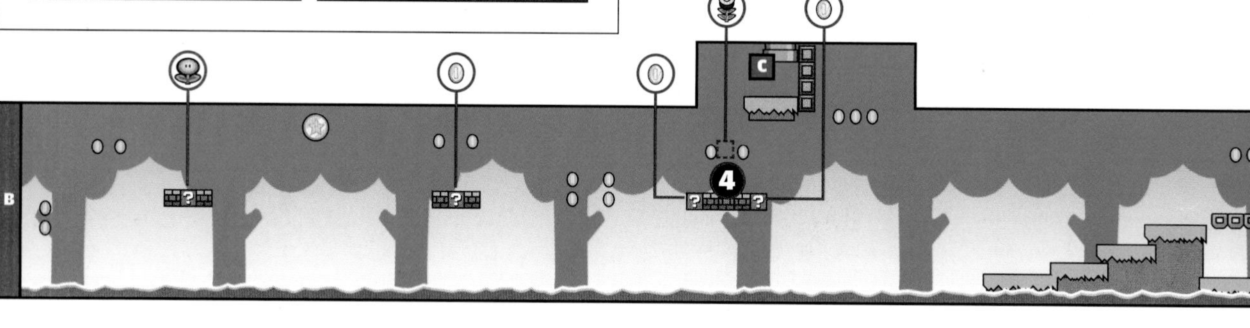

3 When you run out of land, Dorrie will appear to offer you a ride through the remainder of the stage. You can reach high items and platforms by jumping from her head, but to get the Star Coin you'll need to bounce off of a Scuttlebug's back. If you Ground-Pound Dorrie, she'll lower her head and speed up. But with her head low, you may not be able to reach certain items. Ground-Pound her again to have her return to normal.

4 Leap from Dorrie's head to the platform at point 4, and hit the Invisible Block to send a vine skyward. Climb it to a pipe that will take you directly to the level's red-flag exit.

5 Stomp the two hanging spiders, then drop to the floating platforms and dash over the gaps to grab the Star Coin without risk of falling.

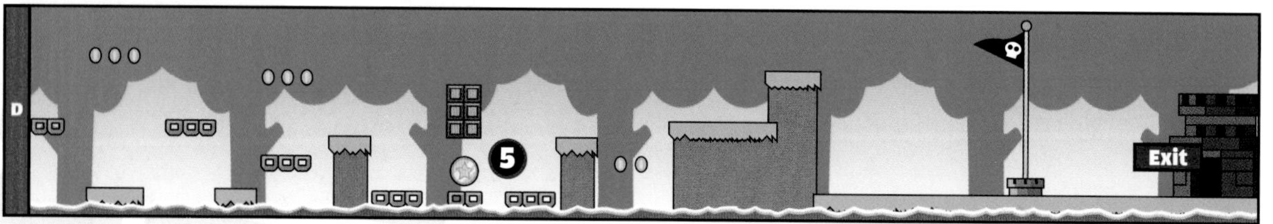

World 4-2

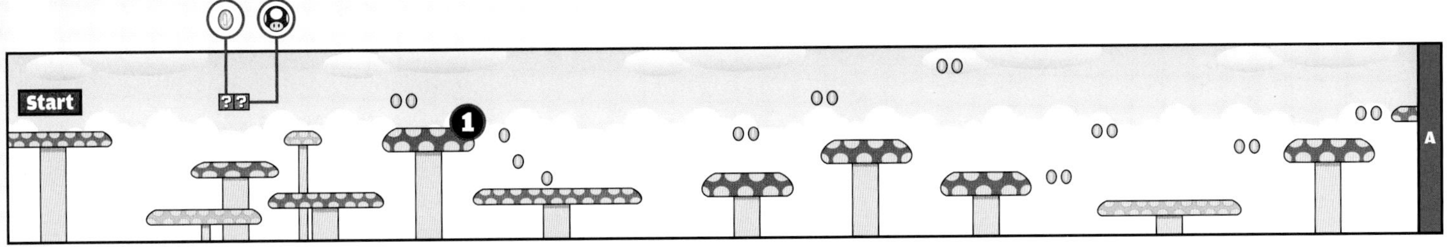

1 When you step on a purple mushroom platform, it will tilt dramatically to whichever side you're standing on. If you want to straighten it out, either jump repeatedly or stand in the dead center.

2 You can get this 1-Up Mushroom only by Ground-Pounding the block from above and chasing it down on the wobbly purple mushroom platform.

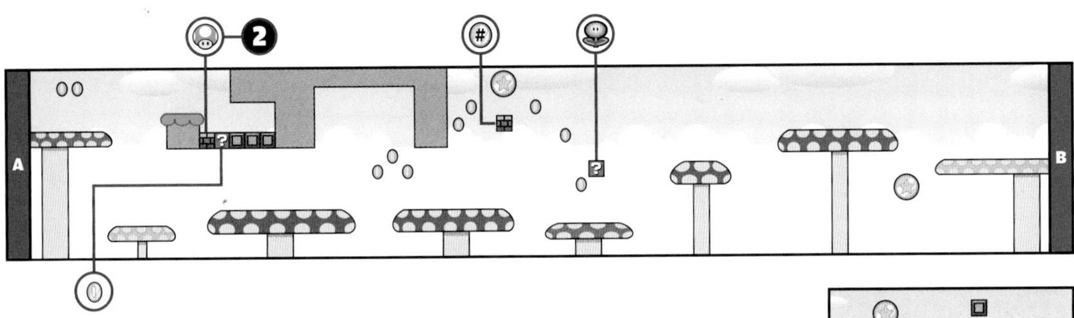

3 Red-Coin Ring

Grab the first four red coins, then ride the left edge of the second purple mushroom platform to get the fifth. Before you slide off, jump right to the final three.

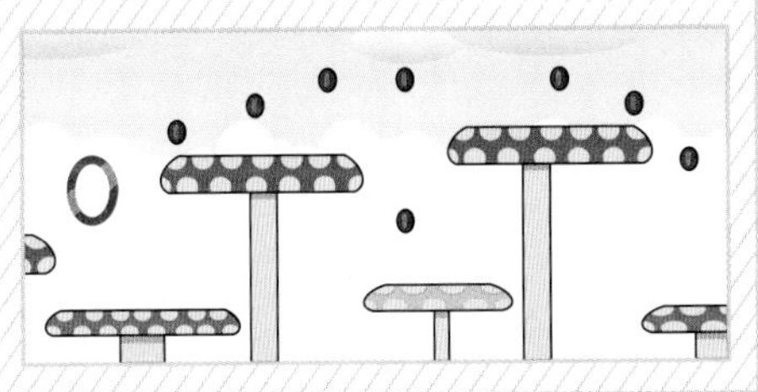

4 Don't Ground-Pound the block at point 4 as you pass! Instead slide off the purple mushroom platform and jump beneath the block to reveal an Invisible Block. Leap from that to punch the Vine Block, then climb into the clouds. There you'll find a second Vine Block that will take you to a Star Coin you can easily long-jump to.

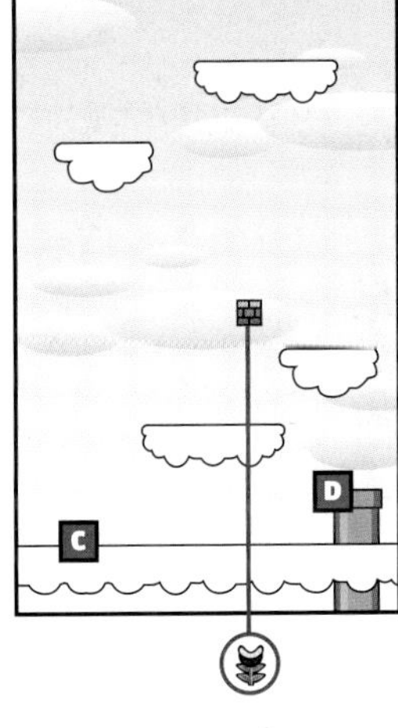

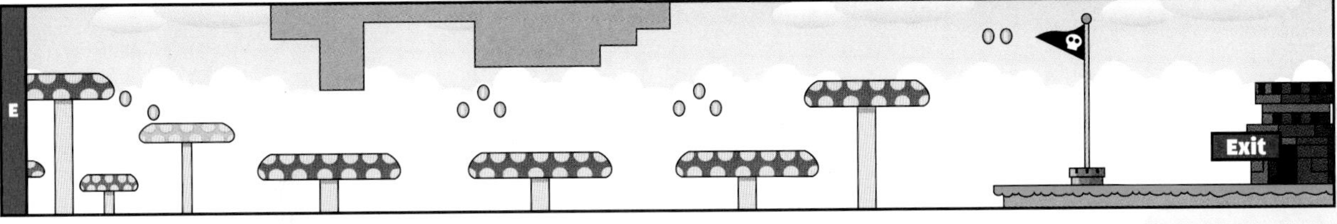

World 4-3

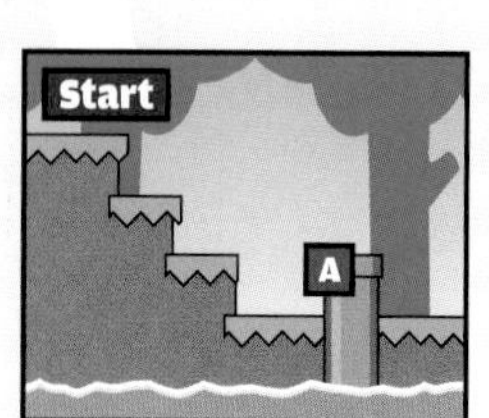

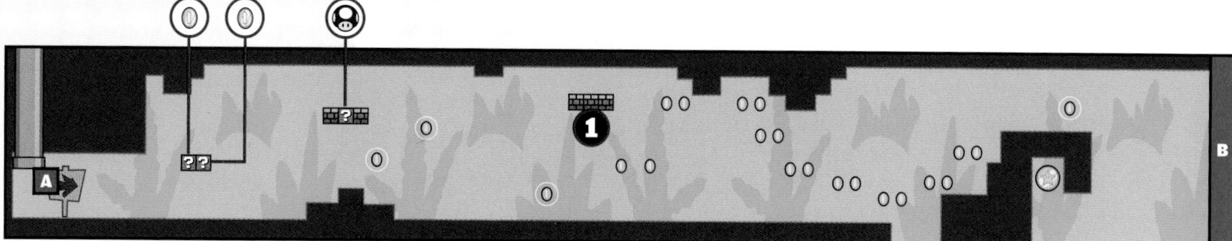

1 Swim to the far-right side of the screen after the Mega Unagi makes its first appearance. That's the only way you'll have enough time to swim beneath the ledge and grab the first Star Coin without being crushed when the scrolling screen catches up with you.

2 Red-Coin Ring

The black areas on the map conceal small snapping eels. To get the coins without being bit, always take the coin farthest from the Unagi first, then swim in to get the nearer one after the Unagi strikes and misses.

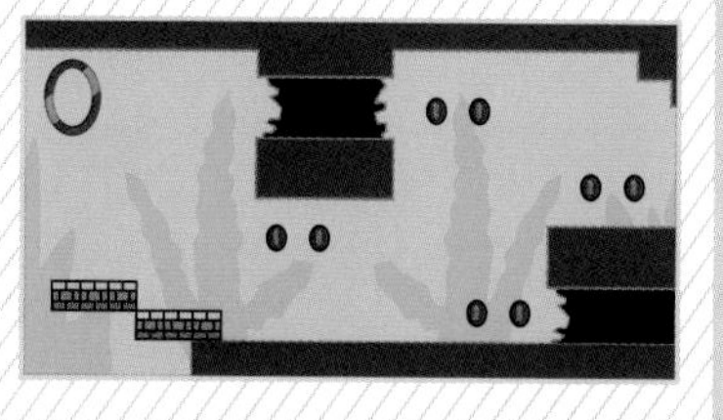

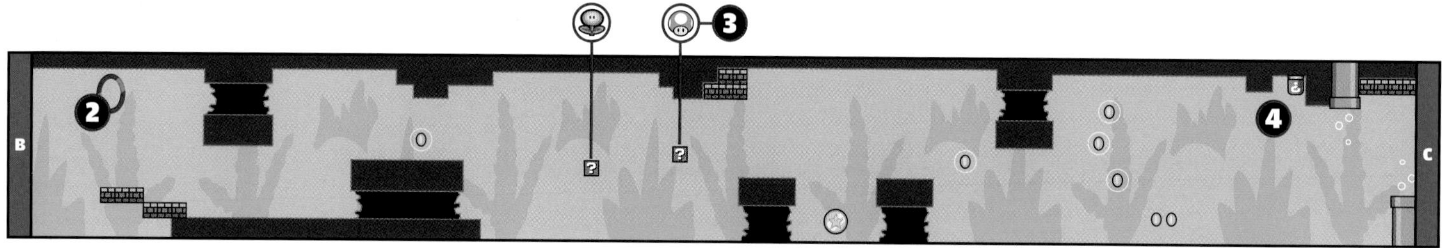

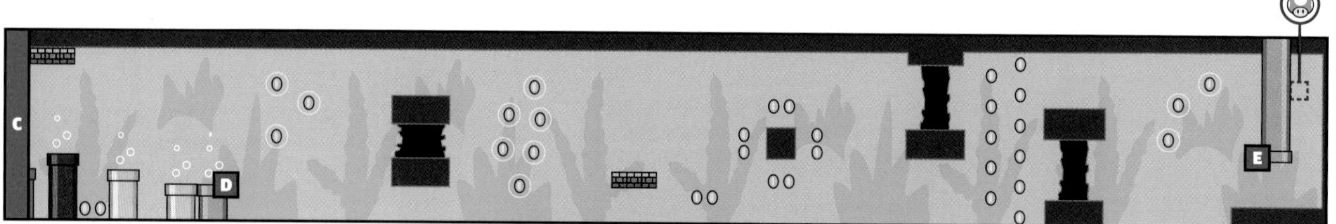

3 Whenever you see normal blocks on this level, you know a Mega Unagi will be along shortly to smash them. So if you want the 1-Up at point 3, you'll need to swim at the right side of the screen and hit it as soon as it scrolls into view.

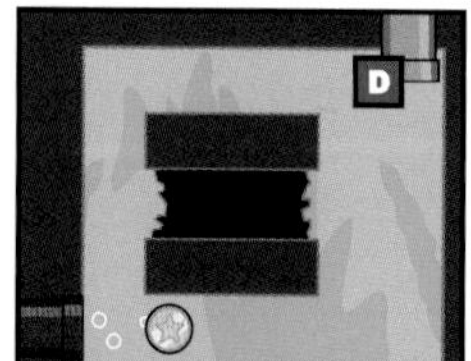

4 The Bubble Kill Switch

When you see the ? Switch on the ceiling, punch it quickly before the Mega Unagi appears. The switch will shut off the air from the pipes, allowing you to glide safely beneath the eel. The final pipe leads to a room where the third Star Coin is—you'll need to move quickly to get into it before the bubbles return. In the room below, get the Star Coin by dropping into the red pipe's bubbles from above.

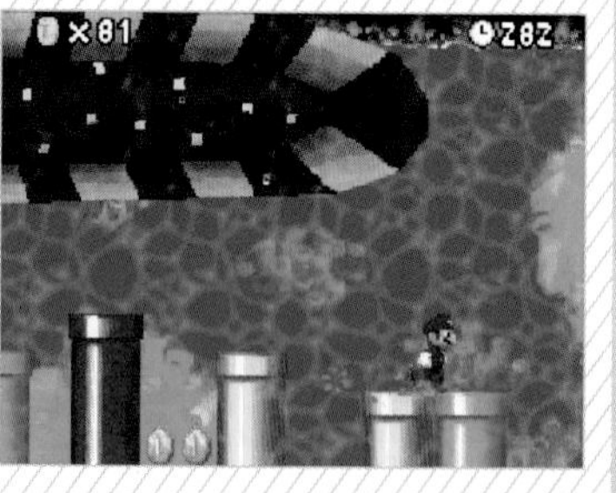

World 4 Tower

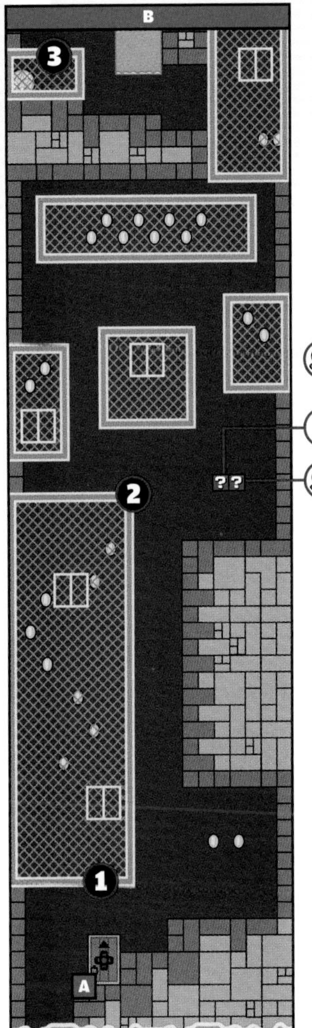

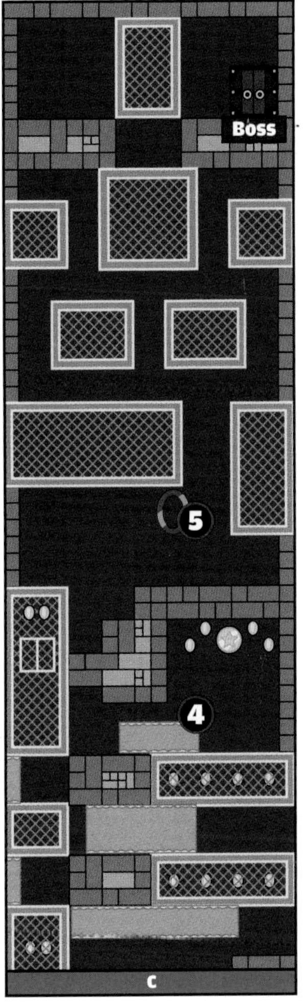

1 An ever-rising pool of lava won't give you much time to make decisions in this stage. Study the map and plan your route carefully to get the three Star Coins without being boiled.

2 You'll have time to safely reach the power-ups to the right if you jump from the edge of the fence, grab the goods, then jump from the ? Blocks and onto the fence above them.

3 The first Star Coin is behind the fence, and if you're on the wrong side you'll need to jump to the gate above it. This takes valuable time, so plan ahead and reverse yourself at one of the gates along the way.

4 After jumping off the moving platform to grab the Star Coin, position yourself at the left edge of the same platform and crouch under the ledge to return to the fences.

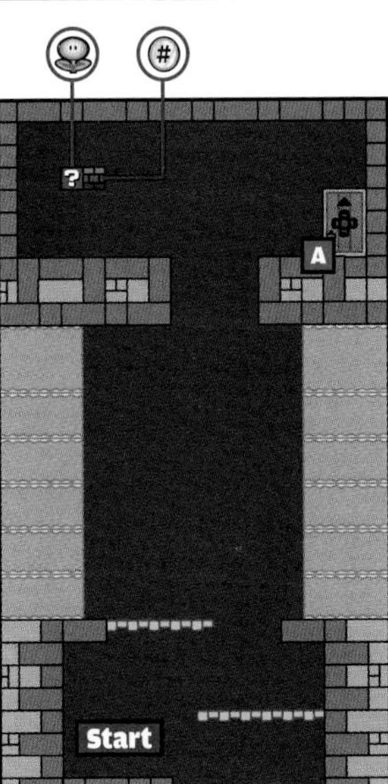

5 Red-Coin Ring

If you try to get the red coins by jumping from the fences to the left or right of the coins, you'll travel in an arc that will take you right over them. Instead, jump from low on the fence that's to the right of the ring to get the first coin, then hit the other coin pairs by jumping into them from below.

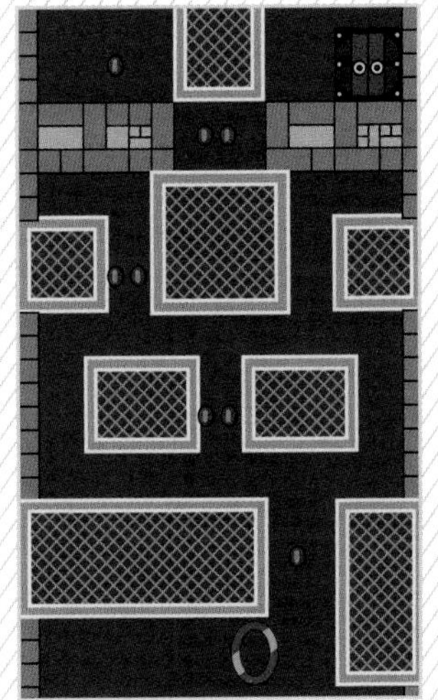

Boss

Bowser Jr. is onto your tricks, and will curl into his spiked shell as soon as you try to jump over him. The best way to defeat him now is by jumping on the Koopa shells he slides at you, and kicking them back. They'll knock him over, allowing you to get a stomp in without impaling yourself.

World 4-4

1 You can stomp on the heads of the Wigglers without taking damage, but you can't harm them unless you use a Koopa shell. Don't go out of your way to kill them when it isn't necessary, though; they can come in handy as platforms that allow for slightly higher jumps.

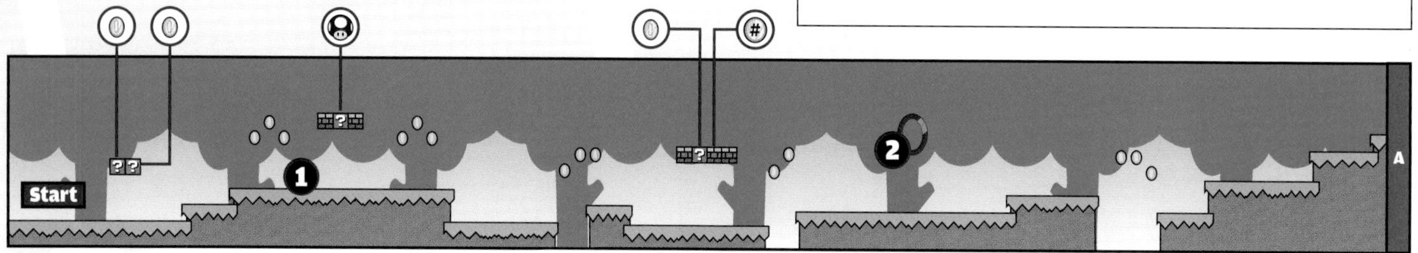

2 Red-Coin Ring

The highest red coins are just a little beyond Mario's reach, but you can get them by bouncing off of the Wiggler that roams on the ledge beneath the ring.

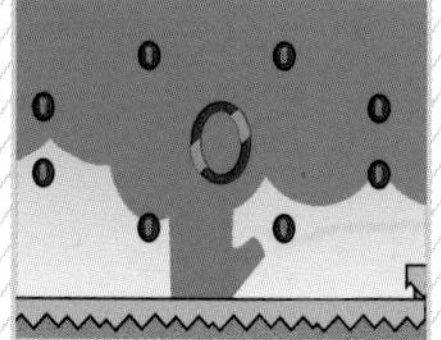

3 To get the first Star Coin, grab a Koopa shell on the ledge above it and kick the shell left. It will ricochet off the wall and take out the Wiggler on the ledge below.

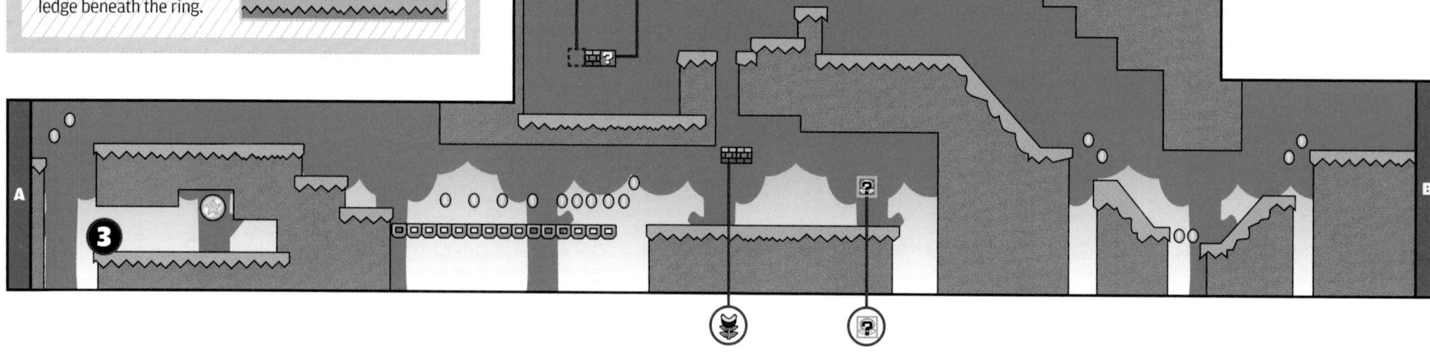

4 To get the second Star Coin, slide down the wall to the left and Wall-Jump to the pipe when you grab the coin. Hold the Control Pad left as you jump, or you'll slide off of the pipe when you land.

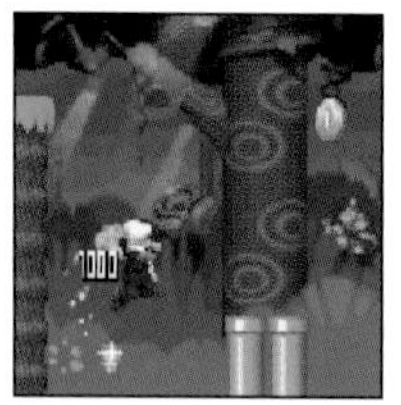

5 If you brought in a Mini Mushroom (or got one from the Roulette Block), you can use it to enter pipe C. Ride the Wiggler until it turns right, then fall off its back and slip into the second pipe from the left to find a Mega Mushroom and plenty of pipes to smash.

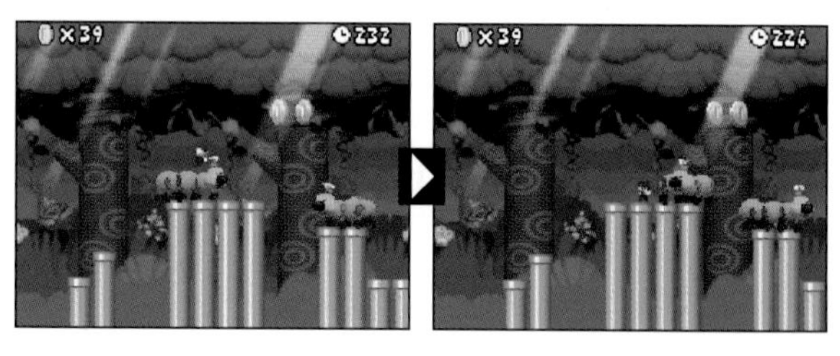

6 Jump onto the top Koopa Paratroopa and bounce straight up so you can stomp through the entire column of Koopa Paratroopas to nab a 1-Up. Don't forget that you're over a bottomless pit—be sure to bounce to the right after hitting the last one.

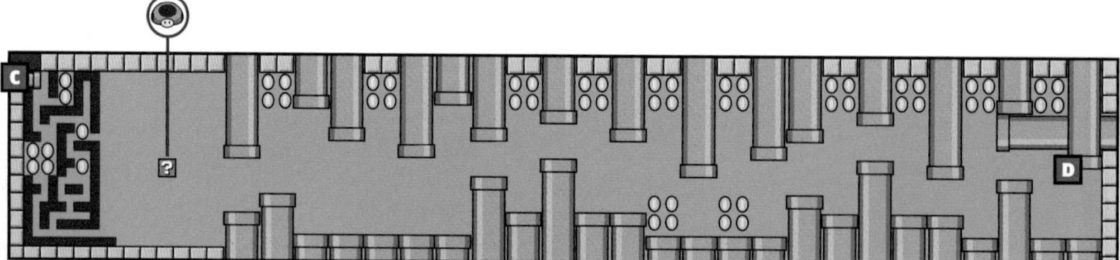

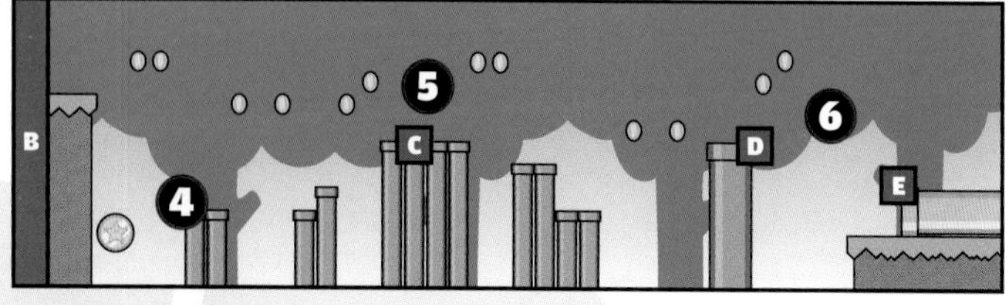

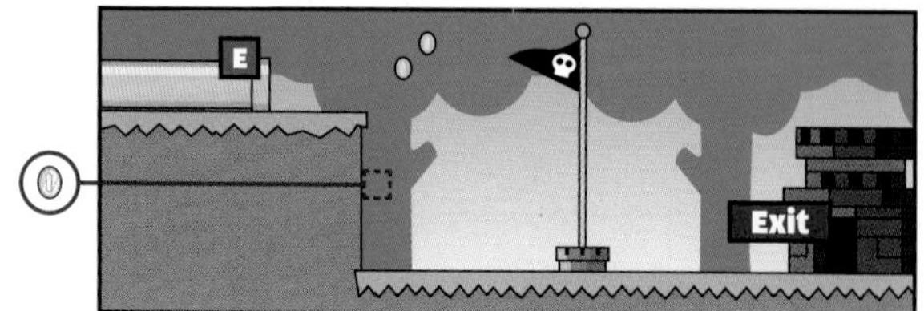

World 4-A

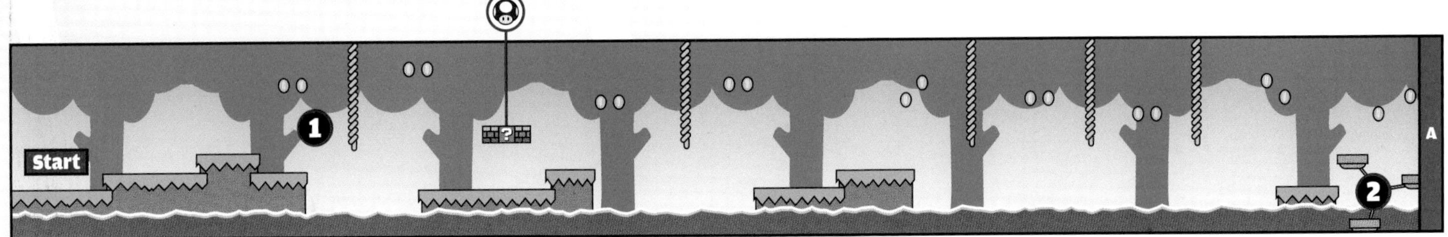

1 Jump onto the hanging vines and press left or right to set them swinging. When jumping from vine to vine, it's best to stay near the bottoms, or your jump could overshoot the next vine entirely.

2 You'll need to use the water wheels at point 2 to cross the poisonous pools in this stage. Step on the farthest-right platform to spin the water wheel in that direction, then jump to an upper platform before your feet touch poison.

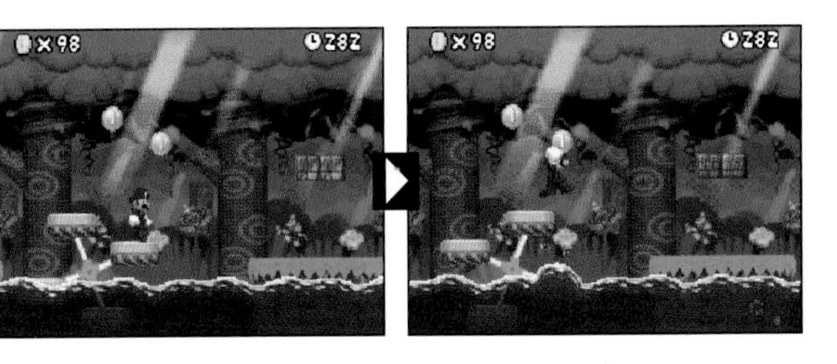

3 Step on the left platform of the water wheel to run the wheel into the cliff, then jump from the top platform, bounce off a Koopa Paratroopa, and grab the vine at point 3. Set it swinging to jump to the pipe that's up and to the right.

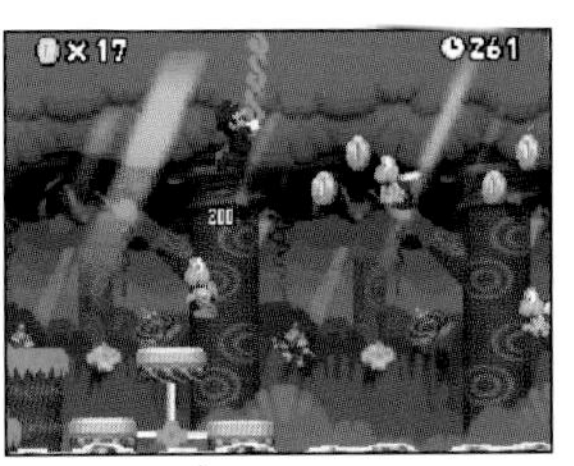

4 The Koopa-Guarded P Switch

Grab the red Koopa shell and hit the P Switch when there are no Koopas on the platform below you. When you land on that platform, kick your Koopa shell in either direction and run along after it (watch out for the ricochet) to complete a 1-Up chain as you snag the coins.

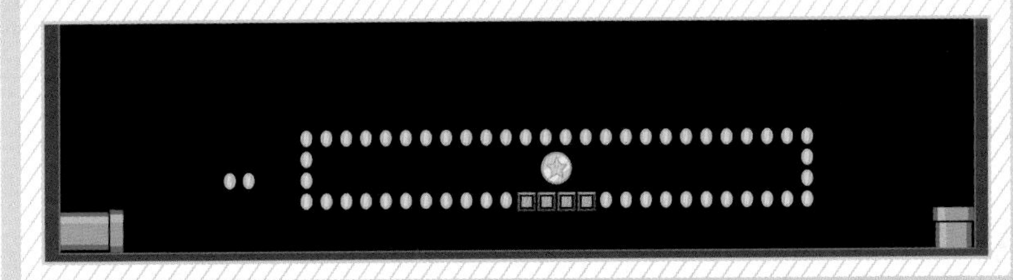

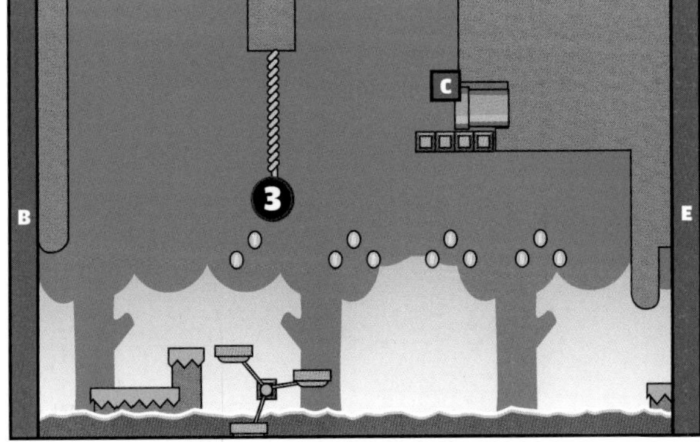

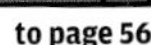

to page 56

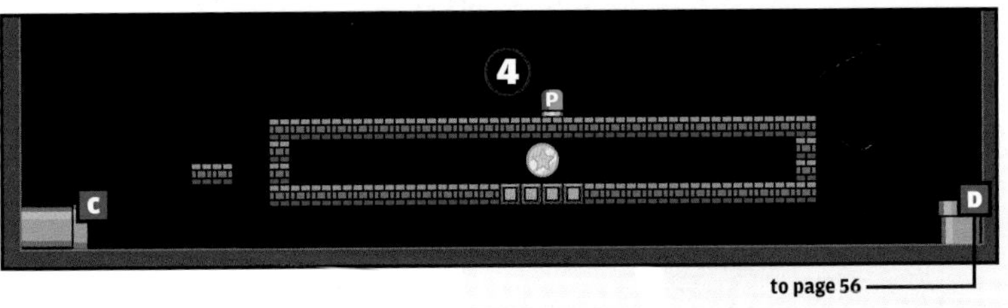

to page 56

from page 55

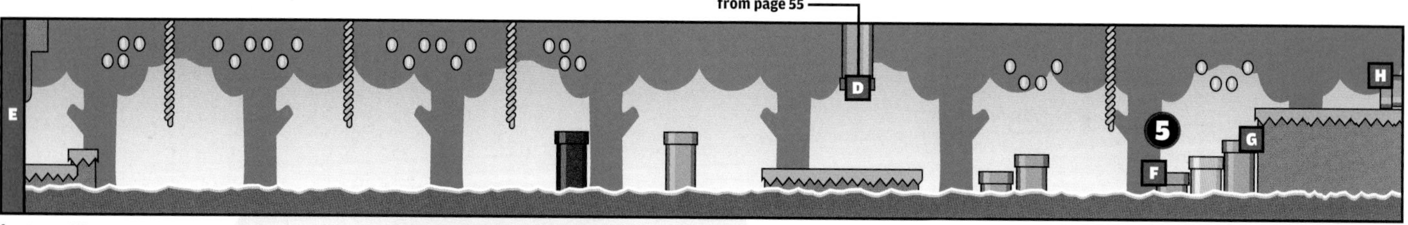

from page 55

5 When you reach the stairway of pipes, crouch at the first green pipe to enter an underground area. Pause for a moment before you approach the Star Coin, or you'll walk right into a Piranha Plant ambush.

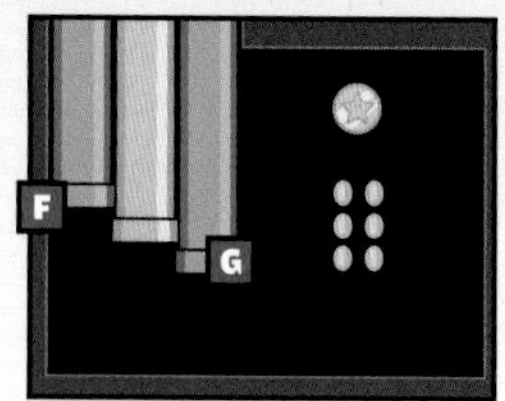

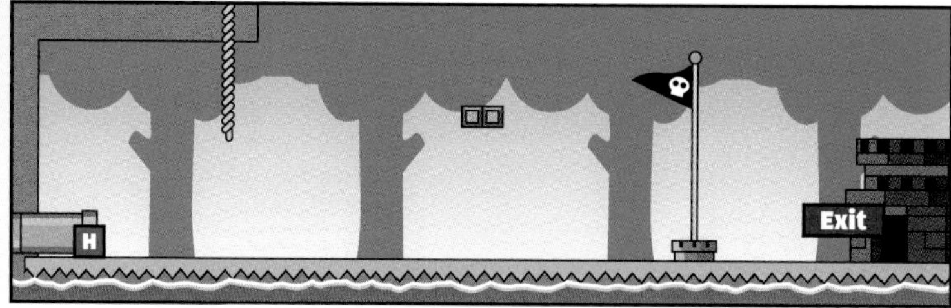

World 4 Ghost House

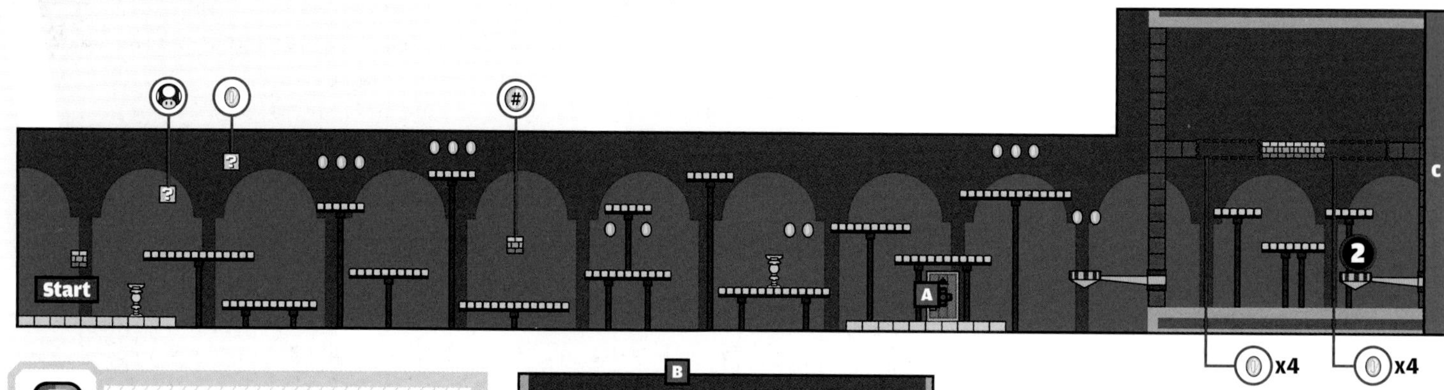

1 Dangling ? Blocks

Hit the ? Switch to drop a bunch of ? Blocks into this room. The one to the left of the switch holds a power-up, and you can ride any block to the room above.

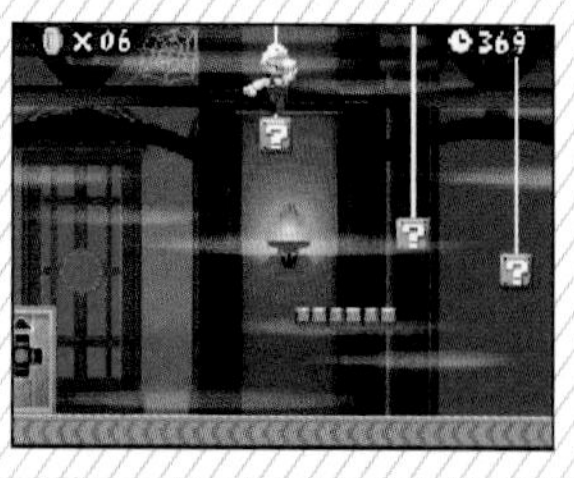

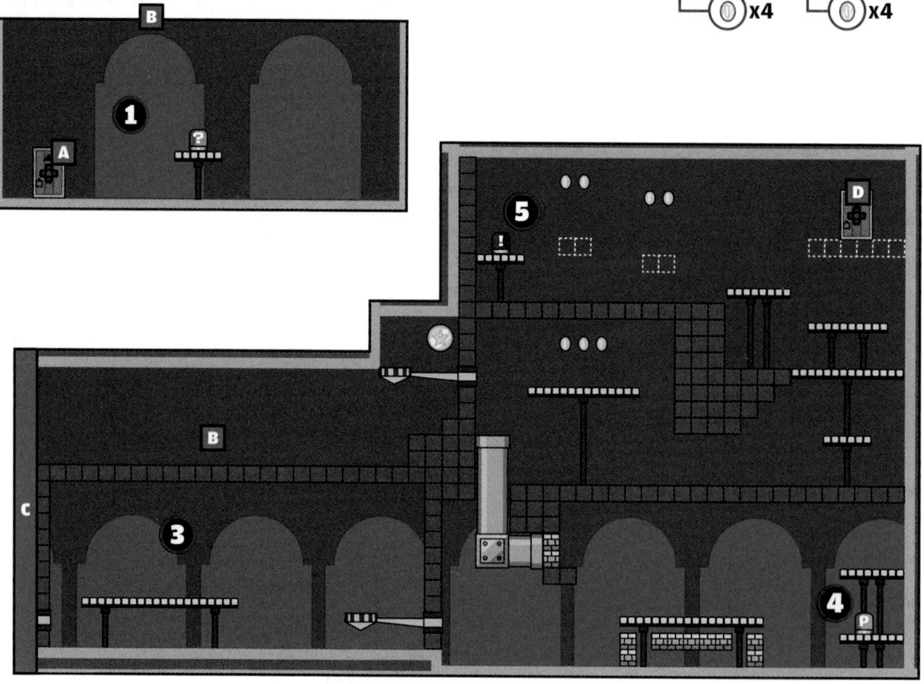

2 The hinged devices on this stage will take you through the walls, but it's a one-way trip. If you want to get the first Star Coin, make sure you've snagged it (by punching through the blocks above) before you step onto the hinged contraption near the Star Coin or at point 2.

3 Like their smaller cousins, Balloon Boos won't move while you're looking at them. But they will react to your gaze by sucking in air to grow to massive sizes, and won't shrink again until you turn your back.

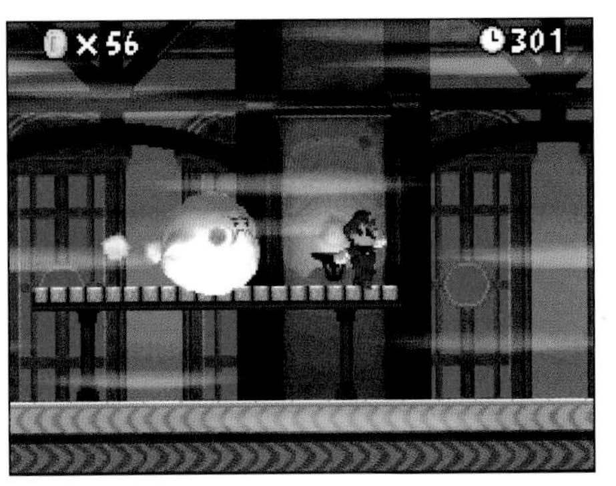

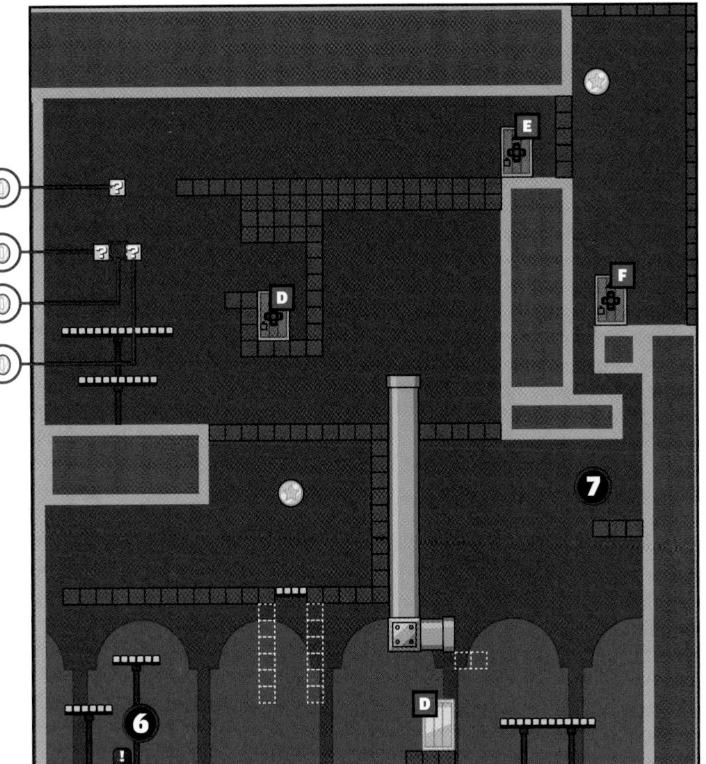

4 The P-Switch Route

If you're heading this direction, you'll need to use the P Switch to transform the pipe-obstructing blocks into coins.

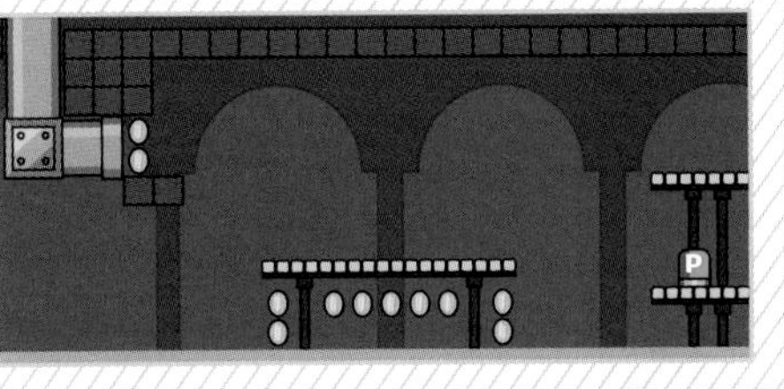

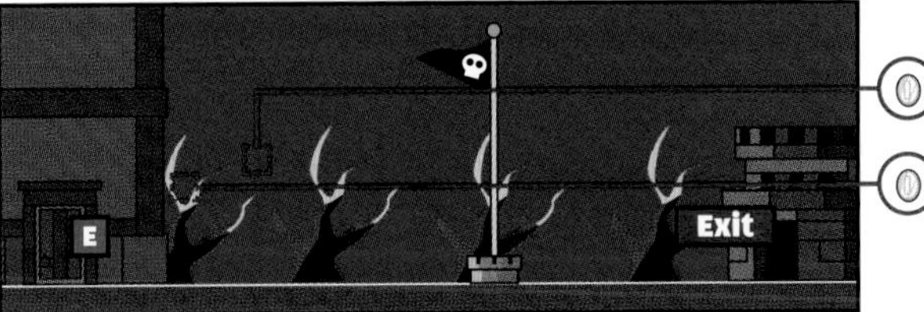

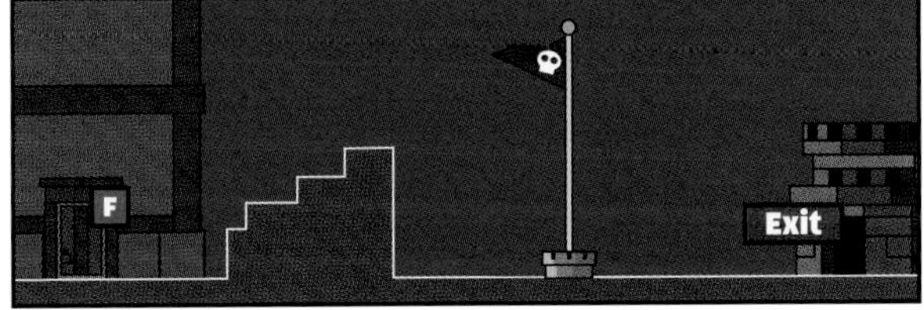

5 ! Switch to the Door

The ! Switch in this room will make all of the outlined blocks become solid, giving you a ledge from which to open the door and proceed.

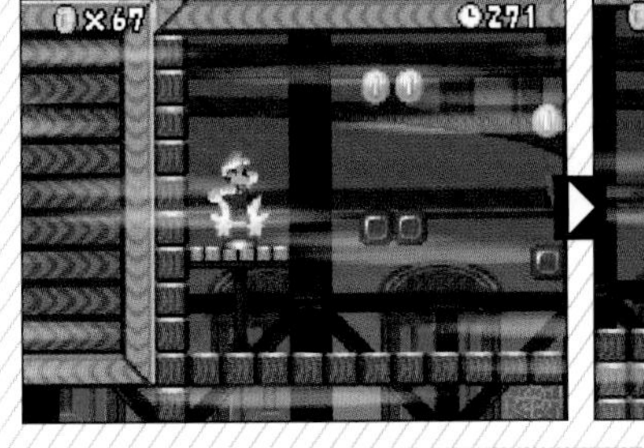

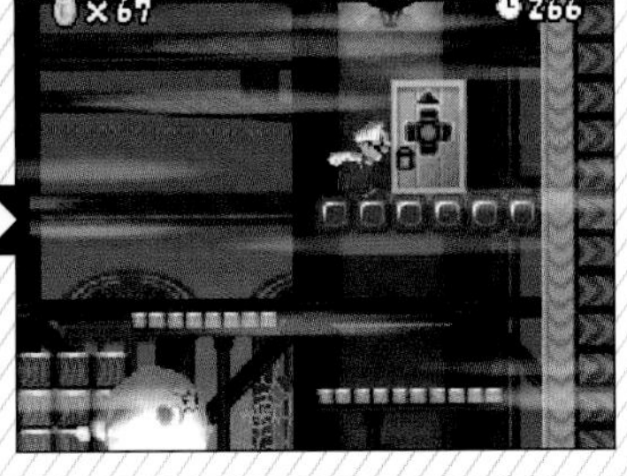

6 ! Switch to the Star Coin

This ! Switch at point 6 creates a ledge at the lip of the pipe so you can proceed, and also creates two walls of red blocks that you can Wall-Jump between to reach a Star Coin.

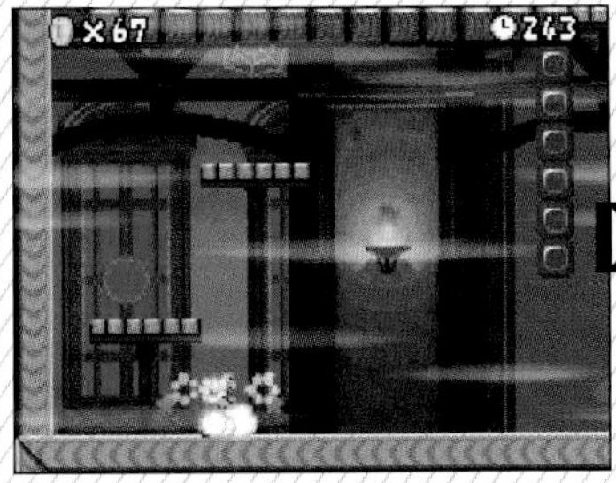

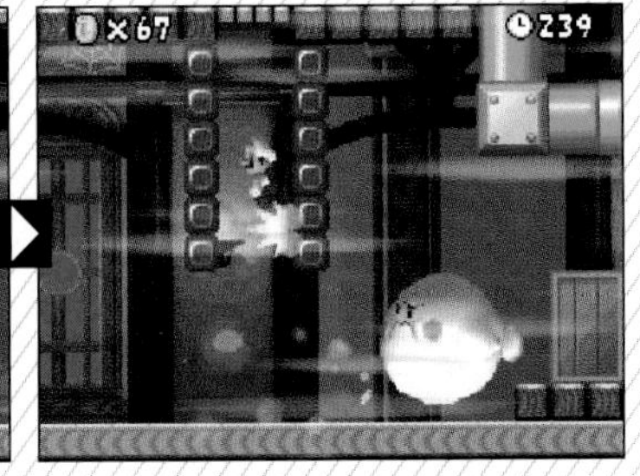

7 Only Mini Mario can reach the final Star Coin and the red-flag exit to a warp cannon. There's no Mini Mushroom in this stage, so you'll need to bring one with you. Use the ! Switch to get above the pipe, eat your mushroom, and Wall-Jump as Mini Mario to the ledge at point 7. Continue Wall-Jumping past the exit door and into the final Star Coin.

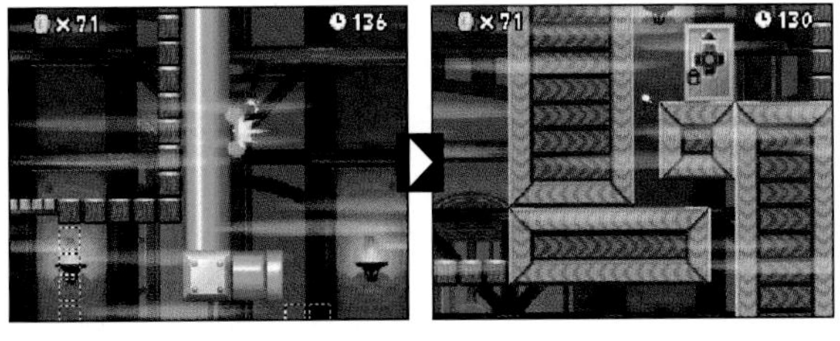

World 4-5

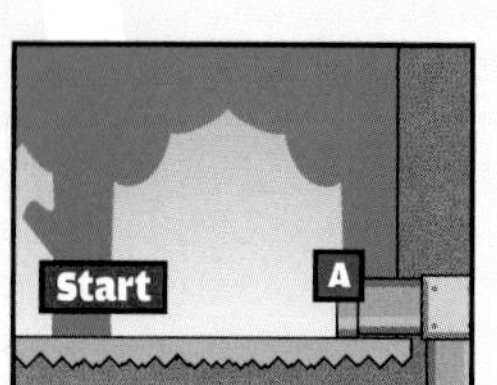

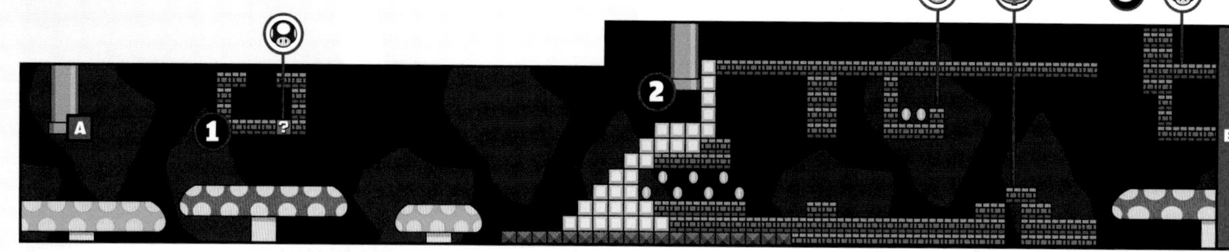

1 You can't smash the blocks at point 1 from below, but you can hit the one the Bob-omb is standing on to knock over the Bob-omb and light its fuse. The blast will destroy a few blocks in either direction.

2 There's a 1-Up loop at point 2, but it will require some careful sculpting. Detonate a few Bob-ombs on or near the fourth step to create a pit at floor level that has an indestructible block on either side. Toss a Koopa shell or a Spiny (found to the right) into the pit—it will bounce from side to side, killing Bob-ombs for 1-Ups.

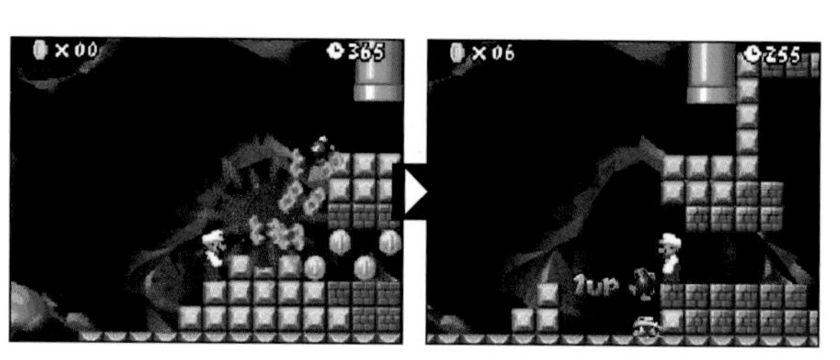

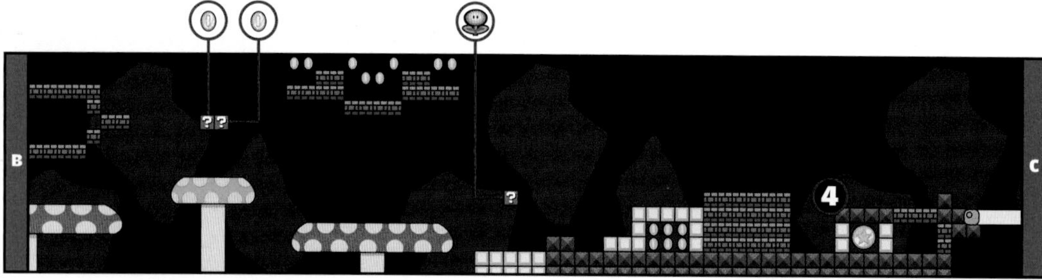

3 The easiest way to get the 1-Up at point 3 is to hit the Bob-ombs in the block structure, then smash the two blocks to the right of the structure. Jump from the top of the ? Blocks onto the structure, then Ground-Pound the block that holds the 1-Up Mushroom.

4 Set off a Bob-omb near the otherwise-indestructible blocks at point 4 to blast open a path to a Star Coin.

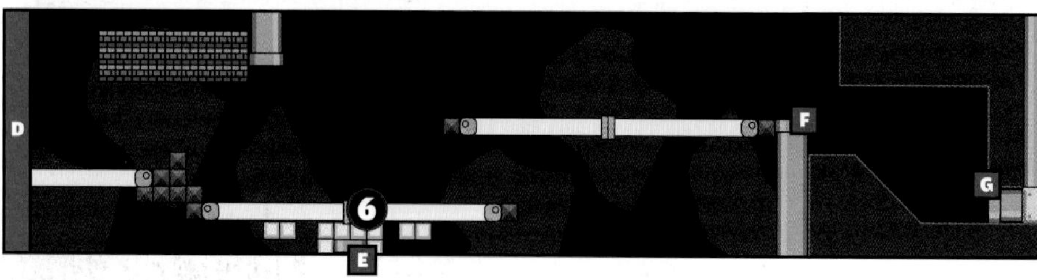

5 Try to hit a Bob-omb so it lands and explodes below the Star Coin. You can then leap into the block structure from the tip of the drawbridge below.

6 Grab a Bob-omb, slip between the drawbridges, and set the Bob-omb on the blocks that cap the pipe. Its blast will destroy the blocks, allowing you to enter the room through the pipe. To get the Star Coin, you can't merely detonate each Bob-omb in its initial position—you'll need to take one to the blocks near the Star Coin.

World 4-6

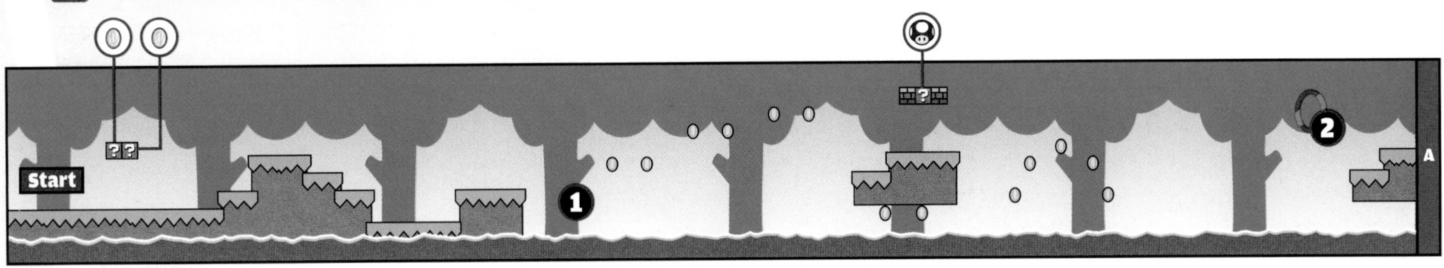

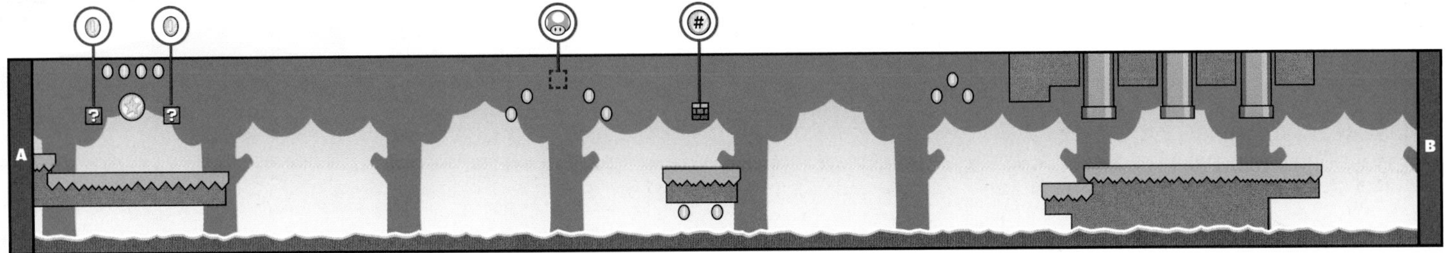

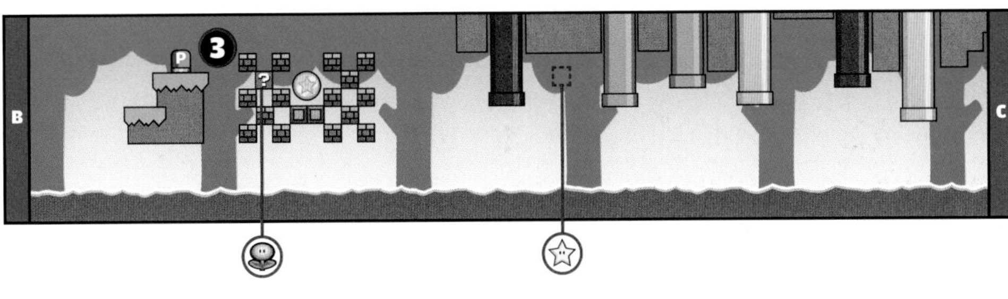

1 This entire stage is one long Dorrie ride. The platforms are spaced far apart, so if you can't keep up with Dorrie when she ducks under ledges (by running on the platforms above), you'll have no chance to recover!

2 Red-Coin Ring

Long-jump through the ring, grab the lone coin on land, then drop off the ledge to the left, Ground-Pound Dorrie, and crouch on her back to collect the rest.

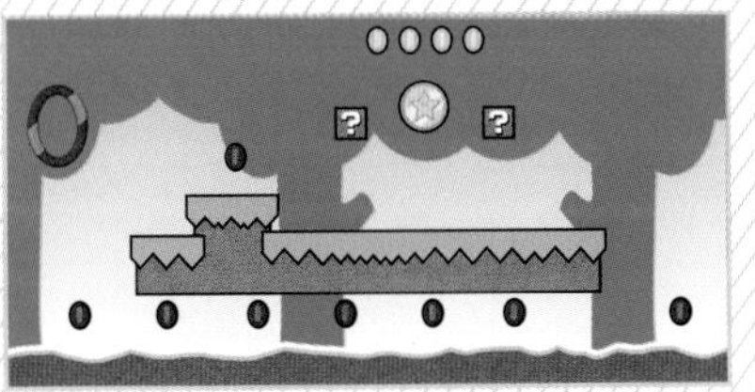

3 P Switch

The P Switch at point 3 will make it easier to reach the ? Block and Star Coin. Be sure to Ground-Pound the ? Block when Dorrie is beneath it.

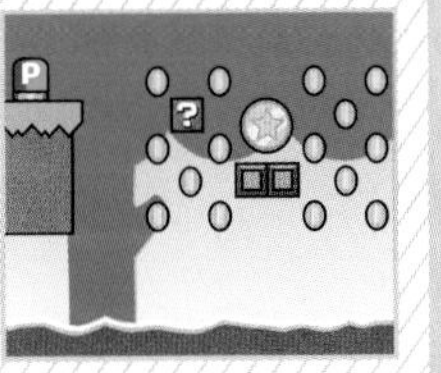

4 ! Switch

After the pipes, Dorrie won't raise her head until slightly past the ! Switch, so you'll need to jump left to hit it. Doing so will create a ledge at the mouth of pipe D.

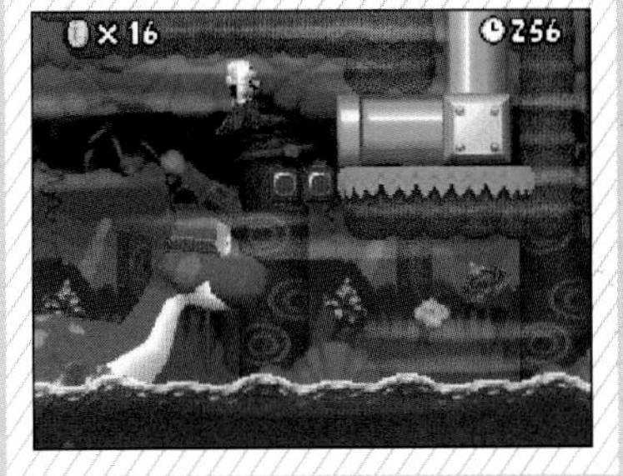

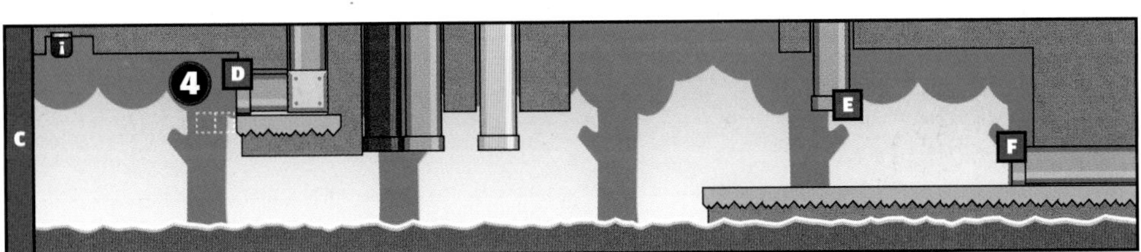

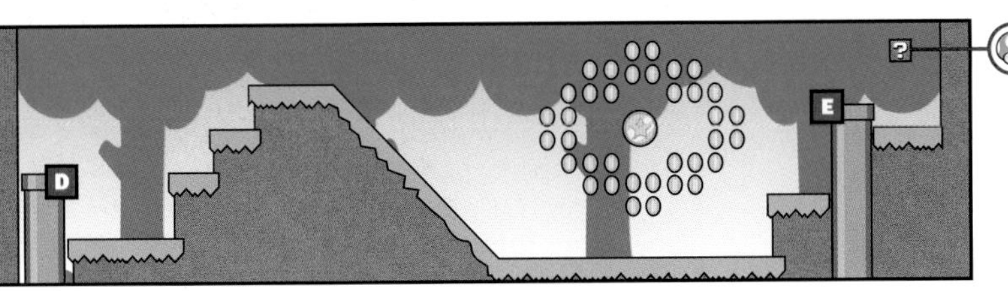

World 4 Castle

1 You'll need to do a running long jump at the apex of the third scythe's swing to reach the first Star Coin.

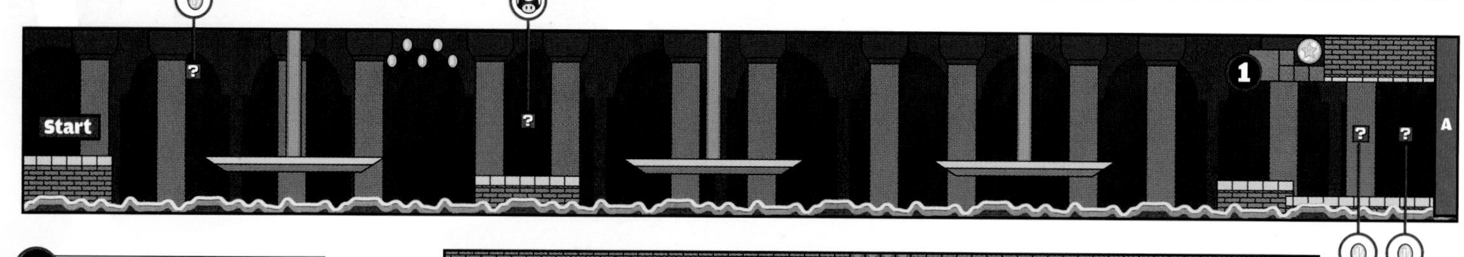

2 Forget the ledges (which are guarded by a Thwomp) and use Wall Jumps to climb to the upper part of the level. Don't get the hidden Starman yet—go back for it after you've completed tip 3.

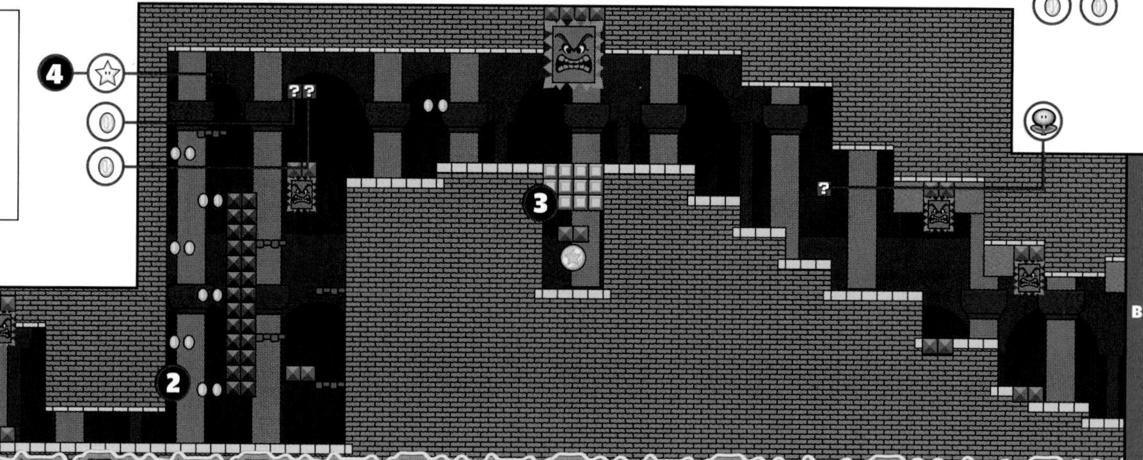

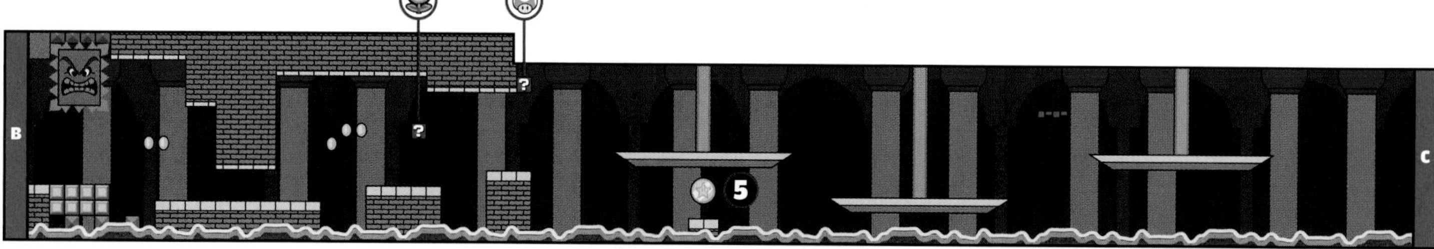

3 Stand near the giant Thwomp as it smashes through three layers of beveled blocks. You can then grab the Star Coin and Wall-Jump out.

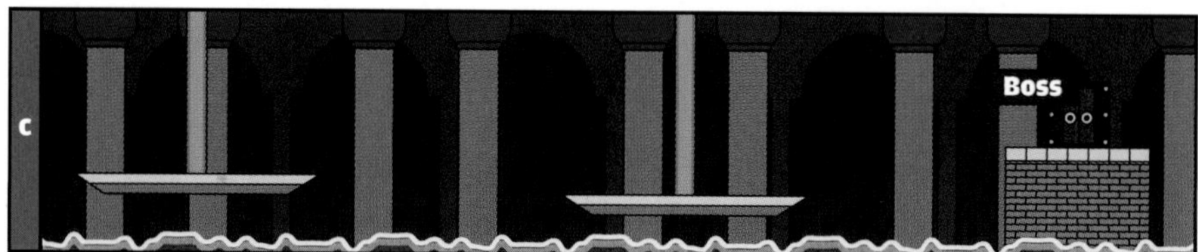

4 Grab the Starman and run all the way down the hill, trampling over the Dry Bones and leaping into each Thwomp. You'll destroy every foe you touch, and earn 1-Ups as you do it.

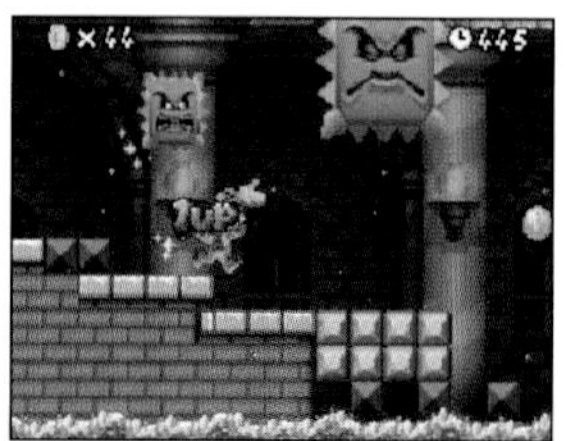

5 Stand on the left side of the swinging platform at point 5 until the platform is at its right apex, then step off onto the Star Coin. Jump straight up to return to the platform before a fireball can catch you.

Boss

You can damage the Mega Goomba only with Ground Pounds. To get high enough, you can use well-timed Wall Jumps or crouch in a crack until the boss runs over you, then hit the ? Switch to make rising platforms appear.

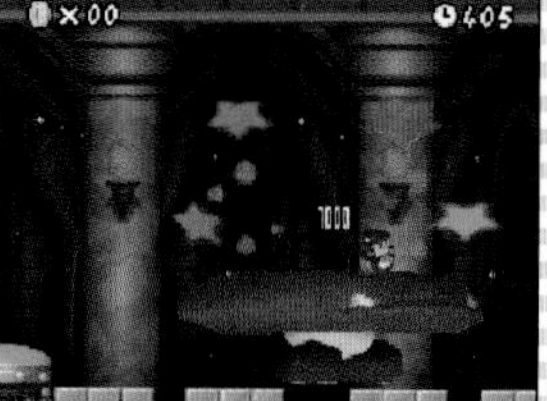

The green platforms will rise only while you're standing on them, so don't try to use them if the Goomba is running right at you—use a Wall Jump or hide in a crack to avoid being crushed.

World 5

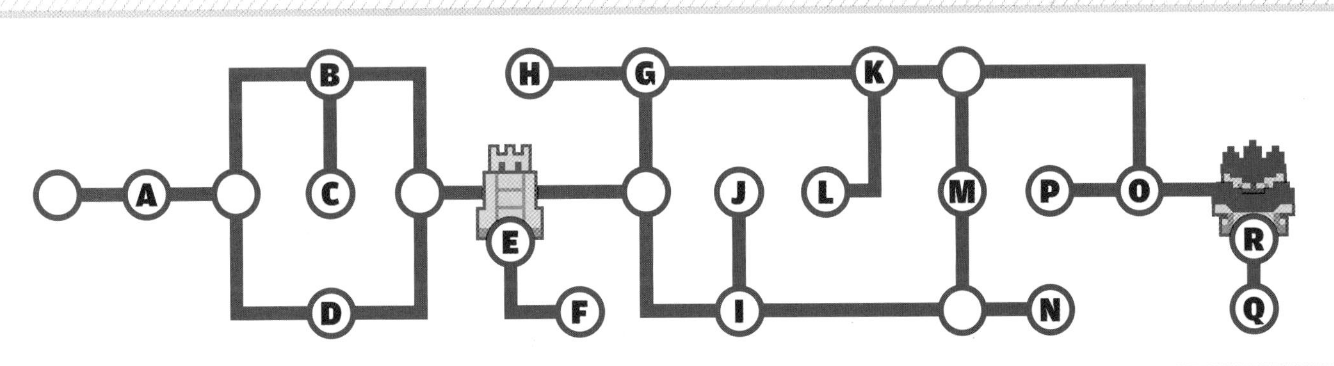

A **World 5-1** (Page 62)

B **World 5-2** (Page 63)

C **Warp Pipe** (Warp to H)

D **World 5-A** (5 Star Coins/Page 64)

E **World 5 Tower** (Page 65)

F **Red Toad House** (5 Star Coins)

G **World 5-3** (Page 66)

H **Warp Pipe** (Warp to C)

I **World 5-B** (5 Star Coins/Page 67)

J **Warp Pipe** (Warp to Q)

K **World 5 Ghost House** (Page 69)

L **Warp Cannon** (To World 8)

M **World 5-C** (Page 70)

N **Orange Toad House** (5 Star Coins)

O **World 5-4** (Page 72)

P **Green Toad House** (5 Star Coins)

Q **Warp Pipe** (Warp to J)

R **World 5 Castle** (Page 73)

World 5-1

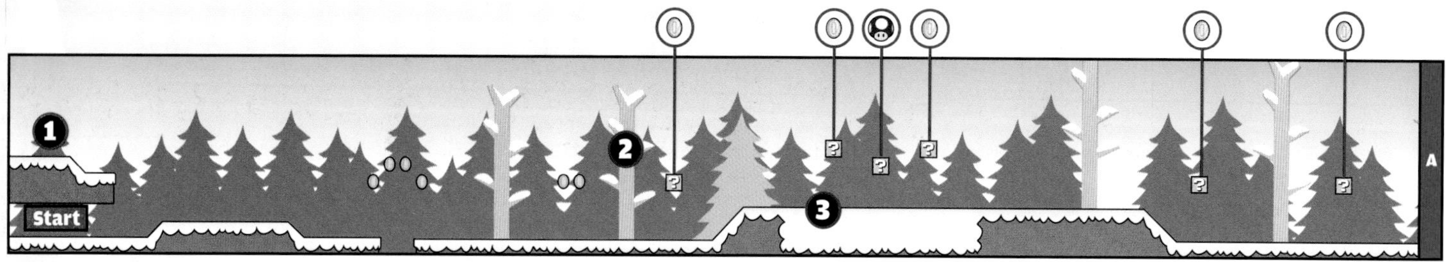

1 Wait for the Snow Spike to throw a snowball, then run along with the snowball as it gathers mass and rolls over foes. Don't run too fast—it's slower than you are, and you'll feel silly if you smack into it.

2 Watch out for accumulations of snow on tree branches. They will fall as you pass, and can bury Mario briefly, exposing him to attacks.

3 The snowdrifts hamper Mario's jumping ability, leaving him vulnerable to enemies and unable to reach the ? Blocks. Jump above the blocks and Ground-Pound down to get their contents.

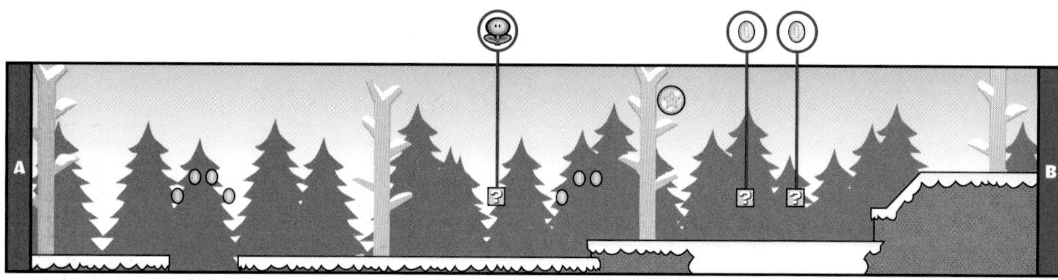

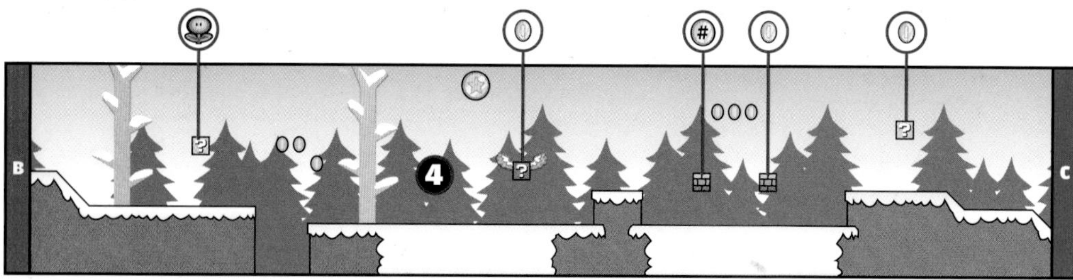

4 To reach the Star Coin, bounce off of the Koopa Paratroopa at the edge of the nearby snowdrift. If you miss, a second chance is on the way—leap onto the winged ? Block and ride it to the Star Coin, or punch it when it's at just the right place to make a permanent step.

World 5-2

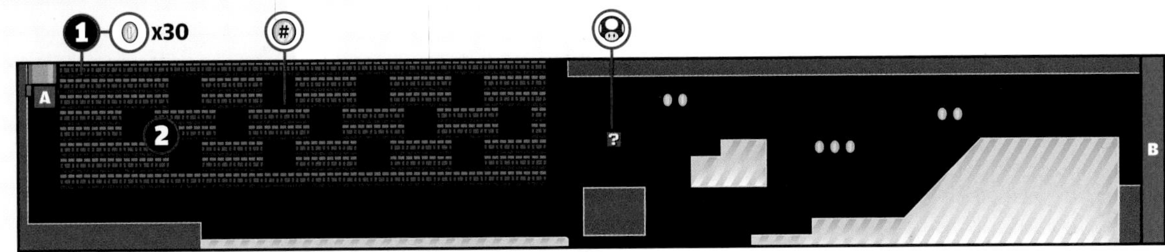

1 There are lots of coins hidden above the massive block structure at the start of the level, but the Spike Tops make it dangerous to punch through it. Instead, make your way to the platform to the right, get a running start, and do a double Wall Jump through the gap.

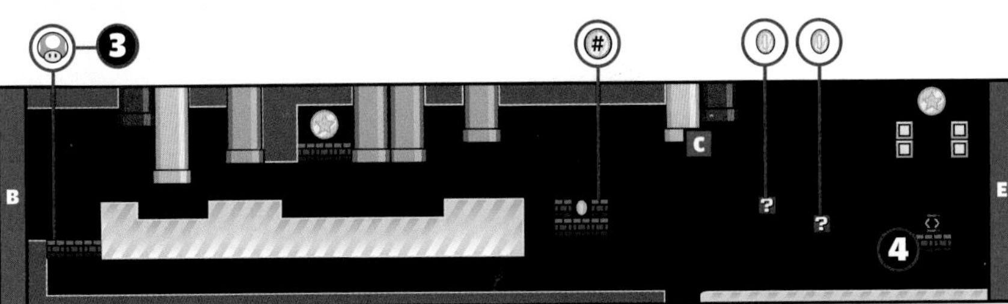

2 Attacking the Spike Tops directly will damage Mario, but you can kill them by punching the blocks they're crawling on.

3 Ground-Pound the 1-Up block at point 3, then run to the right, carefully dodging the Piranha Plants, to catch up with your 'shroom before it slides off the ledge.

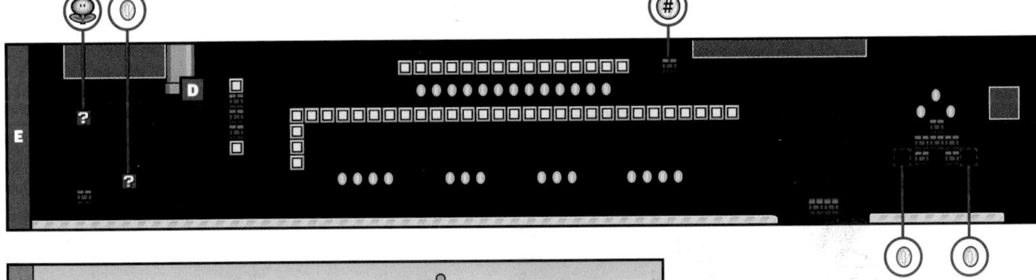

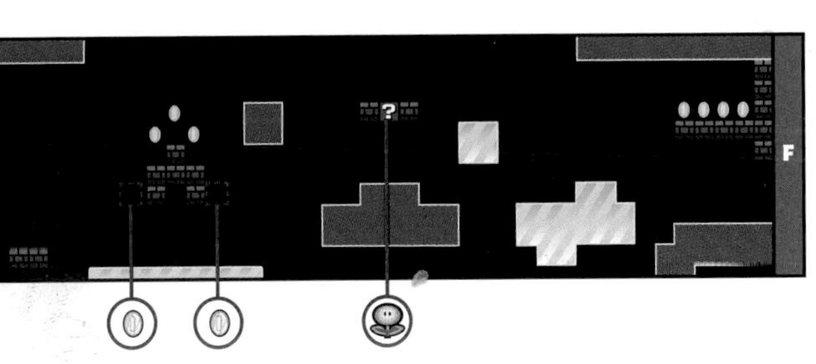

4 When the path is clear, use the spring at point 4 to leap up and grab the Star Coin. Then pick up the spring and take it to the edge of the floor beneath the yellow pipe to the left. Chase down and kill the Moneybags for a 1-Up (if you can), then Wall-Jump off of the pipe to nab a Star Coin.

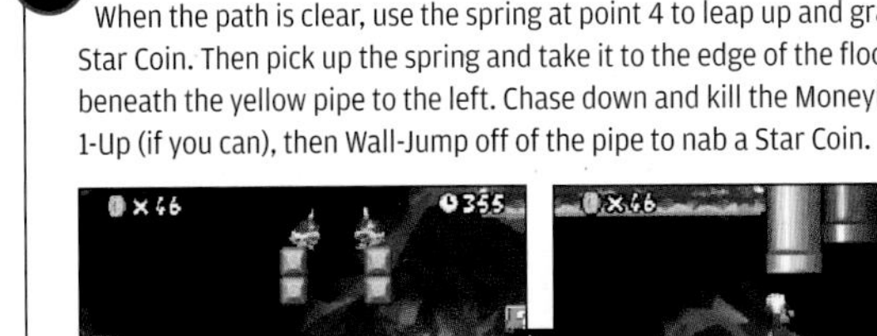

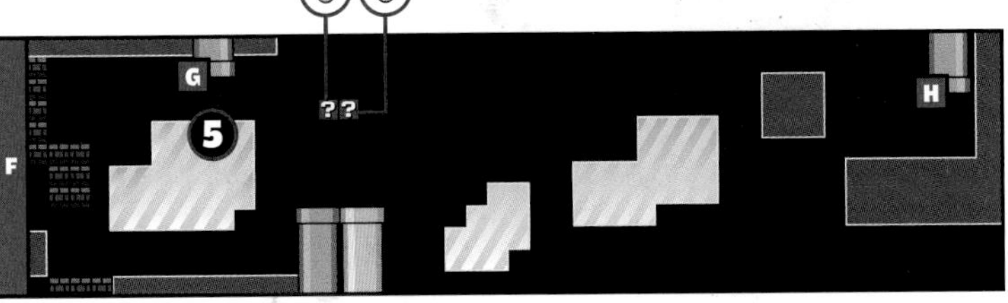

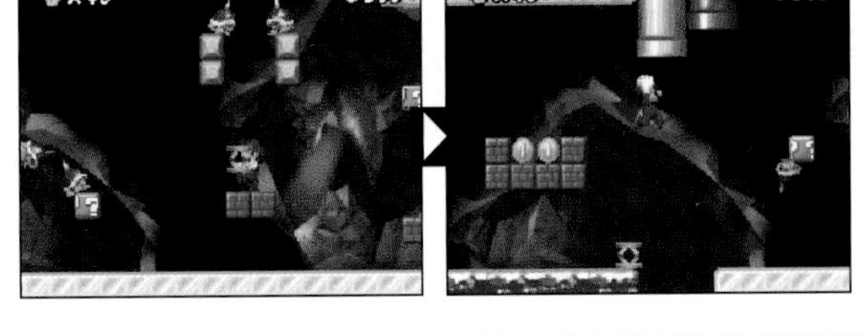

5 If you can get past the Piranha Plant, you can squeeze through its pipe and up to an alternate exit, which leads to a warp pipe that will take you to World 5-3, allowing you to bypass the World 5 tower.

World 5-A

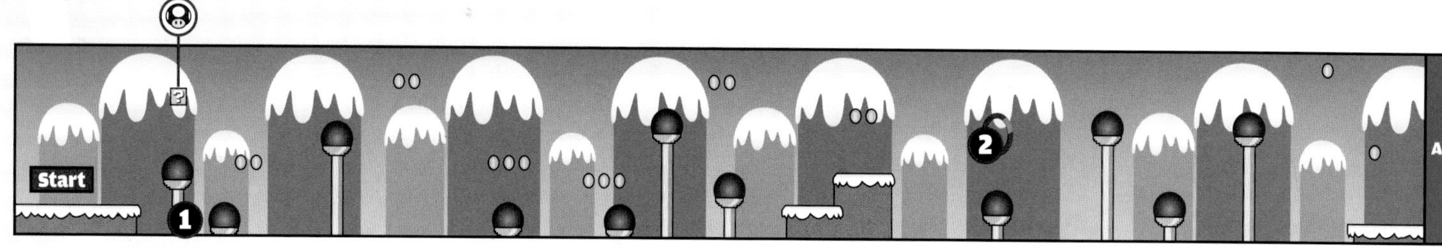

1 The platforms on this stage expand and contract at regular intervals. You don't need to worry about falling if you're standing at the edge when they contract—you'll simply be pulled to the middle. The bad news is that enemies will be too, so be ready to jump up and fight for the limited space!

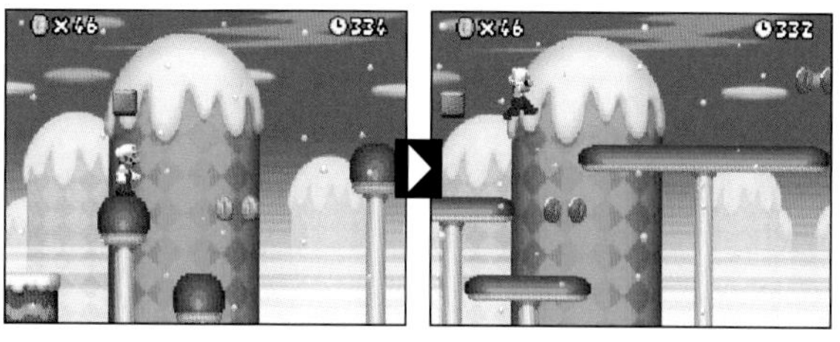

2 Red-Coin Ring

Leap through the red-coin ring and land on the platform just as it's about to expand. That should give you enough time to pick up all the red coins.

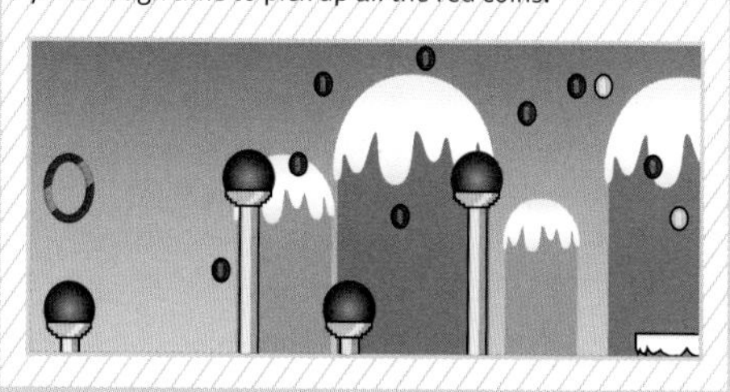

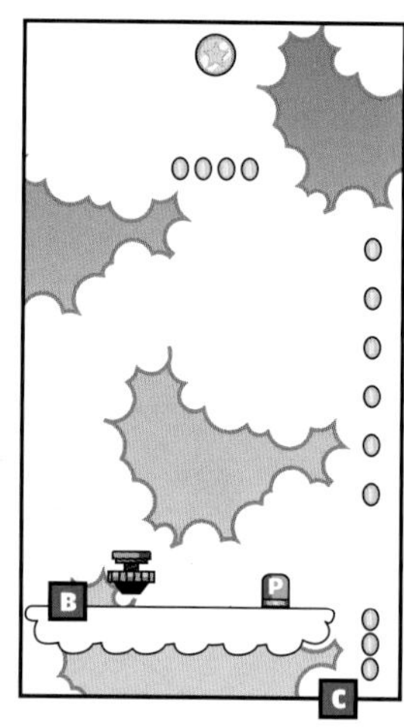

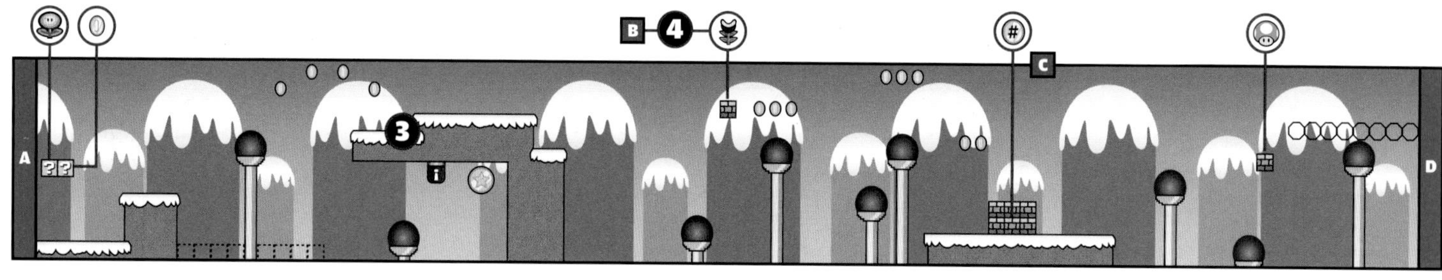

3 The Star Coin

Drop onto the lower platform when it expands, and run to the edge to grab the Star Coin. Wait for it to expand again before you hit the ! Switch, then use the blocks to escape before you run out of time!

4 P Switches in Heaven

When the platform below the block at point 4 expands, jump into the Vine Block to bounce safely to the platform below. Climb the vine to a cloud platform, hit the P Switch, and take the Spin Block for a ride. You'll soar to a coin platform from which you can jump into the second Star Coin.

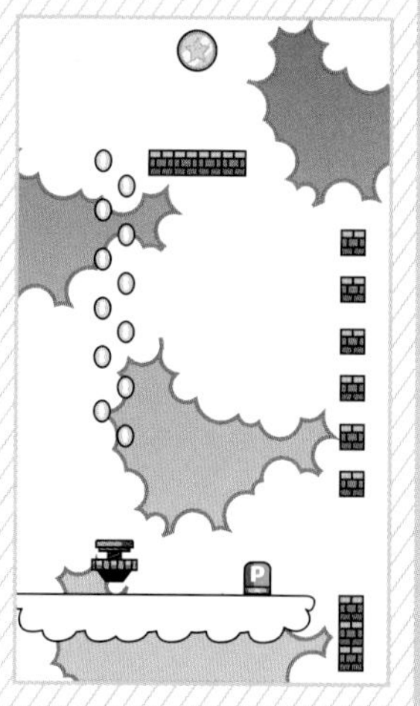

World 5 Tower

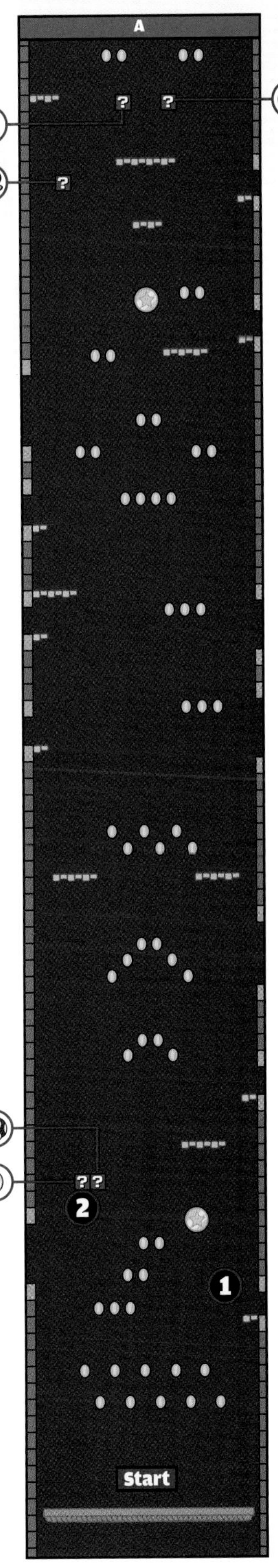

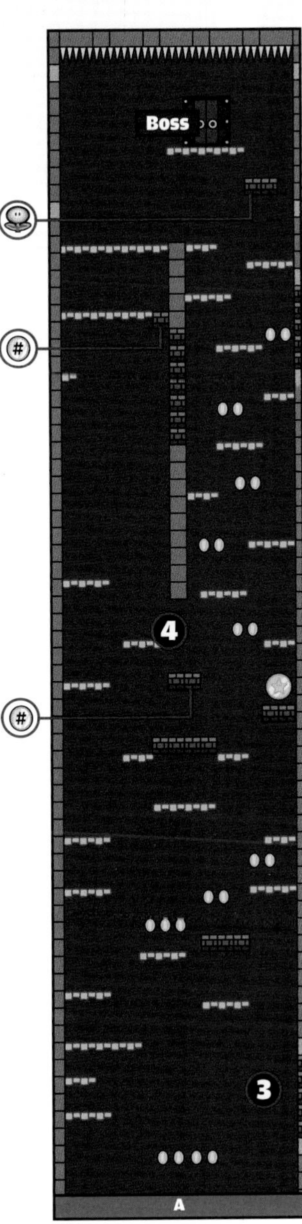

1 The spiked balls that roll through this stage will damage Mario, but they're no friends to the Dry Bones, either. Don't stomp on the Dry Bones (which will make them temporarily invulnerable). The balls will destroy them.

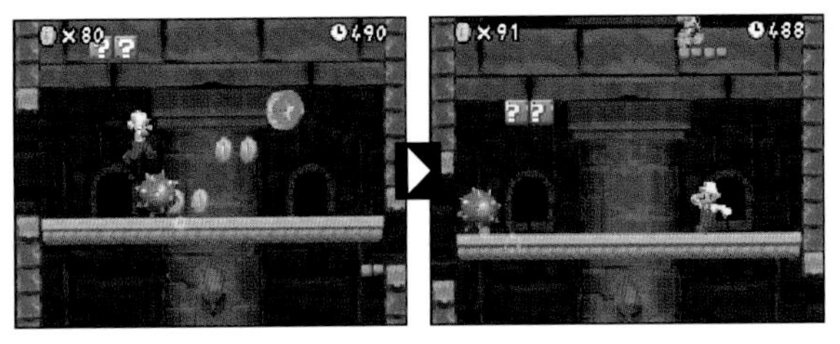

2 Hit the ? Blocks at point 2 as soon as they come within your jumping range. If you wait too long, you could get crushed beneath them. When in doubt, Ground-Pound them from above.

3 The giant spiked ball is too big to jump over comfortably, so you'll need to leap onto the small blue ledges and try to stay a step ahead of the rising platform. If time allows, Ground-Pound the block near the final Star Coin for coins and a Super Mushroom.

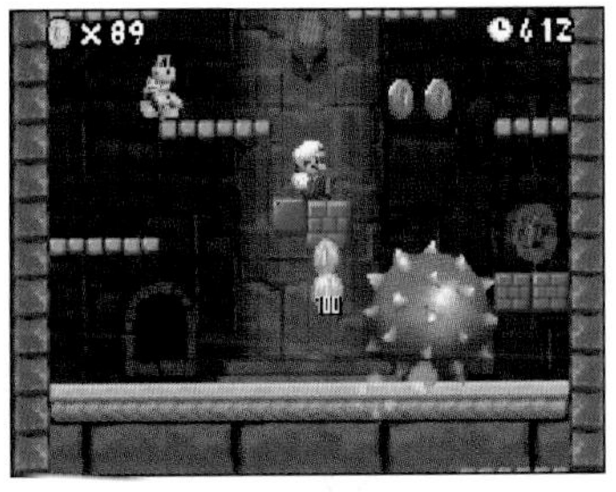

4 When the path splits, the spiked ball will end up on the left side. But don't get cocky if you chose the right side; the ball will roll through the blocks in the divider and crush you if you aren't near the top of the screen. If you choose the left side, Wall-Jump to stay ahead of the ball.

Boss

Unlike the World 4 version of Bowser Jr., this one doesn't throw Koopa shells. This is similar to the World 3 battle. The trick now is merely to time your jumps correctly while maneuvering on slippery ice.

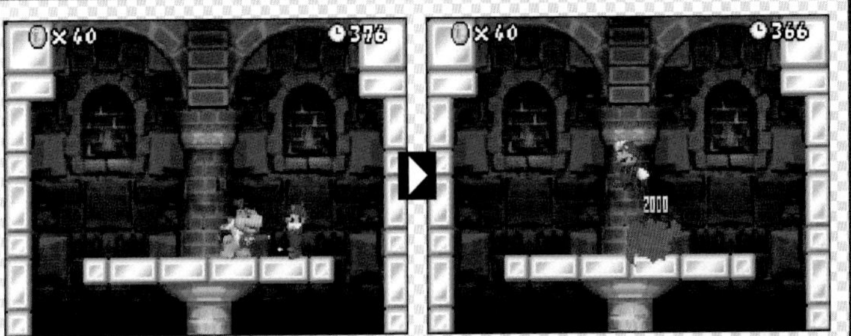

Use the Wall Jump to save yourself if you start sliding off of the edge. There's nothing below the platform, so you can't recover from a fall.

World 5-3

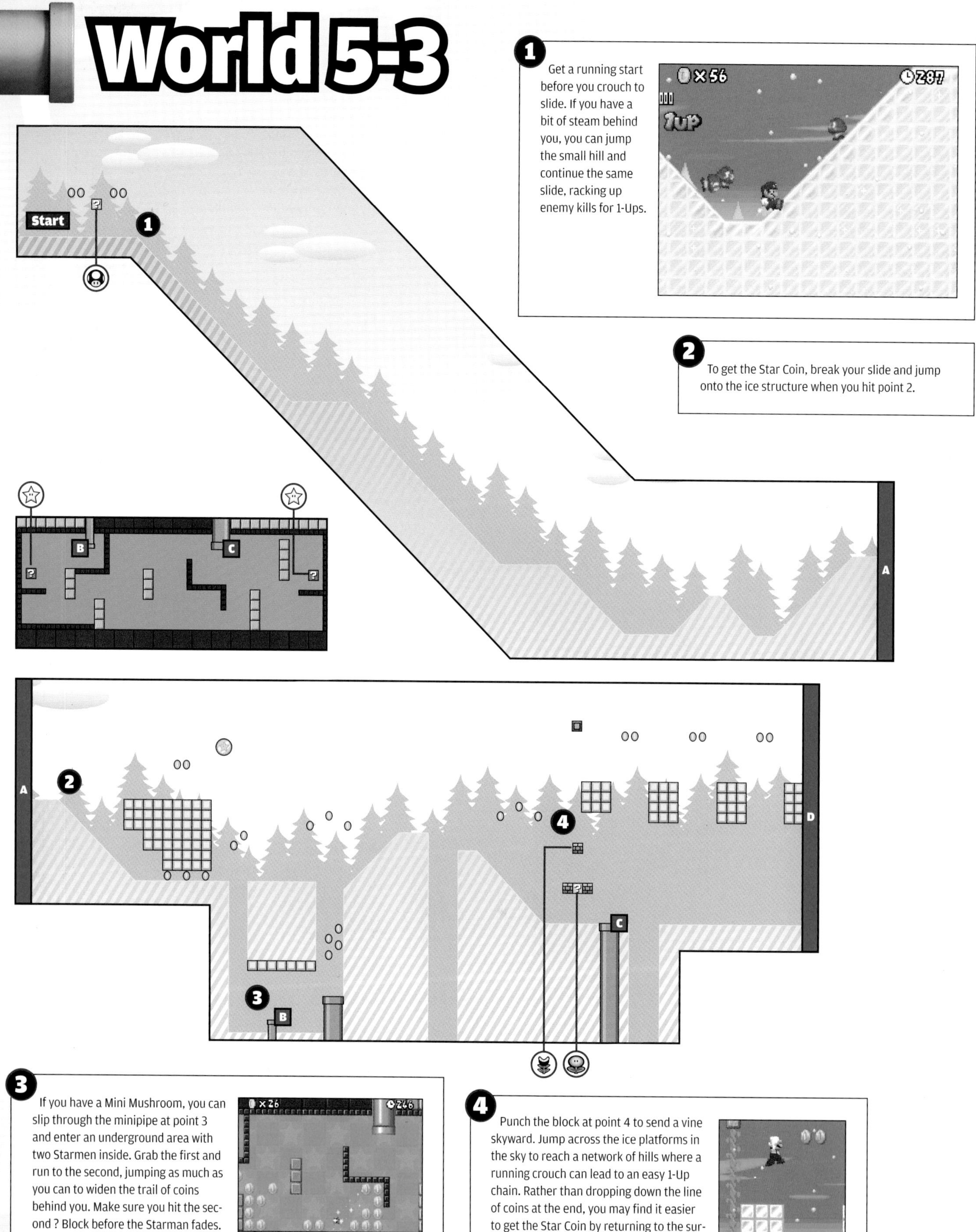

1 Get a running start before you crouch to slide. If you have a bit of steam behind you, you can jump the small hill and continue the same slide, racking up enemy kills for 1-Ups.

2 To get the Star Coin, break your slide and jump onto the ice structure when you hit point 2.

3 If you have a Mini Mushroom, you can slip through the minipipe at point 3 and enter an underground area with two Starmen inside. Grab the first and run to the second, jumping as much as you can to widen the trail of coins behind you. Make sure you hit the second ? Block before the Starman fades.

4 Punch the block at point 4 to send a vine skyward. Jump across the ice platforms in the sky to reach a network of hills where a running crouch can lead to an easy 1-Up chain. Rather than dropping down the line of coins at the end, you may find it easier to get the Star Coin by returning to the surface the way you came (see tip 5).

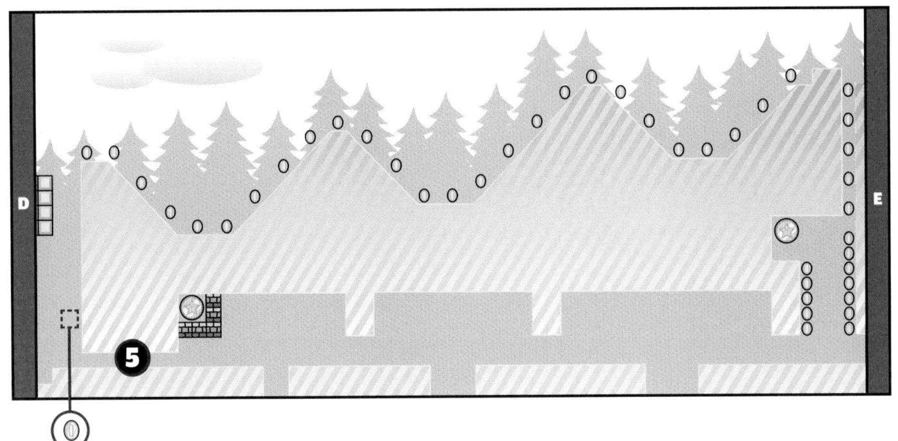

5 To slip through the narrow passage at point 5, dash along the icy plain to the left and jump over the step. Land in a crouch to slide right through the small space. You can return the way you came after you grab the Star Coin, or attempt to continue to the right, defeating the Snailicorns by bouncing off of them until your stomps knock them into a pit. If you're coming from the right, you can defeat them with Koopa shells.

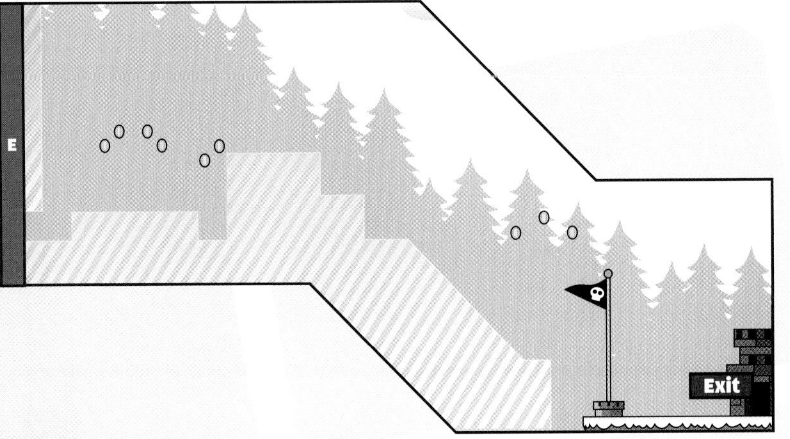

World 5-B

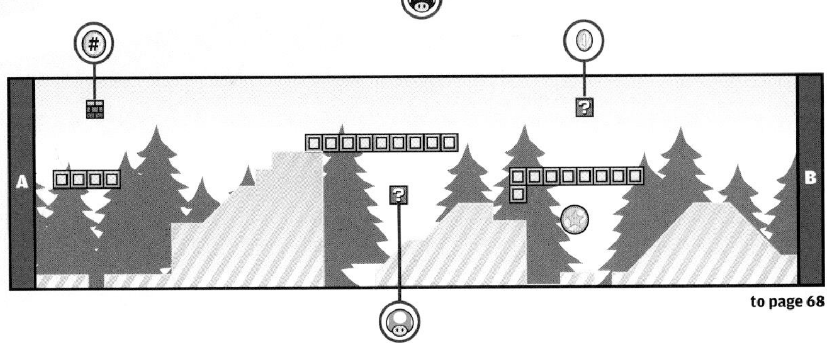

to page 68

1 Slide down the small hill at point 1 and leap at the ramp at the end to reach the icy platforms where the Koopa Paratroopas are. There isn't anything great up there, but you'll have an easier time getting around without the Koopas falling on you.

from page 67

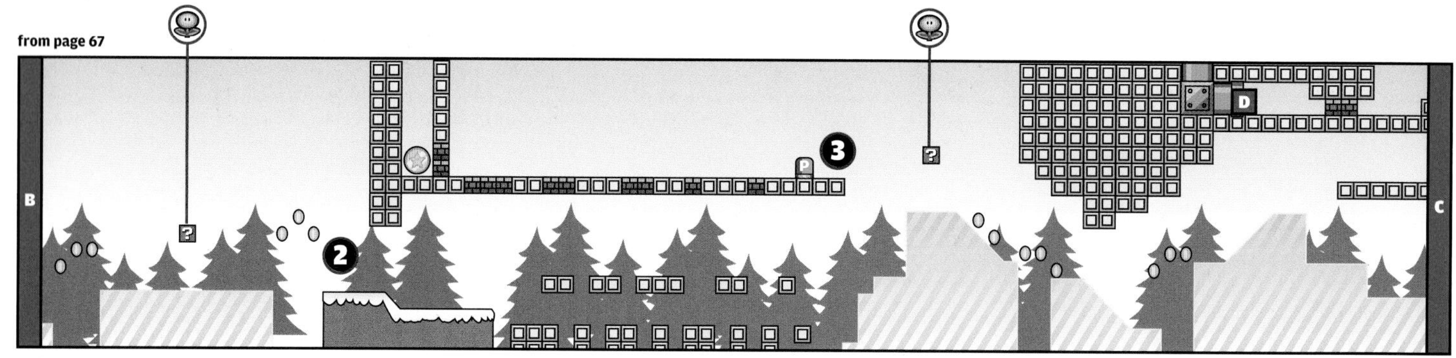

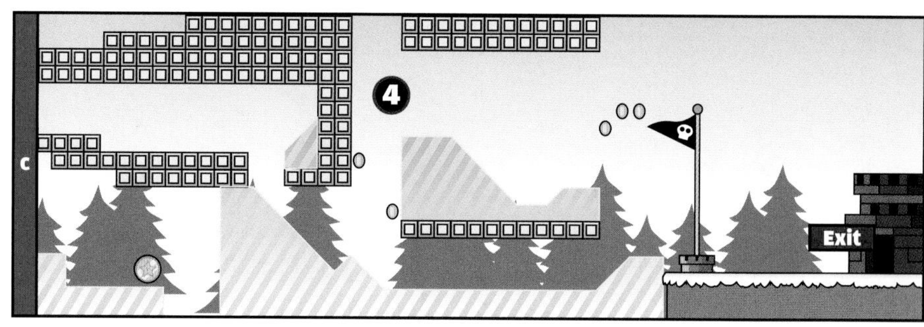

2 Grab the Koopa, kick the shell to the right, and run along with it to collect the 1-Ups. You can dash right over the gaps—you'll end up safe against a wall.

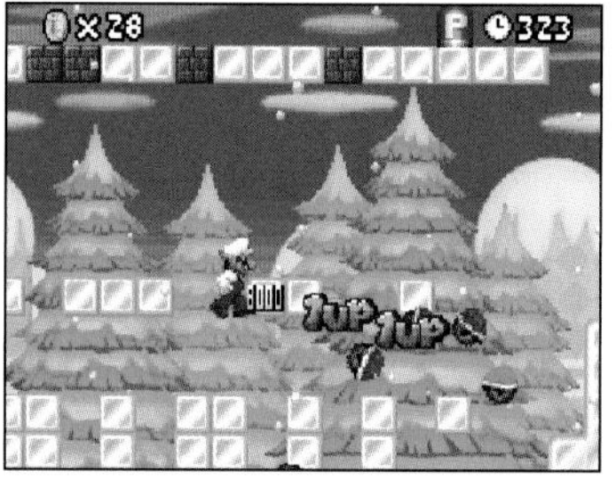

3 P Switch to the Star Coin

Continue past the Star Coin, leap up to the ledge, and hit the P Switch. There's no point dashing frantically across the gaps; you have plenty of time to take it slow.

4 To reach the alternate exit to a warp pipe, you'll need to become Shell Mario. Wall-Jump through the gap near the exit flag, then dash left to draw into your shell, and smash the blocks by the pipe.

World 5 Ghost House

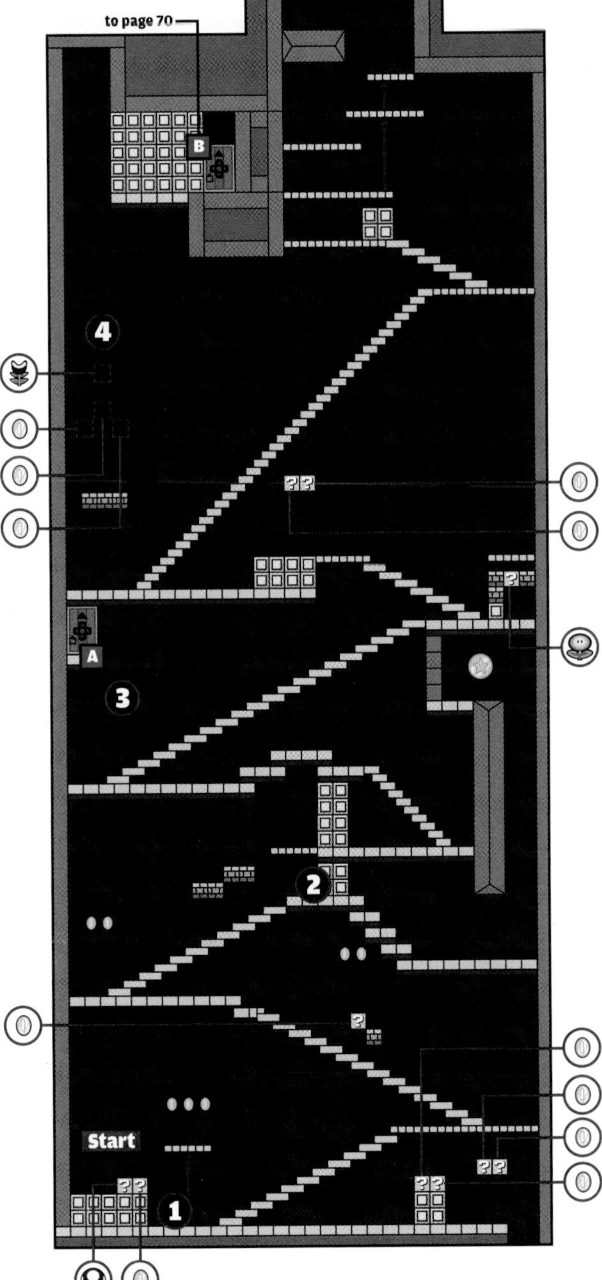

1 Broozers will punch through anything to get at Mario, and you can exploit their zeal by tricking them into smashing block barriers. When their assistance is no longer necessary, terminate them with three head stomps.

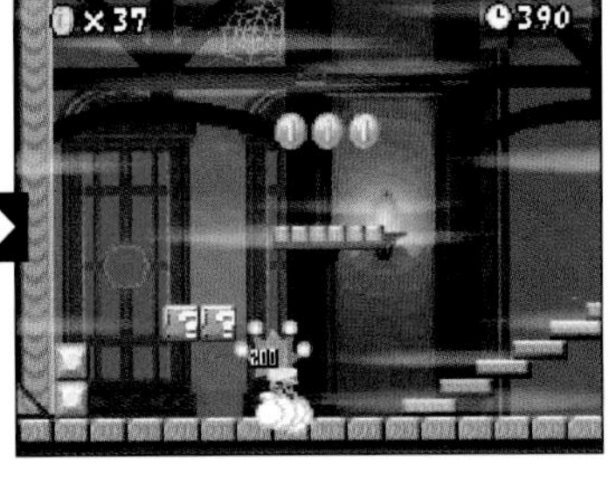

2 To get the first Star Coin, jump above the block barrier at point 2 after dodging the Broozer—it will punch through the barrier for you.

to page 70

3 Bounce off of the Broozer to reach the door at point 3. Inside, act fast—jump to a block ledge and Wall-Jump to the Star Coin before the Broozers can smash all the blocks.

4 The hidden Vine Block at point 4 is so low that if you're Super Mario, you'll need to jump from a crouched position to hit it. Climb it to a door that will ultimately take you to the warp-cannon exit.

5 The platforms in this ghost house seem to be thoroughly haunted, and will rise, fall, and tip from side to side to buck you. If you stay near the middle, you'll be fine.

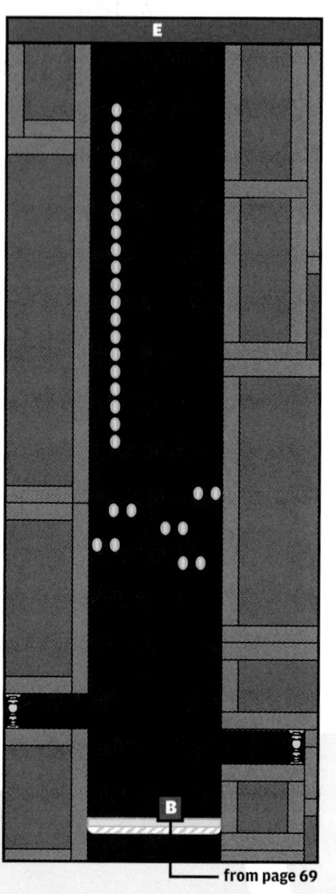

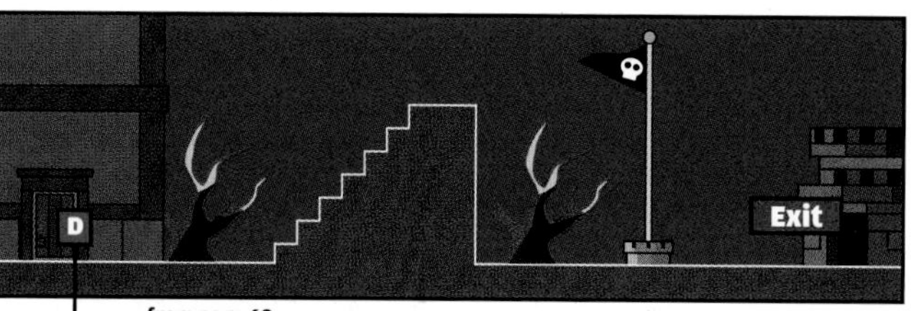

6

When the haunted platform plummets back to the bottom and begins to shoot upward at an accelerated rate, hug the right side of the screen so you can enter the passage at point 6.

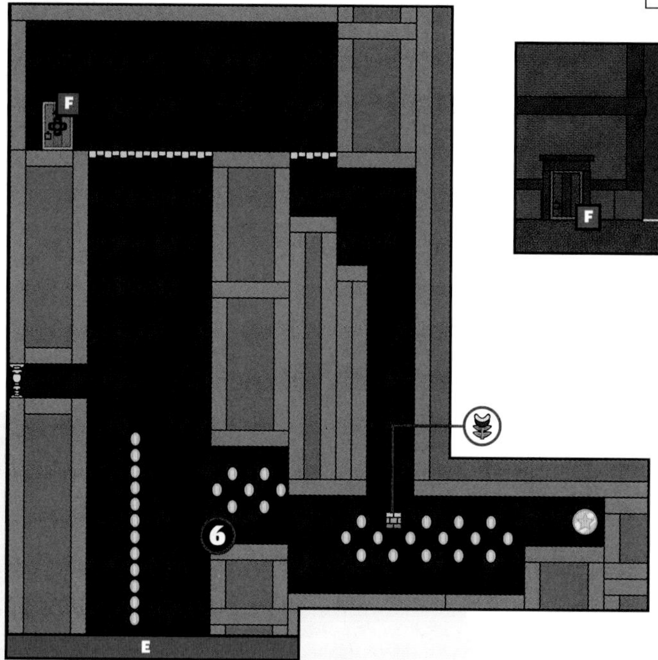

7

Grab the spring from the ? Block, stand on the edge of the block by the flagpole, and set it down. Get a running leap and bounce off of the spring to the top of the flagpole to nab a 1-Up.

World 5-C

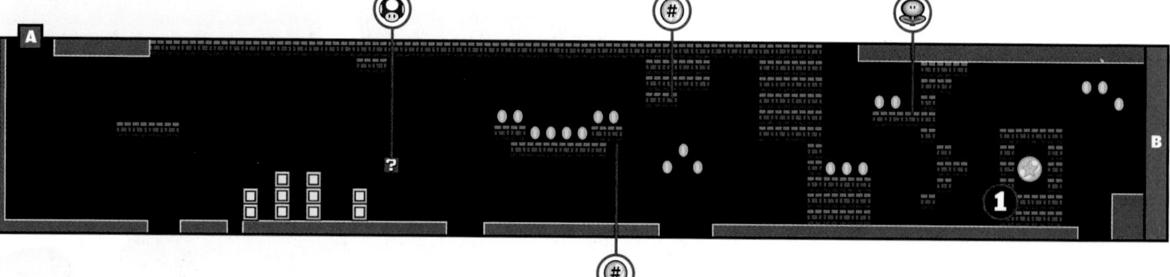

1

After the Broozer smashes a path through the blocks, jump over it and onto the Star Coin platform to trick it into punching through that, too. If the Boo falls off a ledge, you can make it reappear by traveling a few screens to the right.

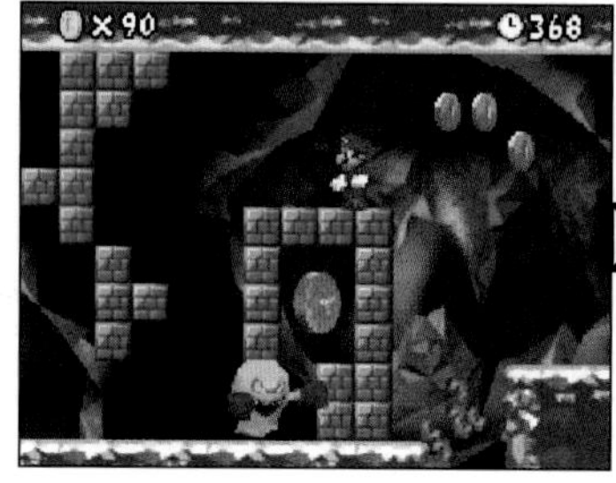

2

Stop the spinning Buzzy Beetle by stomping on it, then kick it into the Star Coin. The Buzzy Beetle moves fast, but if you miss it you can spawn a new one by moving back through the platforms to the left.

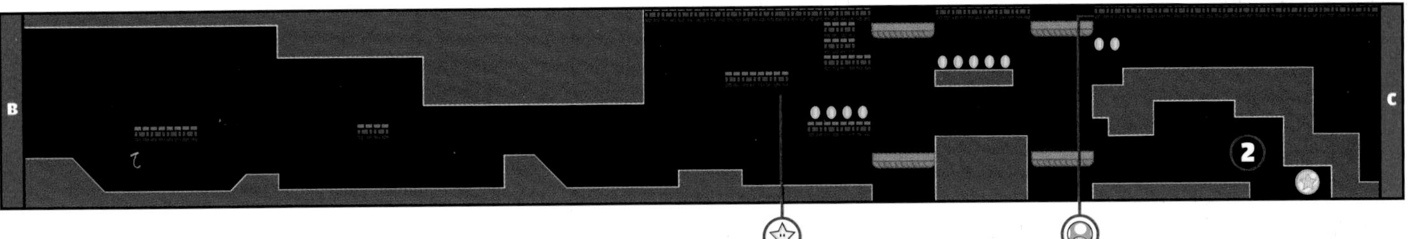

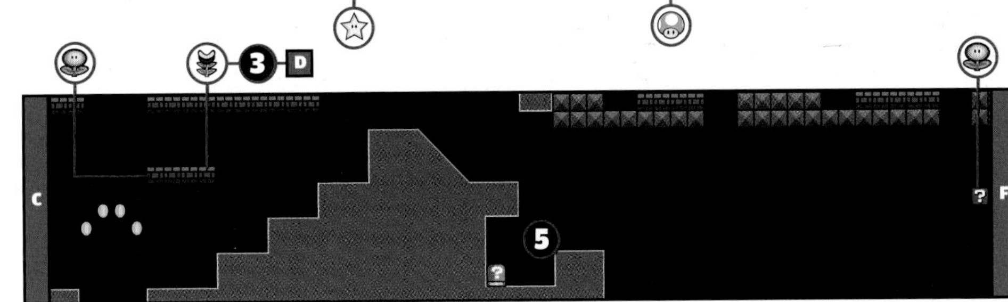

3 This Vine Block can grow all the way from the caves to the sky, but it won't get any farther than the ceiling if you don't smash the blocks above it first!

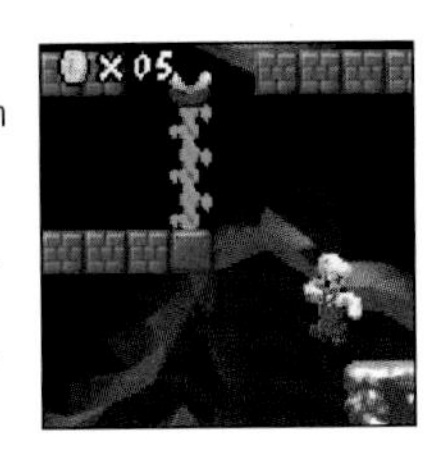

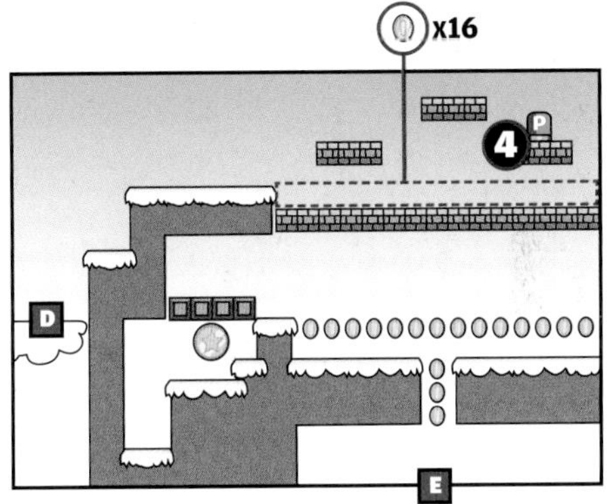

4 P Switch to the Star Coin

The Broozer is the key to getting the third Star Coin. Hit the P Switch when it's on the left side of the brick platform, then jump atop the brown blocks to trick the Broozer into smashing a path to the coin for you. When the P Switch shuts off, drop down the column of coins directly to the level exit.

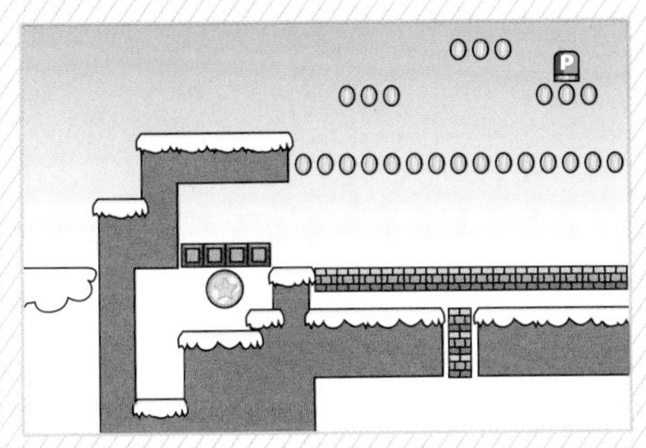

5 ? Switch to the Exit Pipe

Hit the ? Switch to generate a row of red blocks to the exit pipe. Broozers will fall from above and smash it apart, but this ? Switch isn't timed, so you can either dash through quickly or take your time and kill the Broozers.

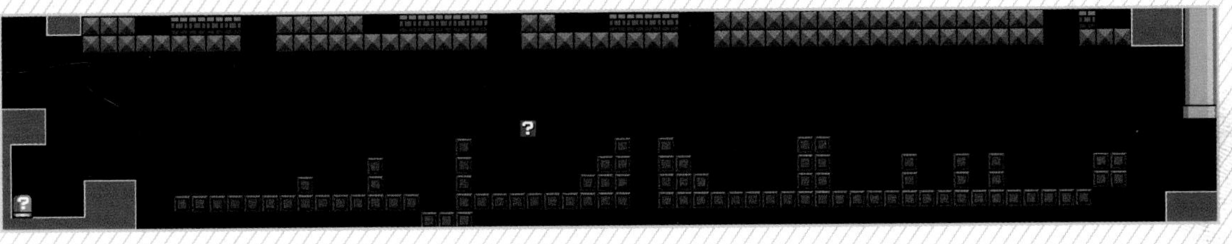

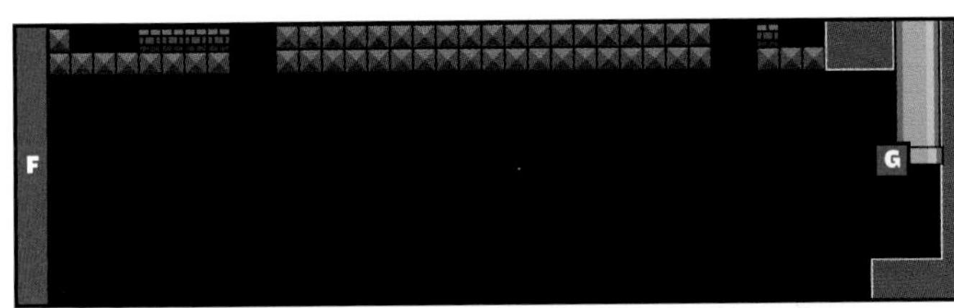

World 5-4

1 Yellow-topped mushroom platforms will sink when you land on them (but will stop automatically at the bottom of the screen). Jump repeatedly to raise a platform high enough that you can jump to the next one.

2 Red-topped mushroom platforms are just the opposite of the yellow-topped ones, rising as you stand on them. Watch out so they don't push you right into a Bullet Bill!

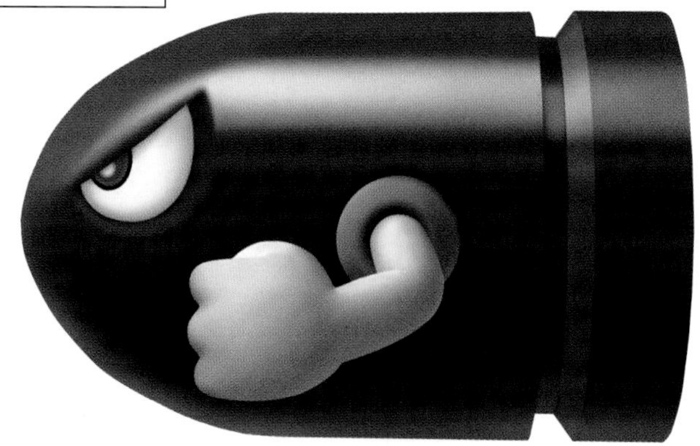

3 Red-Coin Ring

Leap through the red-coin ring and jump as soon as you land on the mushroom platform to grab the top two coins. Sink to the lower pair, then proceed right, using the platforms to get each other coin in turn.

4 The first Star Coin is a gimme, but only Mini Mario can slip through to get the second. Other Mario sizes will need to go around it, stomp the Koopa on the red mushroom platform, and kick the shell to the coin. Watch out for the rebound!

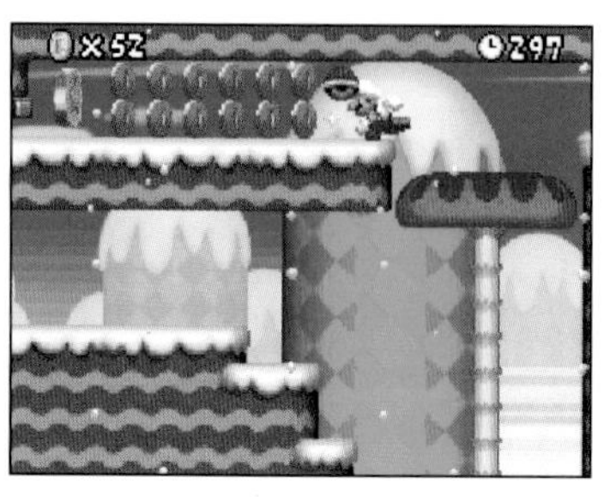

5 Stomp the green Koopa on the ledge and kick its shell to the right to set the 1-Up free. Dodge the shell's rebound as you ride the mushroom platform down and chase ater the 1-Up Mushroom.

6 Hop repeatedly on the red mushroom platform so it can't rise, then step onto the ledge at point 6. You must get the Star Coin from this direction; Invisible Blocks obstruct the path from below.

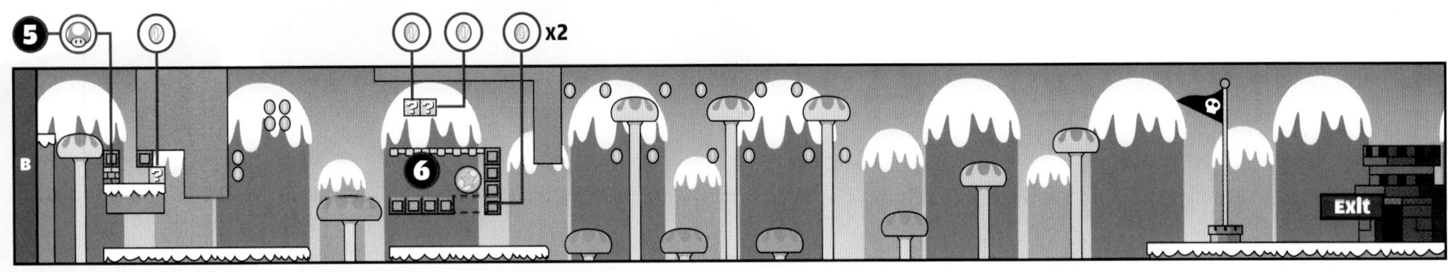

World 5 Castle

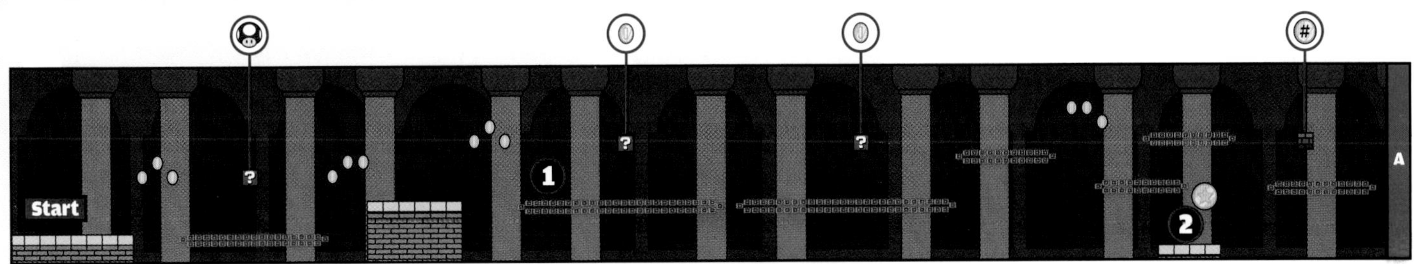

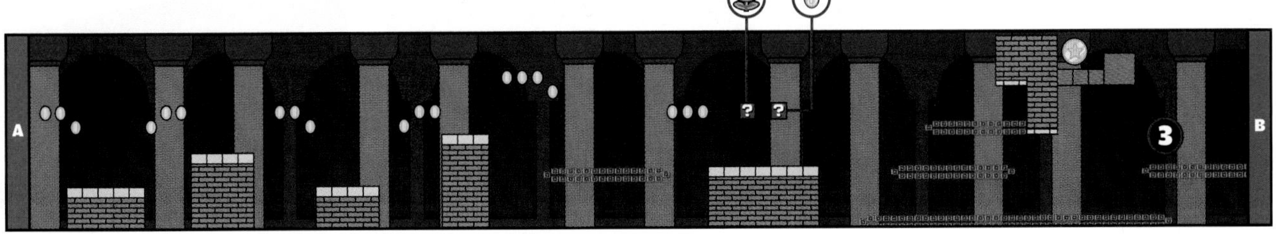

to page 74

1 The conveyor belts will propel you in different directions, so figure out which way they're heading before you jump onto them. If a belt is running toward you, you can still make progress by dashing or jumping forward.

2 Stand still on the conveyor belts above the Star Coin—they'll drop you right on it. Unfortunately, they'll drop the Piranha Plant on it, too, so long-jump to the right as soon as you grab the coin.

3 Wait below and to the right of the Star Coin ledge; the conveyor belts will send a spring your way eventually. If you miss the jump, be patient—another spring will be along soon.

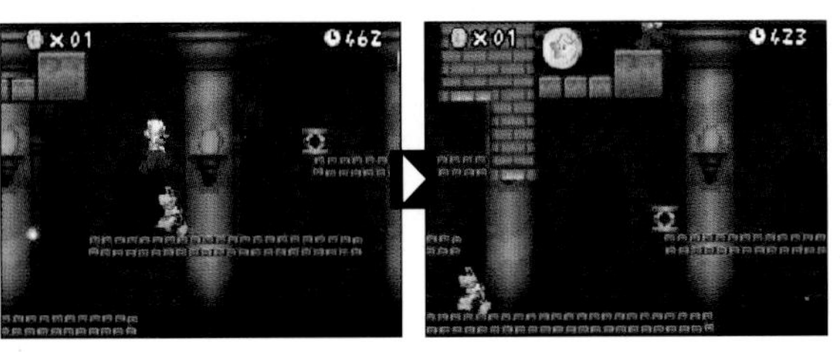

4 Super Dry Bones can shrug off stomps; you can smash them only with a Ground Pound. Instead of engaging them, jump off of them and let the belts carry them away.

5 The Roulette Block at point 5 is the only way to get a Mini Mushroom on this stage. If you're desperate to get the Star Coin and beat the boss as Mini Mario (opening a path to World 7), jump into a pit if you get the wrong power-up, then continue from the nearby checkpoint and test your luck again.

from page 73

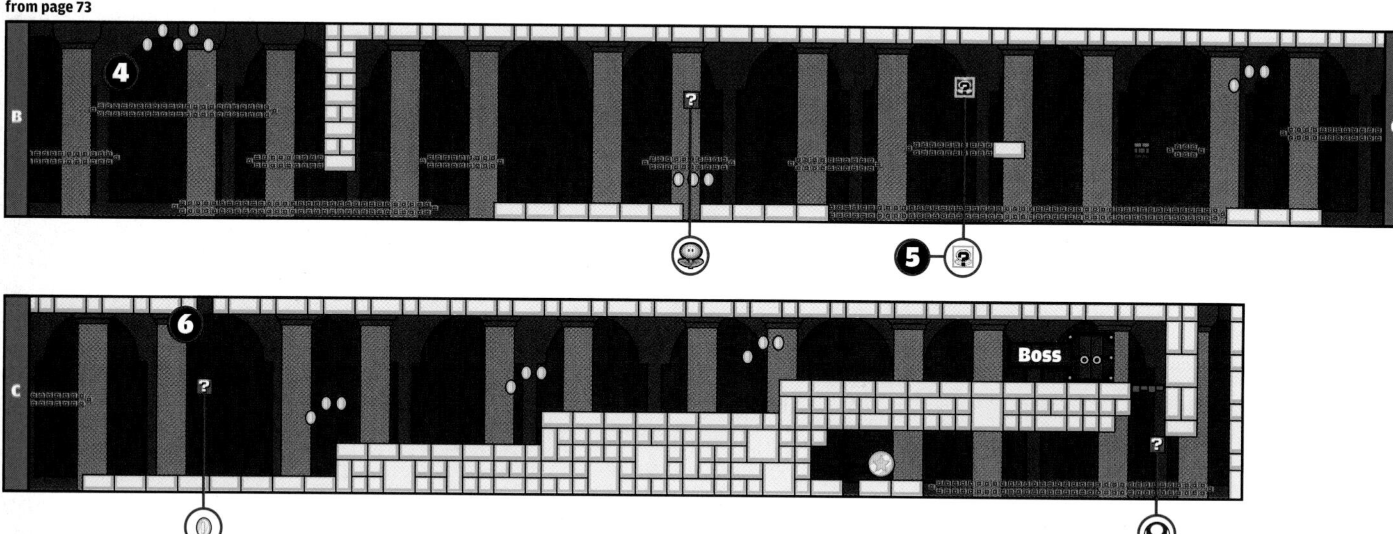

6 As Mini Mario, jump from the ? Block into the gap and do a Wall Jump to get above the ceiling. Move to the right end of the level, where you can grab a Star Coin and, if you want, a Super Mushroom.

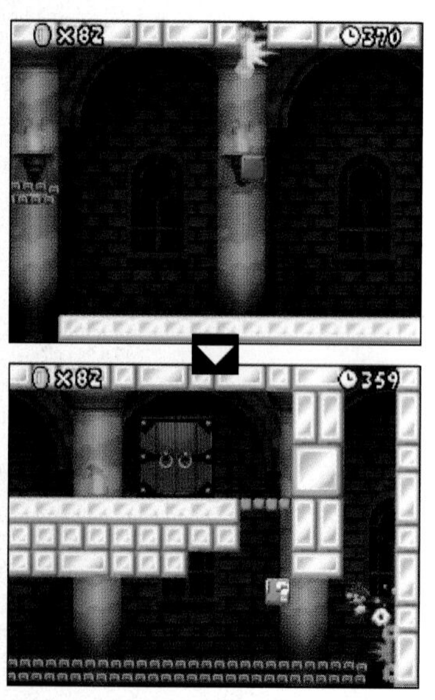

Boss

Dash under Petey Piranha as he flies around the room, attempting to damage you with his own Ground Pounds (to avoid his attacks, run away when he pauses and begins flapping his leaves rapidly). After Petey Piranha Ground-Pounds and misses, he'll fall on his back, allowing you to get above him and stomp or Ground-Pound his head or belly for damage.

After you score a second hit, Petey Piranha will shake up his pattern and jump around the room for a while. Dash beneath his legs to make him return to his usual pattern.

World 6

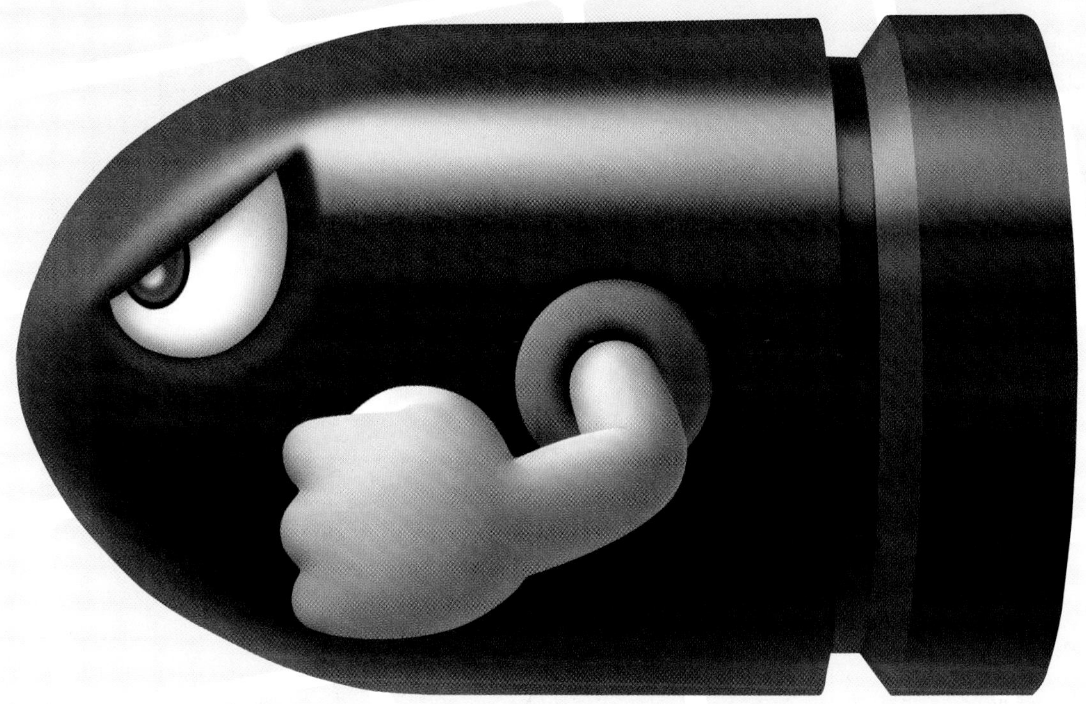

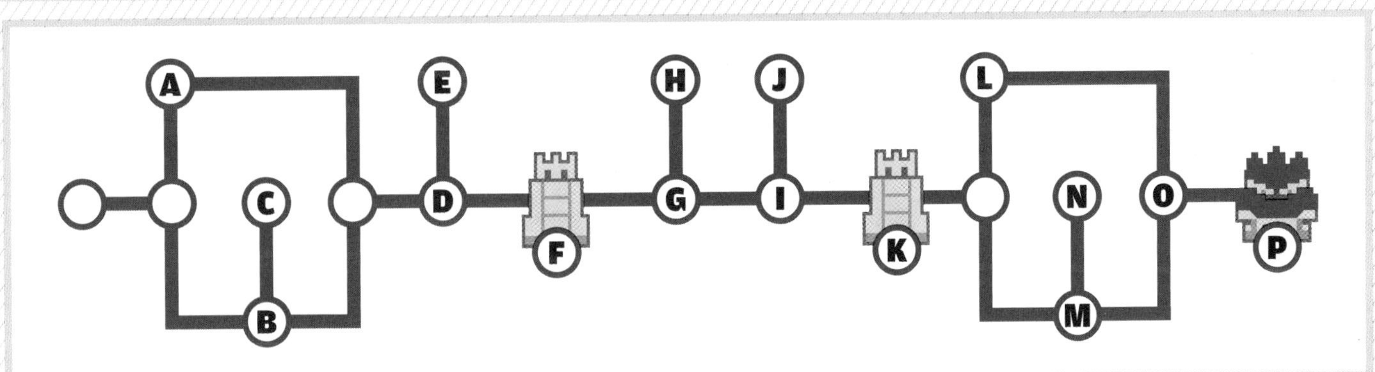

A **World 6-1** (Page 76)

B **World 6-A** (5 Star Coins/Page 77)

C **Red Toad House**

D **World 6-2** (Page 78)

E **Green Toad House** (5 Star Coins)

F **World 6 Tower** (Page 79)

G **World 6-3** (Page 80)

H **Orange Toad House** (5 Star Coins)

I **World 6-4** (Page 81)

J **Red Toad House** (5 Star Coins)

K **World 6 Tower 2** (Page 82)

L **World 6-5** (Page 83)

M **World 6-B** (5 Star Coins/Page 84)

N **Green Toad House**

O **World 6-6** (Page 86)

P **World 6 Castle** (Page 88)

World 6-1

1 Jumping on Bullet Bills is a good way both to defeat an enemy and to bounce to higher areas of this stage. When you tire of timing their blasts, you can stand near the cannons and catch a breather—they won't fire at an adjacent target.

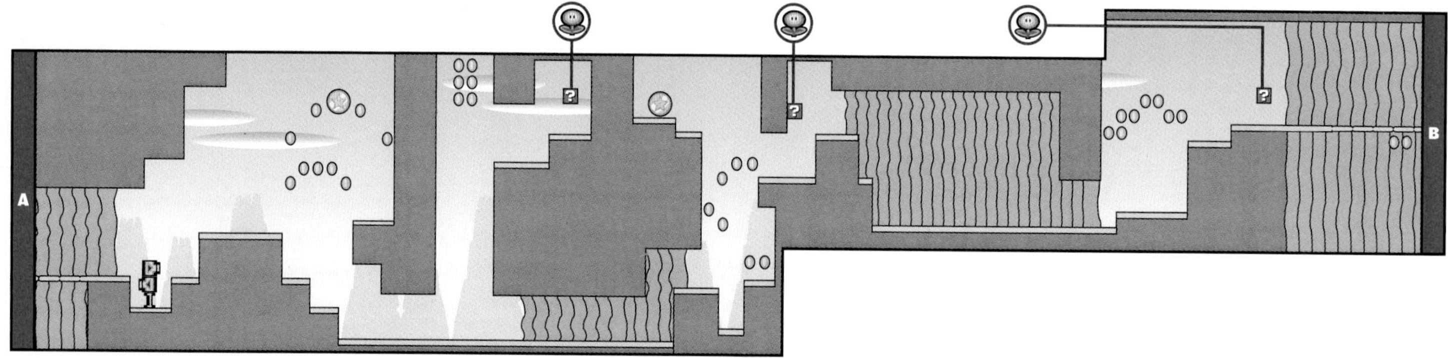

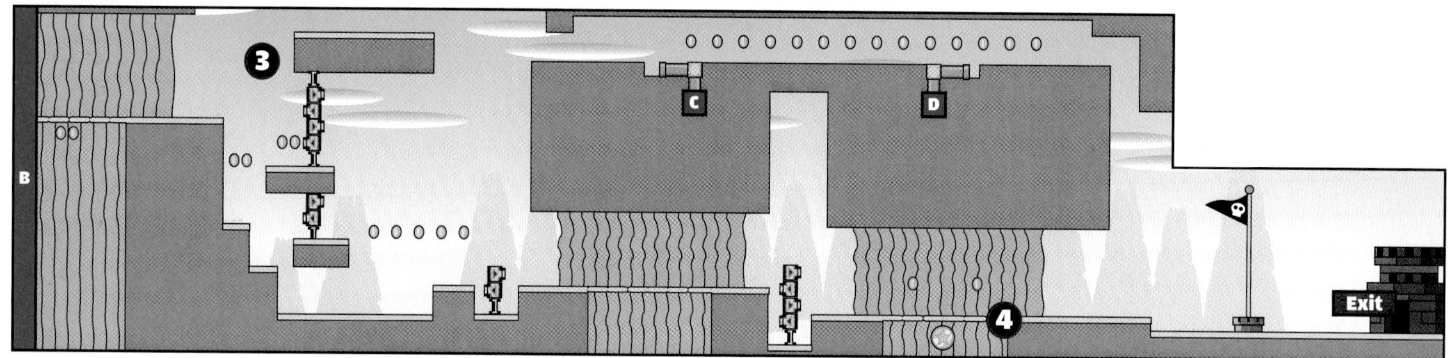

2 Mario must sidle across the thin ledges at point 2, which forces him to move slowly and restricts his jumping ability. To slip under Bullet Bills, press down to hang from your fingertips on the ledge.

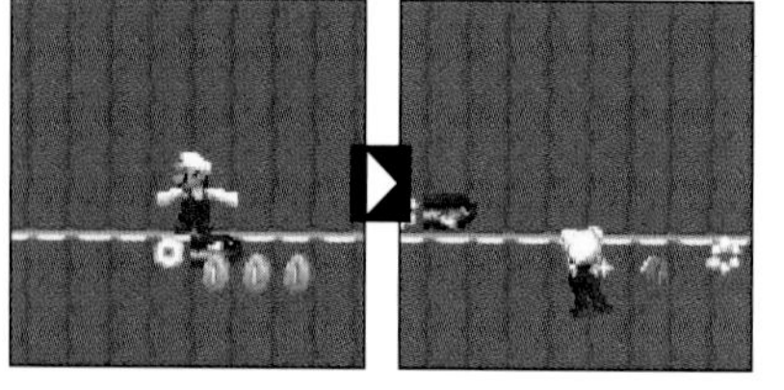

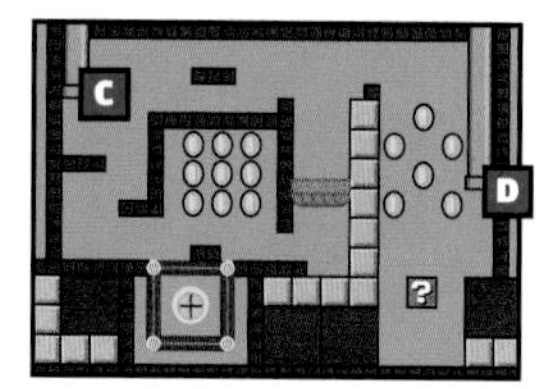

3 By bouncing off of Bullet Bills, you can leap above the ledge and jump to a shortcut that will take you directly to the flagpole. If you're Mini Mario, you can enter a minipipe on the upper level that leads to a room full of Mini Goombas. Dodge them until you get a Starman from the ? Block, then Wall-Jump up the left wall and kill the Goombas for a 1-Up.

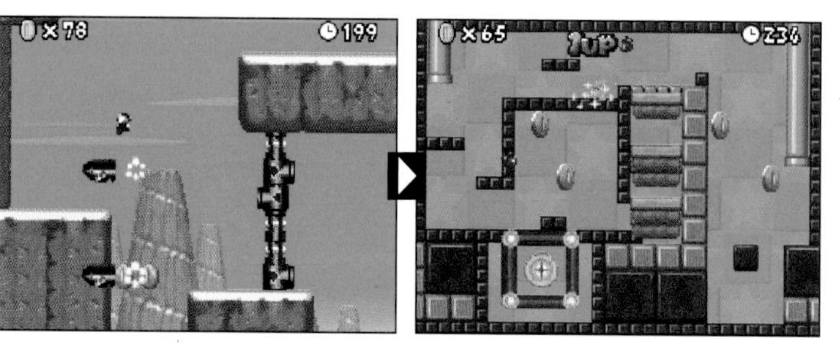

4 If you're coming from the left, sidle past the Star Coin until the Bullet Bill cannons stop firing. You can then head back to grab the coin safely.

World 6-A

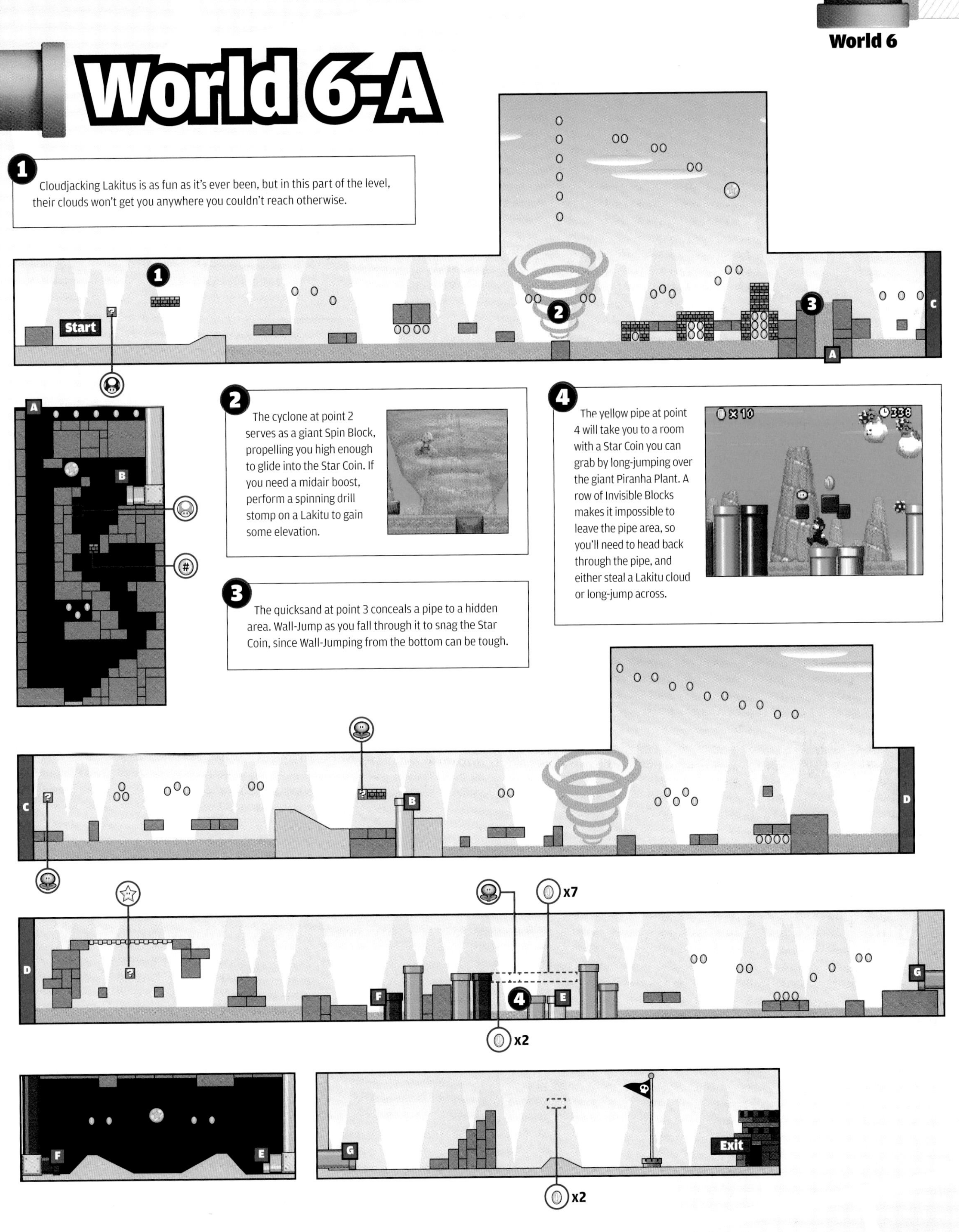

1 Cloudjacking Lakitus is as fun as it's ever been, but in this part of the level, their clouds won't get you anywhere you couldn't reach otherwise.

2 The cyclone at point 2 serves as a giant Spin Block, propelling you high enough to glide into the Star Coin. If you need a midair boost, perform a spinning drill stomp on a Lakitu to gain some elevation.

3 The quicksand at point 3 conceals a pipe to a hidden area. Wall-Jump as you fall through it to snag the Star Coin, since Wall-Jumping from the bottom can be tough.

4 The yellow pipe at point 4 will take you to a room with a Star Coin you can grab by long-jumping over the giant Piranha Plant. A row of Invisible Blocks makes it impossible to leave the pipe area, so you'll need to head back through the pipe, and either steal a Lakitu cloud or long-jump across.

World 6-2

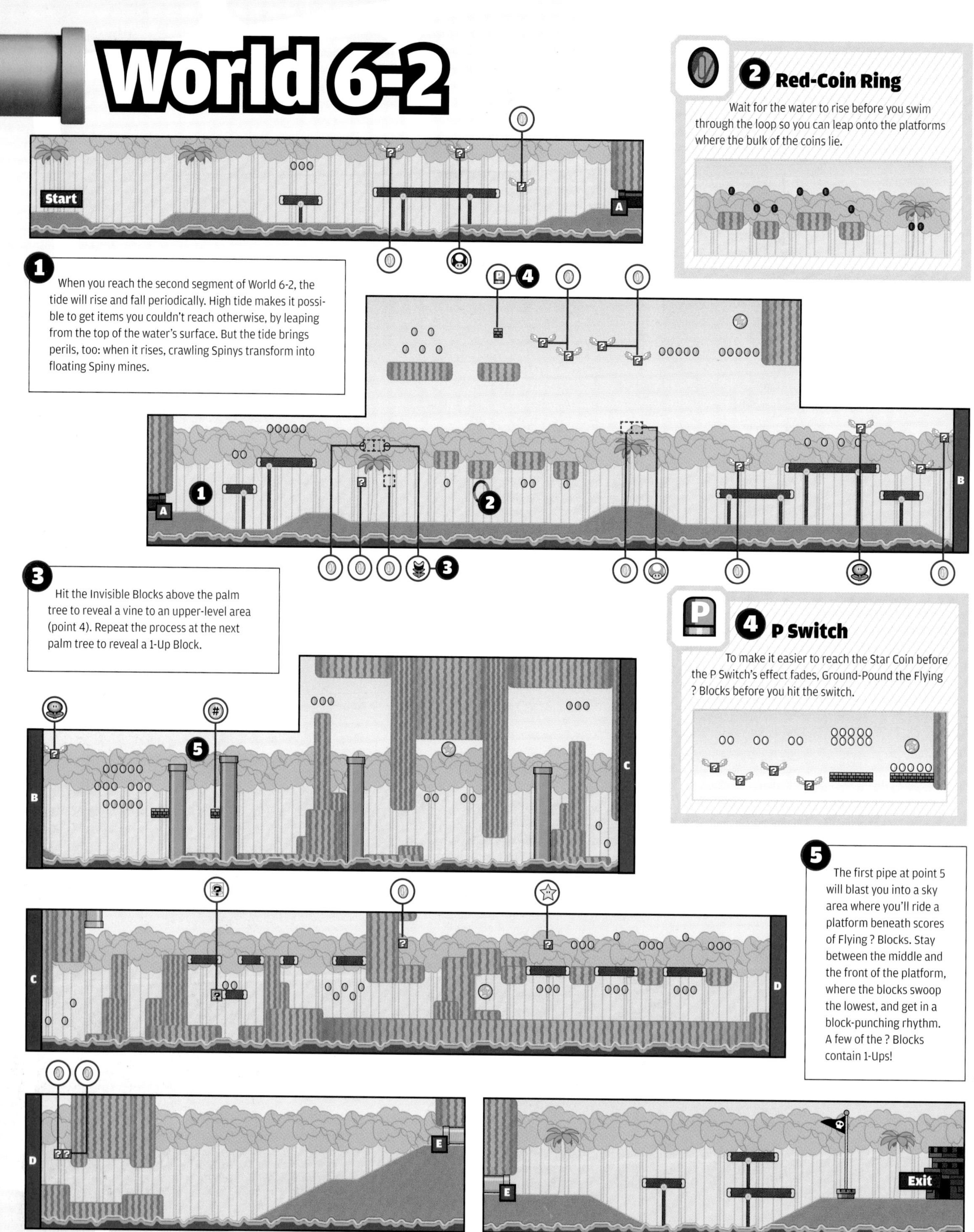

2 Red-Coin Ring

Wait for the water to rise before you swim through the loop so you can leap onto the platforms where the bulk of the coins lie.

1 When you reach the second segment of World 6-2, the tide will rise and fall periodically. High tide makes it possible to get items you couldn't reach otherwise, by leaping from the top of the water's surface. But the tide brings perils, too: when it rises, crawling Spinys transform into floating Spiny mines.

3 Hit the Invisible Blocks above the palm tree to reveal a vine to an upper-level area (point 4). Repeat the process at the next palm tree to reveal a 1-Up Block.

4 P Switch

To make it easier to reach the Star Coin before the P Switch's effect fades, Ground-Pound the Flying ? Blocks before you hit the switch.

5 The first pipe at point 5 will blast you into a sky area where you'll ride a platform beneath scores of Flying ? Blocks. Stay between the middle and the front of the platform, where the blocks swoop the lowest, and get in a block-punching rhythm. A few of the ? Blocks contain 1-Ups!

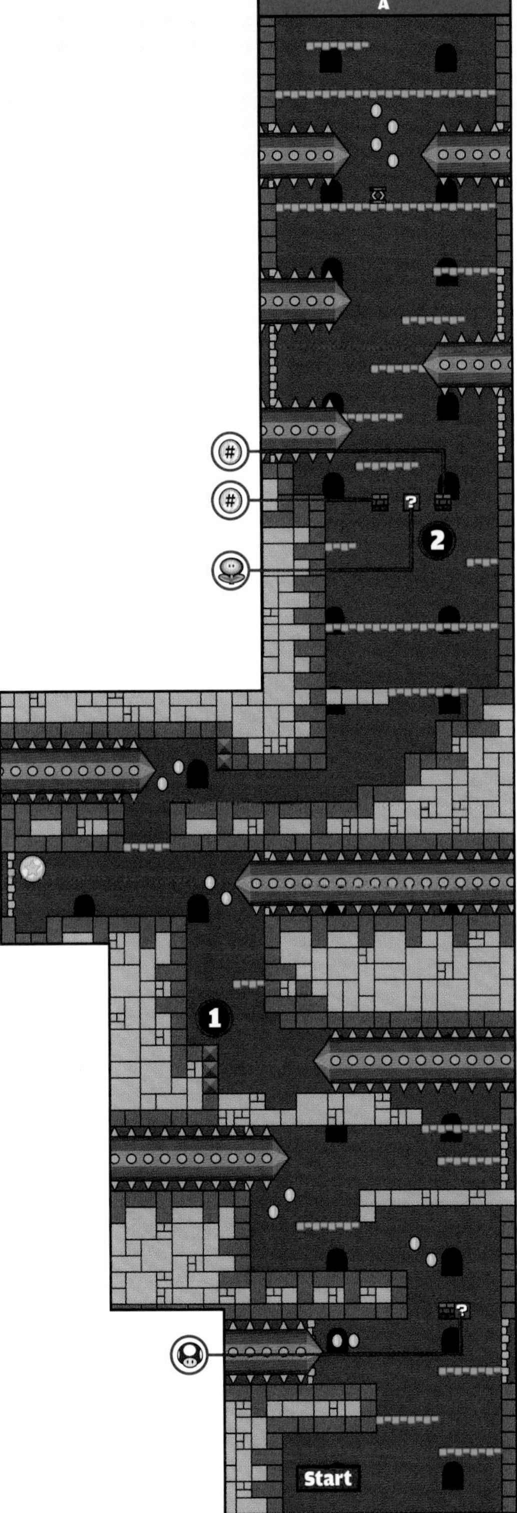

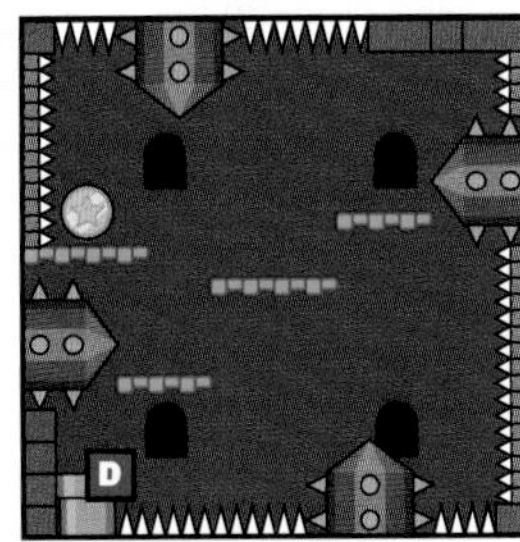

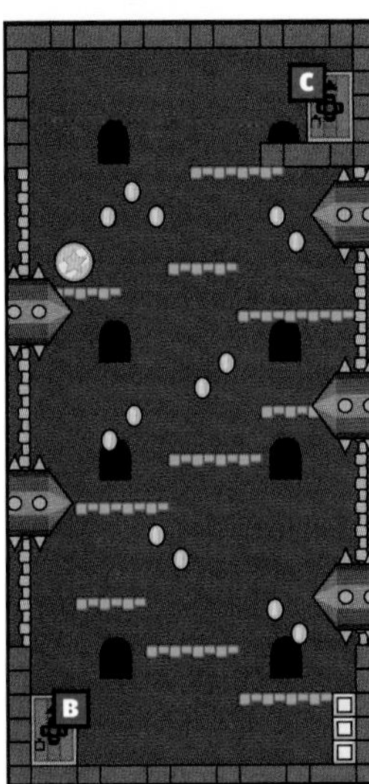

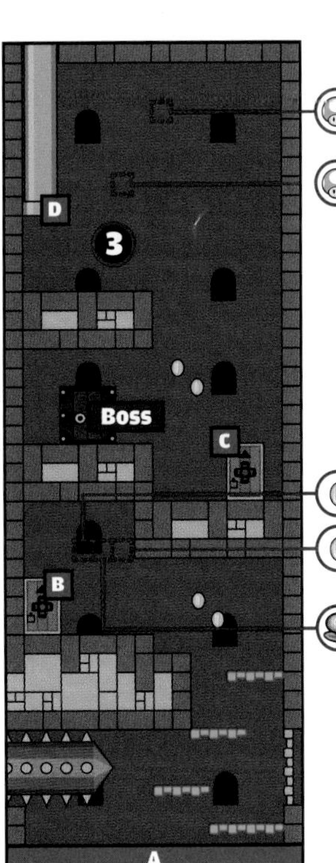

1 Proceed through the tower slowly, moving up only immediately after the spiked pillars retract, and keeping an eye out for places where you can crouch beneath them. At point 1, dash all the way to the end and crouch in the crevasse. Wait for the pillar to retract before you jump for the Star Coin and move on.

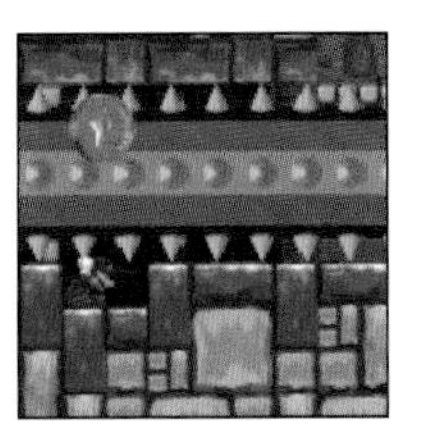

2 Jump atop the Super Dry Bones and hold down the jump button to bounce off of its head and into the ? Block and the Coin Block above.

3 Reaching the pipe above the boss door will take some world-class Wall-Jumping. The walls are pretty far apart, but you can gain height gradually if you do a running jump at the right edge of the ledge where the boss door is and keep at it. If you have a Mini Mushroom, use it to make the task much easier.

Boss

This is a basic Bowser Jr. fight (no Koopa shells) with the added twist of a hanging platform that tilts as you move from side to side. (Mario weighs more than Bowser Jr.? Better lay off the cannoli!) Stay near the center of the platform so it can't tilt far, and use Wall Jumps when necessary to stay off of the spikes.

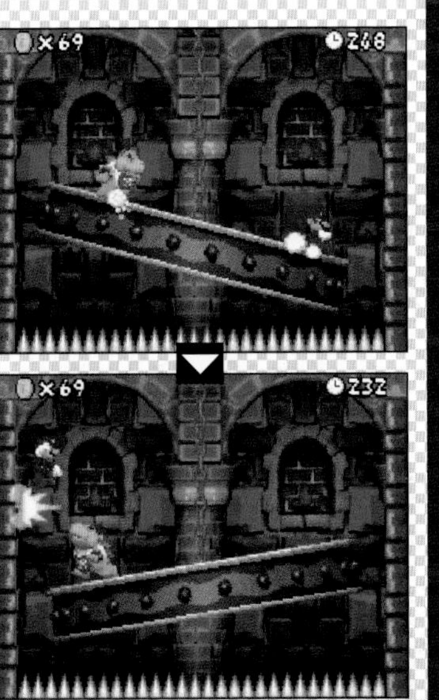

World 6-3

1 If there's one thing Mega Mario loves, it's smashing pipes! Use a Mega Mushroom at point 1 to tear through this stage and earn five easy 1-Ups.

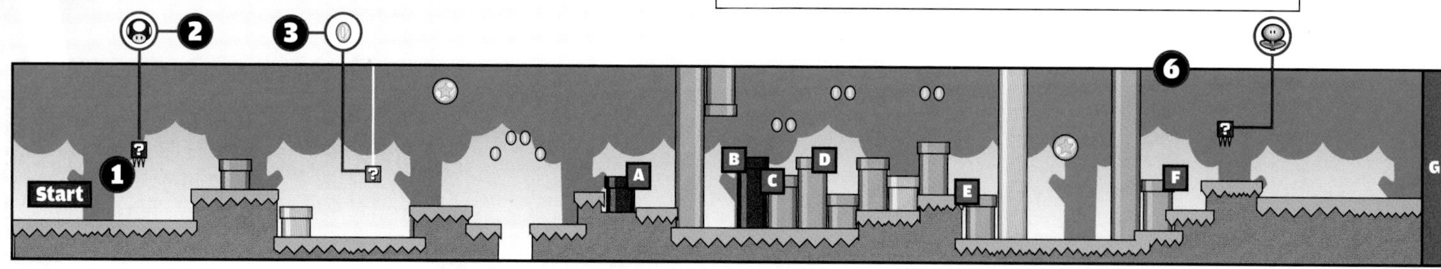

2 Spiked ? Blocks almost always hold power-ups, but they won't give them up easily. Hit the blocks when the spikes are on the opposite side, or you'll be impaled.

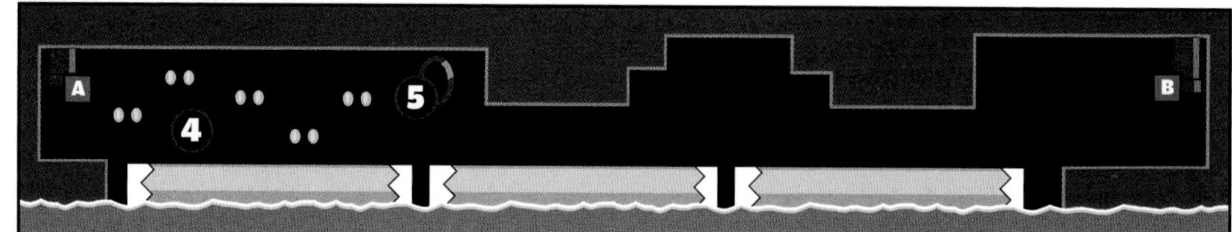

3 You'll get style points for taking point 3's ? Block for a ride, but you can simply hit it instead and long-jump to the Star Coin from its lifeless husk.

4 You can dash safely over these logs, but if you stand on them or walk at normal speeds, they'll begin to roll you toward the screen and into the poison water. Jump to stabilize yourself.

5 Red-Coin Ring

This one couldn't be easier. If you dash over the rolling logs and make two well-timed jumps, you can hit all the coins with time to spare.

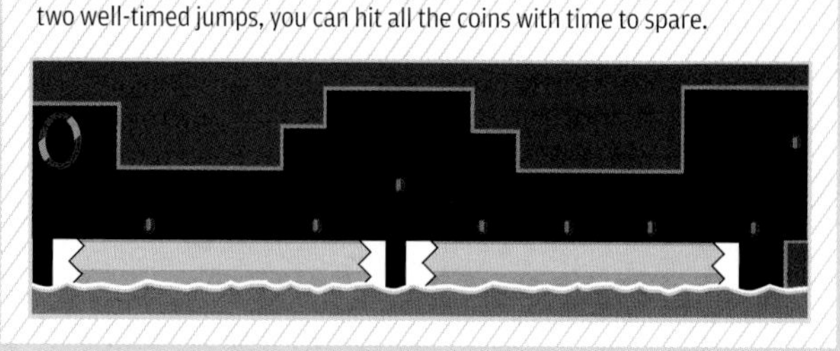

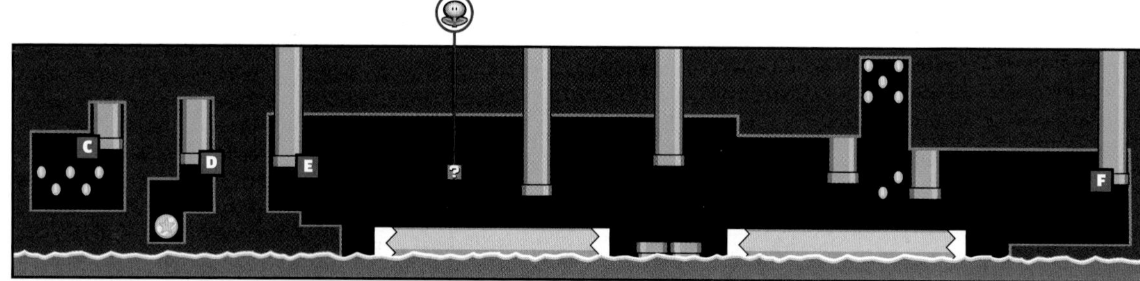

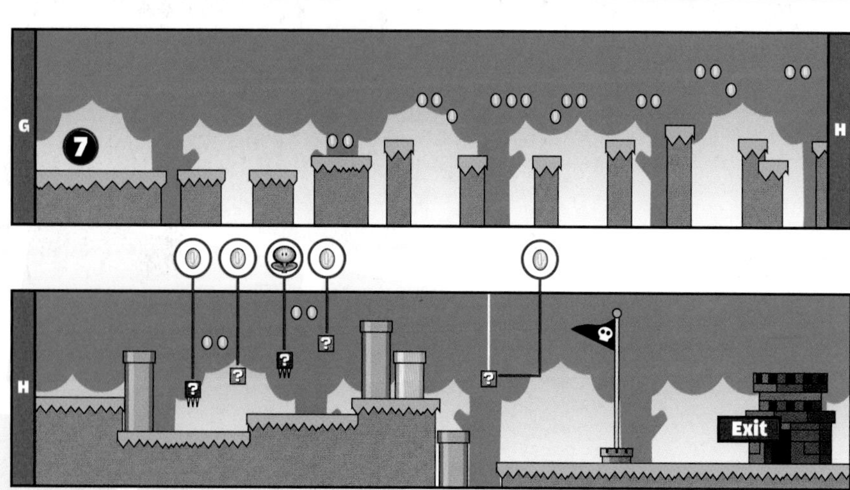

6 Hit this spiked block, then run from the right, jump onto it, and long-jump at its edge to leap over the pipe and into the Star Coin. You can Wall-Jump out afterward. Alternatively, chase the Moneybags left and bounce off of it to get over the pipe.

7 The key to beating the Moneybags is leaping over it and chasing it to the left, where you can trap it against a pipe and blast it with fireballs to earn a 1-Up.

World 6-4

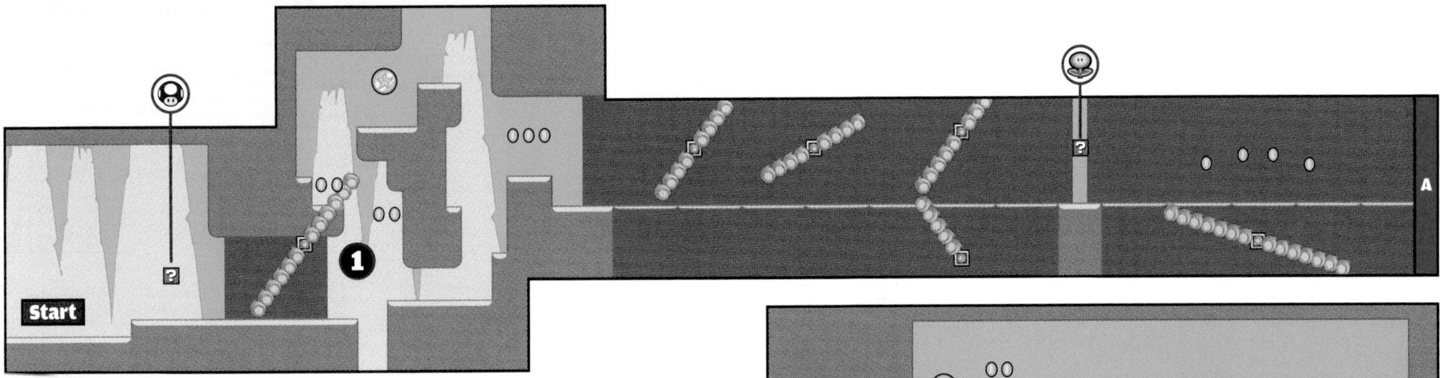

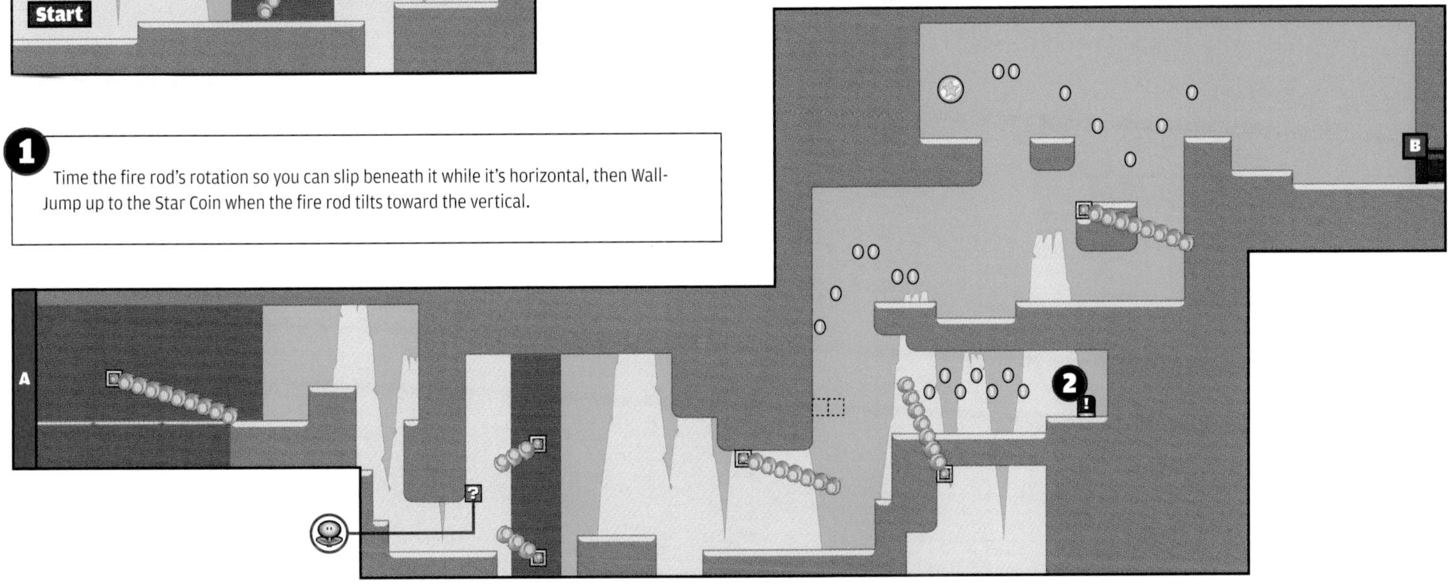

Start

A

B

A

1

Time the fire rod's rotation so you can slip beneath it while it's horizontal, then Wall-Jump up to the Star Coin when the fire rod tilts toward the vertical.

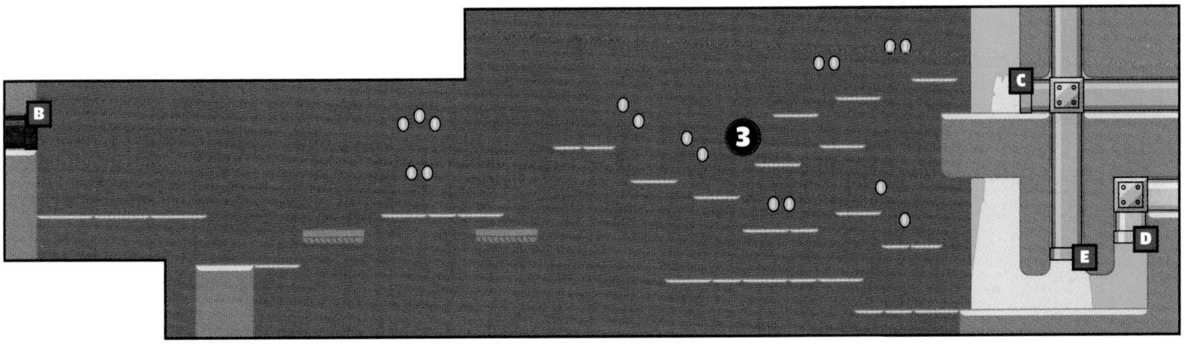

2

B

C

D

E

3

2 ! Switch

You can use this ! Switch to create a ledge up to the next level. But it shouldn't be necessary; you can Wall-Jump up to the next level without it.

3

Be sure to explore the upper part of this area fully, because the higher ledges lead to a different pipe. That pipe makes a loop to a Star Coin before returning to the lower exit pipe.

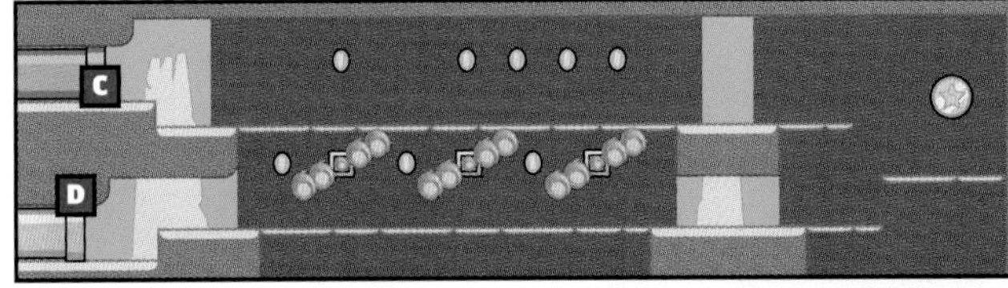

World 6 Tower 2

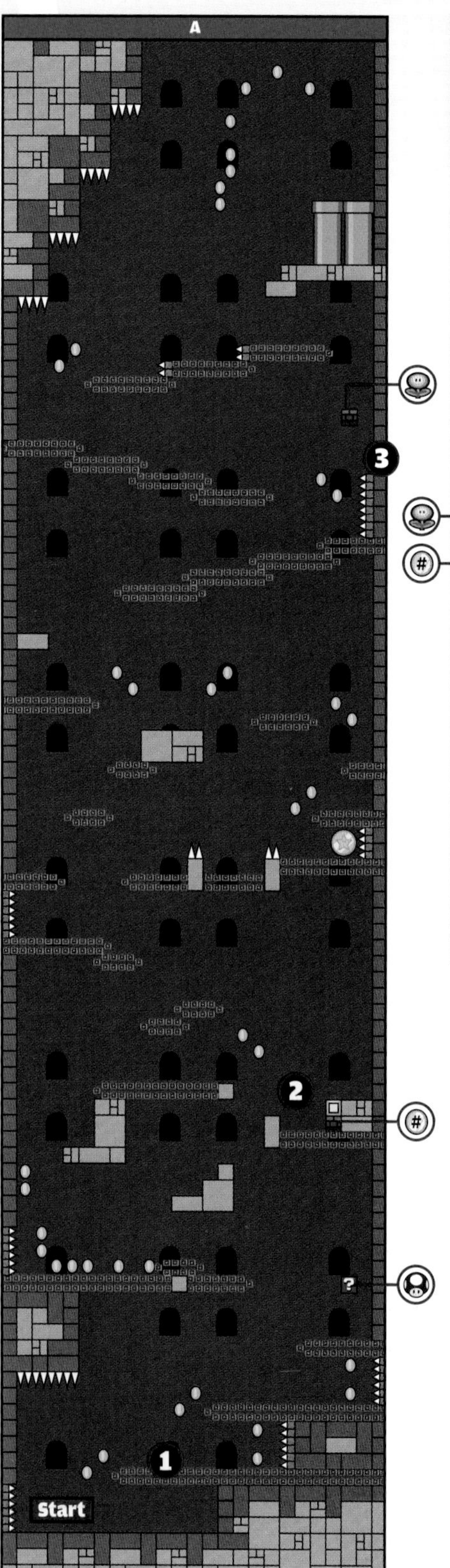

1

The conveyor belts are much harder to navigate here than they were in the previous tower. To pull off delicate maneuvers (such as snagging the first Star Coin), be sure to jump and change direction in midair so you're facing in the opposite direction of the way the belt is running. If you wait to change direction when you land, it may be too late.

2

You'll find a Buzzy Beetle overturned and waiting at the ledge above point 2. Give it a simple kick to the right, and hang around to tally up your winnings from the Coin Block.

3

It's hard not to take damage from the Dry Bones, but you can pick up a power-up at point 3. Just jump on top of the spiked wall (it's safe) and hop slightly to the left to let loose a power-up.

4

When the Spike Tops are out of the way, crouch and let the conveyor belt carry you beneath the Star Coin, where you can punch the blocks above you. You can't get this coin if you aren't at least Super Mario, so you may need to find a power-up and come back for the Star Coin.

Boss

This is the Bowser Jr. variant that throws Koopa shells, so time your jumps carefully to land on the shells and kick them back. The number of times you've jumped on Bowser Jr. determines the speeds at which the Koopa shells slide, so you'll need to account for that when you time your jumps.

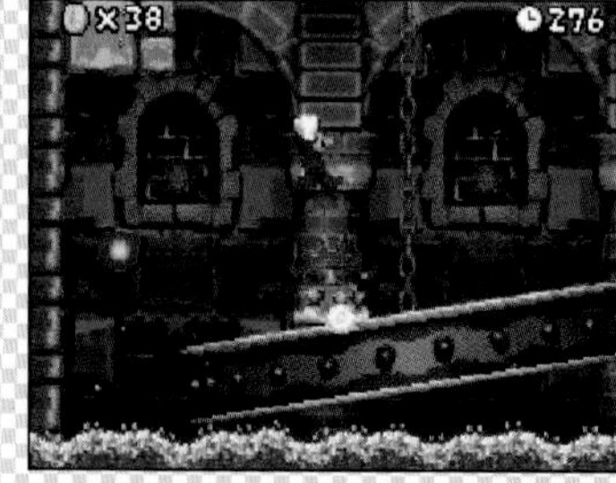

World 6-5

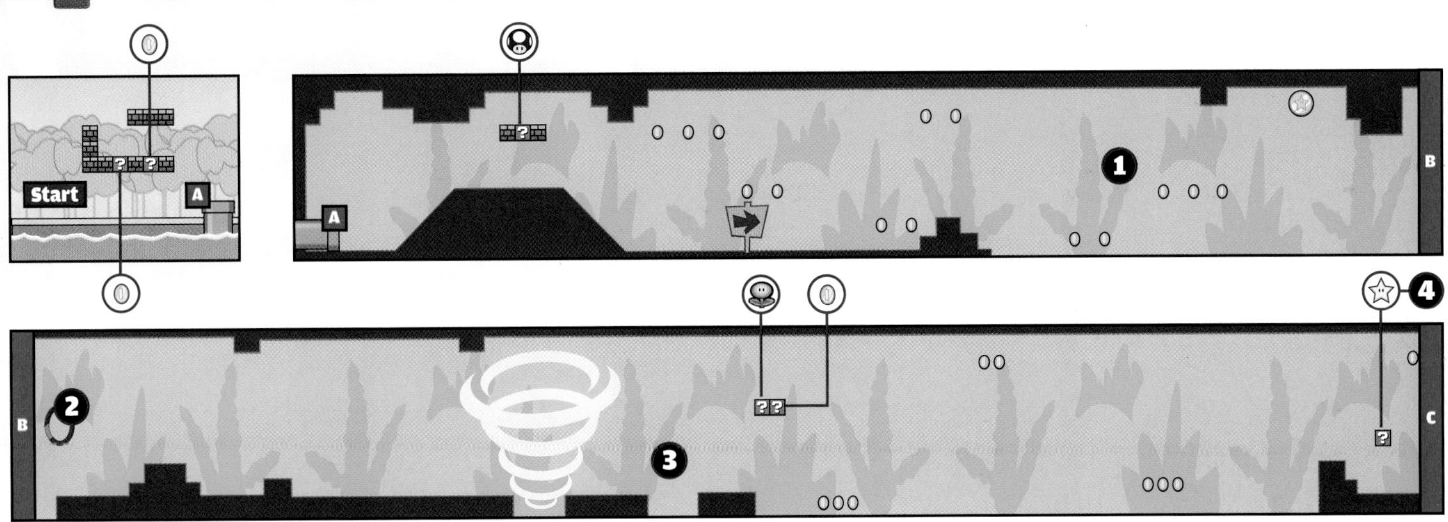

1 Deep-Cheeps actively pursue you, but once you swim past them they'll immediately lose interest. To get the first Star Coin safely, swim toward it to lure the Cheep-Cheeps to you, then sink down and slip underneath them.

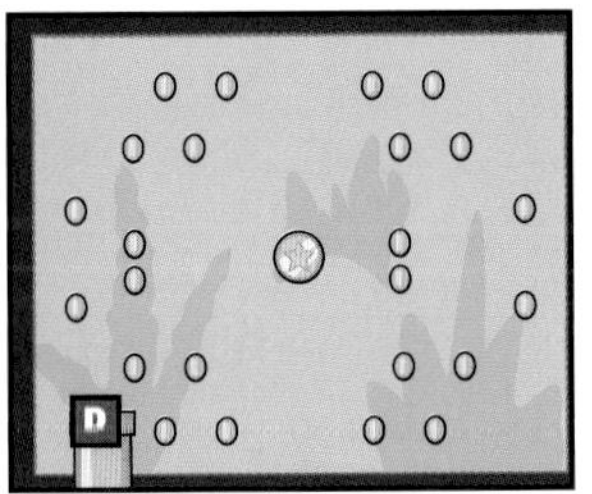

2 Red-Coin Ring

Swimming from top to bottom (or vice versa) is a great way to shake Deep-Cheeps. By dodging successfully, you should be able to claim all eight coins.

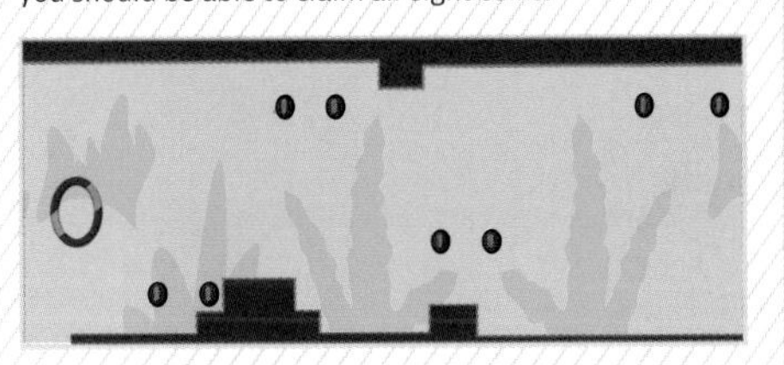

3 If you get caught in a whirlpool, swim rapidly to avoid being sucked into the deep. This will leave you vulnerable to enemies, however, so it's best to wait out the whirlpools and swim through when they abate.

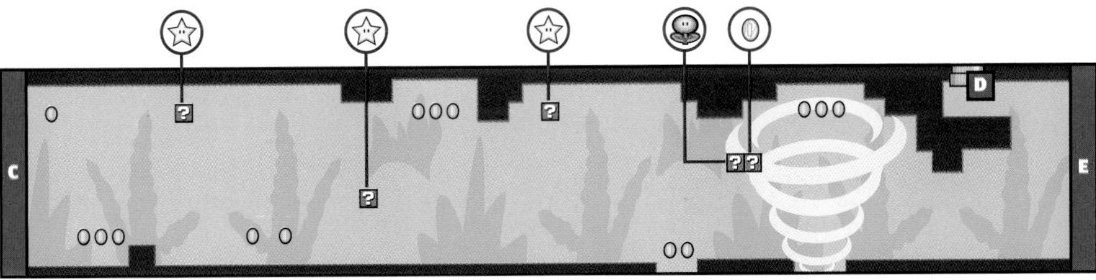

4 You can get Starman after Starman here (but only if you hit subsequent ? Blocks before the current Starman fades). They're spaced close enough together that you have plenty of time to ram Cheep-Cheeps and Deep-Cheeps to earn 1-Ups between Starmen.

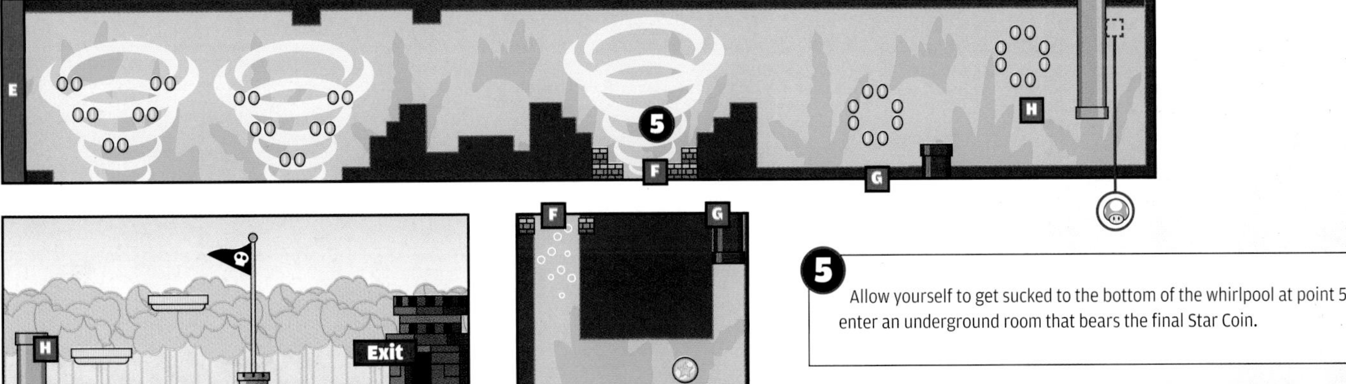

5 Allow yourself to get sucked to the bottom of the whirlpool at point 5 to enter an underground room that bears the final Star Coin.

World 6-B

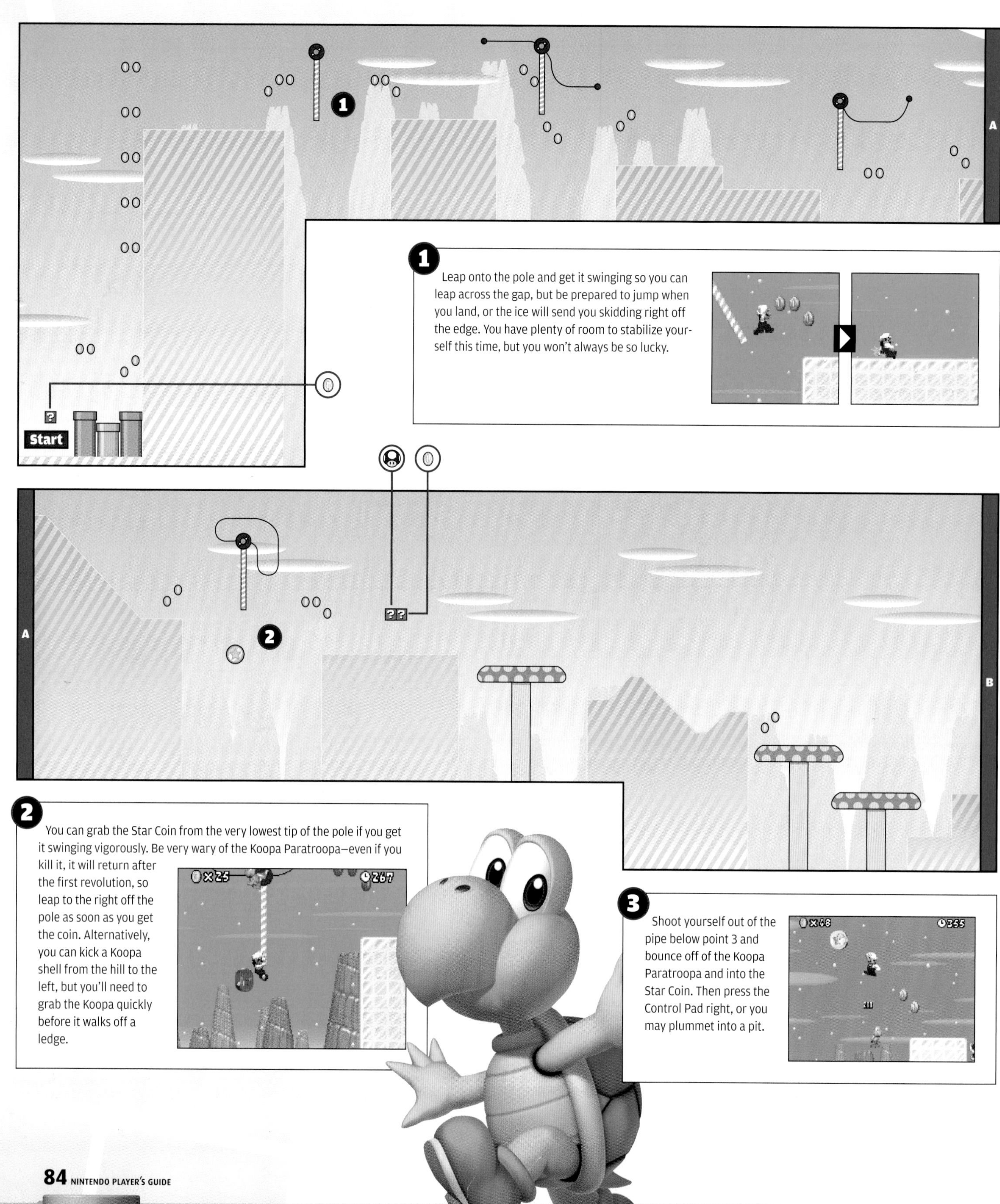

1 Leap onto the pole and get it swinging so you can leap across the gap, but be prepared to jump when you land, or the ice will send you skidding right off the edge. You have plenty of room to stabilize yourself this time, but you won't always be so lucky.

2 You can grab the Star Coin from the very lowest tip of the pole if you get it swinging vigorously. Be very wary of the Koopa Paratroopa—even if you kill it, it will return after the first revolution, so leap to the right off the pole as soon as you get the coin. Alternatively, you can kick a Koopa shell from the hill to the left, but you'll need to grab the Koopa quickly before it walks off a ledge.

3 Shoot yourself out of the pipe below point 3 and bounce off of the Koopa Paratroopa and into the Star Coin. Then press the Control Pad right, or you may plummet into a pit.

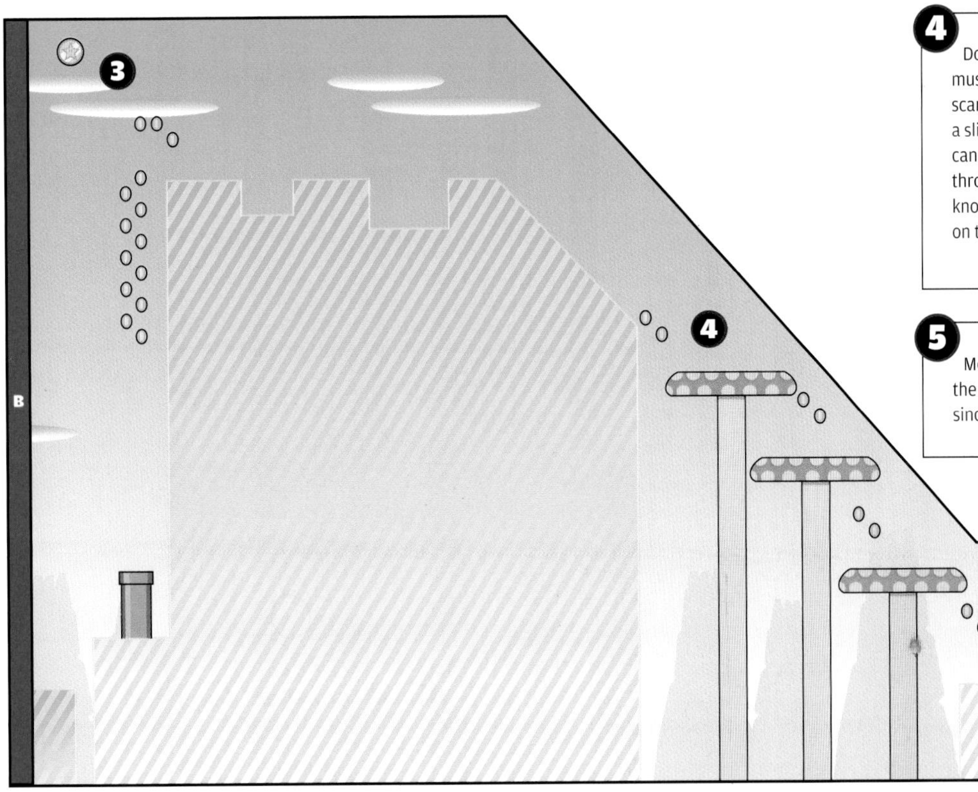

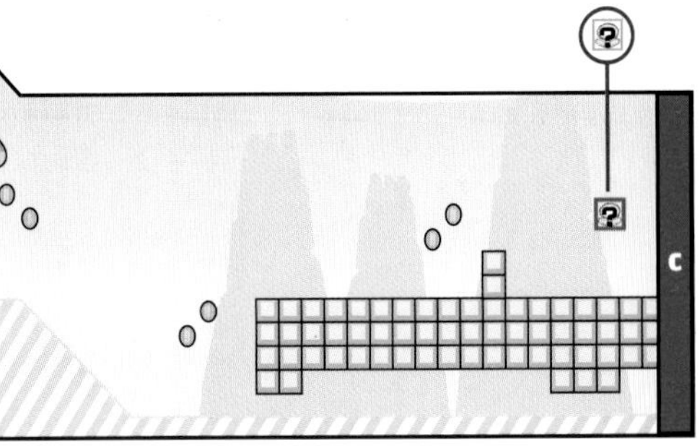

4 Don't let the purple mushroom platforms scare you; if you begin a slide at point 4, you can make it all the way through this area and knock off every enemy on the way.

5 Most of the pipes at point 5 are cannons that will fire you into the air at varying trajectories. The first is the one you want, since it will blast you through the row of coins.

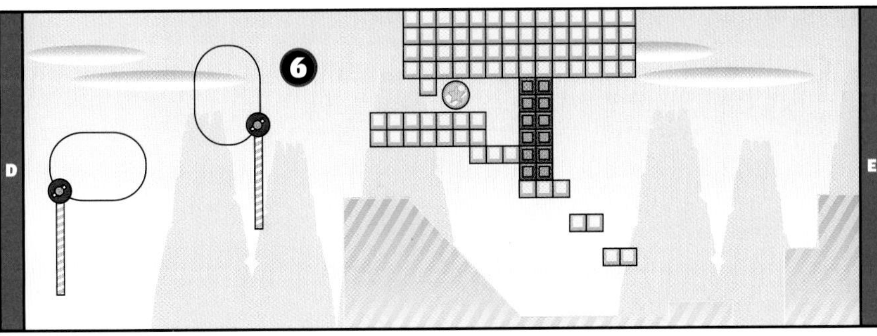

6 Leap off of the second circling pole and crouch when you land to slip through the gap and into the Star Coin. (If you land wrong, you can still dash and crouch under the gap.) Taking the Star Coin will destroy the blocks, allowing you to dash down the ice steps. Be sure to jump at the end, or you'll tumble into a bottomless pit.

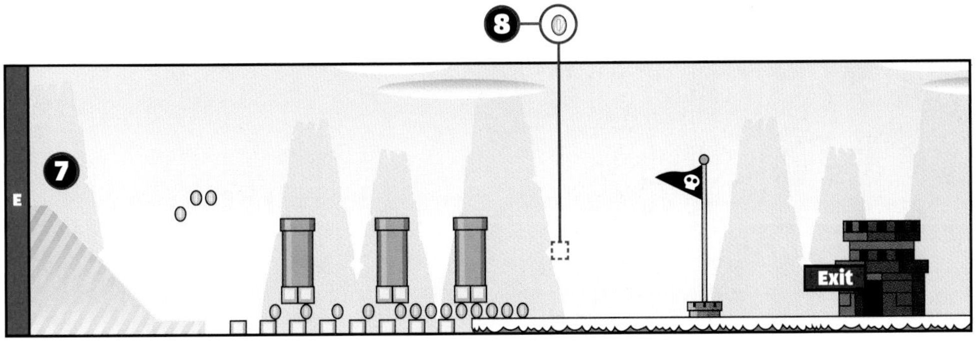

7 Get a bit of a dash going and press down on the Control Pad to slide down the slope, over all the gaps, and through the coins.

8 Punch the Invisible Block and use it to jump onto the first pipe to your left. Squeeze into it; it'll blast you over the flagpole and into a 1-Up.

World 6-6

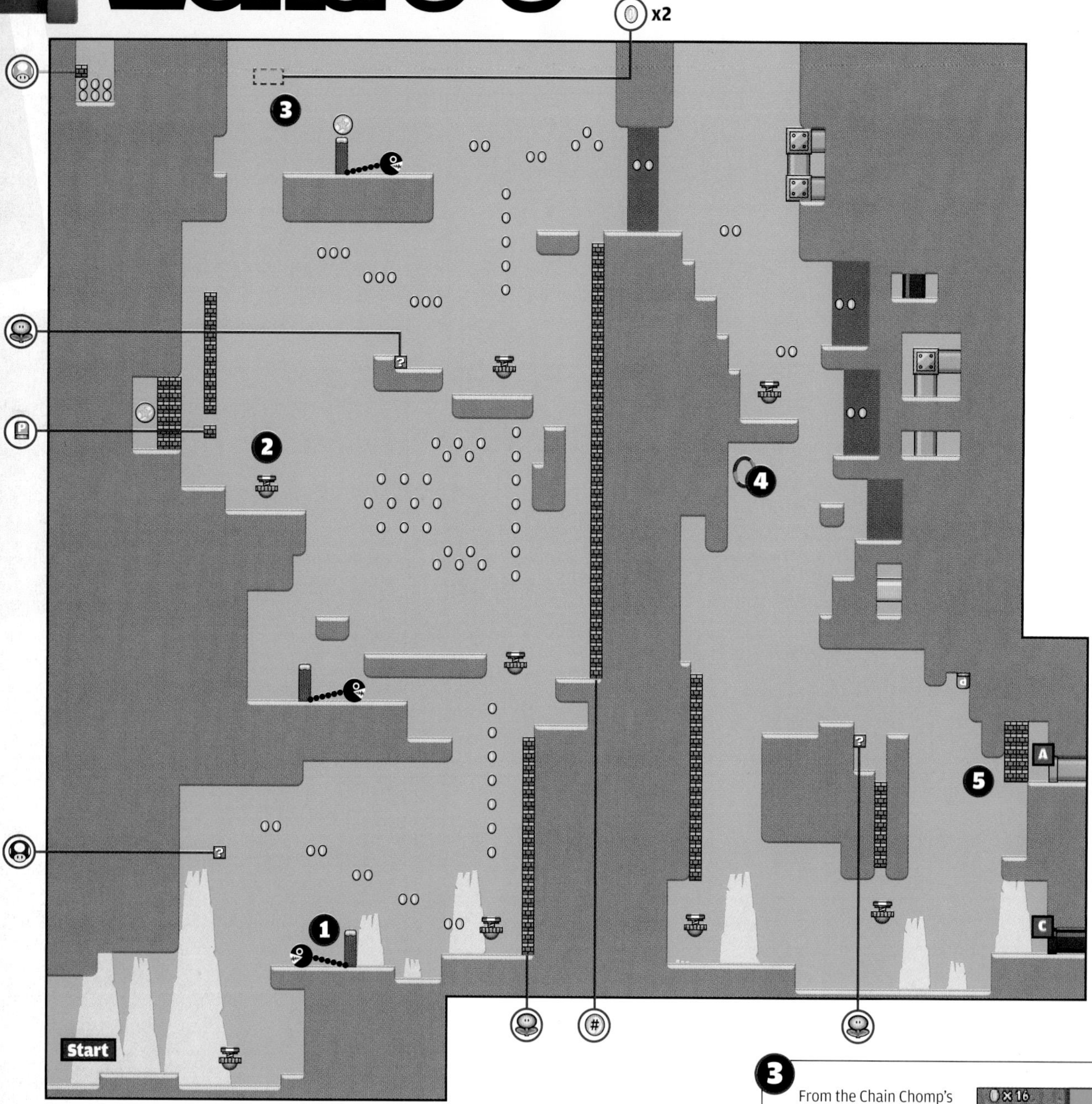

x2

Start

1

You can evade Chain Chomps easily, but if you're feeling sympathetic you can free them by Ground-Pounding the pole they're tied to. After three pounds, they'll flee.

2 P Switch

Use the Spin Block at point 2 to shoot yourself onto the top of the block column, then Ground-Pound through it. The last block will reveal a P Switch, which will let you get the Star Coin and several blue coins above the Spin Block.

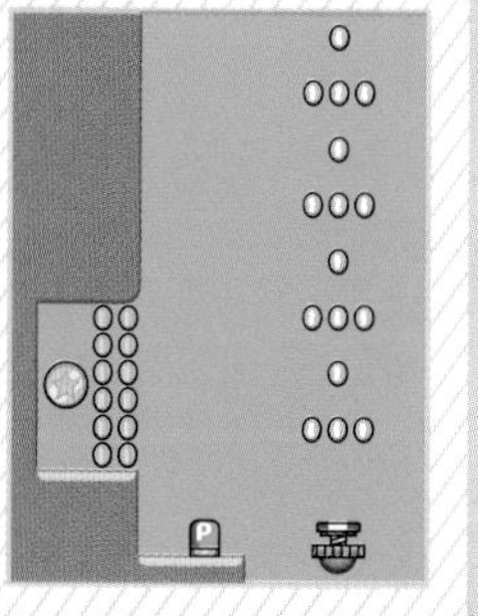

3

From the Chain Chomp's location, run left and do a Wall Jump to reveal an Invisible Block. Do a slightly higher Wall Jump to get above that block, then jump from it over the ceiling to the left. There you'll find a small alcove that holds a 1-Up Mushroom.

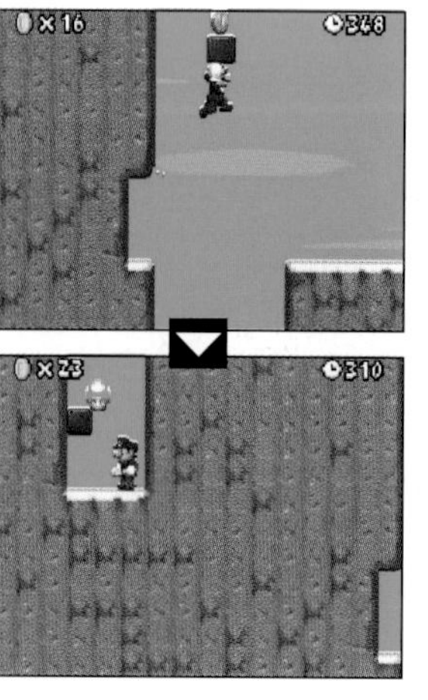

4 Red-Coin Ring

To get the red coins at point 4, start by using the Spin Block above it to set Mario hovering, then glide down through the red-coin ring and into the six coins on the right. Make a sharp left turn, then bounce off of the Koopa and into the final two red coins.

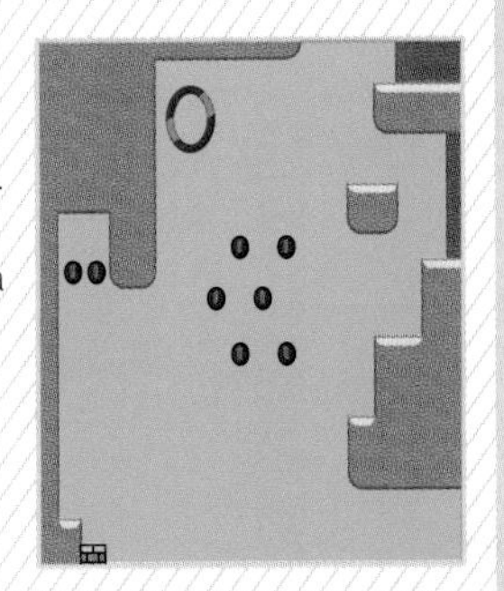

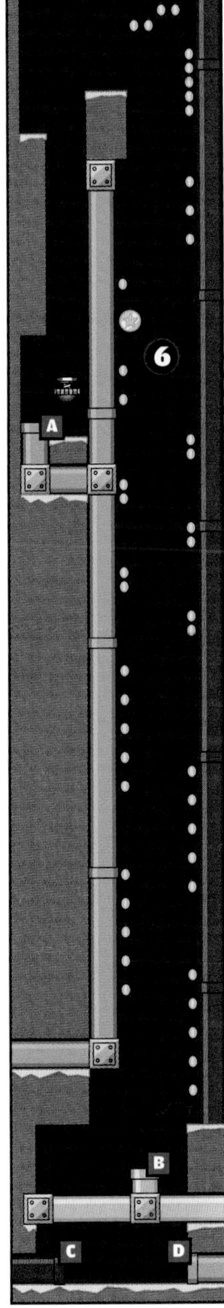

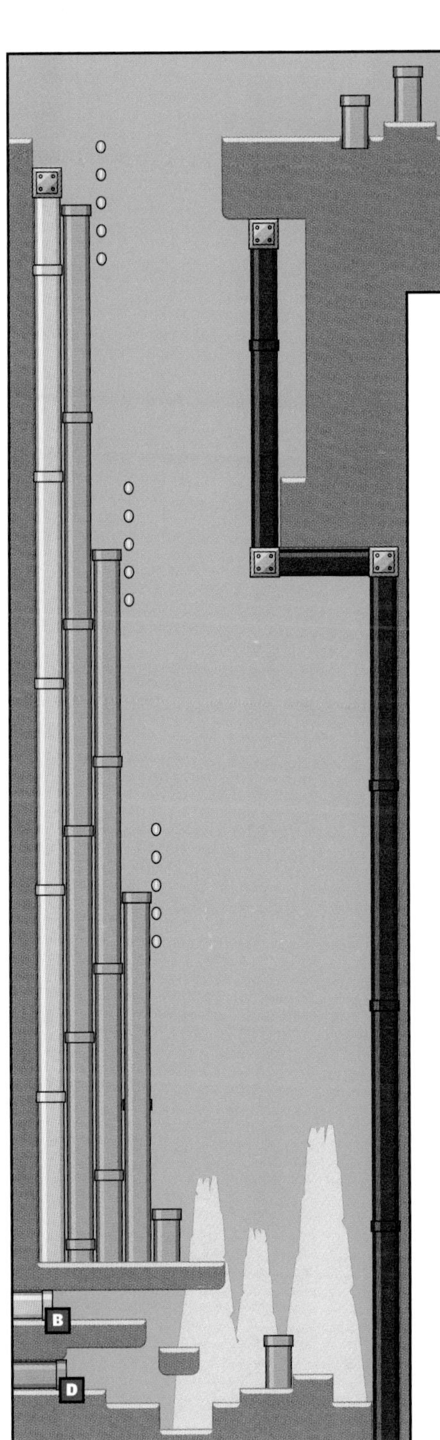

5 Bounce to the Green Pipe

This one is a little tricky. Ground-Pound the column of blocks above the Spin Block, then use that to blast yourself up, hover over to the P Switch, and use a midair spinning drill stomp to bounce off of a flying Koopa Paratroopa and into the switch. Glide to the right and bounce off of the second Koopa to reach the upper green pipe before the coins turn back into blocks.

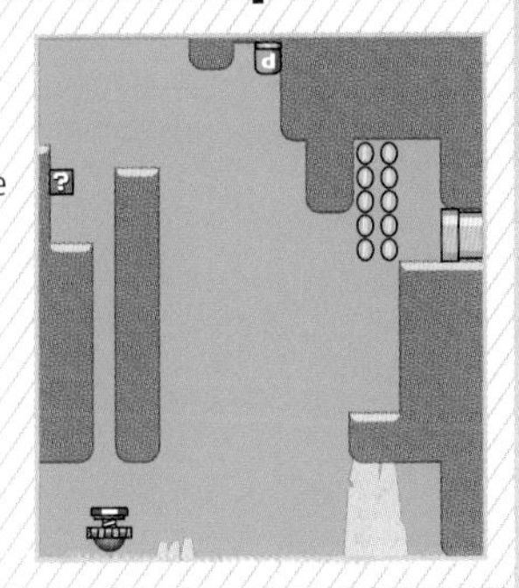

6 It's an extremely long Wall Jump from the bottom of this area to the top, so save yourself the trouble and slide down the left wall to grab the Star Coin on the way down.

7 After using the pipes to blast to the top of this area, enter the third pipe from the left. The pipe cannon will blast you to the top of the flag for a 1-Up. If you're Mini Mario you can get a 1-Up and several hidden coins from the second pipe.

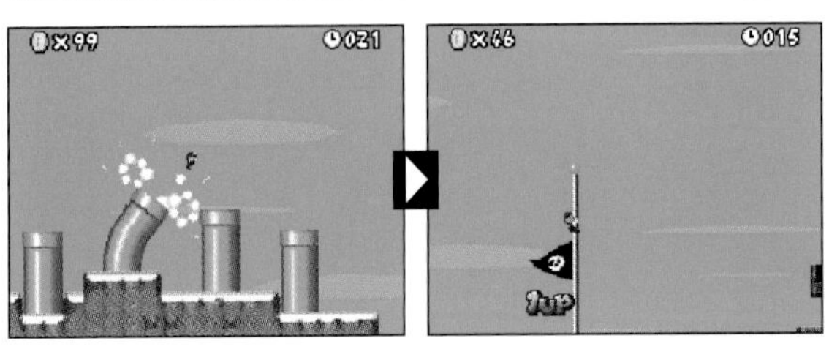

World 6 Castle

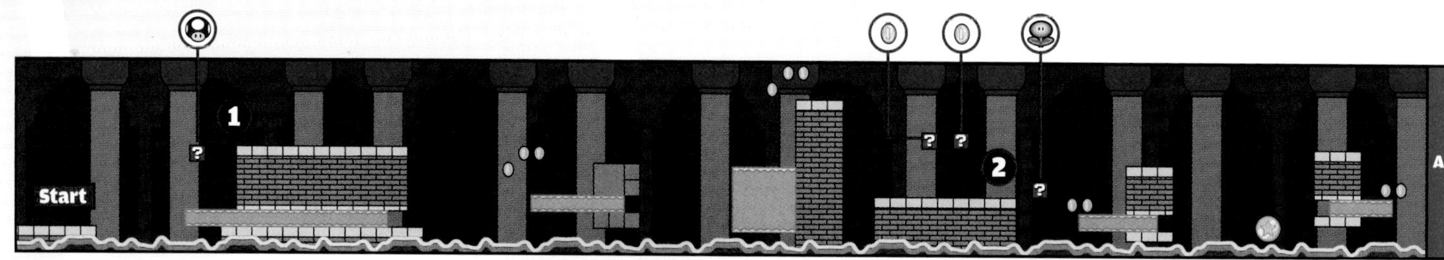

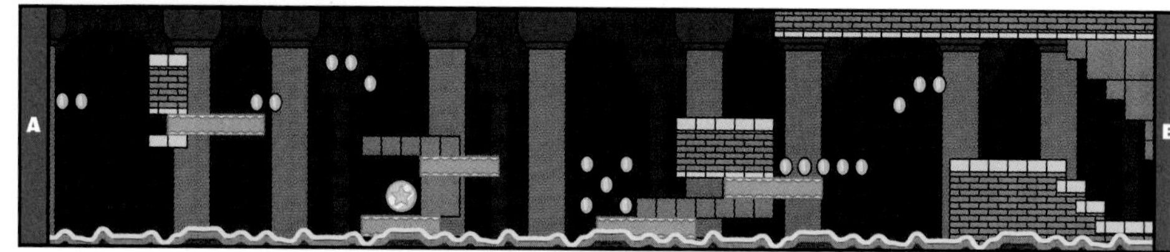

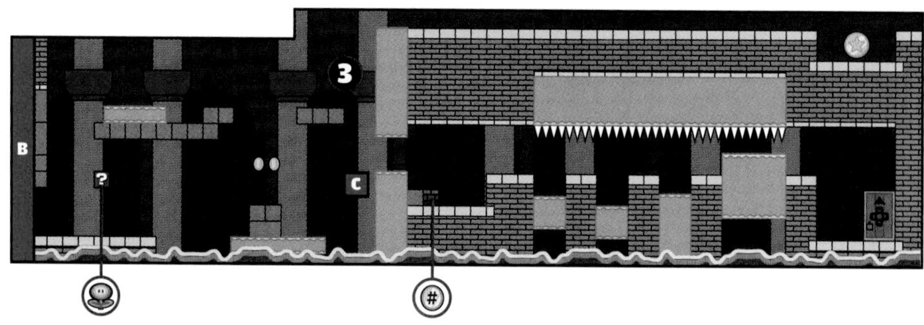

1 Using a Koopa shell to hit the ? Block may be easier and safer than trying to punch the block from the lip of the moving platform, especially if it contains a Fire Flower that won't roll off the block.

2 There's no way to grab the first Star Coin directly. Instead, stomp a Koopa on a nearby ledge and kick its shell into the Star Coin.

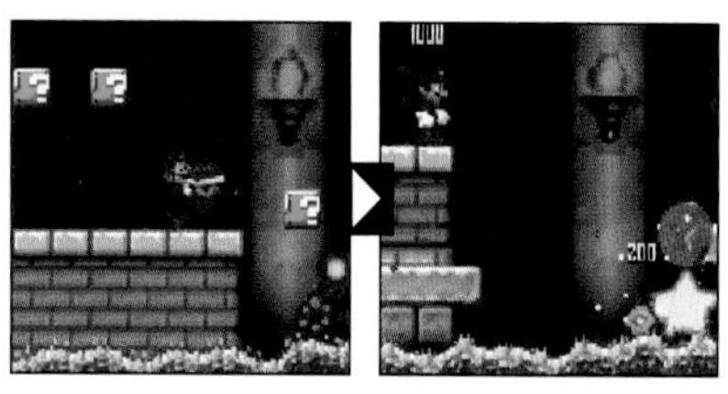

3 After the checkpoint, travel along the upper ledges. On the platform where the Koopa is, you can bounce off of the Koopa to reach the top of the moving column when it's at its lowest point. This will put you on the ceiling, where you can walk to the final Star Coin. On your way back, kick the Koopa into the Coin Block to the right.

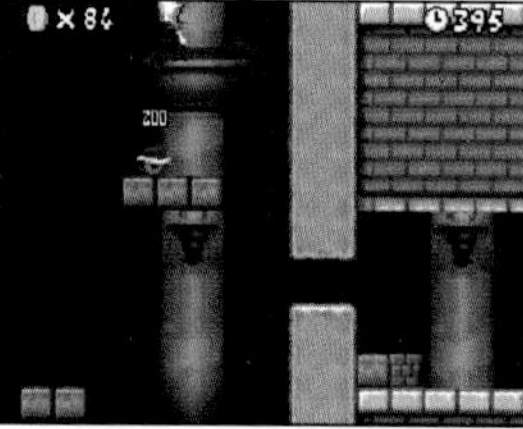

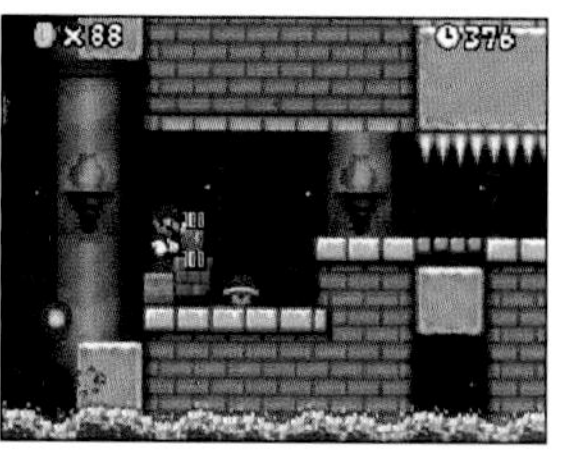

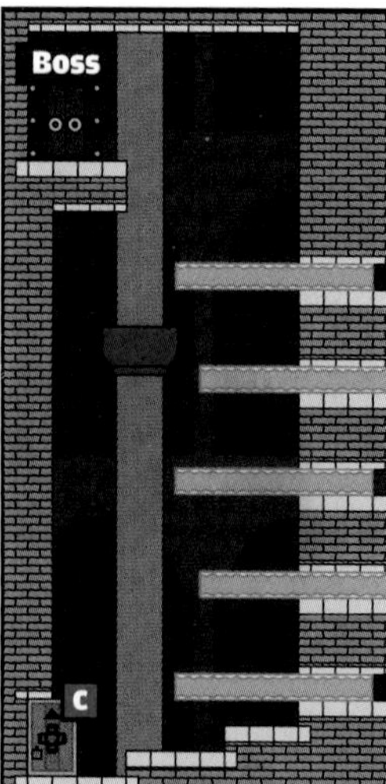

Boss

Jump onto the tank when Monty Tank appears, and stomp him. When the tank is spinning, don't try to attack it—simply crouch in a corner so you'll be safe from the Bullet Bills. To score the decisive final blow, you'll either need to catch a Bob-omb and throw it back at Monty, or jump off of a Bullet Bill or the second turret to reach the highest tier of the tank to perform a stomp attack.

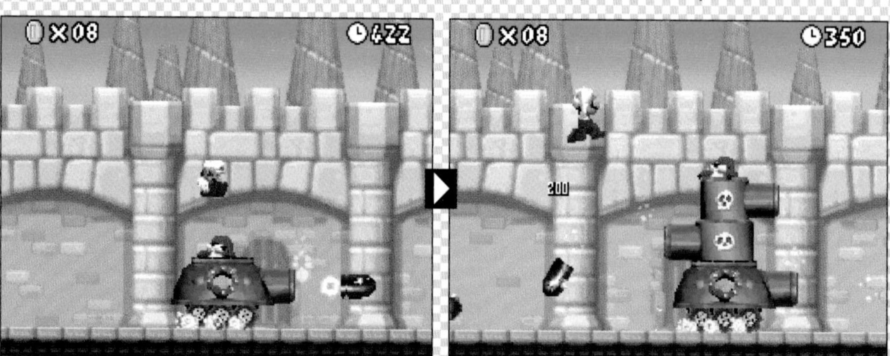

The Bullet Bills aren't much of a threat— you can dodge all of them if you merely crouch. In fact, they often work in your favor, allowing you to leap off of them and onto the top of the tank.

World 7

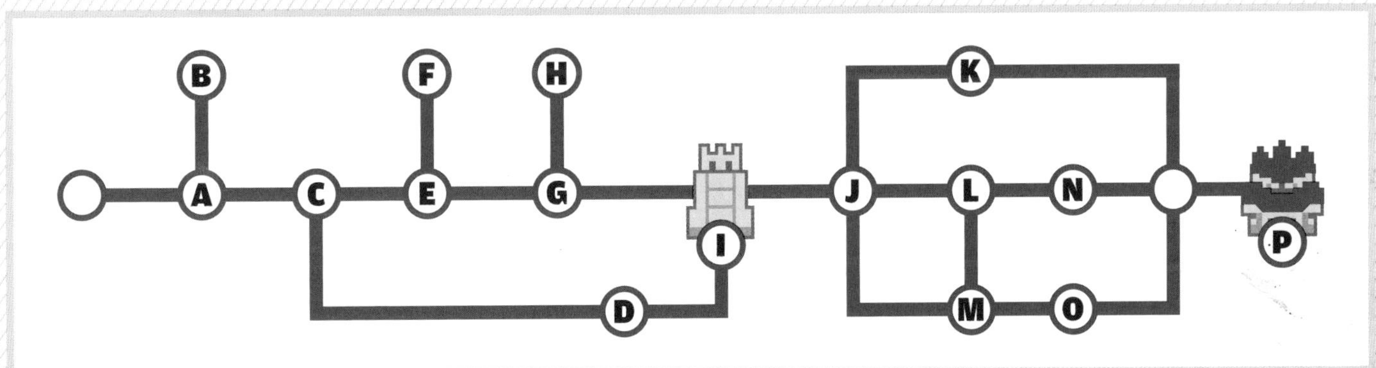

World 7-1

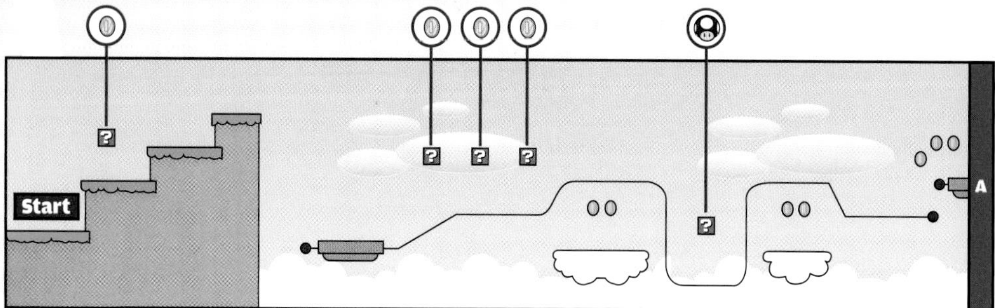

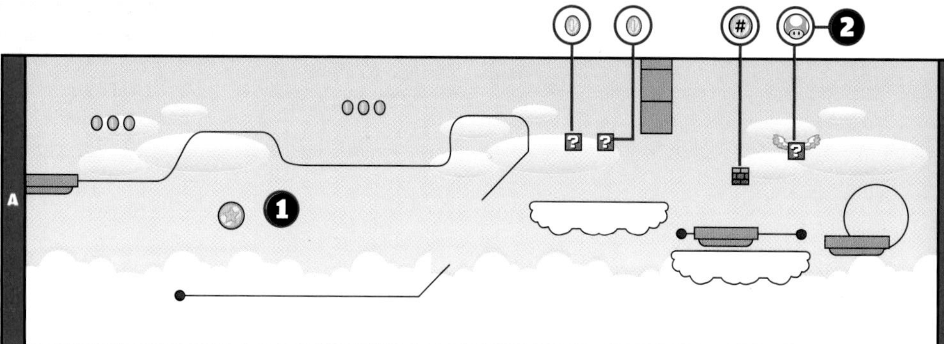

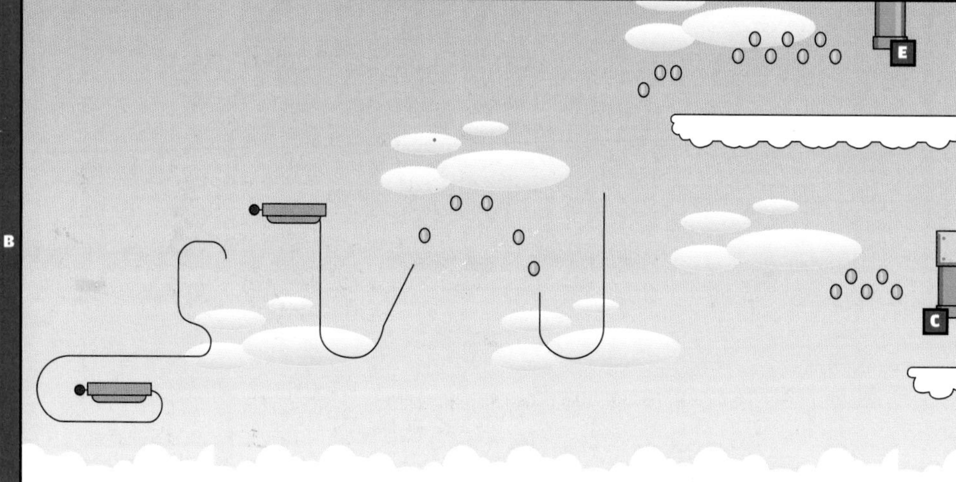

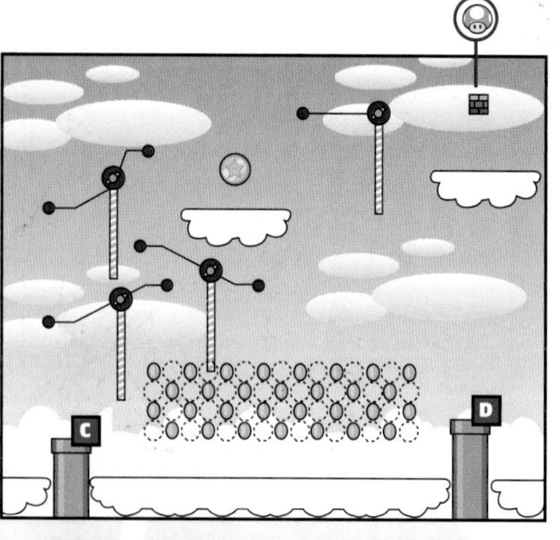

E
3
4
F

1 It looks like the second platform will plummet into the void when it runs out of track, but it will actually drop to a lower track that takes you close to the Star Coin. After claiming the coin, move to the right edge of the platform so you'll be ready to leap to the cloud; this time it *will* fall when it runs out of track.

2 The Flying ? Block that appears at point 2 contains a 1-Up Mushroom, but don't go pounding it yet. Instead, jump onto it (easier said than done, we know) and ride it across the map to a secret pipe that contains a Star Coin, 60 regular coins, and a 1-Up.

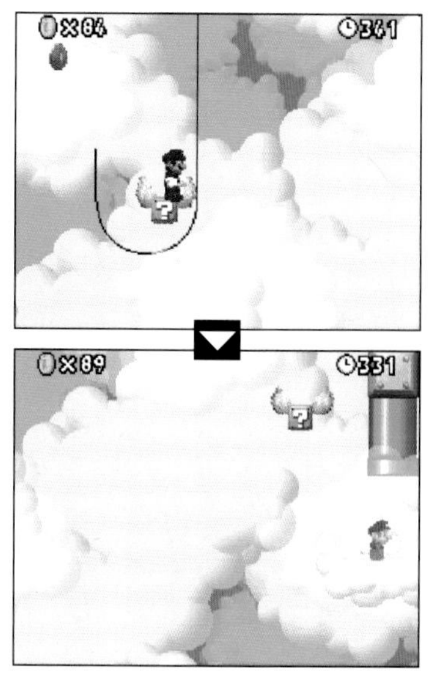

3 In the second part of the stage, take the higher of the two platforms directly to the third Star Coin.

4 At point 4 you'll be pursued by Flame Chomps, but you can defeat them with fireballs or even stomp attacks if you're careful not to touch the chain.

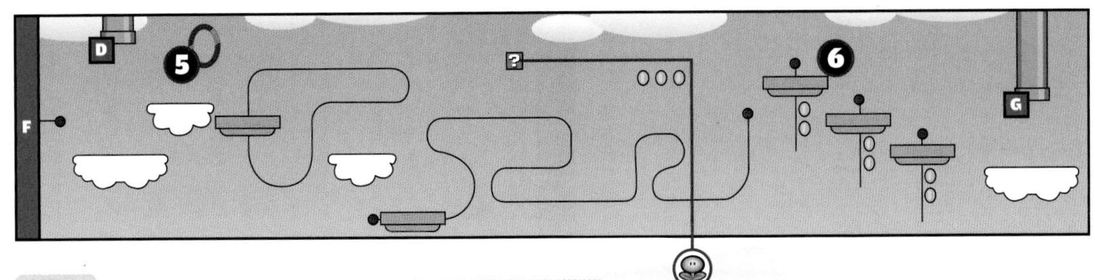

5 Red-Coin Ring

A single rotation of this platform will take you straight through six of the eight coins. After getting the sixth, you can nab the final two with a long jump to the right.

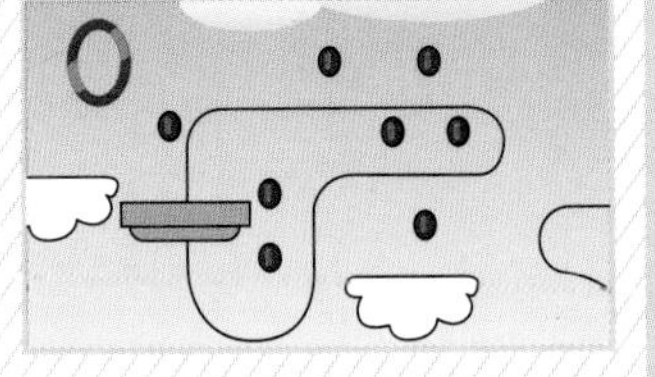

6 There's no bumper at the end of the vertical tracks, so when the platforms fall they won't be coming back. Leap off of them to the exit pipe quickly.

World 7 Ghost House

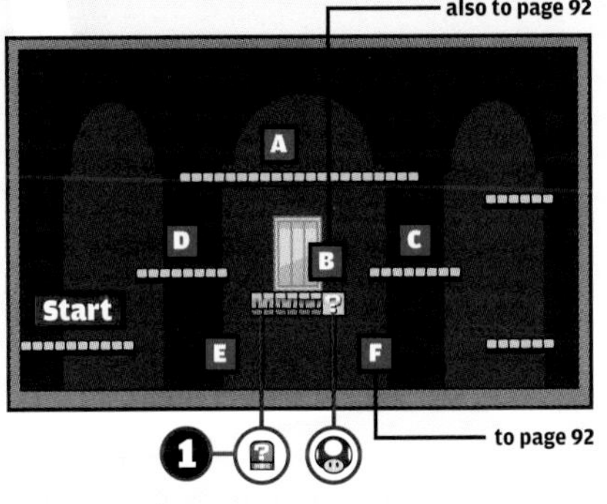

also to page 92

to page 92

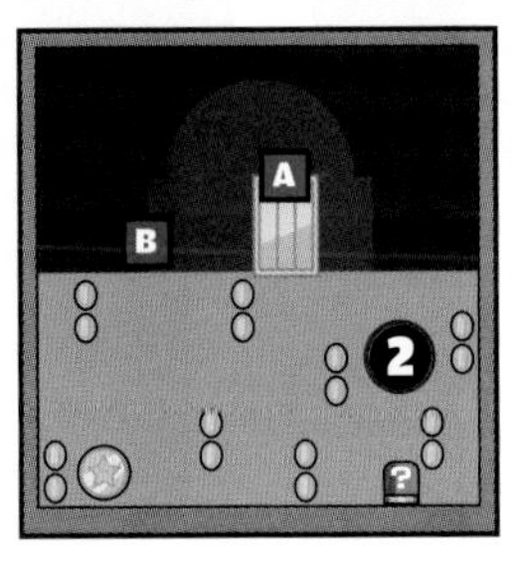

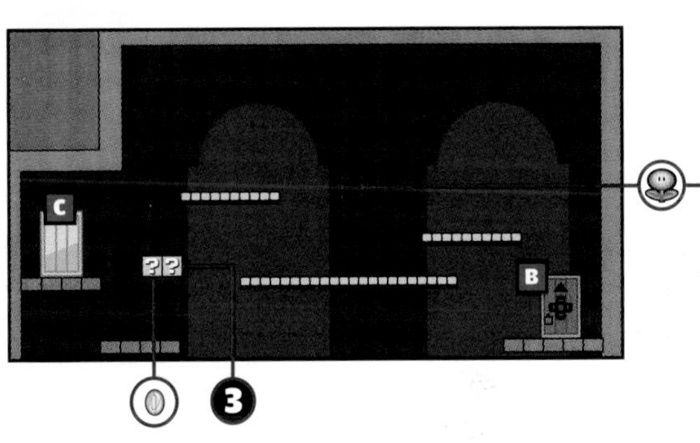

1 Five Hidden Doors

Hit the ? Switch to reveal the doors to the ghost house's five areas. Doors A and D lead to the first two Star Coins, while Door F leads to the final Star Coin and the path to both possible exits.

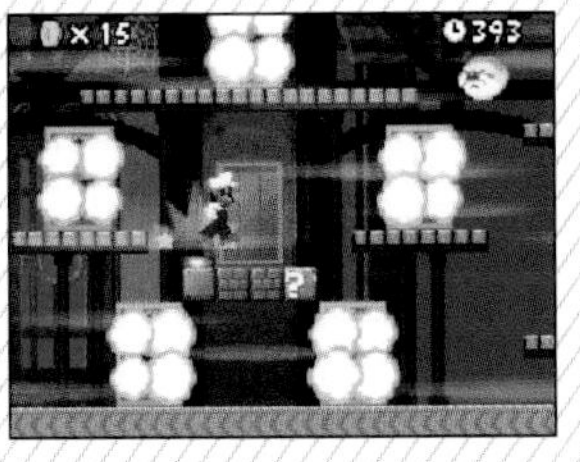

2 Use consecutive Ground Pounds to smash through the gelatin above the Star Coin on the left side of the room, then repeat the process on the right side to hit the ? Switch and make an exit door appear.

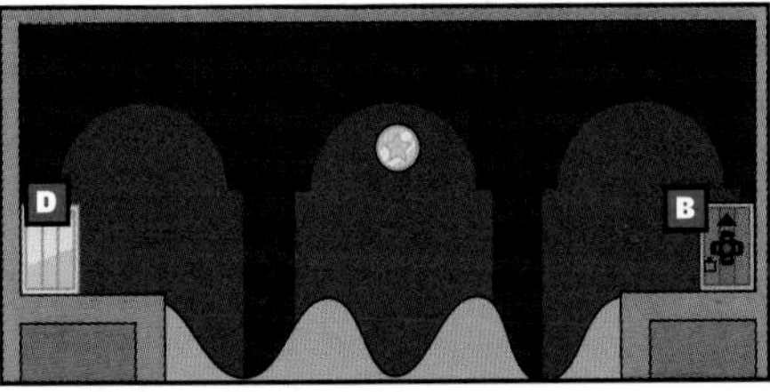

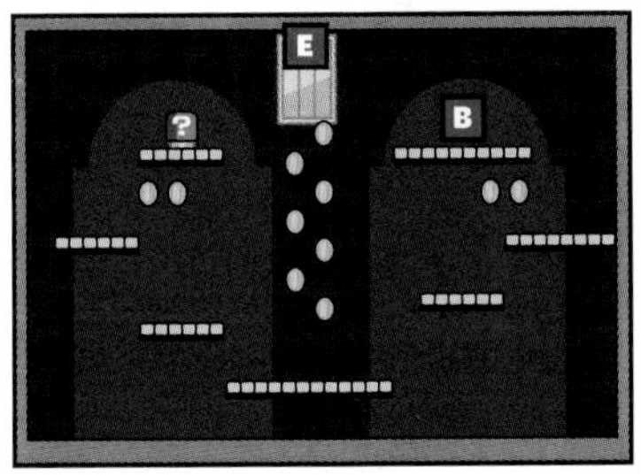

3 The ? Block at point 3 contains a Boo. If you free it, it will torment you—avoid the block.

4 To spot the Invisible Flying ? Block, watch the hands—they'll always point straight at it. Hit it to score a power-up.

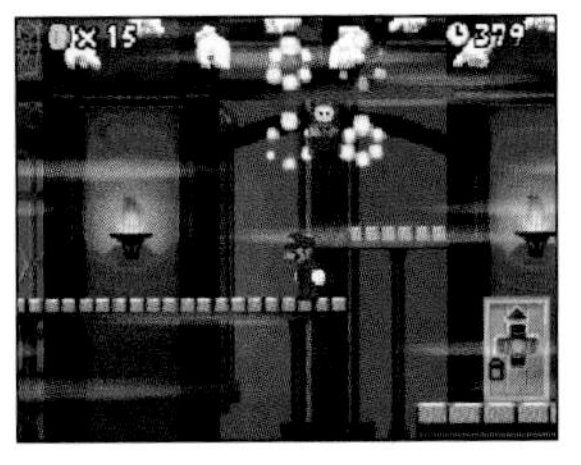

5 Return of the Phantom Hands

The hands are back, and this time they're pointing at an Invisible Flying ? Block that holds a ? Switch. The switch (which you can reach with the spring or a running jump) will make platforms appear at the right side of the room, allowing you to reach door G.

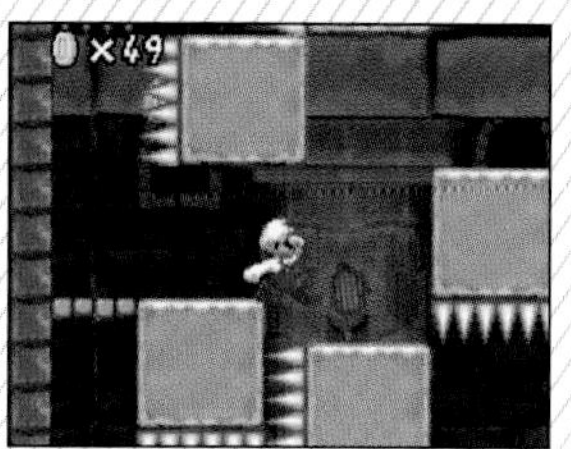

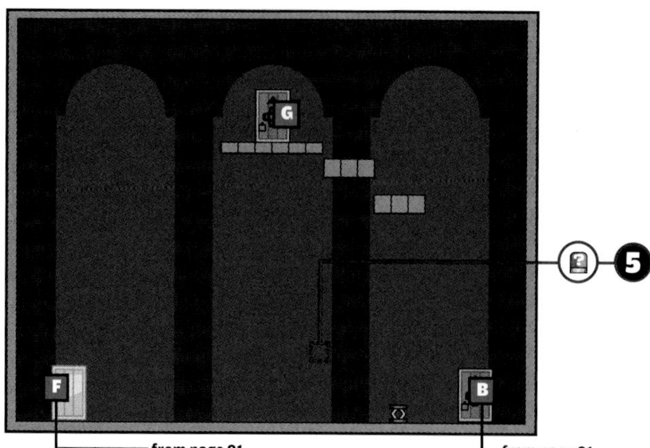

6 A Room Built of Coins

The room behind door G is full of coins, but there is no floor beneath them, so if you dive into them your greed will be swiftly and decisively punished. Doors H and J lead to the level's exits, so pick your destination in advance, hit the P Switch, and make your way to your chosen exit as swiftly as possible. Note that the maps on this page show the coins in their block form.

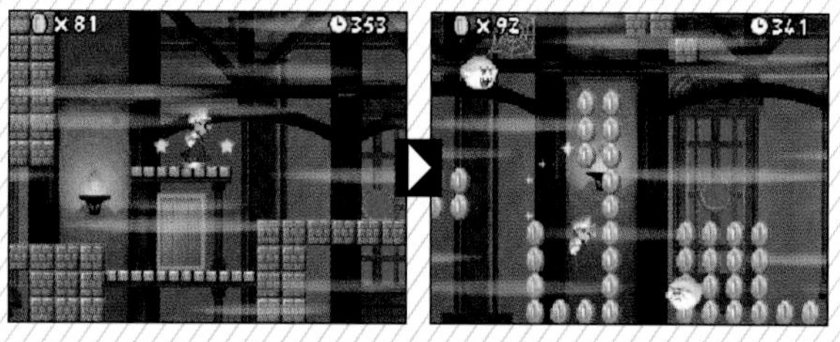

7 Run quickly to the left after you hit the P Switch. One block is shimmering slightly—hit it from below to reveal a Vine Block that leads to the red-flag exit. Alternatively, you can Wall-Jump to it as Mini Mario.

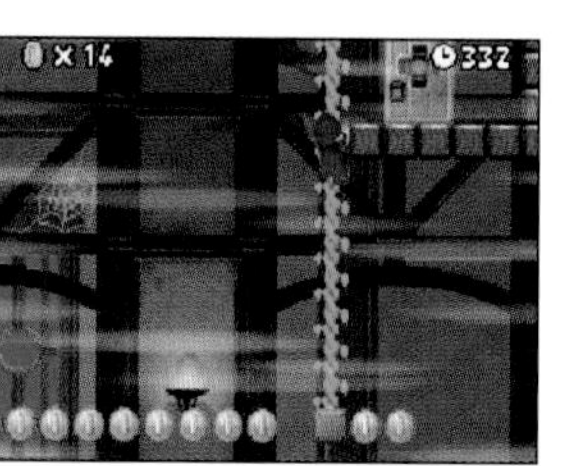

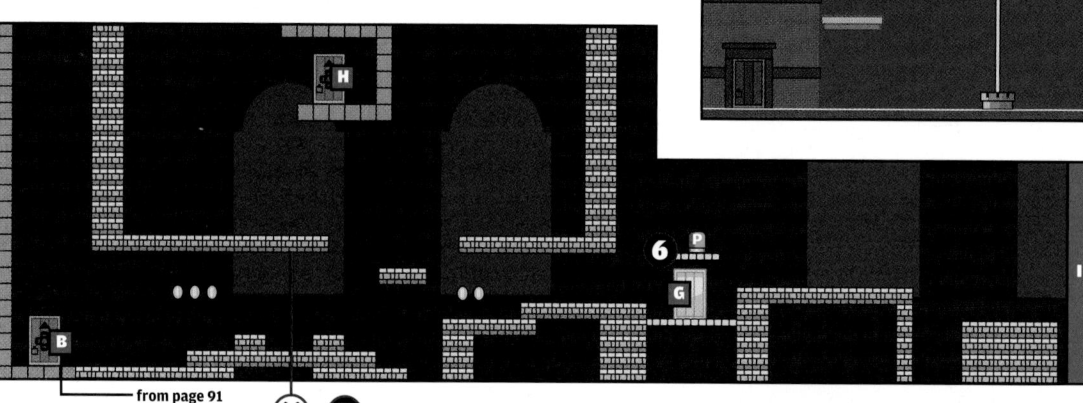

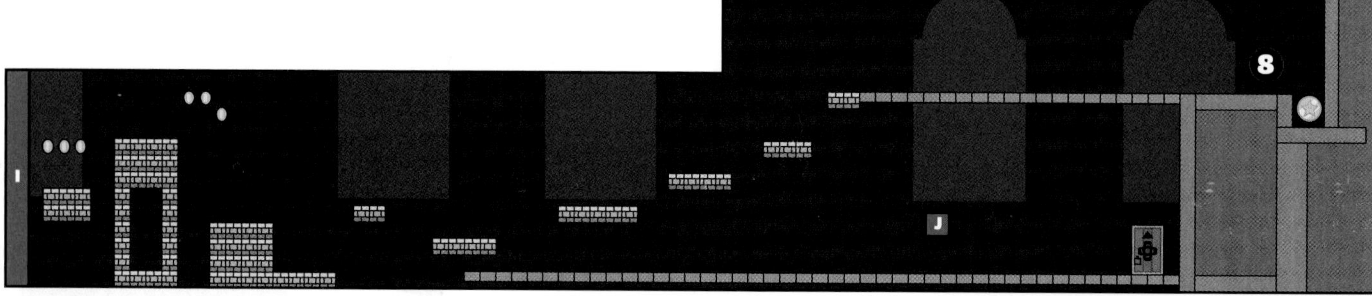

8 After hitting the P Switch, make your way right as quickly as possible, ascending coin platforms even after there's solid ground beneath you. Any slight error will sink your hopes, so you may need to try this several times.

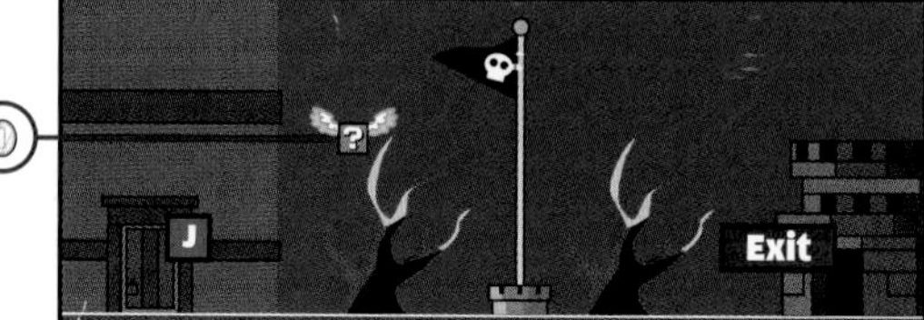

World 7-2

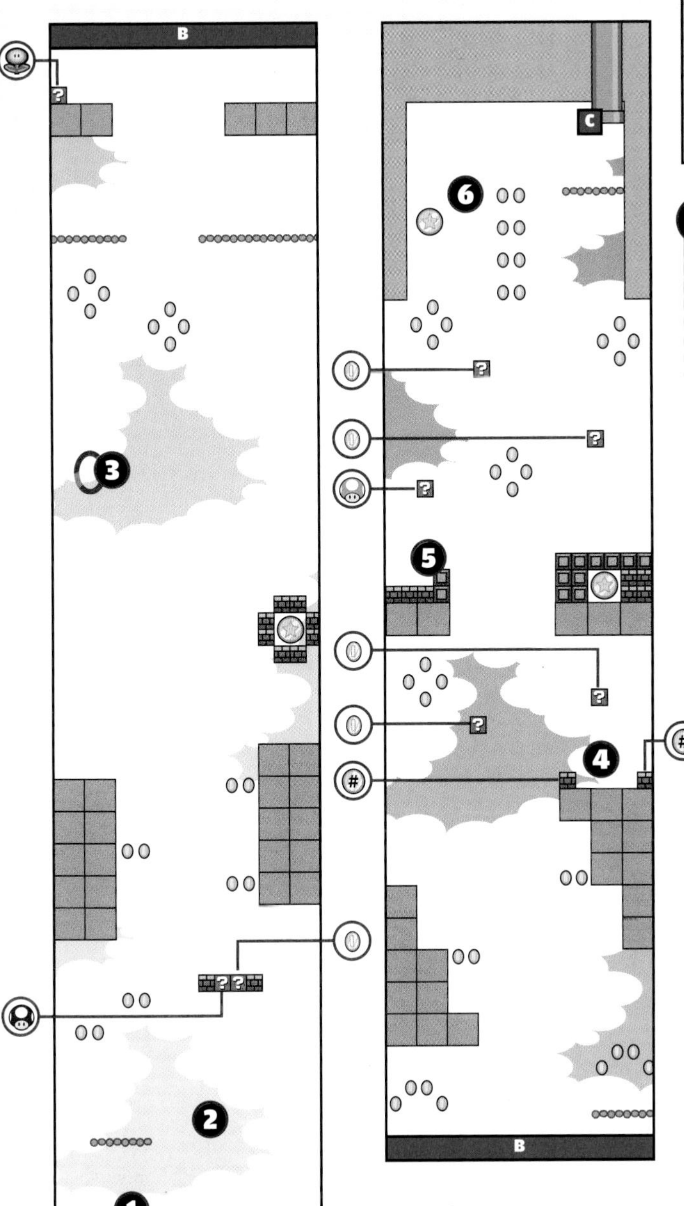

1 You'll ride on a floating platform for the entirety of this stage. If you stand on the middle it will rise straight up, and if you stand on either edge it will head in that direction as it rises. There's no way to reverse direction, so you have only one shot at ? Blocks and Star Coins. Note that if you glide left you'll emerge from the right side of the screen, and vice versa, as will thrown fireballs and Koopa shells.

2 Grab the red Koopa on the ledge and hurl its shell so that it travels in an arc through all the Koopa Paratroopas, earning you a 1-Up in the process.

3 Red-Coin Ring

As soon as you touch the ring, veer left until you emerge on the other side of the screen—that'll save you some time reaching the four redcoins on the right. Afterward, loop back around to the left side of the screen and nab the remaining coins.

4 Launch a Koopa shell onto the platform at point 4; it will bounce back and forth, collecting most of the coins from the Coin Blocks.

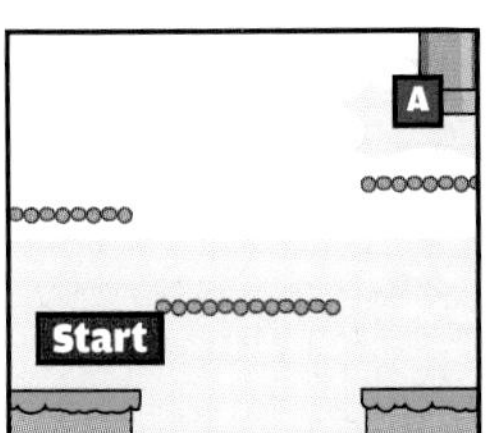

5 You'll need to stomp another Koopa Paratroopa and pick up its shell before you pass the second Star Coin. Kick the shell onto the block platform to the left—it will take care of the rest.

6 The safest way to get the final Star Coin is by tossing a Koopa shell at it. More-adventurous players can jump into the flock of Koopa Paratroopas to the left, bouncing off of them to get the coin and some 1-Ups.

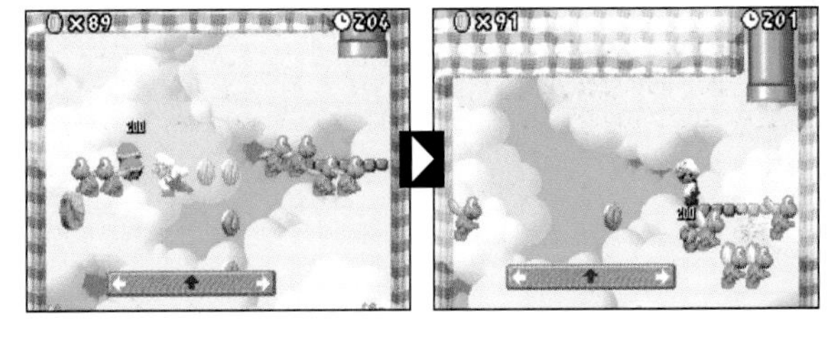

World 7-3

1 It's a rare treat to meet a humongous creature who *doesn't* want to kill you. The giant Wiggler at point 1 is happy to take you on a ride through this level, but you'll need to leap off its back and onto the block platforms to reach the first two Star Coins.

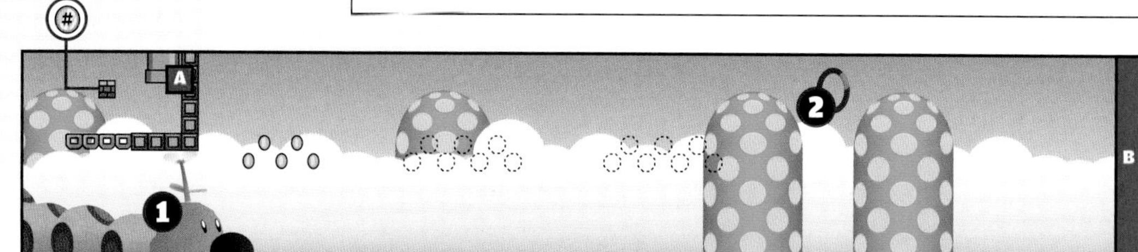

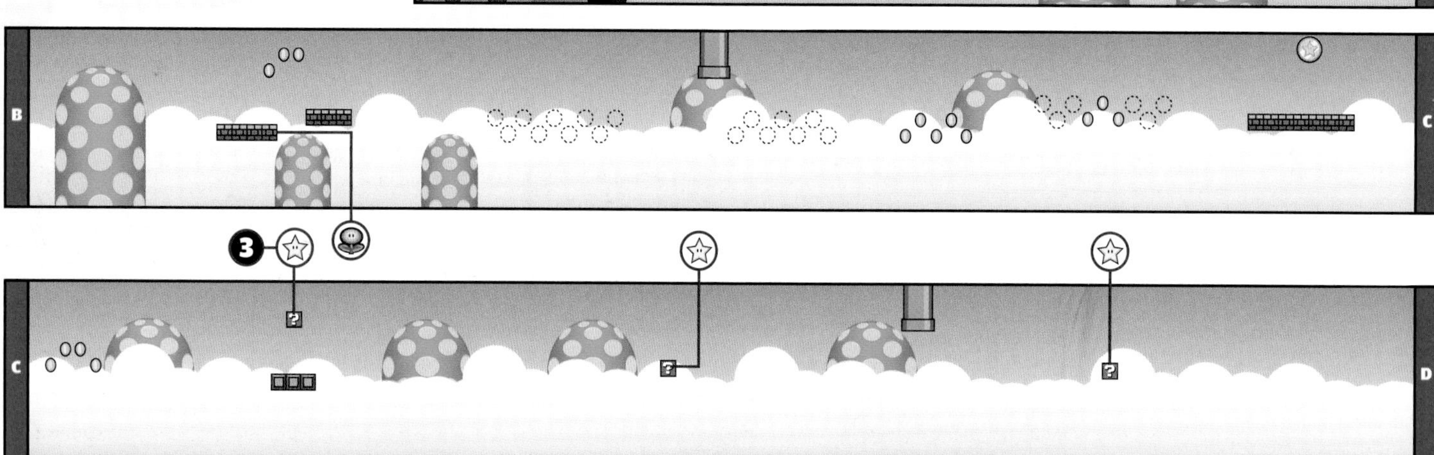

2 Red-Coin Heaven

To reach the red-coin ring, when the Wiggler gyrates, leap off of a segment that is rising. The red coins are all easily grabbed by leaping. Keep Mario moving forward instead of leaving it all to the Wiggler's movement, or you'll run out of time.

3 When you get the Starman at point 3, you'll begin leaving a thick trail of coins in your wake. Grab a few, but continue moving forward so you can keep hitting ? Blocks for more Starmen to continue the fun.

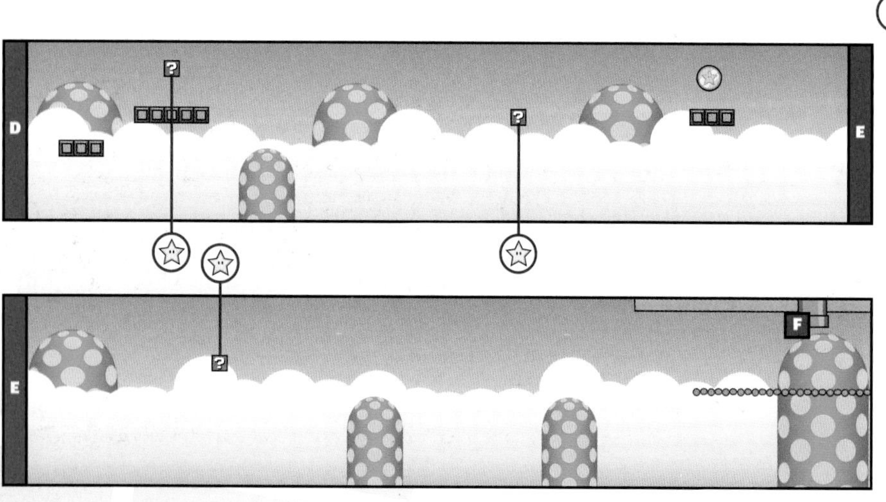

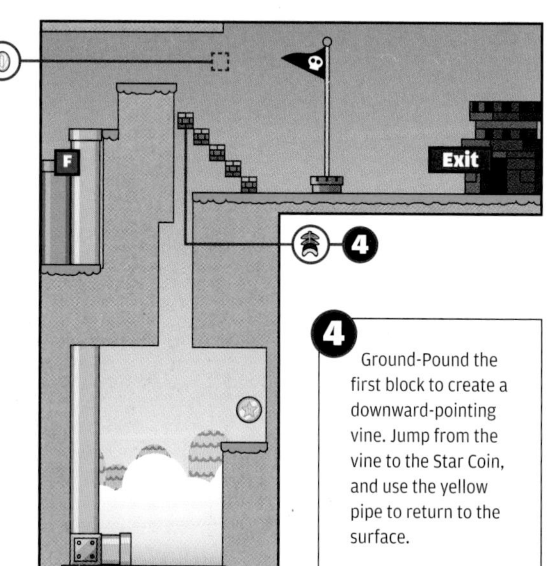

4 Ground-Pound the first block to create a downward-pointing vine. Jump from the vine to the Star Coin, and use the yellow pipe to return to the surface.

World 7 Tower

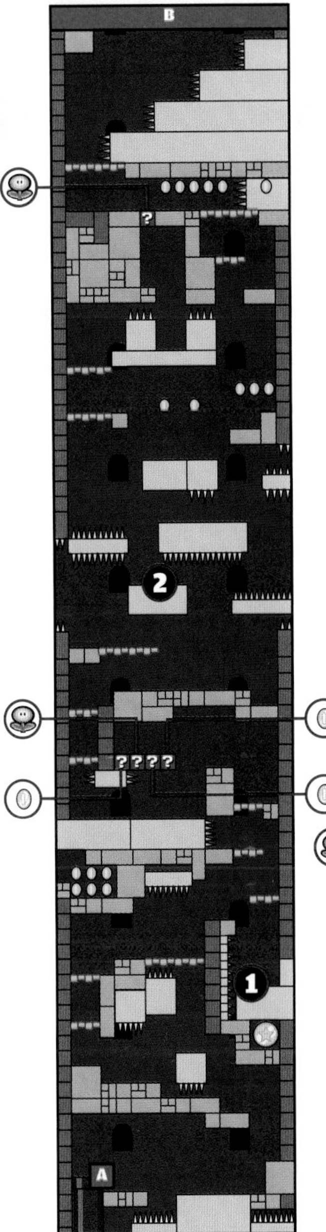

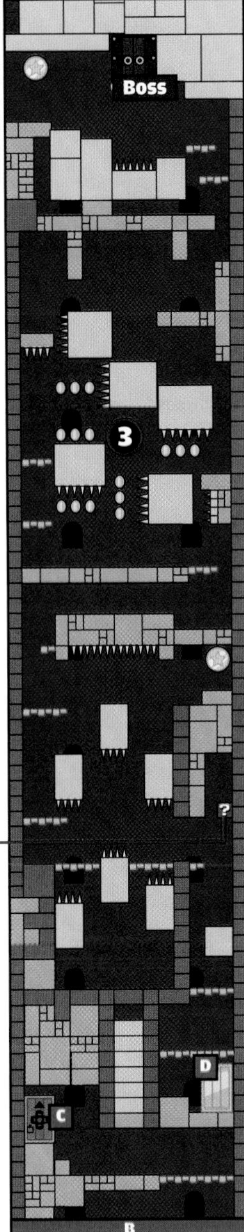

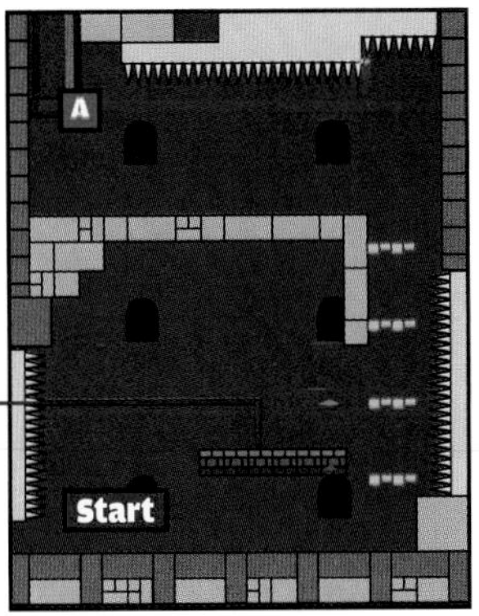

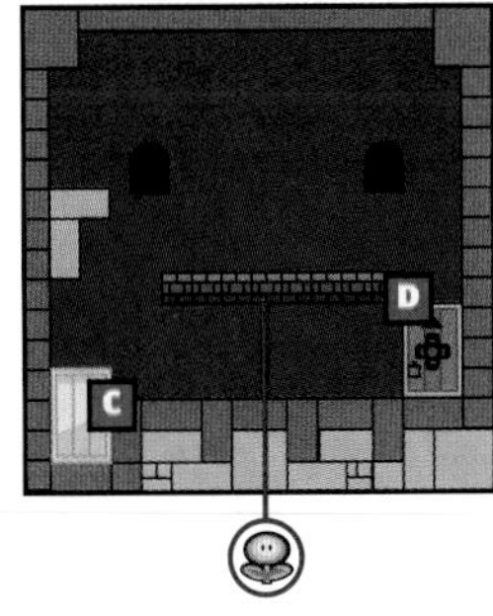

1 The first Star Coin is easy to retrieve, but getting out alive will require patience. The two blocks move at different speeds, so if you mistime your exit, you'll be crushed.

2 Leap onto the platform at point 2 when it's safe, and crouch beneath the rows of spikes. The opportunities to jump to the next-higher platform won't last long, so save time by jumping from a crouching position.

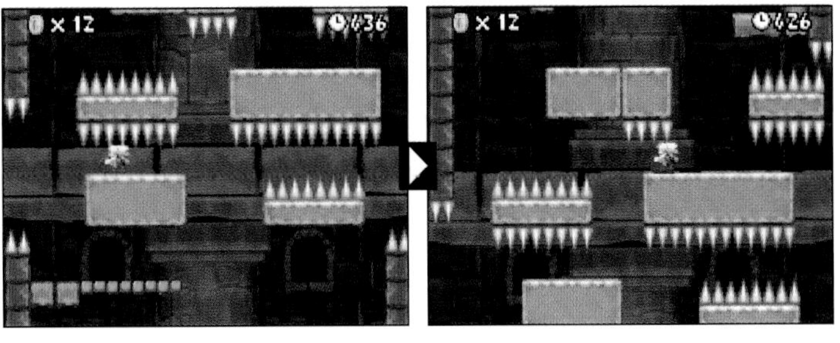

3 Wait until the four lower blocks combine to form a plus sign. When they separate, jump onto the lower-left block, wait for the lower-right block to move left, then run right and up through the gaps.

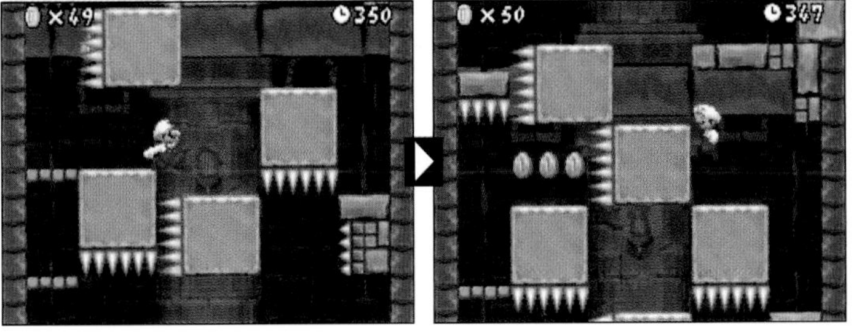

Boss

This is the version of Bowser Jr. that attacks by throwing Koopa shells. Jump onto them and kick them back to knock over Bowser Jr., giving you an opportunity to stomp him for damage.

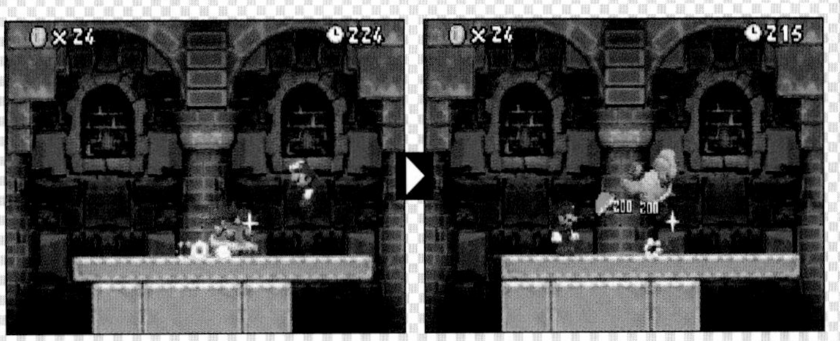

There isn't a lot of room to maneuver on this moving platform, so you'll need to stay close to Bowser Jr. and prepare to jump as soon as he begins to throw. Beware, though—you can't jump on him when he's throwing.

World 7-4

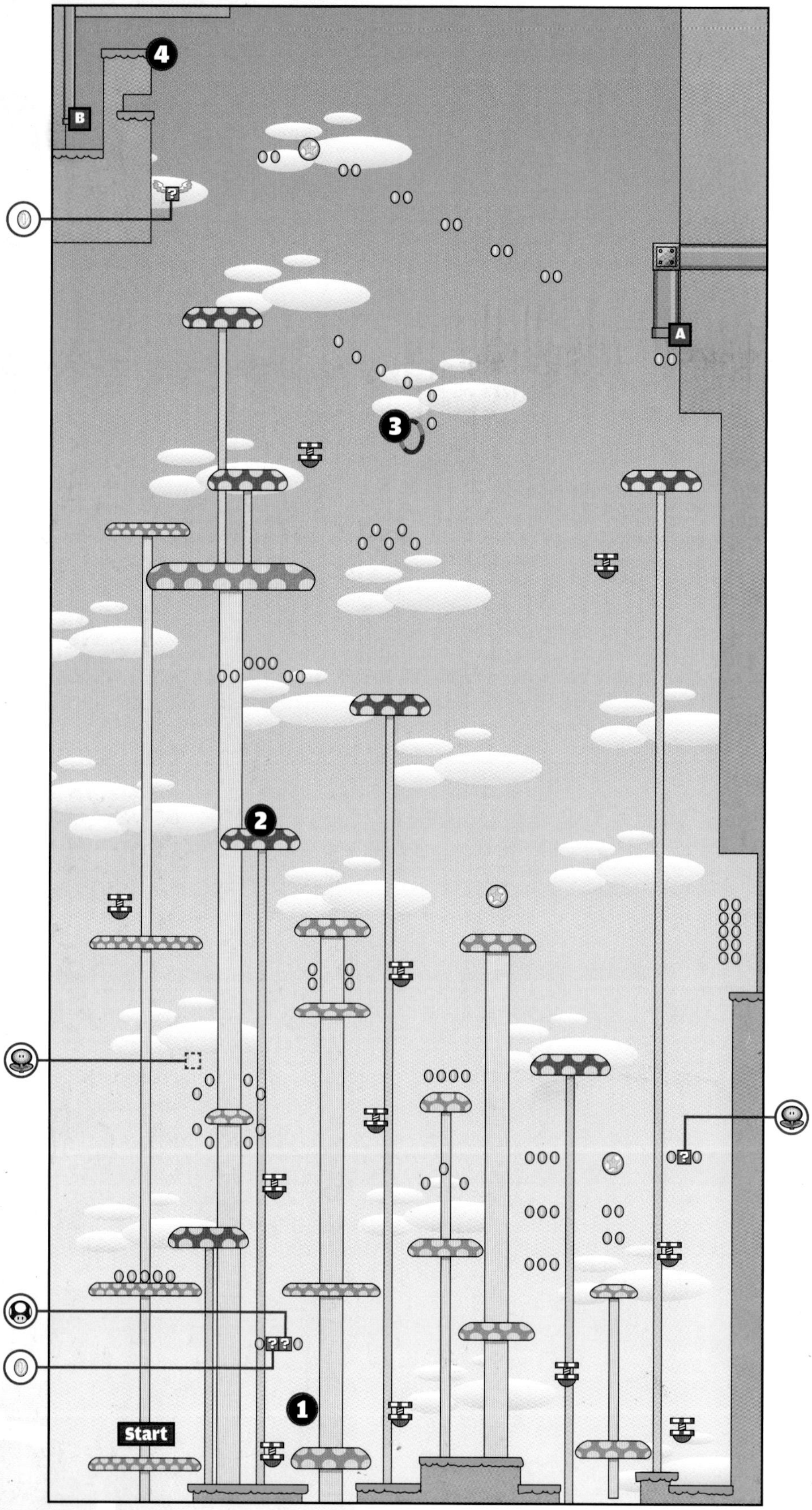

1 To ascend vertically through this stage, jump from Spin Block to Spin Block. To reach the standard exit, aim for the fuchsia mushroom platform below pipe A. There is also an alternate Mini Mario exit at point 4.

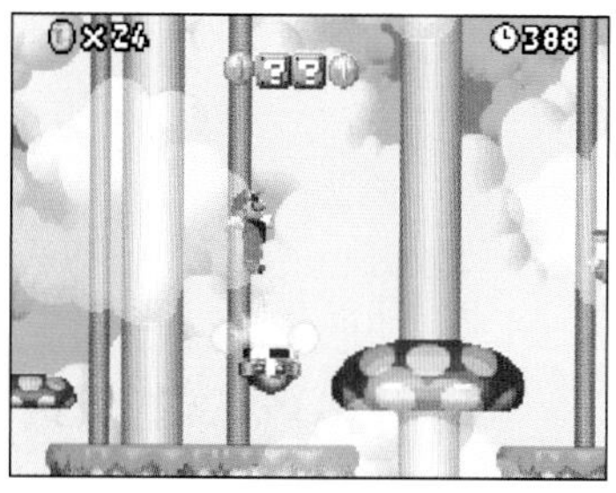

2 The Spin Blocks will take you only so far. At point 2 you'll need to bounce to the fuchsia mushroom platforms.

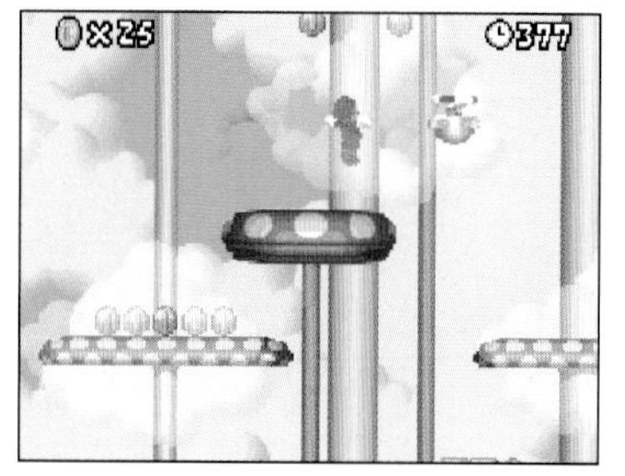

3 Red-Coin Ring

Use the Spin Block to shoot yourself up, and glide along the path of gold coins through the ring. After claiming the lower coins, bounce off the center of the fuchsia mushroom platform to nab the last two.

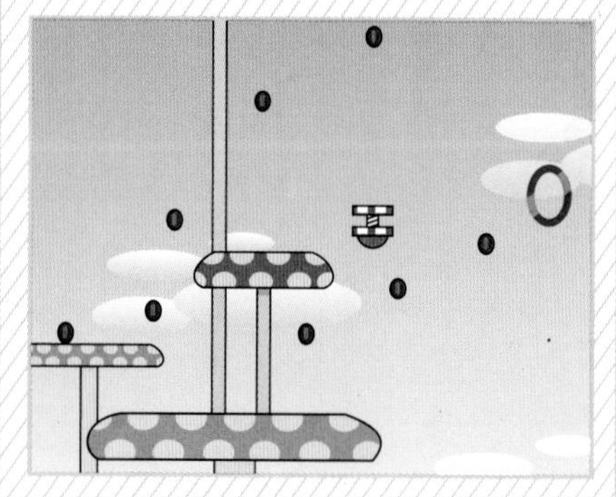

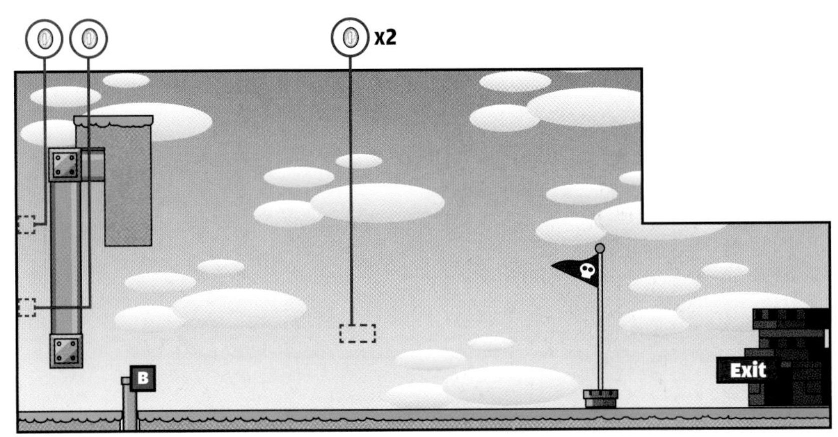

4

As Mini Mario, bounce from the top of the fuchsia mushroom platform onto the Flying ? Block below point 4, then jump from the Flying ? Block into the alcove in the ledge. From there, jump up and right, and change direction in midair to float left to point 4. At the red-flag exit on the other end of the pipe, use Wall Jumps to hit Invisible Blocks to the left of the pipe, and use those as platforms to reach the upper ledge, where a running long jump can take you over the flagpole.

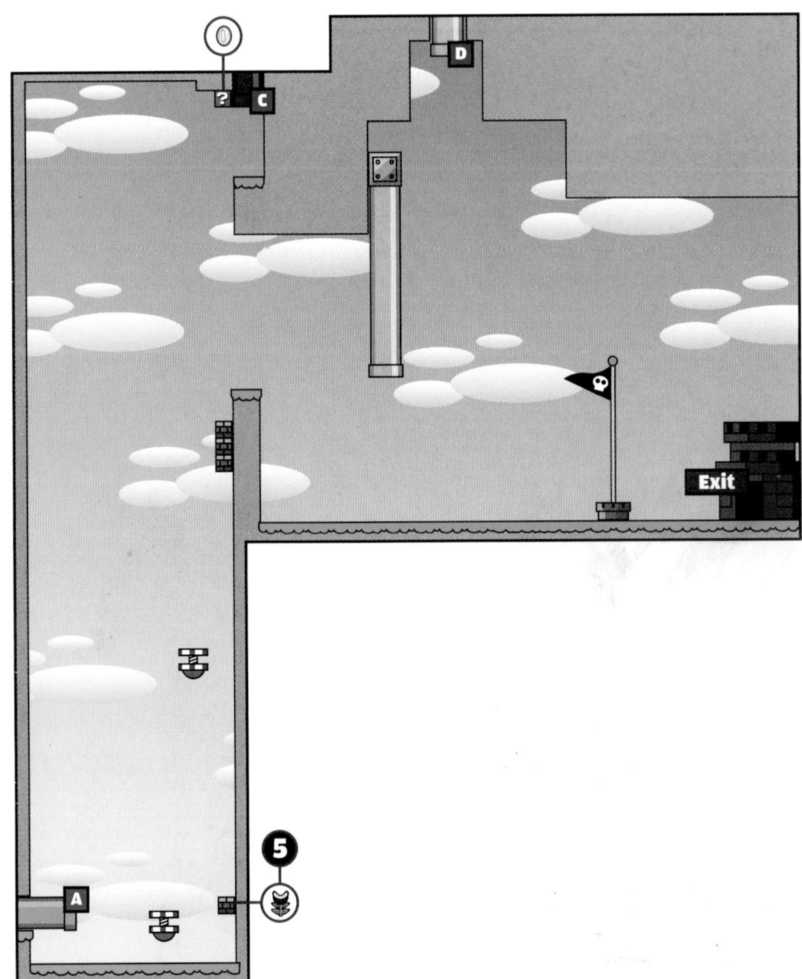

5 Vine to Coin Heaven

Don't hit the Vine Block until you've used the Spin Blocks to reach the upper part of the stage and Ground-Pounded the blocks that obstruct the vine's path. Then return to the surface to hit the Vine Block from below and climb the vine to pipe C.

Use the Spin Blocks to hit the P Switch at the top of the next area, then press down to enter a spinning dive, and follow the trail of coins to the bottom. (If you glide, you'll run out of time after claiming only a few.)

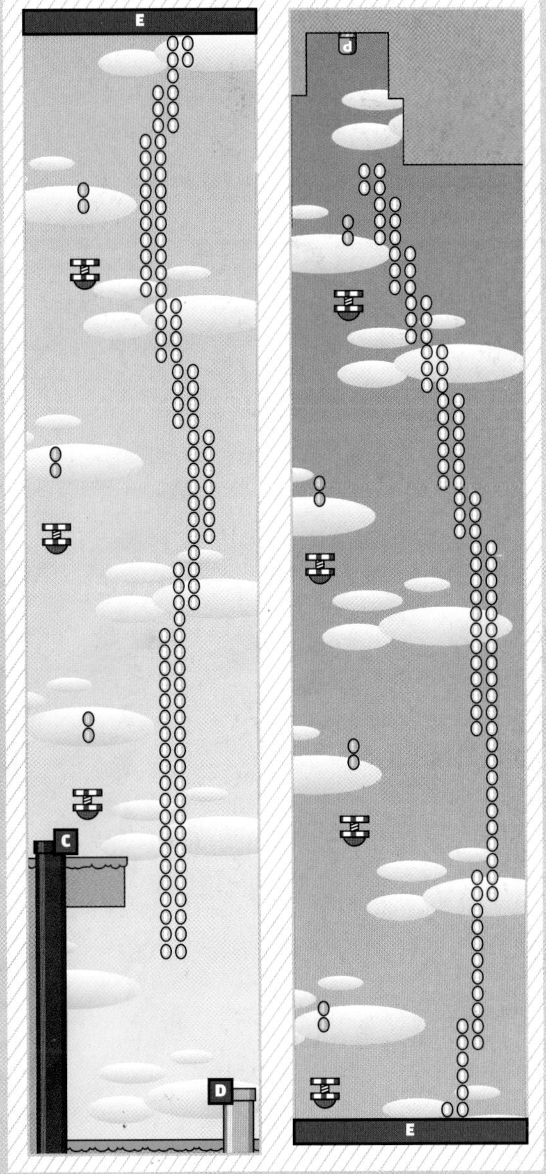

World 7-5

1 To get the first Star Coin, grab a Bob-omb on the steps to the left and toss it onto the ledge at point 1. Alternatively, you can stand below the coin and bounce off of Bullet Bills to smash the blocks beneath it.

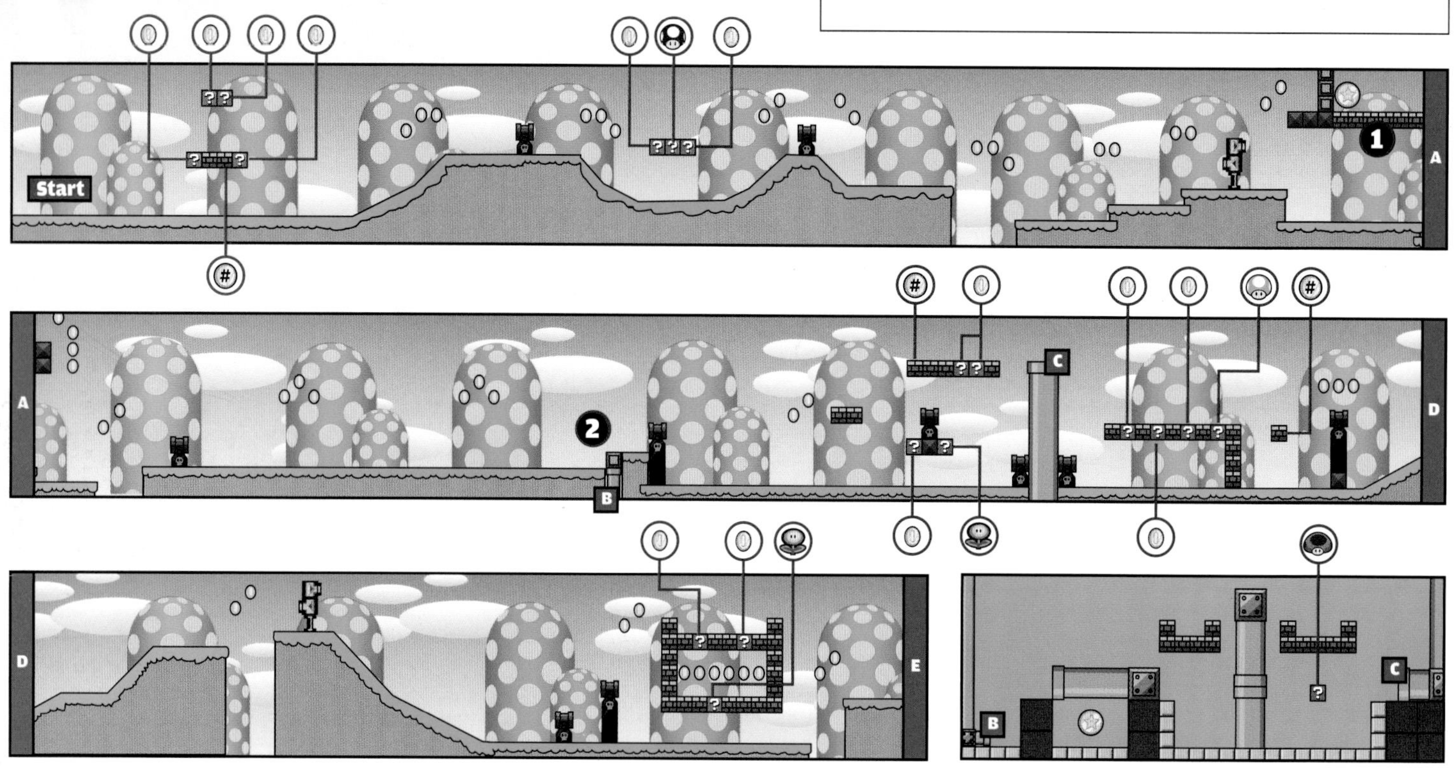

2 If you're Mini Mario, Ground-Pound a Bob-omb and kick it to the block at the lip of the minipipe. Inside you'll find a Mega Mushroom, which you can use to push aside the pipe over the Star Coin.

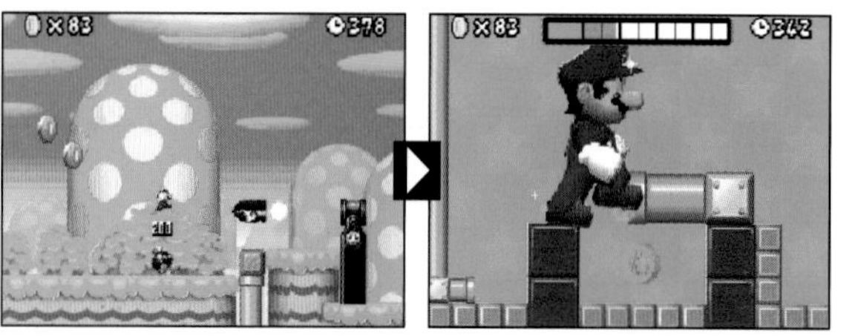

3 You can score some 1-Ups at point 3, but it won't be easy. Grab a Bob-omb from the area to the left and toss it onto the platform to destroy the Coin Blocks. You can then jump off of the Bullet Bills continually.

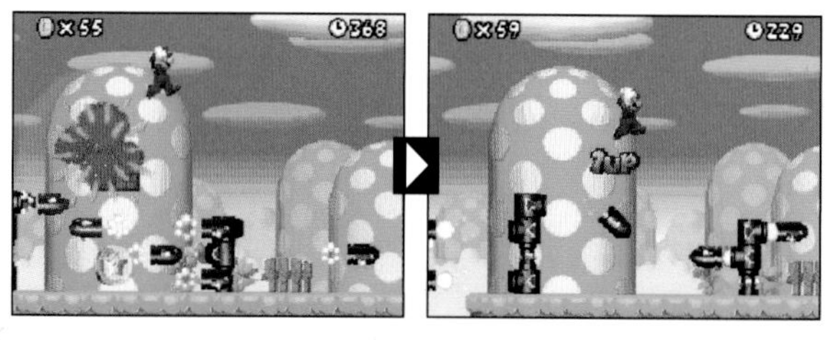

4 Blasting through the blocks at point 4 is extremely difficult since you have only two Bob-ombs to work with (one at point 4 and one to the left). Set the first Bob-omb on the pipe side of the second step to clear a place for the second Bob-omb. Or pop a Mega Mushroom to make things a lot easier.

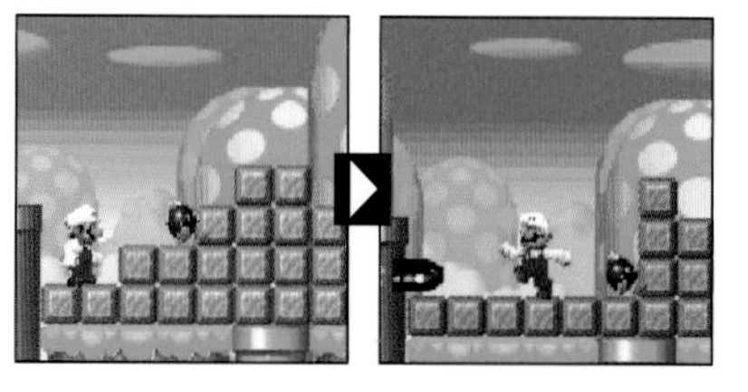

5 Wait for the cannon to fire a Banzai Bill toward the flag, and use a running long jump to bounce off of it and over the flagpole.

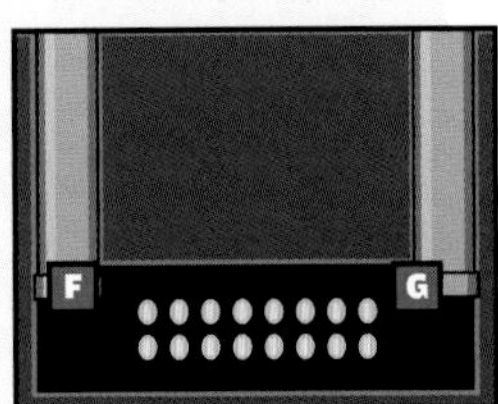

World 7-6

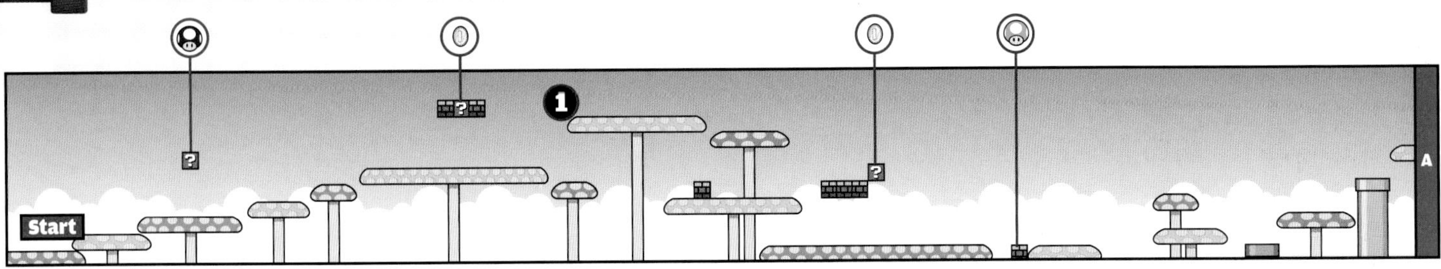

1 Grab a Koopa shell from the platform to the left of point 1, then jump onto the platform at point 1 and kick the shell to the right. Follow it as it earns a 1-Up from kills, and looses a 1-Up Mushroom from the block at the end.

2 Break the block above the Vine Block, then hit the Vine Block from below to create a vine to an upper area where a wobbly mushroom platform will take you to a Star Coin. If you can avoid being bucked off the 'shroom, you can reach the red-flag exit through the pipe at the end.

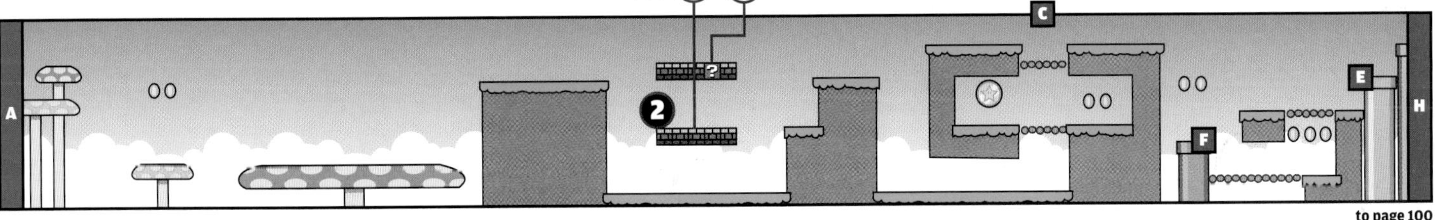

to page 100

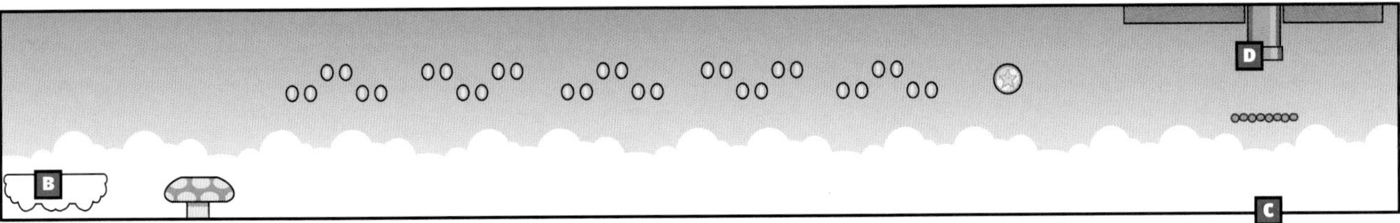

to page 100

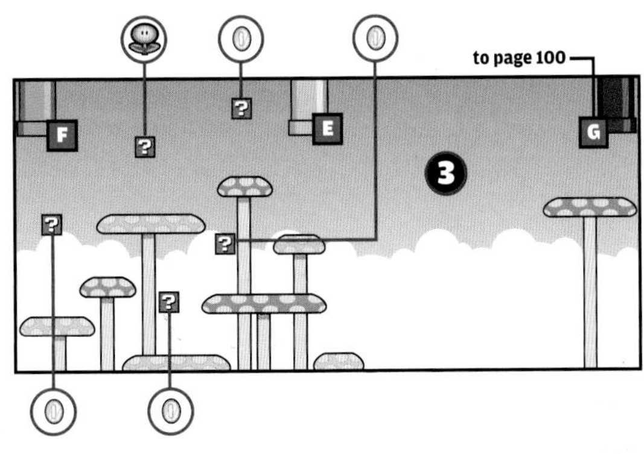

3 To reach the stage's final Star Coin, pass through pipe E and bounce across three Koopa Paratroopas to reach the red exit pipe. You'll emerge directly beneath the coin.

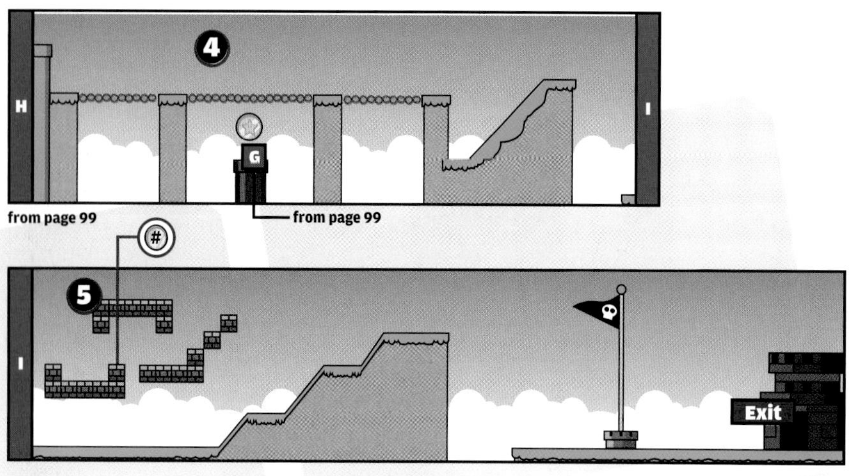

4 Skilled Koopa-stompers can score 1-Ups at point 4 by jumping on each Koopa Paratroopa twice. When you're done, take a shell with you.

5 Throw your Koopa shell at point 5 to clear out the Koopas and drain the Coin Block of its loot.

World 7-A

1 Many of the pipes in this level are empty. In the first area, travel through the pipe at point 1 to proceed, or through the pipe to the right (after making a ledge of Invisible Blocks) to a Star Coin.

2 The pipe below the column of coins is a cannon that will blast you straight up. After collecting the coins, fire yourself up again, slide down the wall, and Wall-Jump into the pipe at point 2 to net a Star Coin.

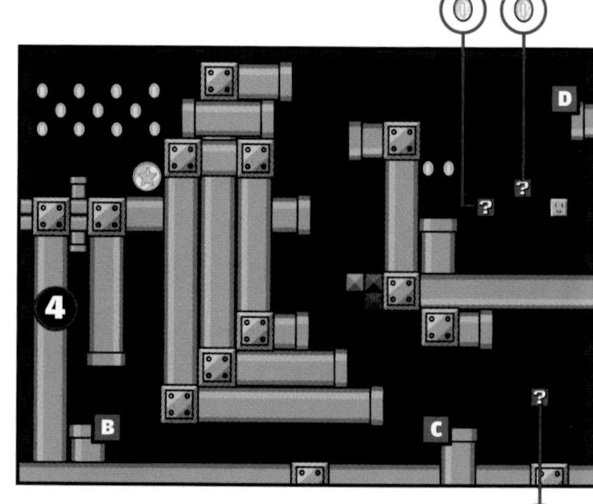

3 Hit Invisible Blocks to fill in the gaps on the purple platform, and grab a Koopa shell from above. Kick it left along the purple platform to hit the block that bears the 1-Up Mushroom.

4 In the first part of the area, proceed through the pipe below pipe B, wait for the Piranha Plant to withdraw, then jump through pipe B. Make your way to the right to grab a Mini Mushroom, and use that to Wall-Jump at point 4 to reach the final Star Coin.

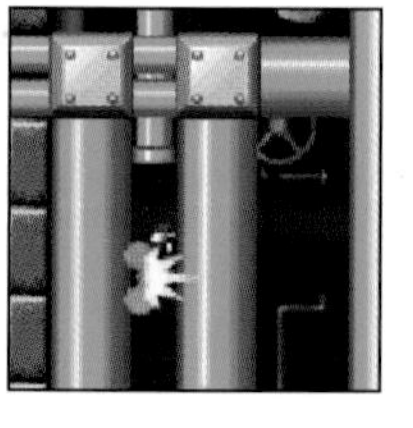

World 7-7

1 The little platforms at point 1 will fall when you put your weight on them. On this stage, you'll often need to let them fall so you can leap off of them and onto lower items such as Star Coins.

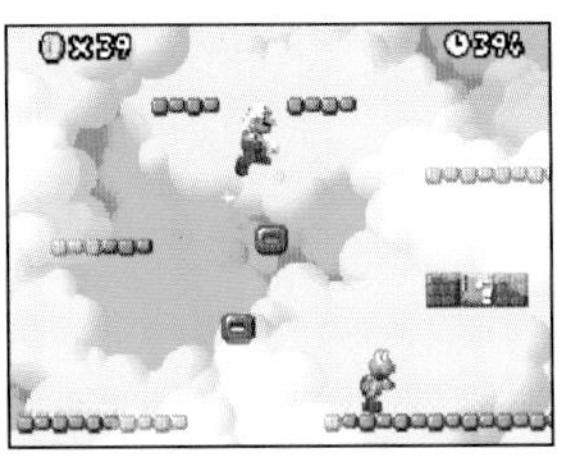

2 Stomp the Koopa at point 2 and kick it to the right to break the block and reveal a 1-Up Mushroom.

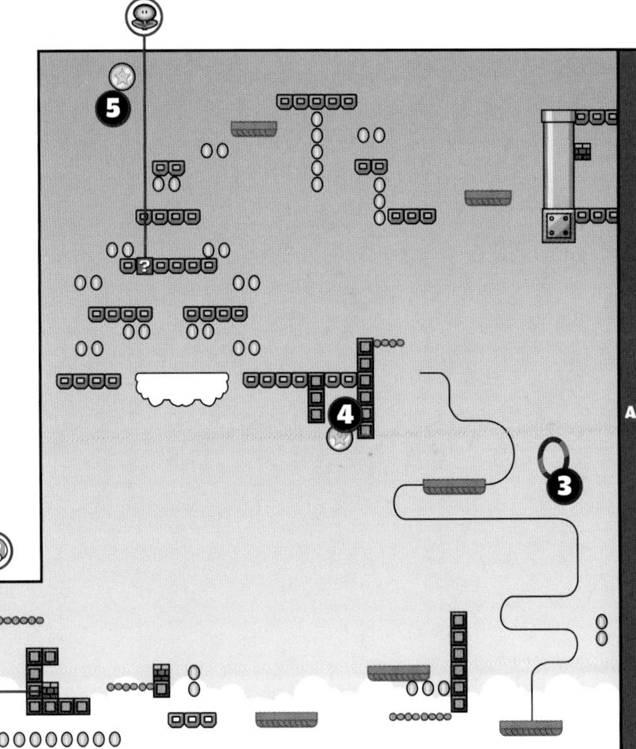

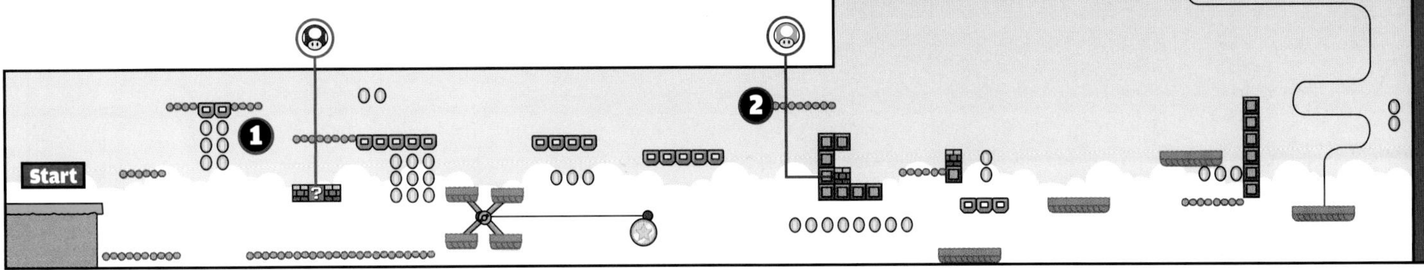

3 Red-Coin Ring

Don't expect the platform to carry you into the red coins—it will carry you below them, and you can snag each of the first six with well-timed jumps. A long jump at the end will take you to the final two.

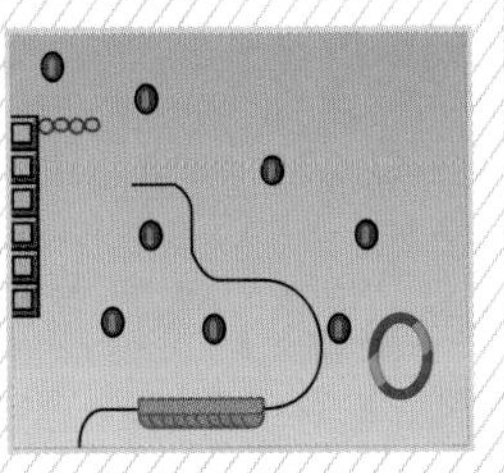

4 Stand on a platform and wait for it to fall. After it takes you through the Star Coin, you can Wall-Jump off of the right wall to get back on track.

5 Make your way to the highest platform and hop on it repeatedly so it won't fall. When the Star Coin scrolls into view, leap into it from the platform.

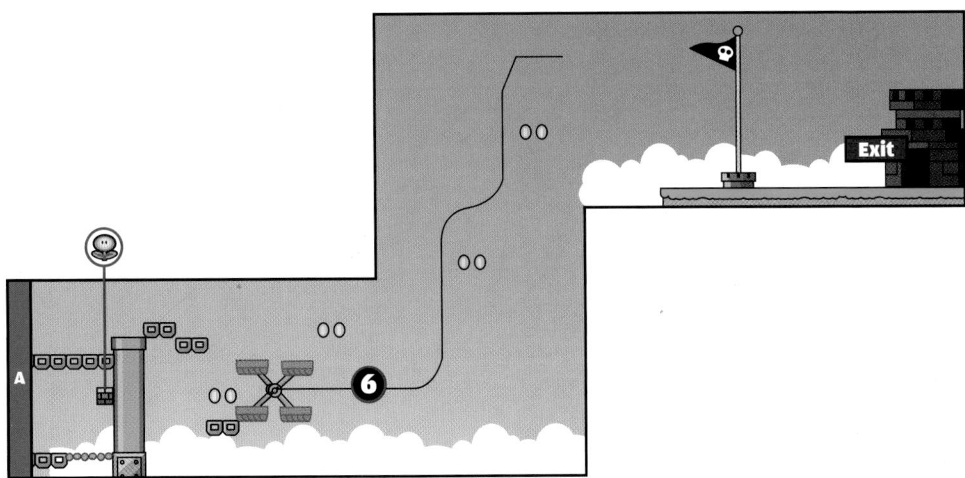

6 Keep jumping to platforms on the right side of the platform wheel to move it along the track. When you get to the end, leap from the top to the flagpole.

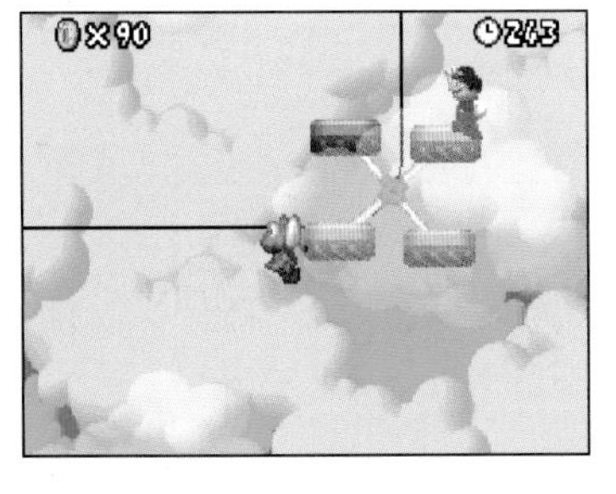

World 7 Castle

1 You'll ride serpentine platforms like this one throughout the level. The platforms change direction abruptly, so stay near the middle to keep your options open.

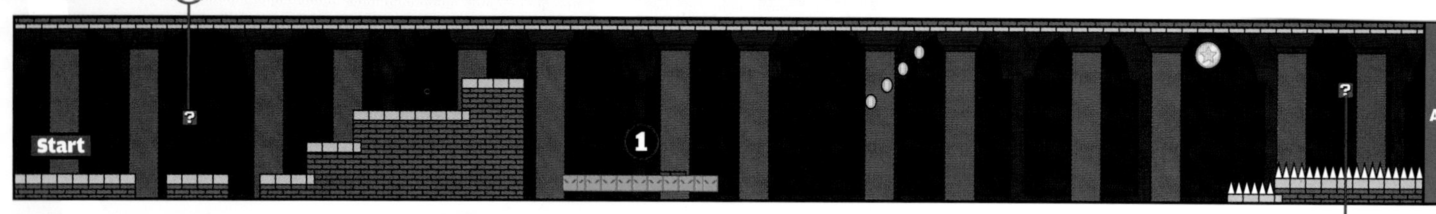

2 In this part of the stage, spiked balls spin around central pivot blocks that Mario can stand on safely. This is the place to wait while your lunatic platform does loops around the pivot blocks.

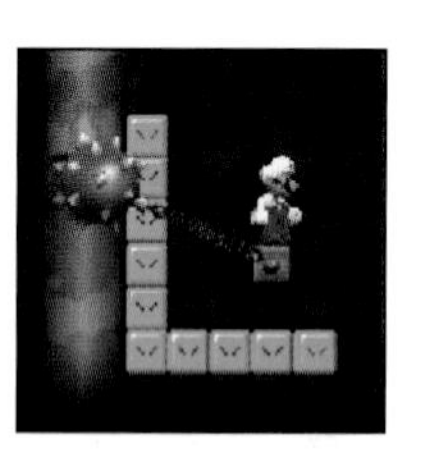

3 Drop on the Star Coin at point 3 as early as you can, and wait on the pivot block while your platform screws around. Jump straight up onto it as soon as the head is about to pass over you—it's a lot easier than trying to leap onto the tail.

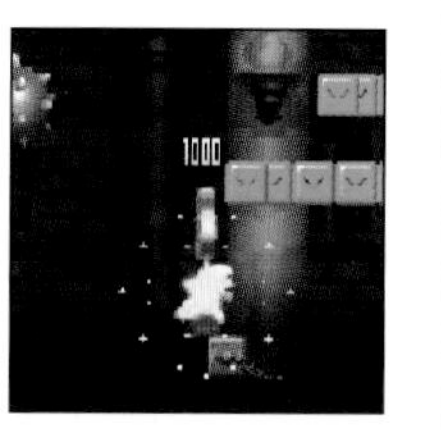

4 Stay near the head of the platform so you'll have plenty of space to fall back and wait out the flames. Afterward, run toward the head to ensure you have space for the next time.

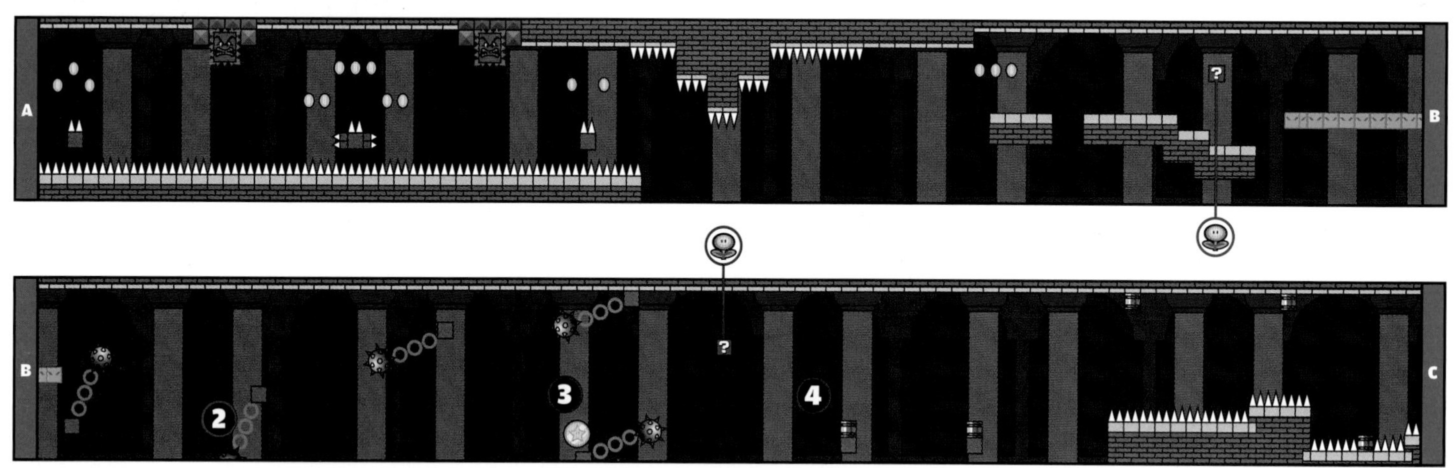

5 With no Koopa shell to kick, you'll need to ride your platform as it crumbles and falls, then long-jump to the ledge as soon as you're low enough to hit the Star Coin in midair. Yikes!

Boss

Lakithunder throws Spinys at Mario and occasionally swoops down for a direct attack. That's your chance to get in a stomp, but your timing must be good—you'll clear Lakithunder only at the very height of your jump. After he takes his second hit, he'll retaliate by sending a flurry of lightning bolts down at you. Keep moving so he can't get a bead on you, and resume your normal pattern after the final bolt strikes. If the situation gets dire, find the Invisible Block at the far left of the room—it contains a power-up.

Lakithunder has lots of Spinys to throw, but they won't last long on the ground—eventually they'll fall through the gaps in the platform.

World 8

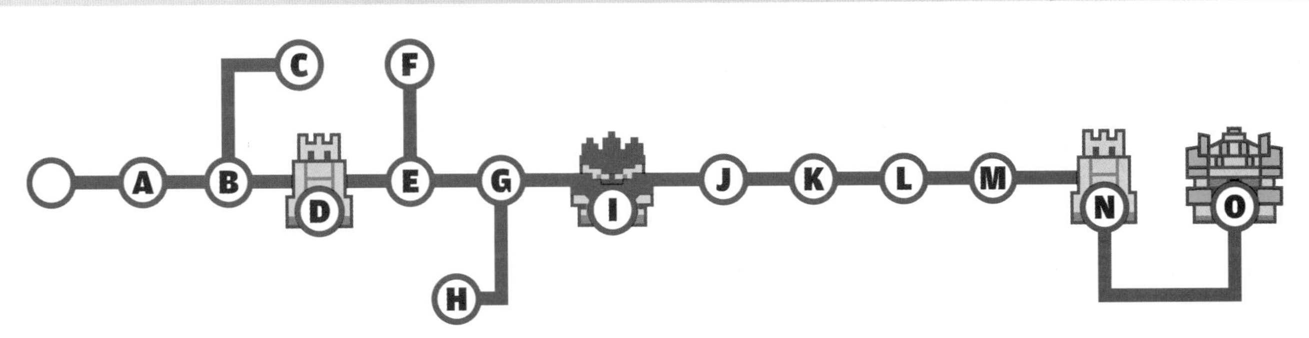

World 8-1

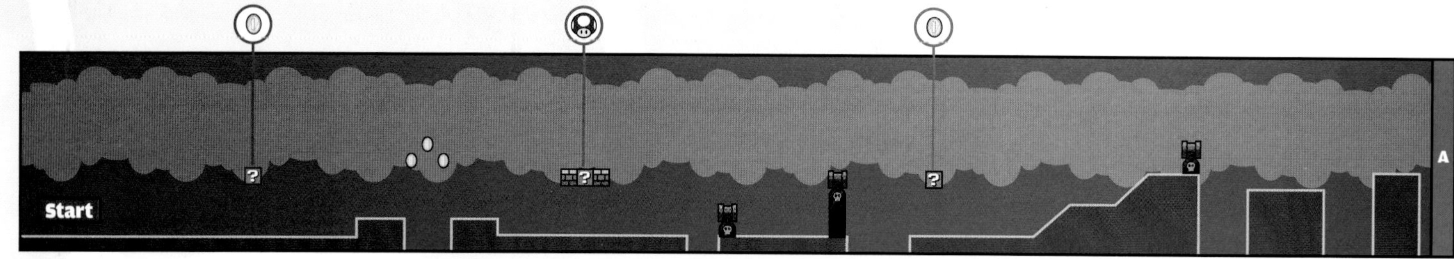

1 Hit the ? Block from beneath to reveal a spring. If you jump on it you'll be able to see the Star Coin, but to get the coin you'll need to pick up the spring and place it on the pair of blocks a short distance to the right.

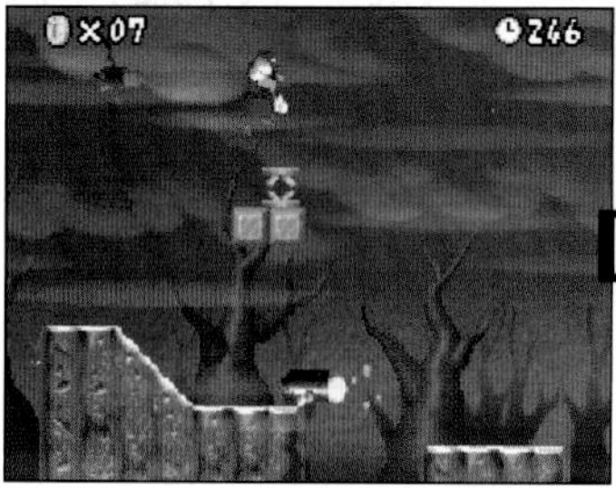

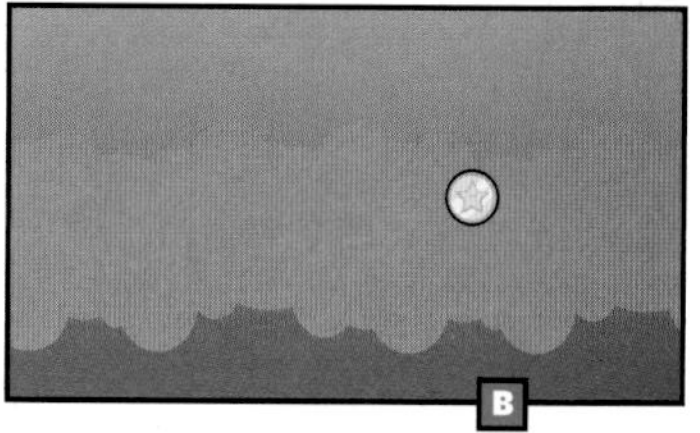

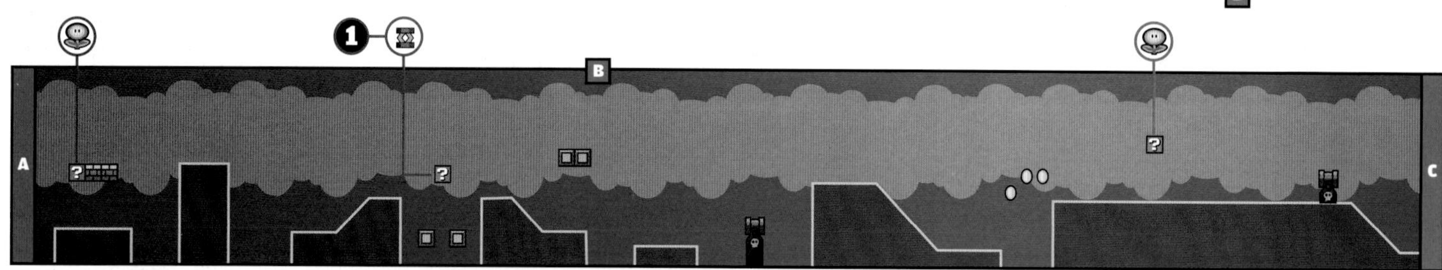

2 Bounce off of the Bullet Bills to reach the second Star Coin. Don't let the Boos get in the way—lure them to the left so you can jump while facing them.

3 Wait for the cannon to fire past the Star Coin, then drop onto the coin and wait for it to fire again before you Wall-Jump up. To get above the flagpole, wait until the cannon fires, jump onto the platform to the right, and hop onto the Banzai Bill.

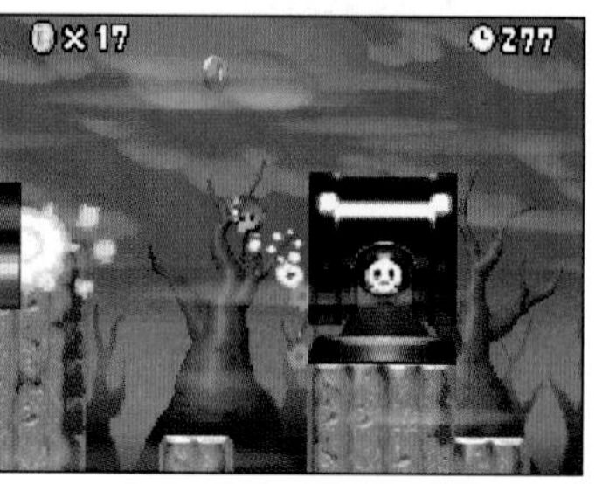

World 8-2

1 Raise the Water

Hit the ? Switches scattered throughout this stage to raise the water level. That will give you a limited amount of time to swim to the top and find the next pipe.

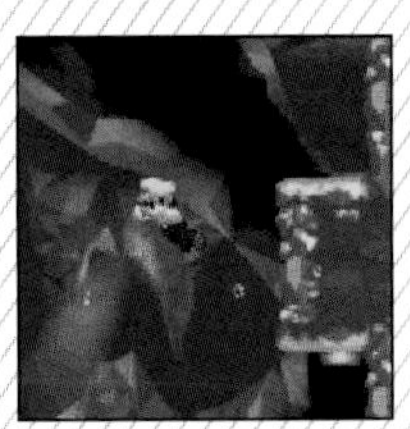

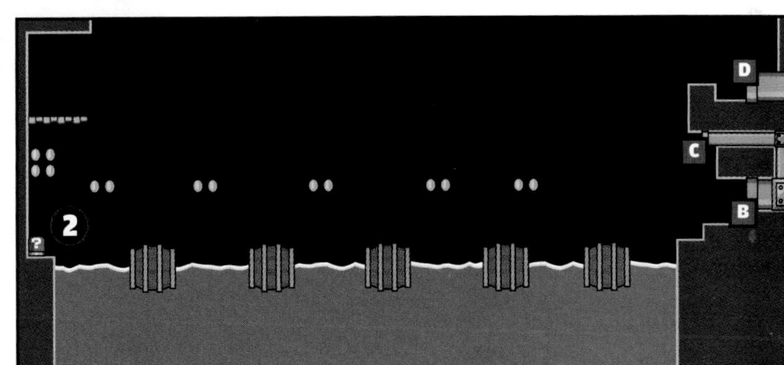

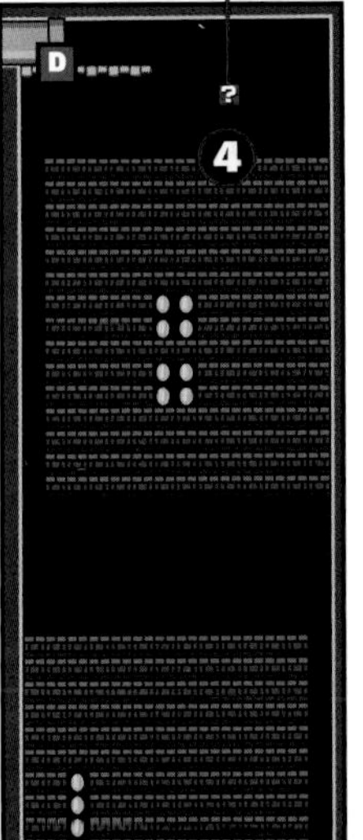

2 Jump across the barrels to the left, stomping as many Skeeters as you can along the way, and hit the ? Switch to raise the water level. You can then jump across the barrels to the exit pipe or, if you're Mini Mario, run along the water's surface into a pipe that leads to a bonus area.

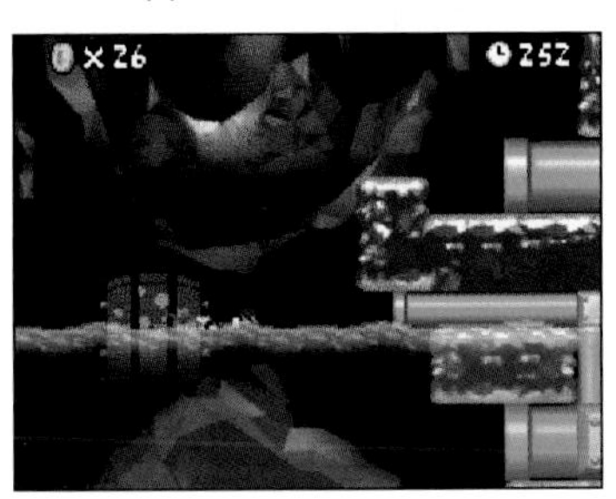

3 Grab the Starman and dash through all of the Mini Goombas to earn 1-Ups before the Starman fades.

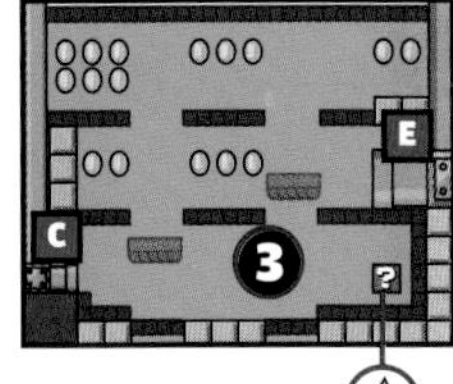

4 Consult the map to tell where you should Ground-Pound to drop into the coin groups and the Star Coin. If you have a Mega Mushroom, this is a great place to use it to score several 1-Ups.

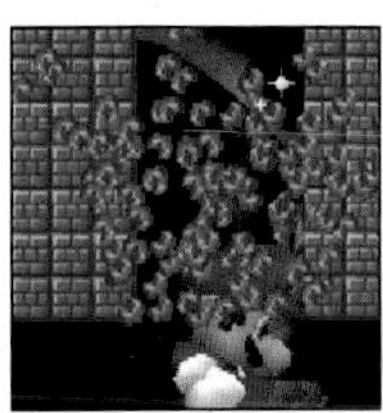

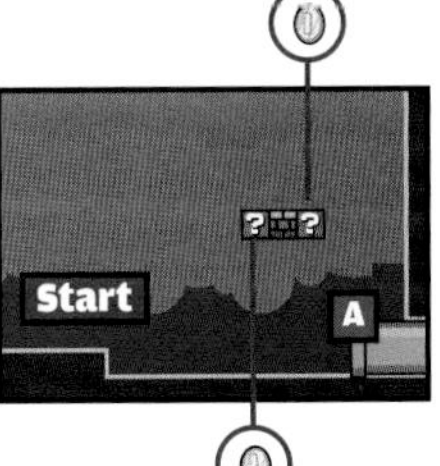

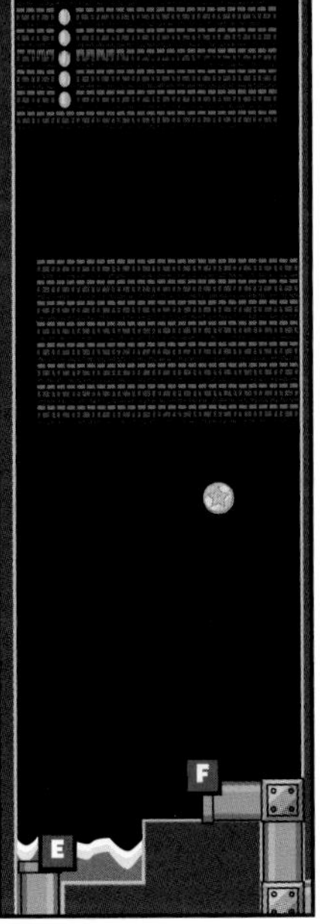

5 The water level won't rise quite high enough to let you jump into the second Star Coin. You'll need to Wall-Jump into it (though normal Mario can't) or bounce off of a Skeeter to reach it.

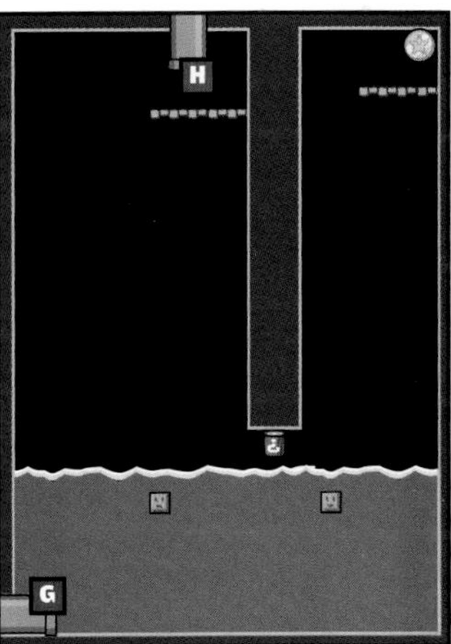

World 8 Tower

1 Get in front of the row of spikes and crouch. The moving platform will push you through the coins and to the other side.

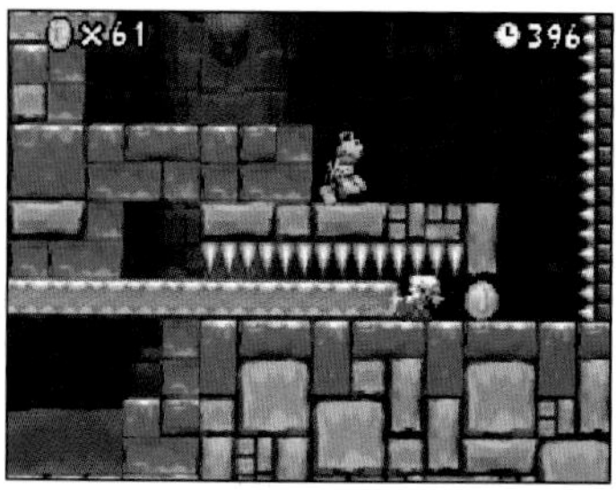

2 When there's a gap between the Spike Tops, leap onto the platform and crouch to take it for a ride. Leap up to the second Star Coin, then crouch again; the upper platform will push you out of the cramped space.

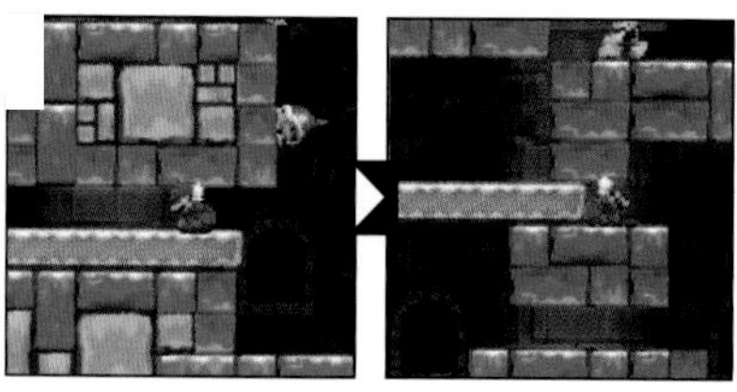

3 Jump off of the Dry Bones or the Flying ? Block to hit the Invisible Blocks. You can then Wall-Jump onto them and into the Star Coin.

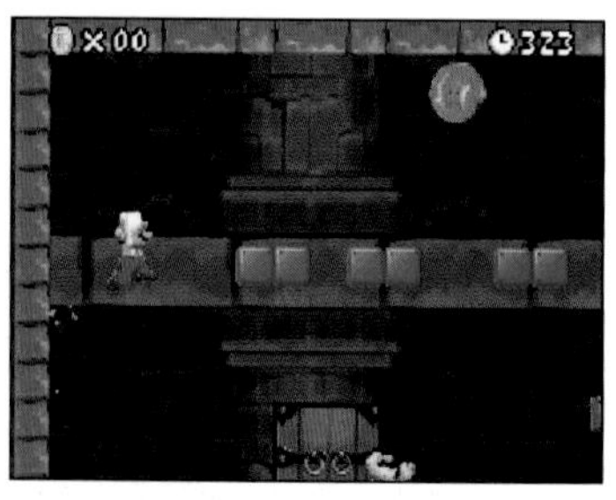

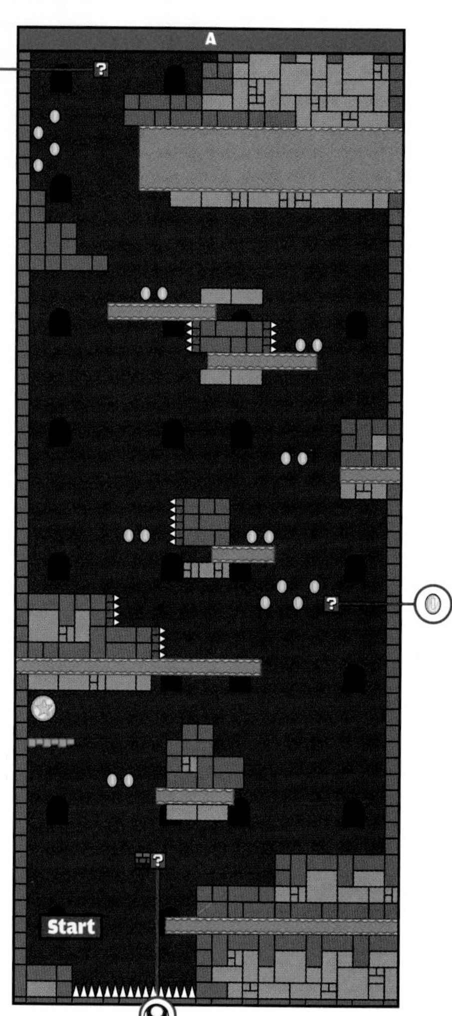

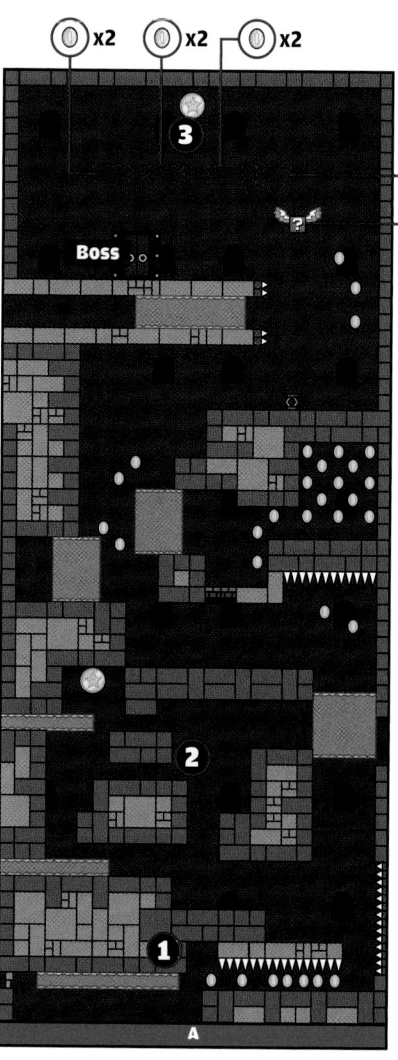

Boss

There are lots of environmental obstacles to contend with in this battle. Moving platforms and the torch flames make it dangerous to stray from the middle of the battlefield, so that's where you should do your fighting. When you knock over Bowser Jr. and go in for the stomp, don't get suckered into jumping into the flame!

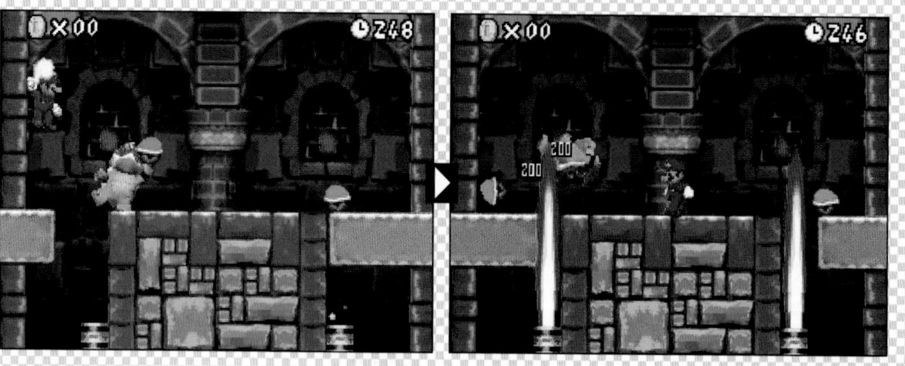

World 8-3

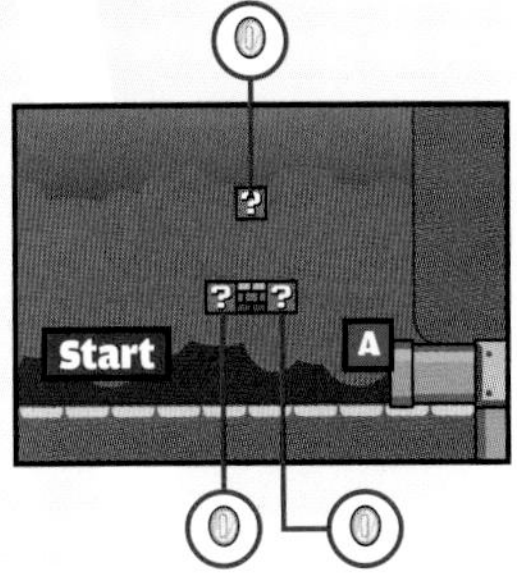

1 Swim along the edges of the reef so you'll be out of the Unagi's range. Alternatively, approach to lure them out, then swim past them when they retreat.

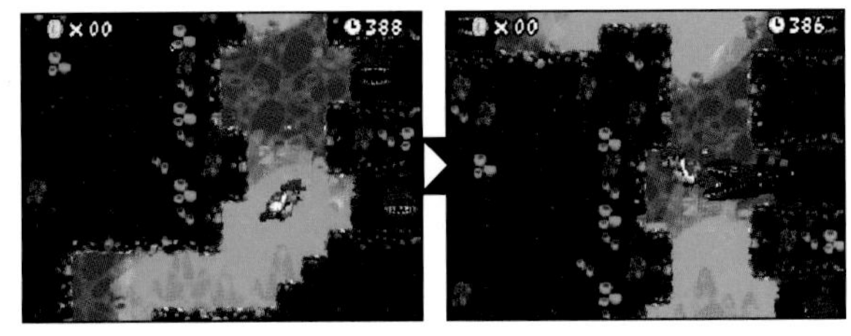

2 Red-Coin Ring

Swim to the left of the ring so you'll be heading to the right when you activate it. Wait for the Unagi to pass overhead, then swim through the ring, get the top one of the lowest coin groups to lure the Unagi out, then drop for the other two. Swim like a madman to collect the other five.

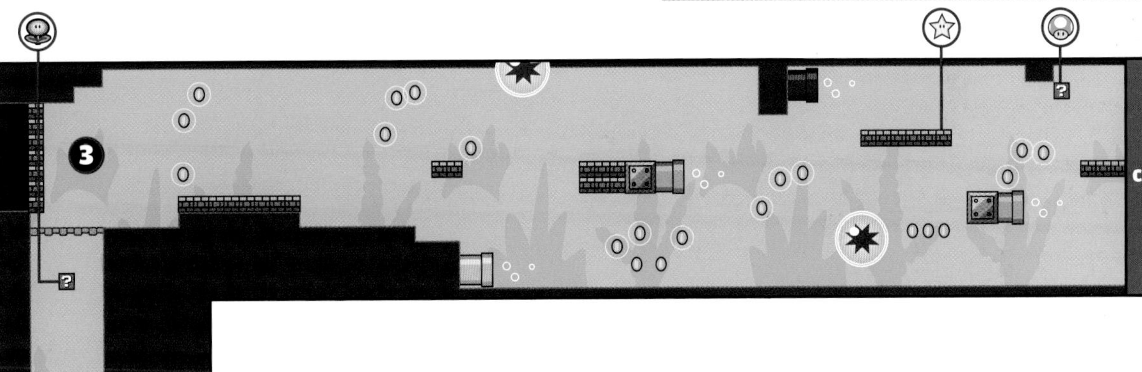

3 When you enter the horizontal area, a Mega Unagi will begin a long and dogged pursuit of Mario. Use the air bubbles blown from the pipes to get a speed boost, and check the map to identify the few items that are worth going for—you'll want to boost for the Starman and Star Coin. Beware of sea anemones, which will bounce you right into the Unagi's maw!

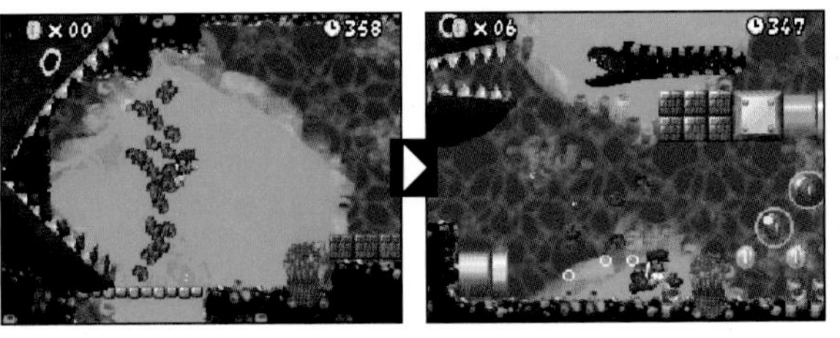

4 P-Switch Coins

Don't get greedy here; grab as many coins as you can without turning around and losing your momentum.

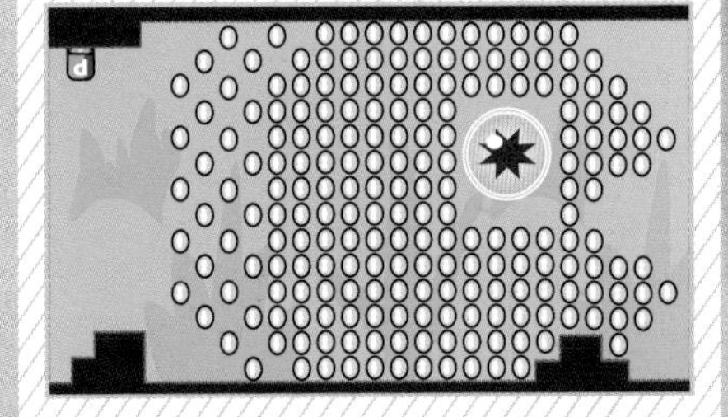

to page 108

from page 107

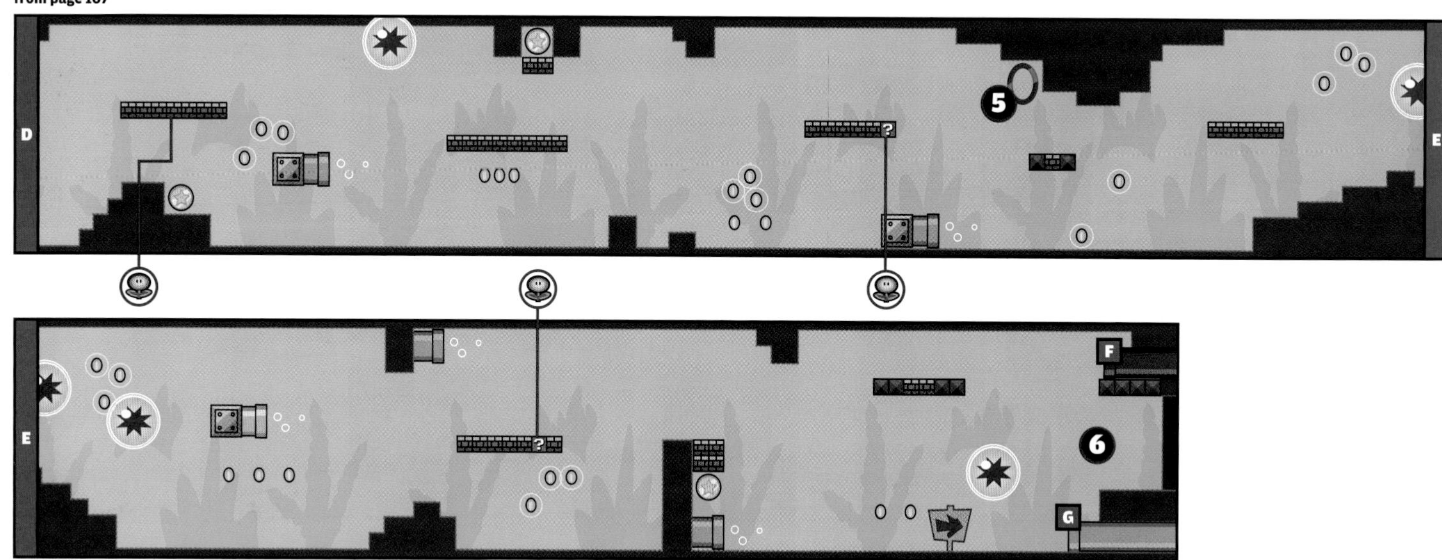

5 Red Coins While on the Run

You'll need to be Shell Mario to grab all of the coins at point 5 without losing too much momentum when you turn around. You may want to save your bubble-powered boost for the Star Coin.

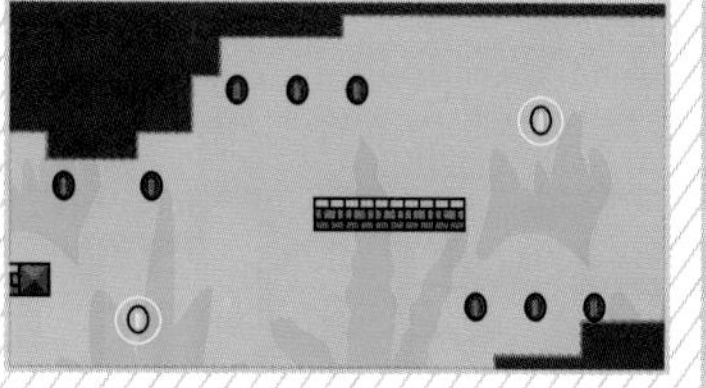

6 Choose the top pipe to exit so you'll have a chance at getting a 1-Up from the flagpole by doing a running long jump and bouncing off of a Koopa Paratoopa.

World 8-4

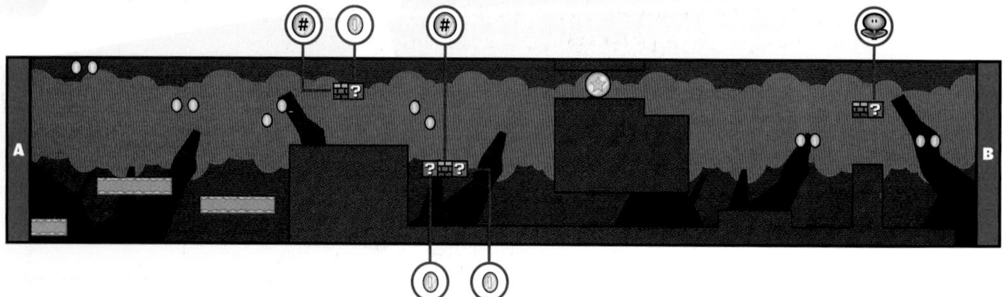

1 You won't get to see the Scuttlebugs coming the way you have in past stages. They drop from the top of the screen, hesitate only briefly, then dive onto you. Keep your eyes on the top of the screen so you'll know when to dodge.

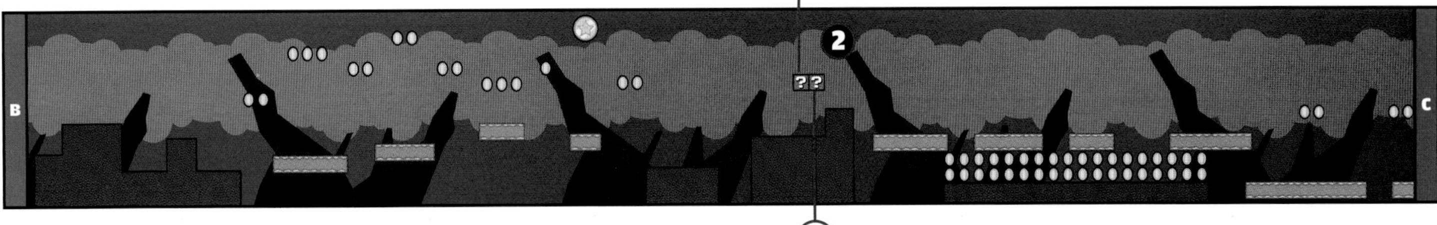

2

When you get the Starman at point 2, try to collect all of the coins without worrying about the spiders. If you have a Mini Mushroom, you can step onto the miniature pipe from the platform to its right.

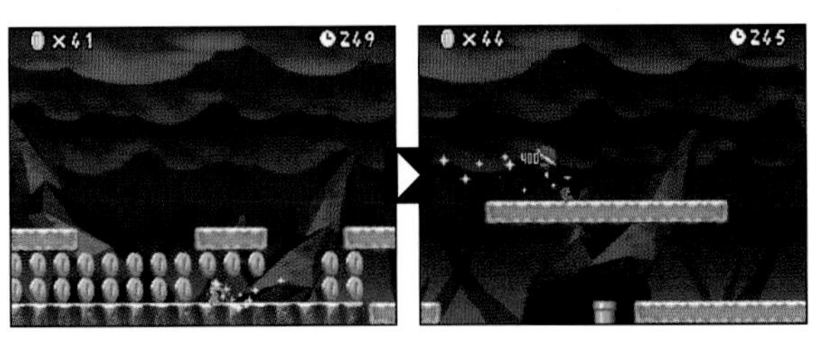

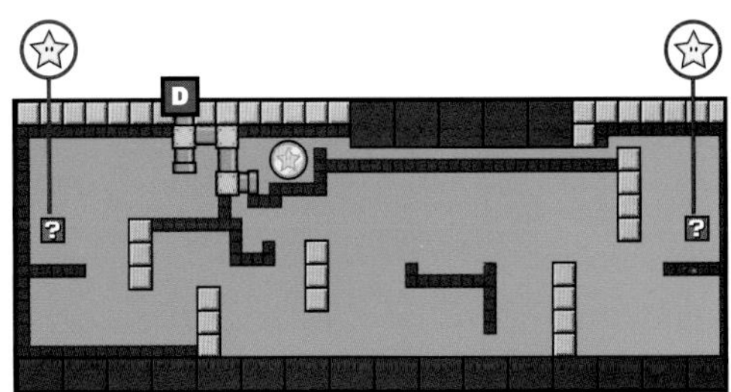

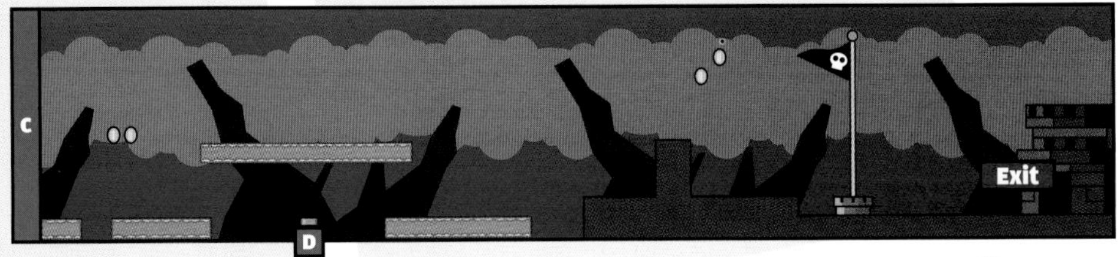

World 8 Castle

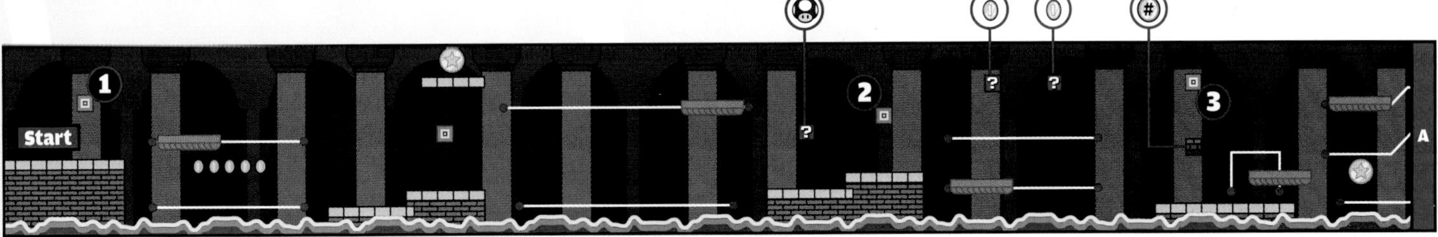

to page 110

1

There are two platform tracks across many of the pits, and you can switch the platform from track to track by hitting the red-and-yellow blocks.

2

Cross the pit to point 2 with the platform on the lower track, then hit the red-and-yellow block to move the platform to the upper track. Jump onto the platform from the ? Block and ride it to the Star Coin.

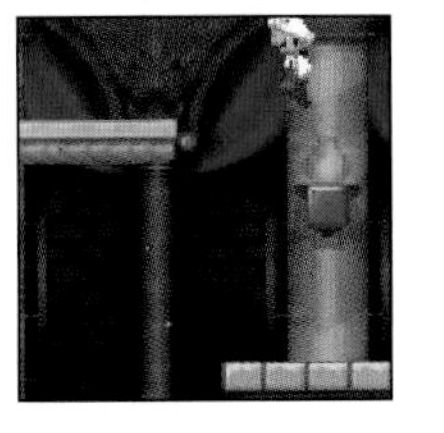

3

Use the red-and-yellow block at point 3 to create a platform on the short track, and jump from that to the platform on the right. When that one runs out of track, it will drop onto the track that leads to the Star Coin.

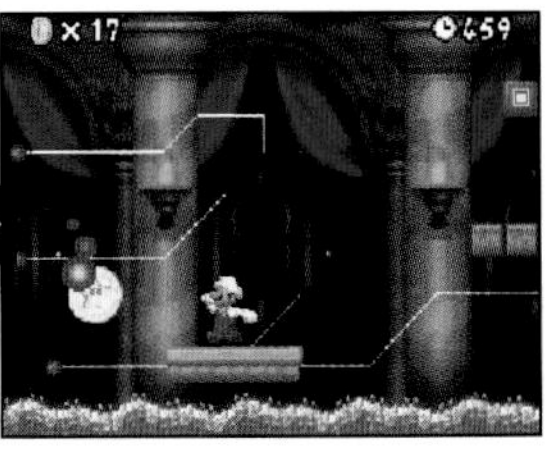

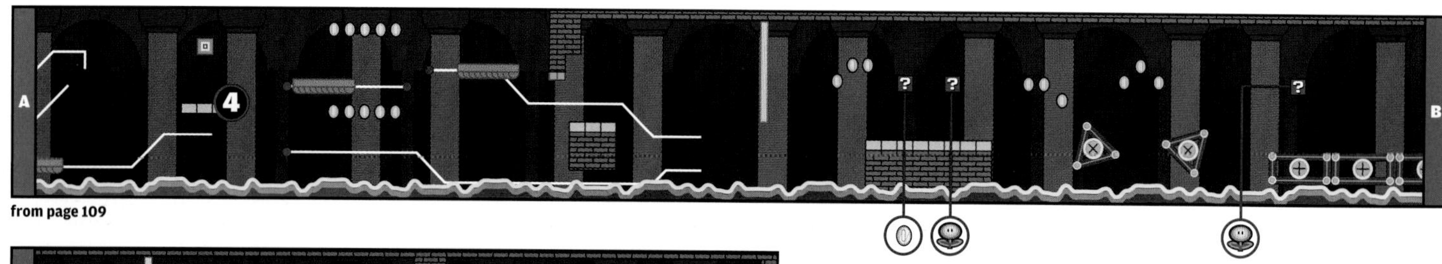

from page 109

4 You can progress to the end of the level by using either the upper or lower platform, but to obtain the final Star Coin you have to set the red-and-yellow block at point 4 to the lower platform. There's no turning back from the boss door, so if you choose the wrong platform, you'll have to start the level over to acquire the Star Coin.

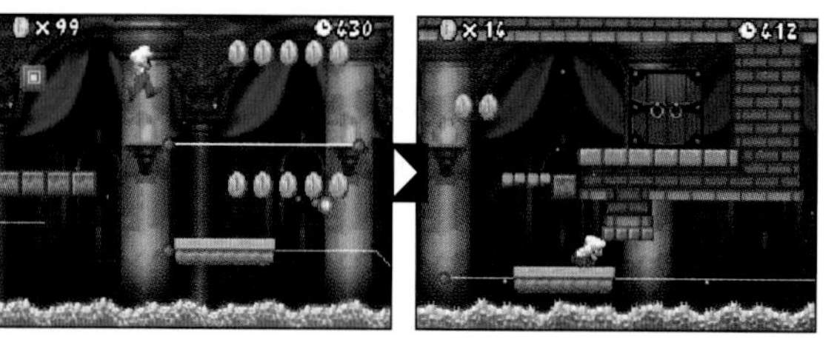

Boss

The skeletal version of Bowser can throw bones as well as fireballs. The arc of the bones makes it tough to leap over him, so it may be easier to dodge for a while until Bowser does a high jump, then dash beneath him to the skull switch.

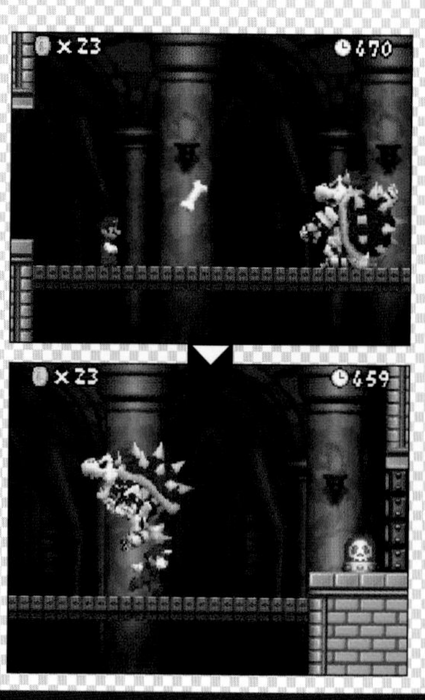

World 8-5

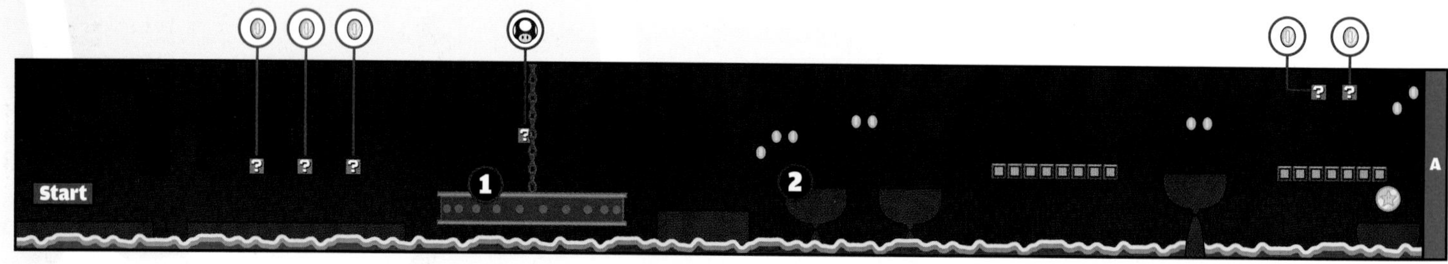

1 The hanging platforms will tilt toward whichever side Mario is standing on, and if you're close to the edges you may slide right into the lava. Jump to stabilize yourself, or dash to the center.

2 The rocks at point 2 will tilt under your weight, and will ultimately break off of their stems and into the lava. It doesn't matter how quickly you jump off or where you step; once your feet touch the rocks, they'll begin to collapse.

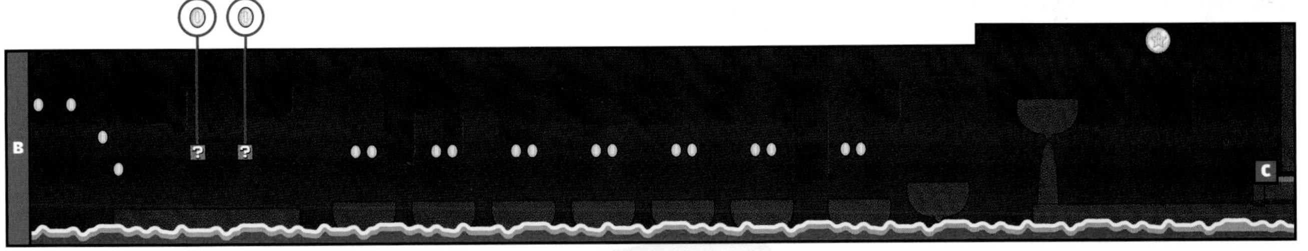

3 Grab the red Koopa shell, and toss it from the platform at point 3 to hit a block. Leap quickly to the center of the hanging platform to catch up with the 1-Up Mushroom.

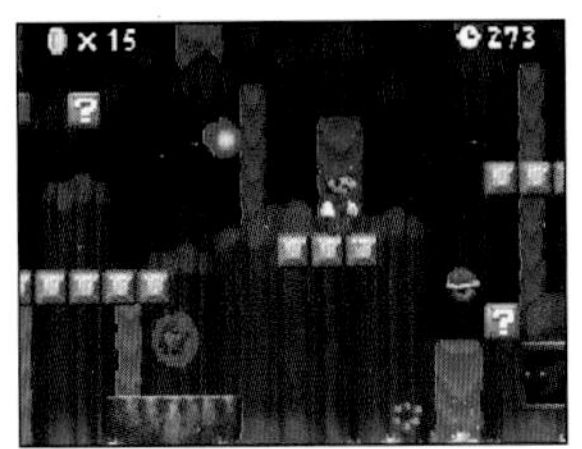

4 Grab a Koopa shell and, from the center of point 4's hanging platform, kick it left to hit the Star Coin.

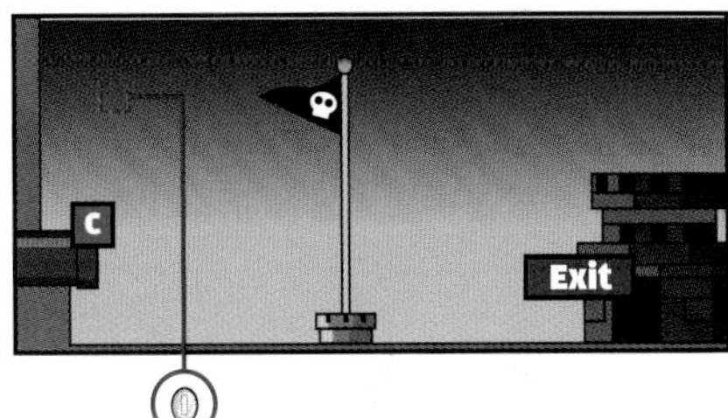

World 8-6

to page 112

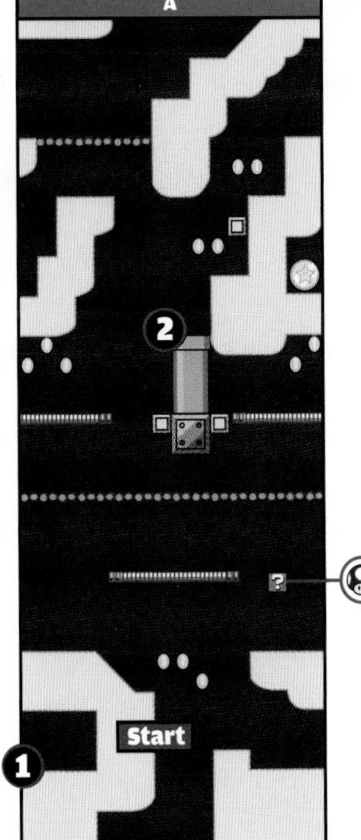

1 Whenever you run through the side of the screen, you'll reappear on the other side. Whenever you're facing a dead end, run through the side of the screen—you'll find a path to proceed on the other side.

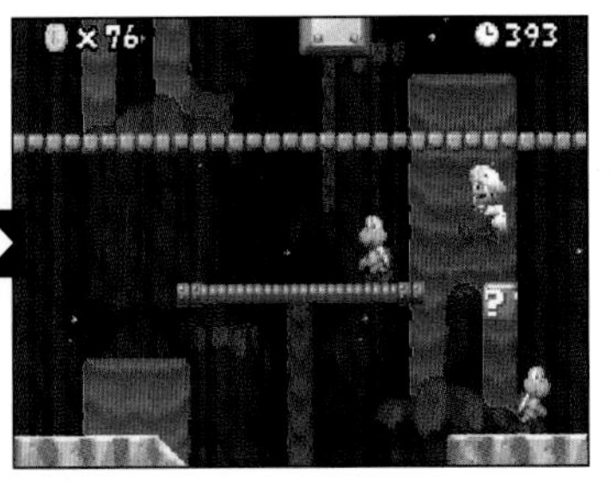

2 Squeeze into the pipe at point 2; it will blast you to a ledge you can't reach via standard jumps. Drop to the other side, run through the screen, and grab the Star Coin.

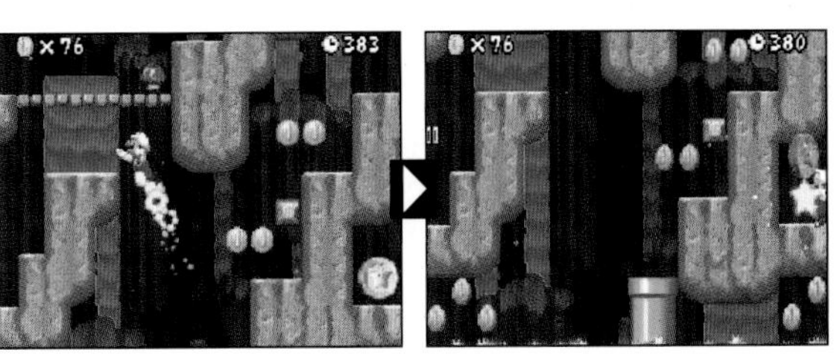

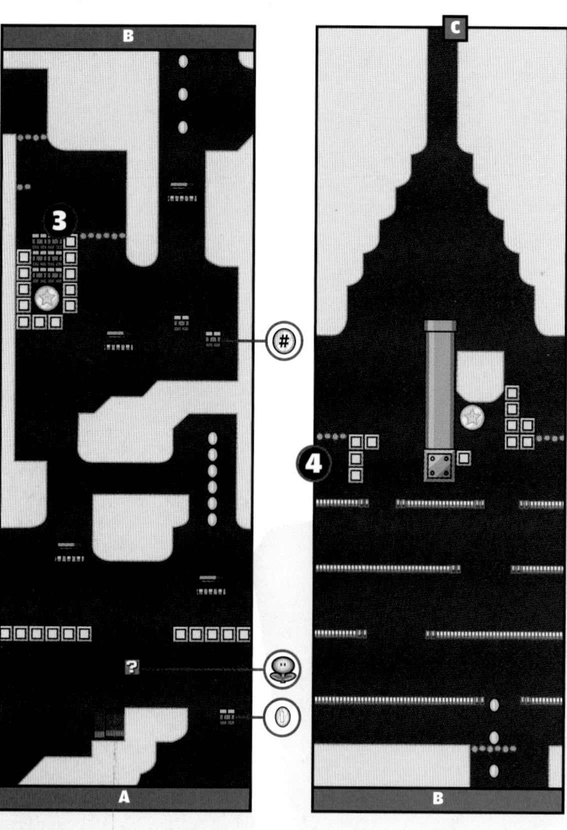

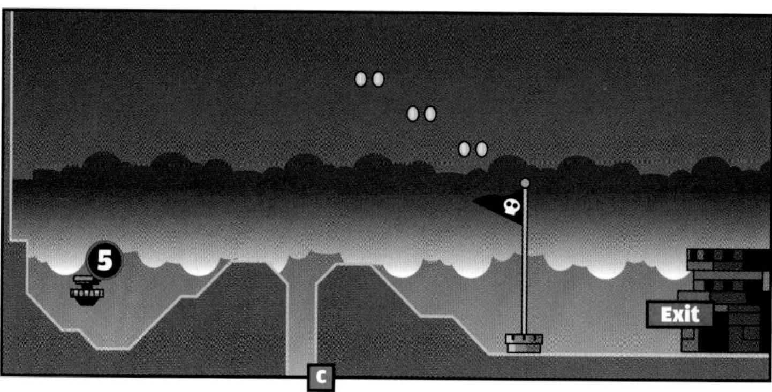

3 Unless the lava is nipping at your heels, you should have enough time to get above the Star Coin by using the Spin Block. Then do a spinning drill stomp to destroy the blocks in the way.

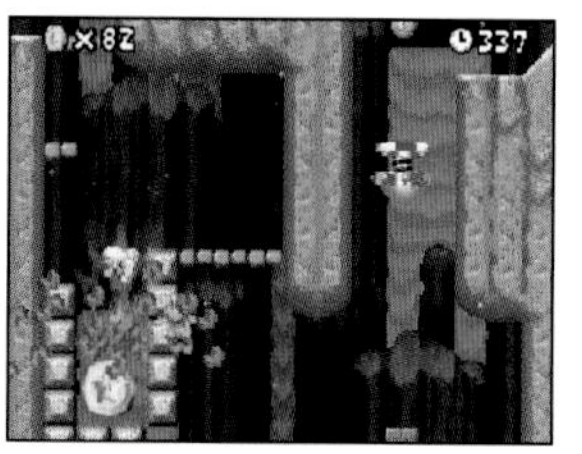

4 Getting the Star Coin near point 4 is easy, but getting back out alive isn't. If you aren't standard Mario, take a hit from a Spiny so you can slip beneath the pipe and get back on track quickly.

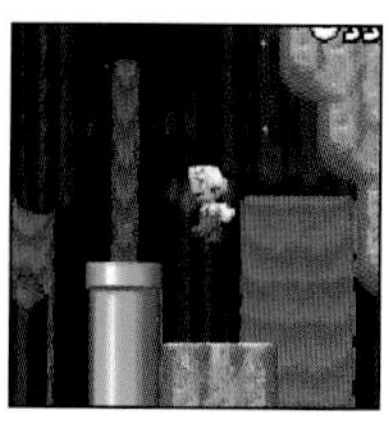

5 Hold right on the Control Pad as you blast off a Spin Block to reach the top of the flagpole.

World 8-7

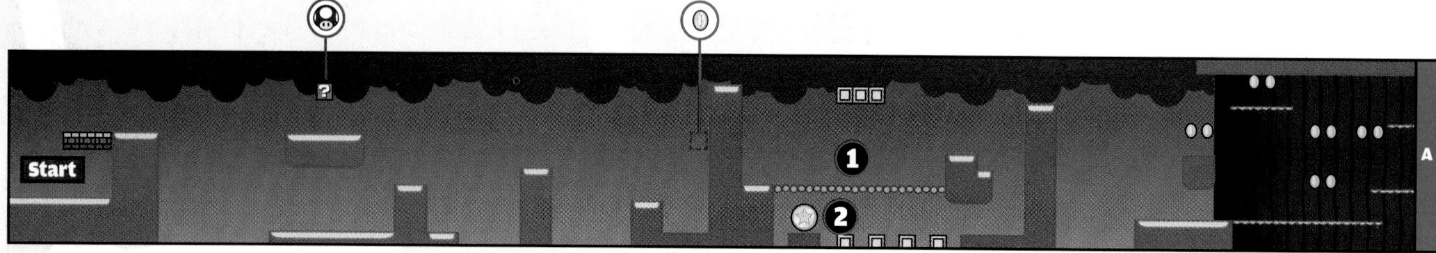

1 When the Sumo Bro jumps, jump along with him or you'll be stunned by the tremor when he lands. Then jump on his head while he recovers from the jump.

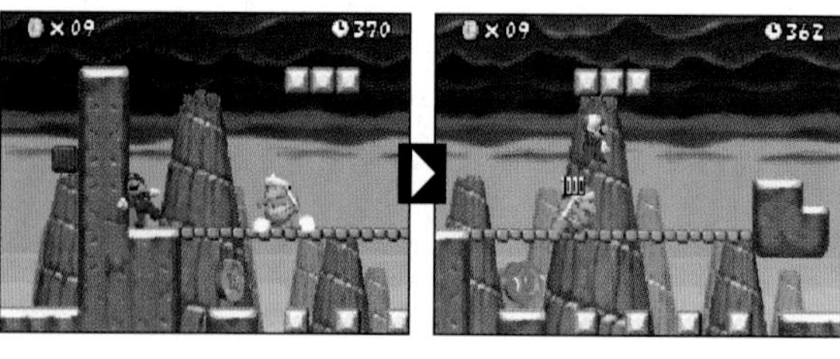

2 Run across the gaps at point 2 to grab the Star Coin. Jump to the bridge as soon as you touch the coin to avoid sliding off the ledge.

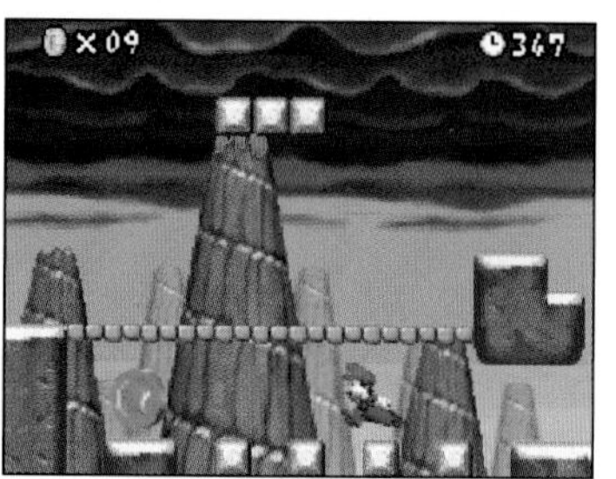

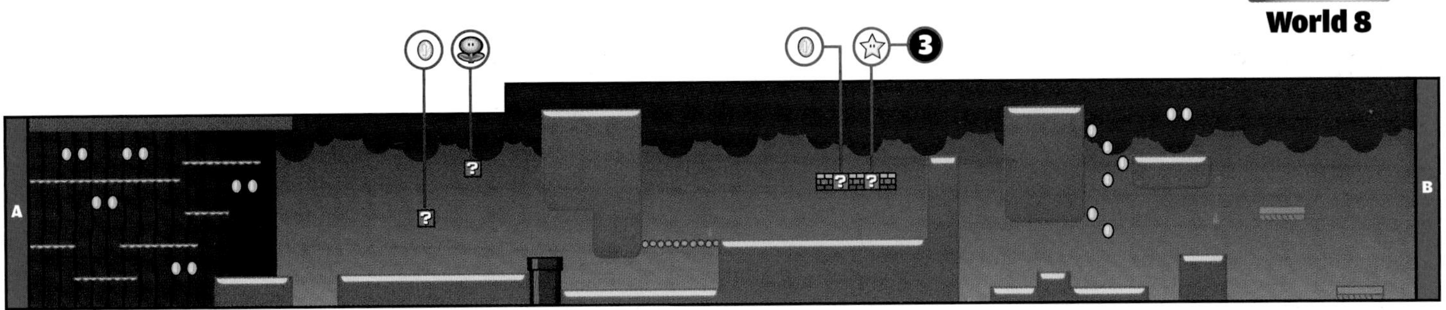

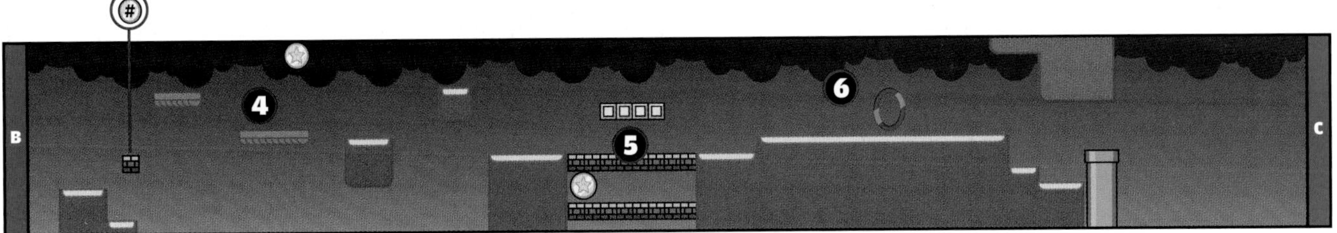

3 Wait for the lower Fire Bro to throw a fireball, then run to punch his block from below. Grab the Starman and use it to take out the other bro, then drop to the right, Wall-Jump along the path of coins, hit the Koopa on the platform, then step off to the left to complete a Starman 1-Up chain.

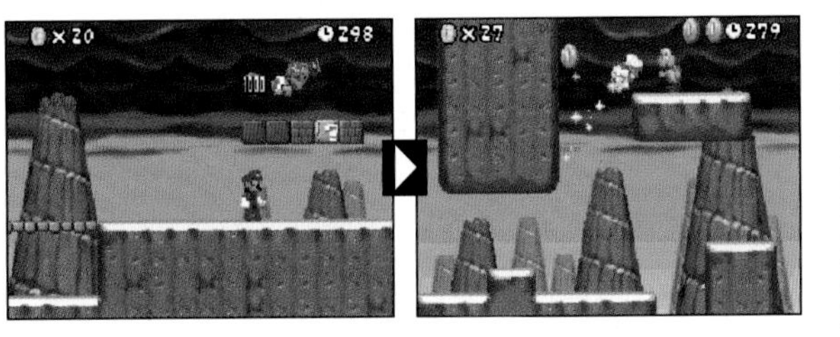

4 Jump onto the left platform and wait until it's at the apex of its rise, then jump off onto the Boomerang Bro's head. If there's a boomerang, be ready to dodge it on the return trip!

5 Hesitate at point 5 and dodge the hammers that the Sumo Bro throws. When he does his stomp attack, he'll punch right through the blocks, allowing you to initiate a stomp. If you're standard Mario, hold off until the Hammer Bro punches through to the Star Coin.

6 Blast through the Coins

Leap over the red-coin ring and stomp the Boomerang Bro before you trigger the ring. Collecting the coins is easy, because the pipe cannon will shoot you through most of them.

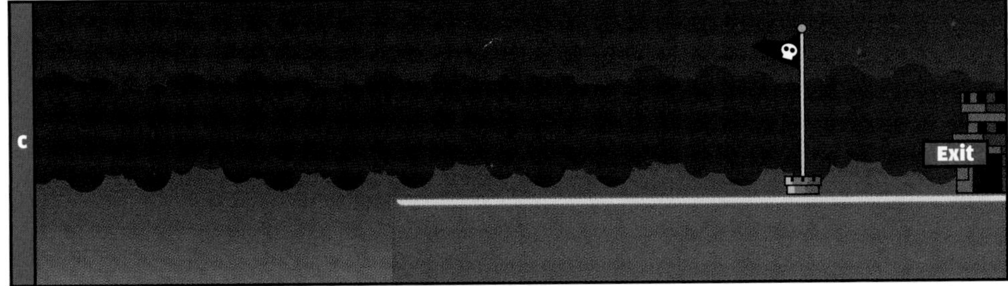

World 8-8

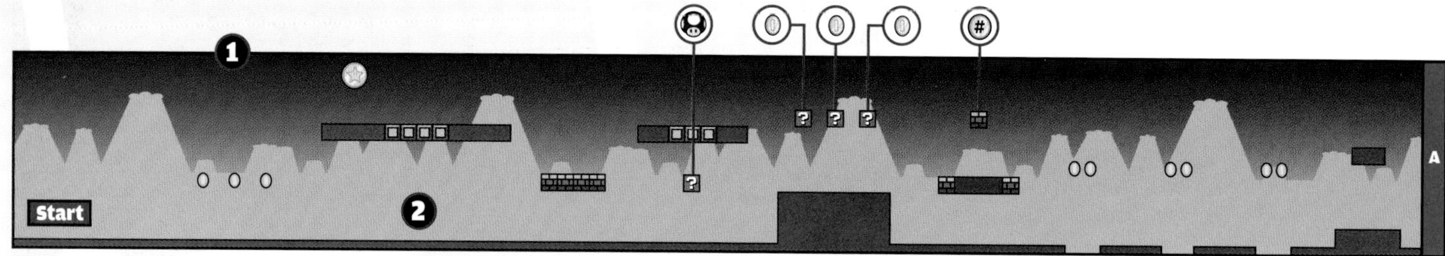

1 Intermittent waves of volcanic debris will rain from the sky on this level, but you'll be safe under the darker-colored blocks. The falling rocks can destroy normal and ? Blocks, however, so it will be a race to claim their contents before they're demolished.

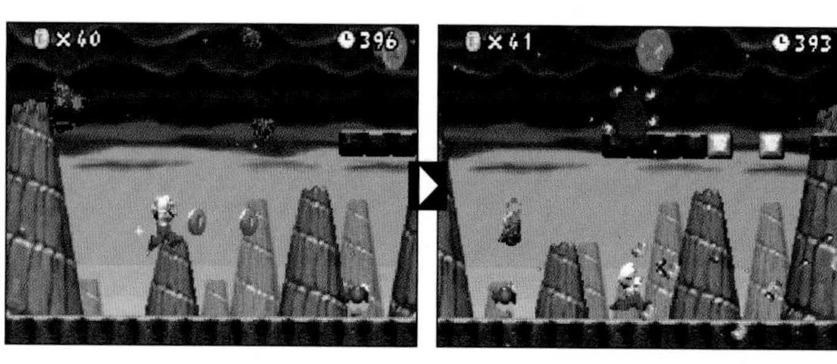

2 The volcanic ash will light the fuses of the Kab-ombs, and send them charging at you full-throttle. Stomp them as soon as they appear, even though they might be easier to evade, simply to head off a future threat.

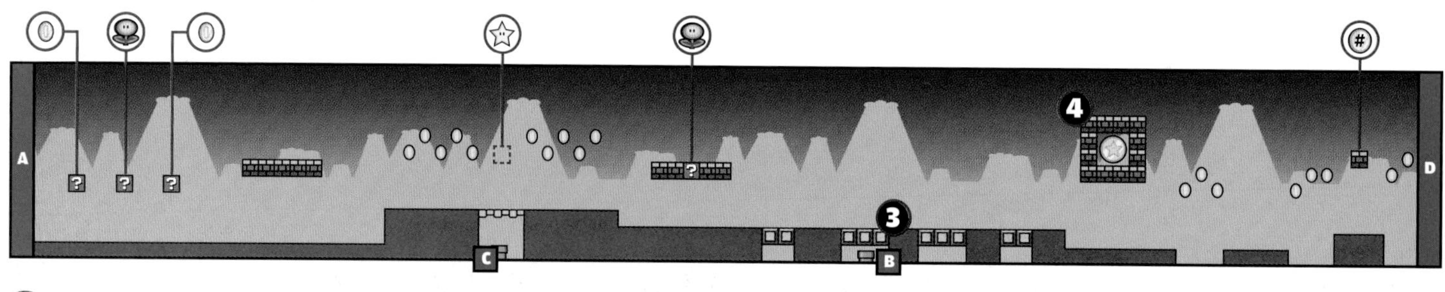

3 If you look carefully, you'll notice a tiny pipe below the blocks at point 3. If you have a Mini Mushroom, dodge for a while and let the volcanic debris smash through the blocks. You can then squeeze into a Mini Mario maze that contains a Star Coin.

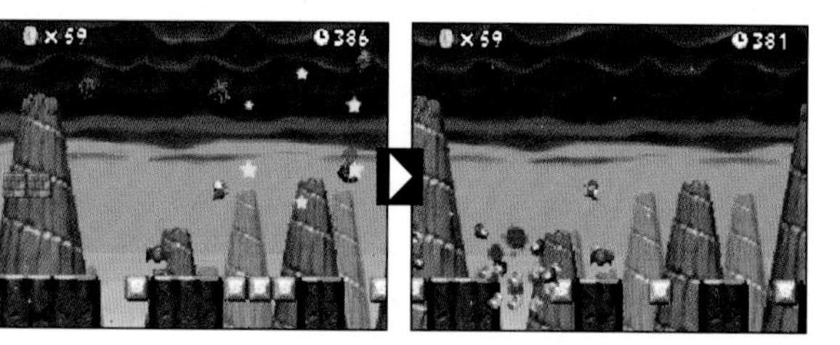

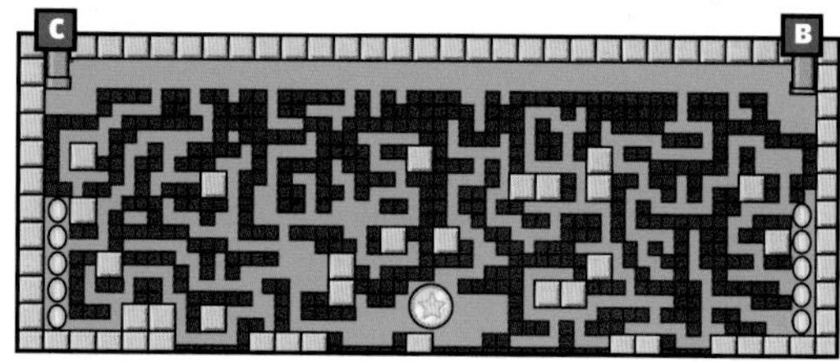

4 The Star Coin at point 4 is surrounded by blocks that Mario can't destroy, but that the falling rocks can. Wait under the coin and let the volcano do your dirty work.

5 Volcanic rain will disintegrate the platform at point 5 as you cross it. Try to stomp the Kab-ombs early, wait for the debris to abate briefly, then make a frantic running leap to the top of the flagpole.

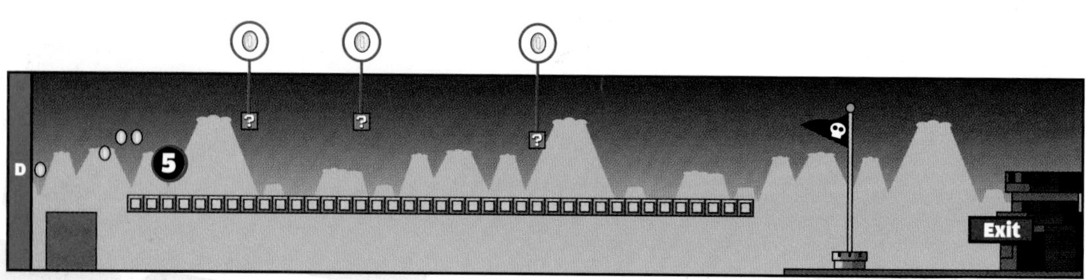

World 8 Tower 2

1 That serpentine green platform thing has returned! As a general rule, stay toward the front of it, since it's easier to fall back to dodge an obstacle than it is to run forward.

2 The platform proceeds vertically through much of this stage, and it can be tricky to keep up with it. As soon as it takes a vertical turn, leap onto its head.

3 Red-Coin Ring

The trick to this one is to pick the right moment to jump into the ring. Don't leap for it early; wait for the platform to pass underneath the ring, heading left. Its course will then take you directly under all of the coins except the last one, which you'll need to jump to the right for, then reverse direction in midair to land safely on your platform.

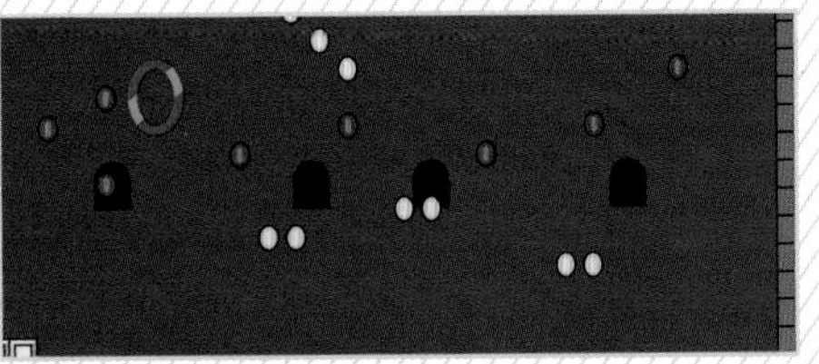

4 Jump onto the upper ledge at point 4 so you can grab the Star Coin, and run through the fire rods to catch up with your platform at the end. When you're back on your platform, jump onto its head immediately, or you'll take damage by a spiked ball that rolls down from above.

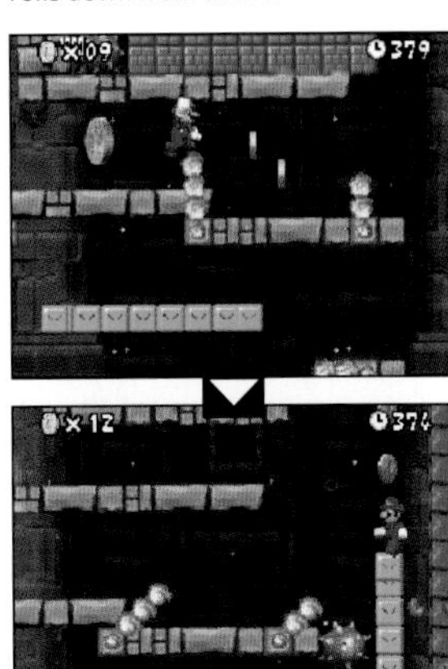

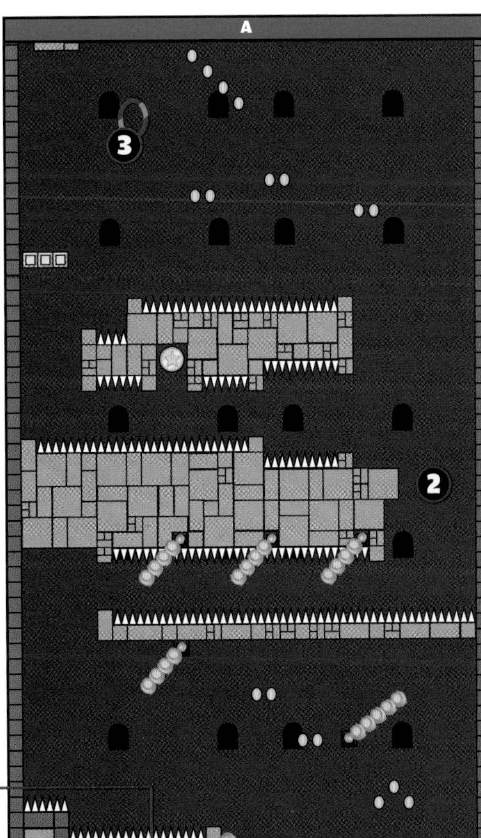

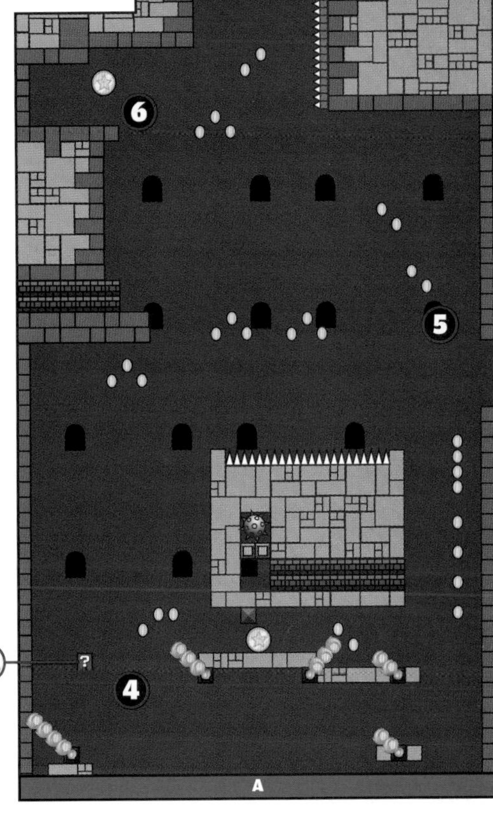

5 When block pieces begin to rain onto your platform, you know a spiked ball is coming. Stay at the head of your platform to avoid it, until your platform turns toward the ball. At that point you'll want to be one or two segments away from the head.

6 When the spiked ball falls onto your platform, jump over it and then immediately leap onto the ledge where the Star Coin is. Long-jump from there back onto your ride. Make your way swiftly to its head, or you'll be sunk.

Boss

Bowser Jr. will use every trick in the book during your final duel. He'll charge at you and then enter his shell (it's still easy to jump over him), he'll throw fast-moving Koopa shells, and he'll shake up his pattern by jumping after he's taken two hits. He hasn't used that last trick in a while, so don't get suckered into jumping after the second hit!

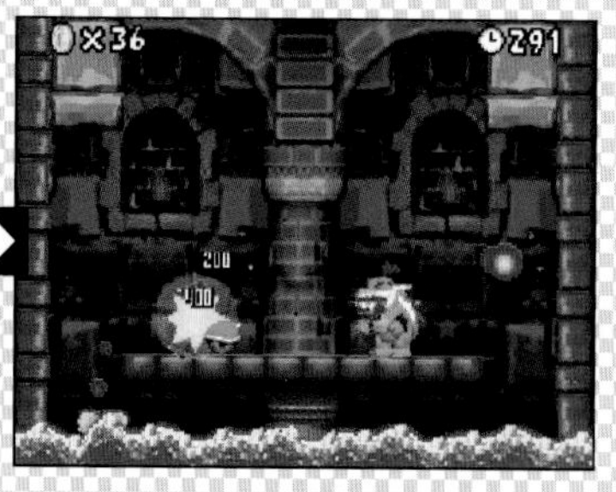

Bowser's Castle

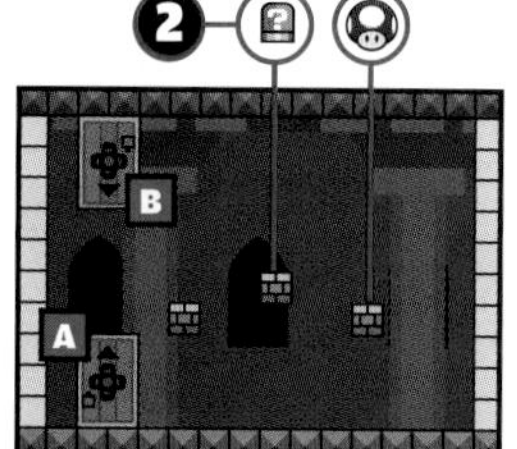

1 Pause at point 1 for a second, and wait till the fireball pops up from the lava and begins to fall. Then jump through the coins and dash over the gaps.

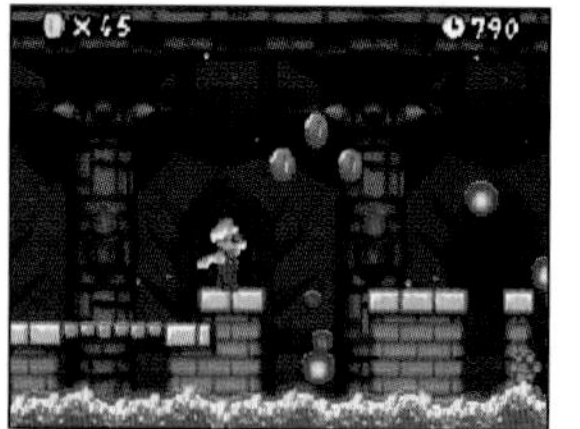

2 Flip the Castle

The ? Switch at point 2 is the first of several switches that will flip the entire castle upside down. This is disorienting, but you can keep your bearings by remembering that the floor is purple and the ceiling is blue. Our maps are presented with the orientation at which you first enter each area.

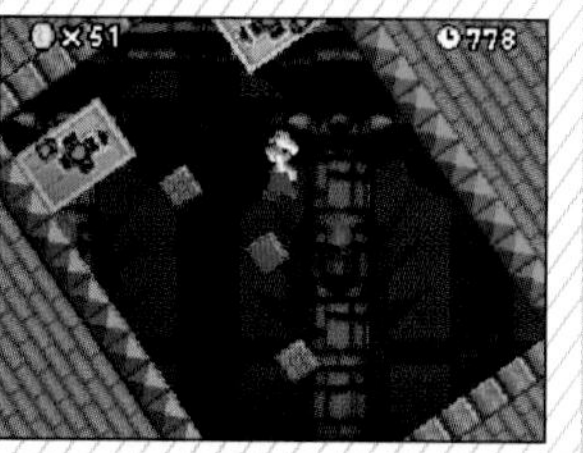

3 Watch out for the torches in this room; when you see sparks, they're about to fire. Do a long jump over a torch to reach door C, or you'll smack into a block. You'll need to use the same trick in the next area to get under the Whomp and hit the ? Switch.

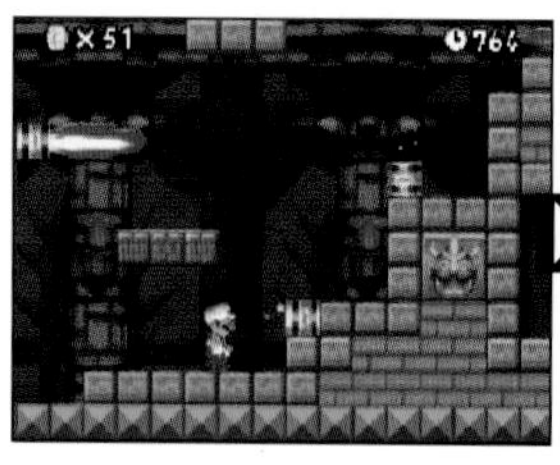

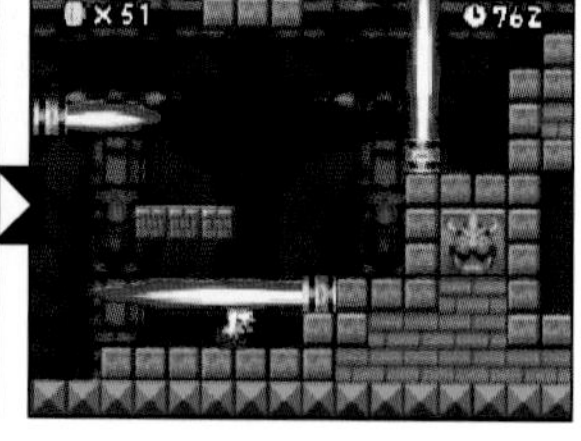

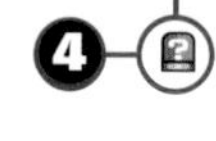

4 Activate the Platform

Before you step through E, make your way to the far-left end of the level and hit the ? Switch to make a platform appear below door G. After completing tip 6, you can use that platform to reach a Star Coin.

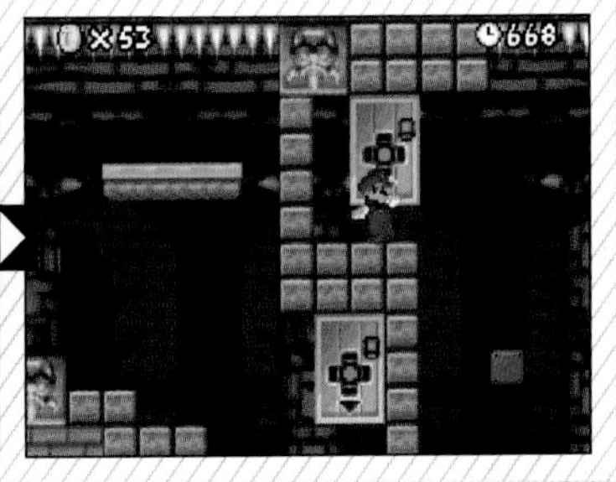

5

The torch in front of door E never shuts off, so you'll need to do a dash-ing crouch to slide beneath it.

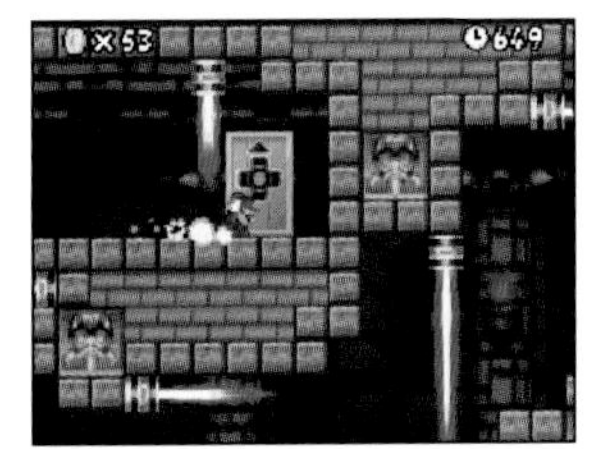

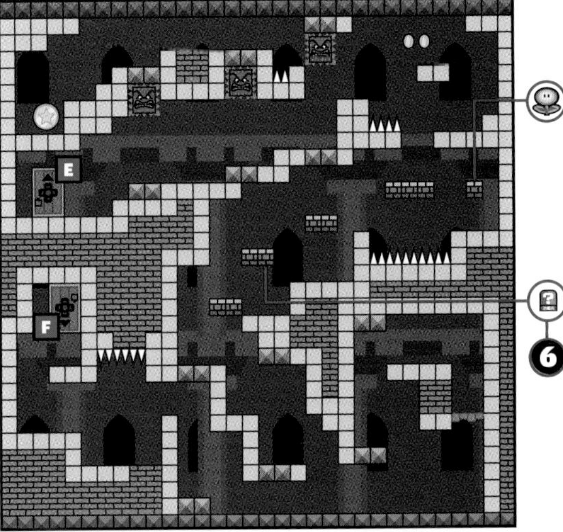

6 Flip the Castle Again

The Star Coin and Thwomps will remain in the upper-left corner regardless of the castle's orientation, so grab the coin now to save time, or wait till after you hit the ? Switch if you're having trouble with the rhythm. When the castle flips, make your way to door F, where you can ride the platform you generated in tip 4 to reach the room that holds the second Star Coin.

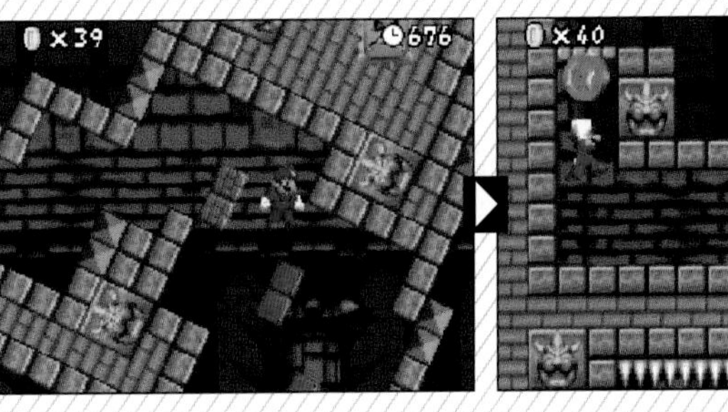

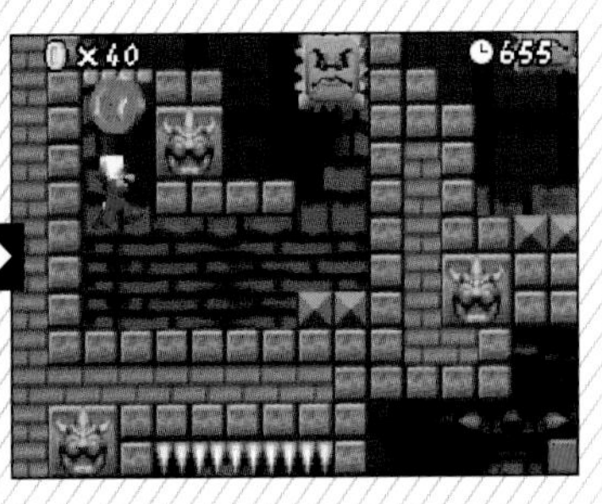

7

If you've muted your DS, turn the volume up now. In this final stretch of the castle, you'll be presented with multiple platforms upon which to travel. If you hear a buzzer as you progress to the right, you've chosen the wrong route and the area will repeat endlessly until you get it right. In the first section, dash across the lowest level; you'll hear the happy chime of a correct selection.

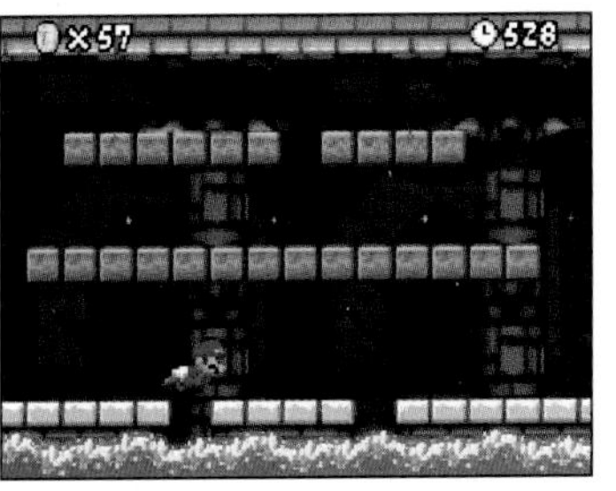

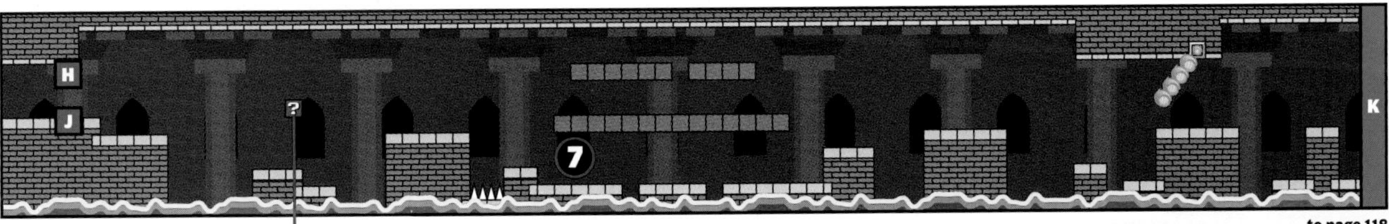

to page 118

from page 117

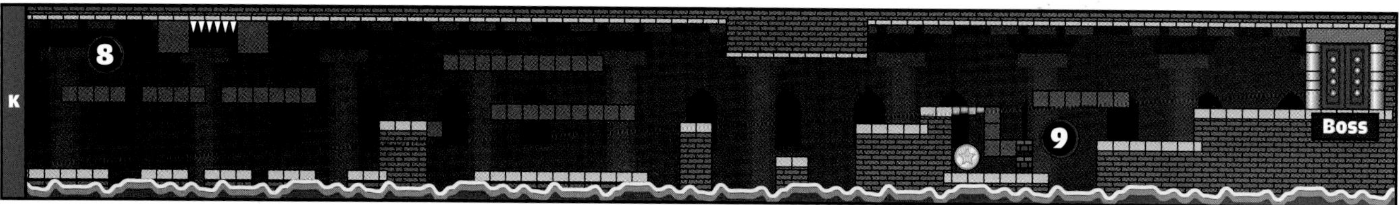

8

This time, take the high road and dash over the gaps. You're not done yet, though; drop into the next section, step off the block onto the floor, then jump up so you're on the center platform. You should hear a second chime as you run over that platform. If you chose the wrong route, you'll end up back at point 8.

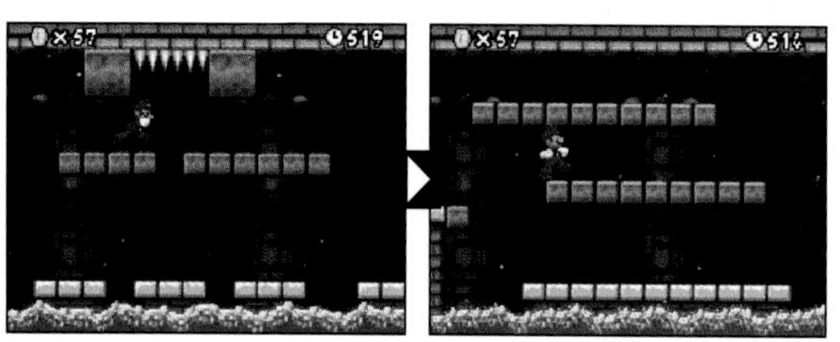

9

Ground-Pound the blocks, then get a running start from the ledge where the boss door is, dash over the lava, and crouch to slide under the gap to the final Star Coin.

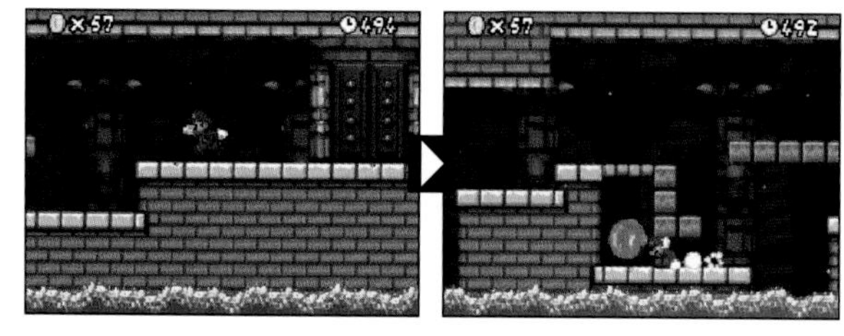

Boss

In the final battle to save the princess, you'll face both Bowser Jr. and a freshly resurrected Bowser Sr. It's virtually impossible to get past Bowser Sr. without defeating his son, even if you're willing to take a hit doing it. Instead, focus on besting Bowser Jr. by kicking back his Koopa shells while dodging his dad's heat-seeking fireballs. When you jump on the fallen Bowser Jr., make sure the bounce won't knock you into a fireball!

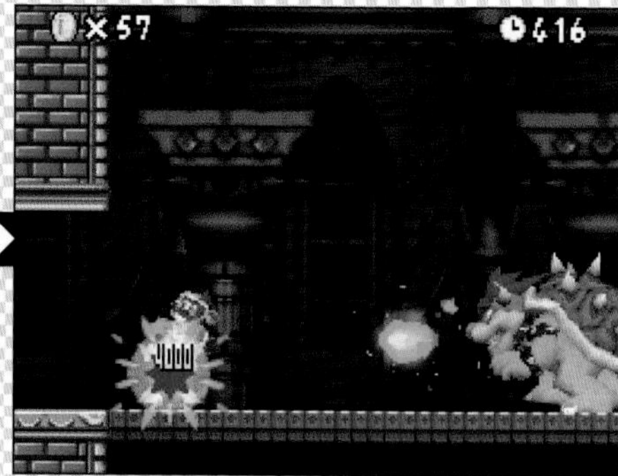

Try to stay on the left side of Bowser Jr. so you'll have more room to stomp his shells and kick them back. The blue fireballs will follow you, but they move slowly and cannot change direction if you jump over them. Treat this as a standard Bowser Jr. fight—don't let the elder Bowser's presence psych you out.

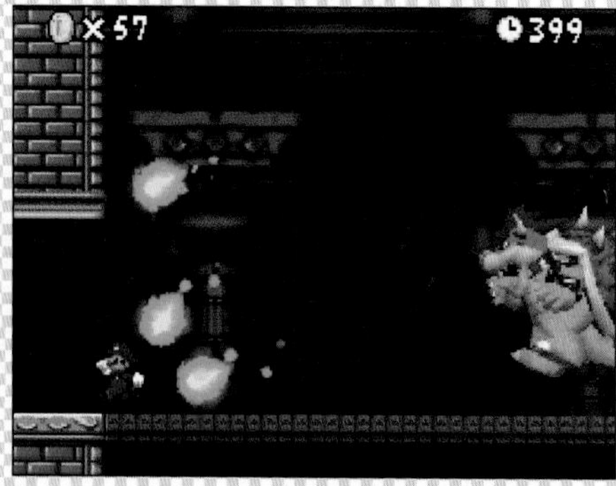

After you defeat Bowser Jr., his father will take off the kid gloves. He now has two attacks: firing three heat-seeking blue fireballs, and filling the screen with normal red fireballs. They're easier to dodge if you're farther back, but you'll need to stay fairly close to your foe so you can dash to the skull switch when Bowser jumps.

You'll know Bowser's about to make a big jump because he'll crouch slightly to build up strength. That's your cue to begin dashing! Don't ever try to jump over him or dash under his little jumps; he'll knock you back every time.

Multiplayer & Minigames

Mario vs. Luigi

Mario and Luigi often set their sibling rivalry aside to work together, but they're a pair of scrappers at heart. Have at it in this one-on-one version of the single-player game.

Wireless Connection

When you play Mario vs. Luigi mode, you'll have the choice of playing against another New Super Mario Bros. owner or an opponent who doesn't have a copy of the game. The game loads more quickly if both players have a copy, but is identical otherwise. The player who starts the game can choose the mode, select his preferred character (Mario and Luigi have the same set of abilities), and wait for a friend to show up. If your opponent has his own copy of the game, he should select the same mode and choose the opposite brother to make a connection. An opponent who doesn't have a copy of the game will need to choose the DS Download Play option from the Nintendo DS menu screen. When both players have agreed to compete, the player who started the game can select the rules of engagement.

Mario vs. Luigi — It's brother vs. brother in a race for stars!

Collect Stars to Win

The goal of Mario vs. Luigi is to collect the stars that appear throughout the stage at timed intervals. But that isn't the only way to win–if a series of unfortunate "accidents" should happen to whittle away your brother's remaining lives, you'll win by default.

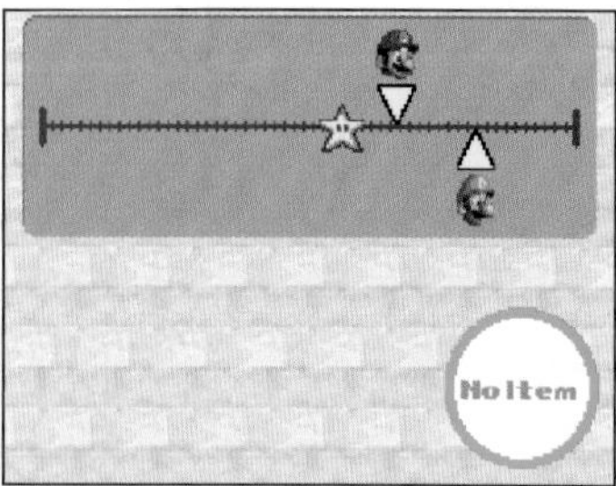

The levels in this mode loop endlessly, so it will often be easier to reach the right side of an area by running to the left. The automap shows the positions of both players and all of the stars on the field.

Dish Out Some Brotherly Love

A star isn't lost to you just because your brother got to it first. Any time you damage your brother, he'll drop one of his stars and you can claim it for yourself. Don't dash madly after every new star–clever players should hit ? Blocks or accumulate coins (you need only eight) to win power-ups that will give you an offensive advantage. The techniques listed below are among the best ways to hurt your bro.

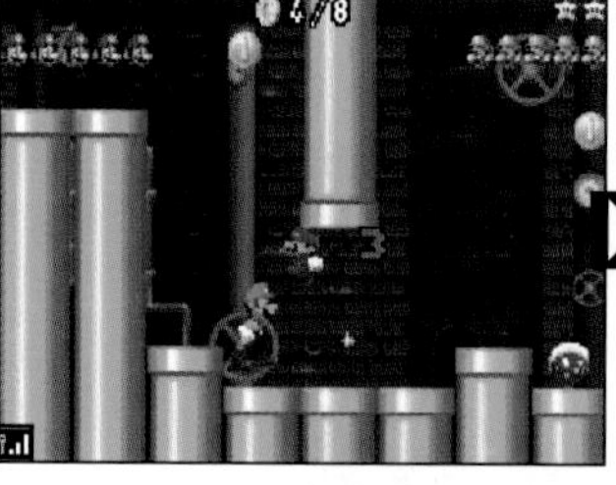

Hit from Below

Jump into a block your brother is standing on—you'll knock him over and liberate a star.

Jump from Above

Mario and Luigi are as vulnerable to stomps and Ground Pounds as any normal foes.

Fire Flower

The Fire Flower is the ultimate weapon in Mario vs. Luigi mode. If you can trap your opponent in a tight spot, you can blast him repeatedly to knock all of his stars away.

Other Enemies

Well-aimed Koopa shells and Bob-ombs can knock out a star *and* deal damage to the brothers. In this mode, the shells of blue Koopas will allow you to become Shell Mario or Shell Luigi.

Starman

The Starman does double duty, allowing you to damage your brother with a touch and protecting you from any damage he might cause.

Size Matters

Mega Mario (or Luigi) can knock stars free with ease. The Mini Mushroom will allow you to squeeze through tight spots and dodge certain attacks more easily.

Battle Levels

From pipe mazes to ice floes, terrain is a significant factor.

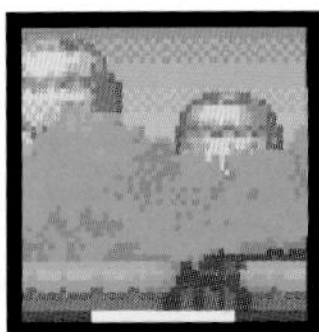

Grass

This is a typically bucolic World-1 level. The ? Blocks and coins are easy to find, and there are no particular perils to worry about . . . except for your brother's fratricidal tendencies.

Stars often spawn in dangerous spots in this level, and you may need to make a leap of faith into a walled pit and Wall-Jump out. This can be suicide if your brother is waiting above, so either let him go for it first, or wait till he's far enough away that you're assured of a safe return trip.

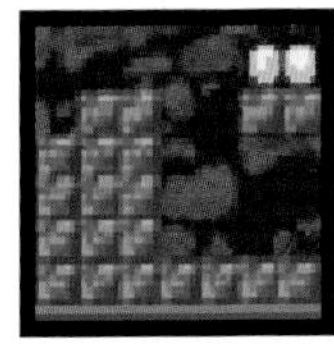

Bricks

This level is made up of blocks that large characters can smash through, giving powered-up characters a big advantage. The ? Blocks don't contain power-ups, so collecting coins is key.

The moving platforms on this stage will let you get above the ceiling, which is a great way to run through the stage quickly or beat a hasty retreat. Getting powered-up is vital, so fight hard for coins, and force the power up out of its block. Power-ups earned from coins fall from the top of the screen—make sure your brother isn't around to steal them!

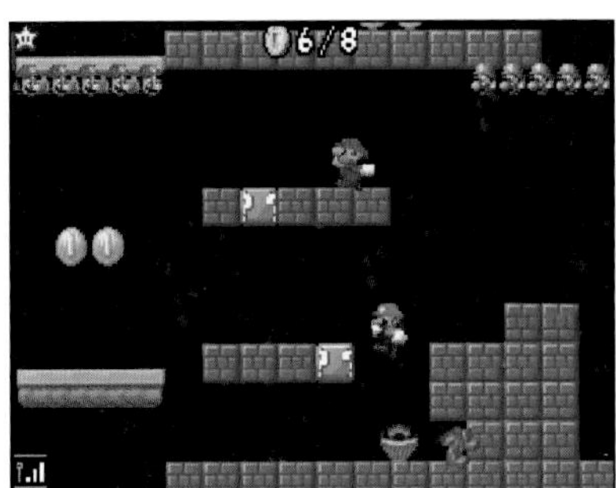

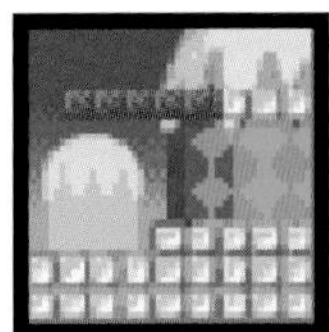

Ice

This is one slippery stage! Although you're probably used to maneuvering on ice, it's a different story when your brother is hurling fireballs or Koopa shells your way.

This level scrolls higher than the others, and there are plenty of coins hiding in the sky. The Spin Block is key, since stars often spawn above it and you can glide into several coins up there. (Getting above your brother for a spinning drill stomp is pretty nice, too.) The stage's other highlight is the blue-shelled Koopas—stomp them for an easy Shell Mario (or Luigi) power-up.

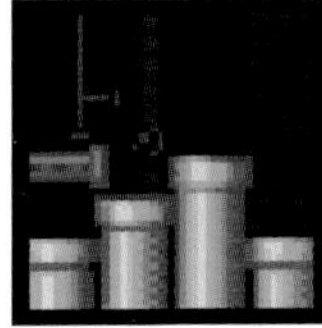

Pipes

This level is composed entirely of pipes. Only the red and yellow pipes can be used to reach other parts of the stage; the green ones are all solid.

If you're being chased in this level, going through a pipe will help you escape, since it makes you temporarily invulnerable. If your opponent follows, you can go right back through the same pipe, and be ready with a trap if he's foolish enough to tail you again.

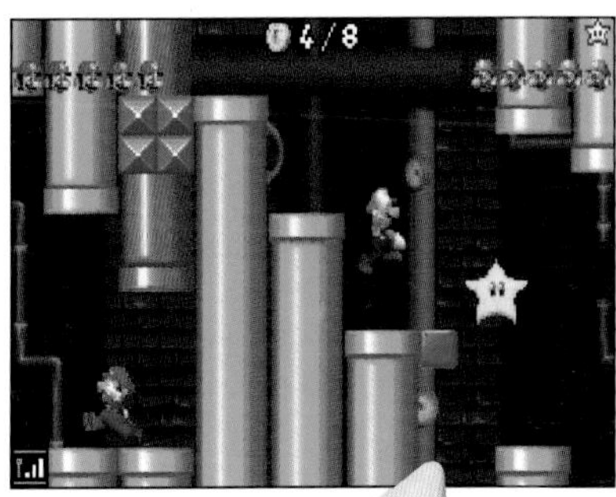

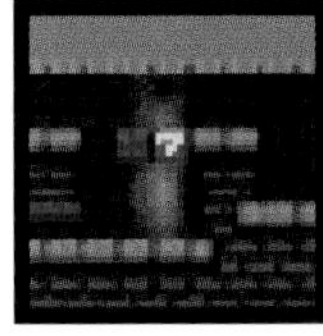

Fortress

With the ceiling constantly pounding downward, this stage is often less about the stars and more about just staying alive!

Beware of the Bob-ombs as you take refuge from the ceiling—they can be dangerous if you're trapped with one in a small alcove. They're powerful but unreliable weapons when used against your brother—the Fire Flower is a better choice, because you can use it to prevent him from reaching safe spots. The Mini Mushroom has its uses, too; it offers good maneuverability and lets you enter a special part of the stage.

Minigames

The Minigames mode offers more than 20 simple touch-screen activities. Challenge them solo or use them as the basis of a minigame tournament for up to four players.

Single-Player

Select Minigames from the main menu screen. You'll see a list of the categories on the left, and the icons of individual games on the right. Make your selection with the stylus to bring up a detailed description of the game. Not every game can be played solo, but there are a few single-player exclusives in the mix. There are no NPC opponents, so your goal is merely to top previous high scores.

Vs. Battle

Choose Vs. Battle to set up a group or join one that a friend has already established. You can then set the terms of the tourney: how many points you wish to play to, how many points each game is worth, and how the games are selected. You can allow the computer to choose the games randomly, or select them individually each time—the player with the lowest score will always get to make the choice. In Vs. Battle, the final category of games will be "1 on 1" instead of "Variety."

Action

Race the clock solo or test your stylus skills against your friends.

Snowball Slalom

Use the stylus to roll the snowball to the finish line as quickly as possible. Trouble is, the snowball gathers mass as it rolls. An obstacle that you can avoid easily when it's small poses a major challenge when it fills up half the screen. Use the top screen to get a preview of the terrain ahead, and plan your movements well in advance! Avoid bouncing off walls, as the rebound will dampen your forward momentum.

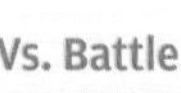

Vs. Battle

In multiplayer races, all players race at the same time. Try to get ahead of your opponents early so you can slow them down or force them into obstacles.

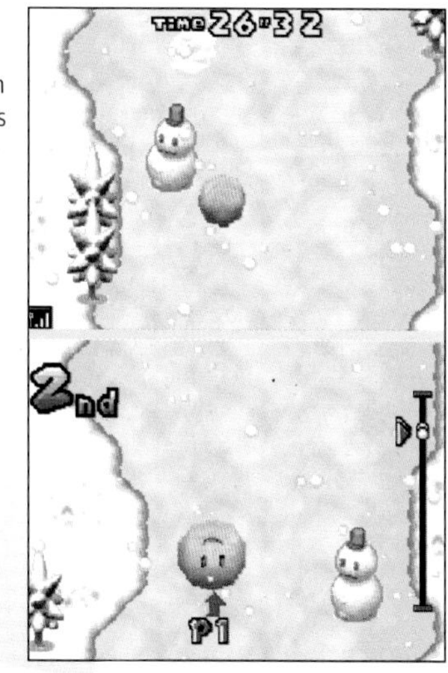

Lakitu Launch Single-Player Only

Position your stylus on the spiky ball in the lower-screen slingshot, and drag it back. When you release the stylus, the spiked ball will go flying into the upper screen. The farther you pull back, the farther the ball will fly. When the countdown clock hits zero, you'll earn points equal to the number of balls in the baskets.

Once the ball leaves the slingshot, a new one will be ready to go, so don't waste time watching them roll around the rim when you could be firing more shots. Try to focus your shots at one basket so it will fill up and sink to the lower screen, making it easier to hit.

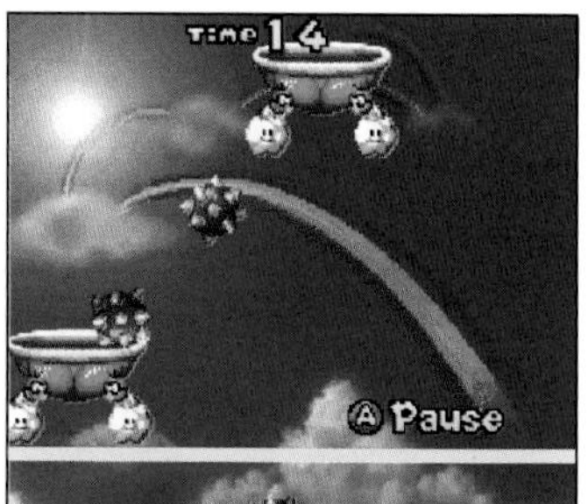

Vs. Lakitu Launch Vs. Battle Only

This game is similar to Lakitu Launch, except each player has his own basket, and you'll give points to your opponent if you land a spiky ball in the wrong one. As in the single-player game, the ball in your slingshot is replaced as soon as it's fired, so you'll want to unleash a rapid-fire flurry of spiked balls instead of carefully aiming each one and watching them bounce around the rims.

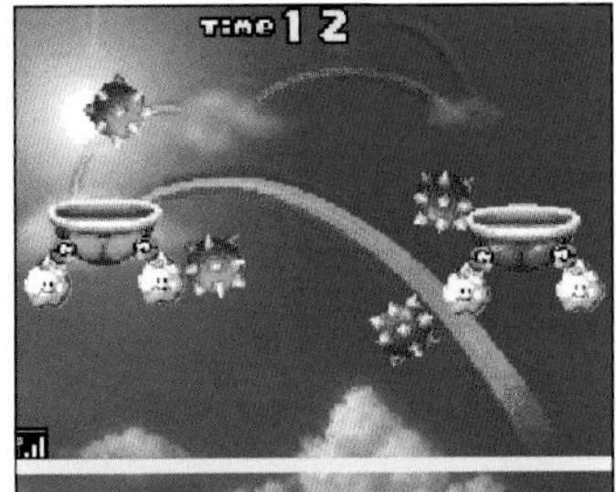

Whack-a-Monty

Tap the screen with the stylus or your finger whenever a Monty Mole pops out of a hole. You'll get one point for each Monty you whack, but you'll lose three each time you hit Luigi by mistake. The game lasts 30 seconds and starts slowly, but the Montys will pick up speed as the game progresses.

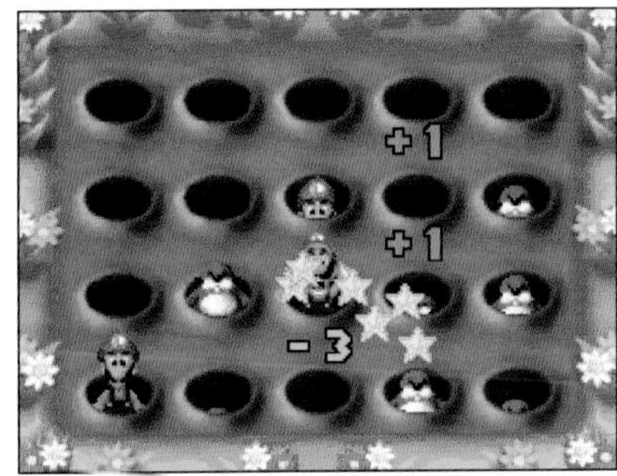

Vs. Battle

When there is more than one player, everyone will compete on the same screen, trying to hit the same Montys first. Don't get flustered and accidentally hit a Luigi!

Balloon Racing

Blow into the Nintendo DS microphone slowly and steadily to send Yoshi progressively higher. Keep an eye on the screen so you can stop blowing when you approach the Shy Guys, and wait for them to pass. You'll lose a balloon if you bump into an enemy, and you have only one balloon to spare before you lose the race.

Vs. Battle

Multiple players compete in the same race at the same time.

Danger Bob-omb! Danger! Single-Player Only

Use the stylus to guide the Bob-omb out of the path of Bowser's fiery breath and the constant volleys of bullets. The longer you last, the more points you'll earn.

There are two ways to move the Bob-omb. You can stab it with your stylus and drag it around the screen, or you can poke your stylus at the position you want the Bob-omb to run to, and it will run straight there. The latter option offers less precision, but prevents the screen from being blocked by the stylus.

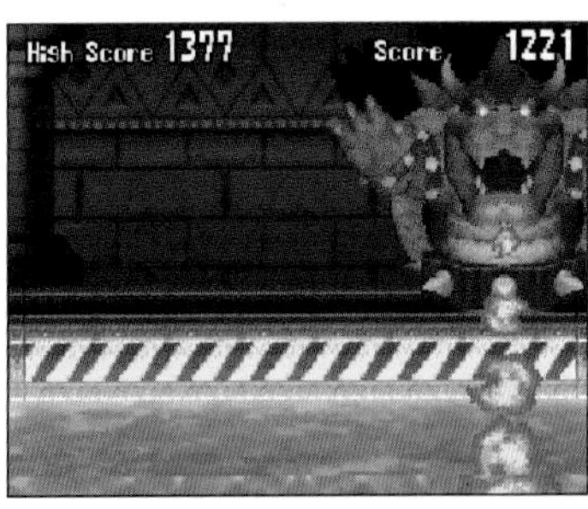

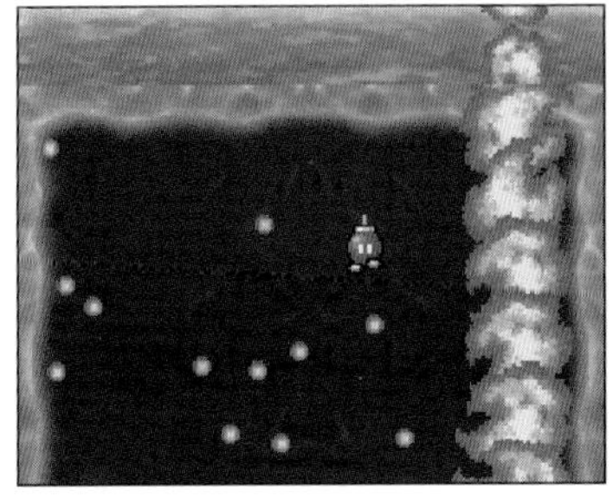

Keep an eye on the top screen to see where Bowser will unleash his next column of fiery breath.

Run Bob-omb! Run! Vs. Battle Only

The multiplayer version of Danger Bob-omb! Danger! puts all the Bob-ombs on the same field of fire. Use the stylus not just to guide your Bob-omb to safety, but also to drive it into other players' Bob-ombs and knock them into bullets. A player is eliminated from the game when his Bob-omb dies three times.

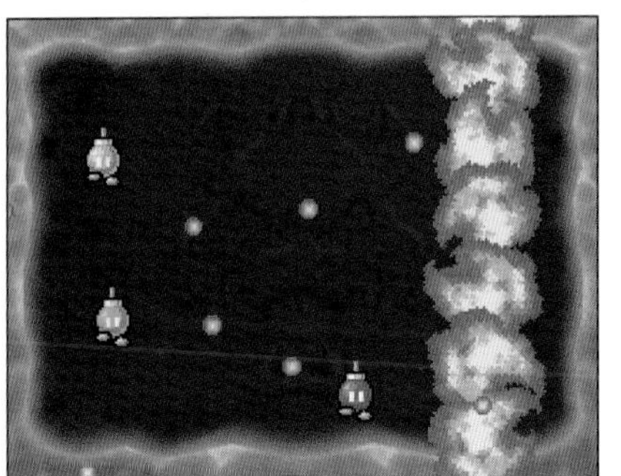

Snowball Slam Vs. Battle Only

It takes at least two players to have a snowball fight, and larger groups will be divided into teams. Tap the stylus in the upper part of the touch screen to throw snowballs, which will travel in a straight line from your character through the reticle. To move your character, either drag him with the stylus or tap a destination in the lower part of the screen. You'll run straight there.

You'll score five points every time you hit an opponent, and one for nailing the snowmen. You can hold only 10 snowballs at once, and if you run out you'll need to restock by running to a snowman (or its remains). Try to count your opponents' shots and be ready to nail them when they run out and have to reload.

Puzzles Test your memory, reflexes, and reasoning skills with these brainteasers.

Wanted!

At the beginning of each round a Wanted sign will appear on the top screen, and your objective is to find the depicted character on the bottom screen. If you find your man, you'll get five seconds added to the clock. If you guess wrong, you'll lose 10 seconds. Try to earn as much time as possible in the easy early rounds!

In later rounds your target may be moving, obstructed, or both. In such cases, wait for a clear shot; wasting a second is a small price to pay to avoid a 10-second penalty. If your target scrolls off the side of the screen, it will reappear on the opposite side.

Vs. Battle

Multiple players compete to find the wanted man first. There are 60 seconds on the clock, and you no longer earn time bonuses or penalties. If you miss your mark, you'll lose a point instead.

Which Wiggler?

Which Wiggler? is similar to the Wanted! game. This time your goal is to match the Wiggler on the top screen to one on the bottom screen. Choosing correctly will add five seconds to your timer, and choosing wrongly will knock 10 seconds off the clock. In later stages the Wigglers will begin moving and curling into strange positions, and will have more-similar body patterns. Before you strike, make sure all four Wiggler body segments (the only part that varies) match the top-screen Wiggler exactly, including their order.

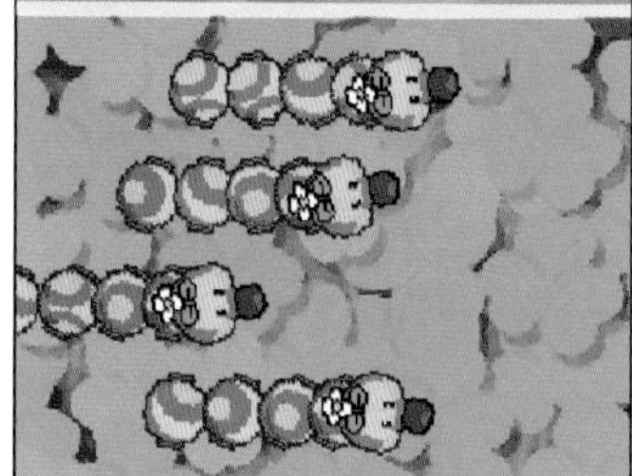

Vs. Battle

Multiple players compete to find the Wiggler first. There are 60 seconds on the clock, and you no longer earn time bonuses or penalties. If you hit the wrong Wiggler, you'll lose a point instead.

Hide and Boo Seek

Track the Boos on the bottom screen, and when the lights go out, rub their positions on the touch screen. The Boos will keep moving for a second, so assume they'll be a bit farther in the direction they were heading when the screen went dark. Use wide stylus scribbles to reveal them—there's no bonus for accuracy, and you might get lucky and expose part of one you didn't know about.

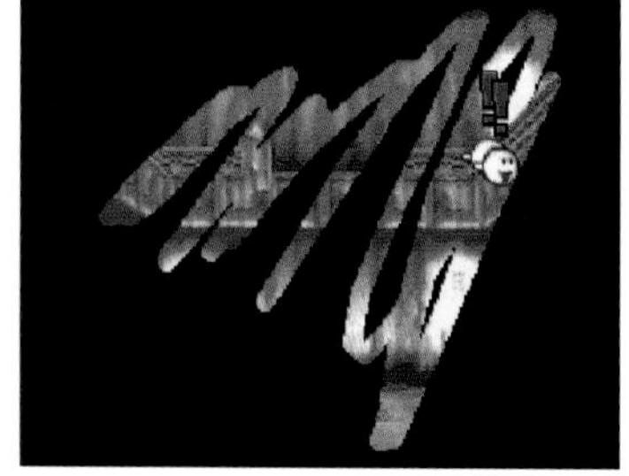

Vs. Battle

Multiple players compete on the same screen, trying to catch the greatest number of Boos. You don't need to hit them all, so focus on the largest concentrations.

Puzzle Panel

Poke a panel on the lower screen to flip that panel and all panels adjacent to it (including diagonally) to match the image on the upper screen. The number on the left shows how many moves you have to complete the puzzle, and the hearts on the right show your remaining chances—you're allowed three mistakes before the game ends. There is no time limit, so consider the consequences of your actions carefully!

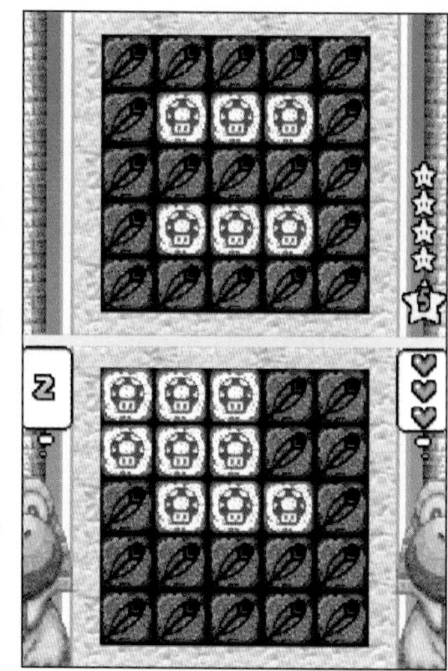

Vs. Battle

Multiple players race to complete the same puzzle first. The game continues for 60 seconds, and all of the puzzles have single-move solutions. If you choose wrong you'll lose a point, but your opponent won't get to see what you did.

Coincentration

Wario will drop 40 coins into 24 boxes, and your job is to pay careful attention to which boxes collect at least one coin. Use your stylus to tap the coin-filled boxes, which will add their coins to your total. If you hit even a single empty box, your game will end. (Usually eight boxes come up empty.) Early on, focus on clearing just one or two rows, then take your chances on the row(s) you ignored.

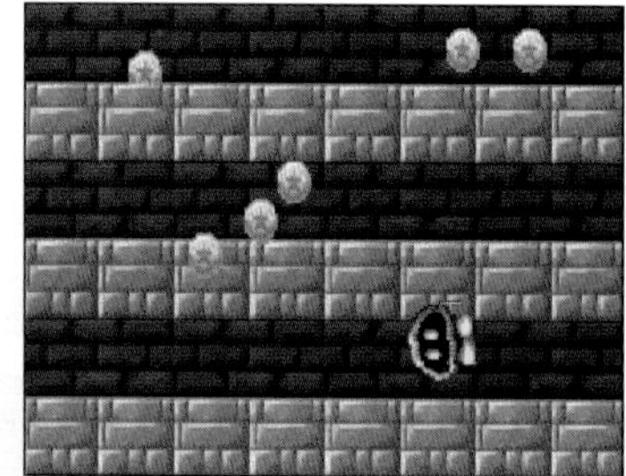

Vs. Battle

Multiple players compete on the same puzzle, taking turns picking one box each. If you pick an empty box, you'll lose two of your collected coins. You can pass once without choosing; save your pass for when the empty boxes outnumber the filled ones.

Loves Me... Vs. Battle Only

In this game players take turns plucking a flower. You're vying to pluck the last petal when it's "Loves me!" and forcing your opponent to pluck the last petal if it's "Loves me not." Each player must pluck between one and three petals during his turn. The key is to figure out early how the flower will end. Stick your opponent with four petals if it's "Loves me!" and five if it's "Loves me not."

Cards

Who knew Luigi ran a casino? These games require luck as well as wits.

Speed Vs. Battle Only

In this multiplayer game, players try to place cards that are one point higher or lower than the common cards at the top of the screen. Players can see an opponent's hand, so figure out what legal moves your opponent has, and cut him off if you can. For example, if a 7 is on the board and someone has a 6, spoil his play by dropping an 8. The first player to use all his cards will be the winner.

Picture Poker

In Picture Poker you get 10 coins with which to play a simplified version of five-card draw. After your opening hand you may bet up to five coins. Then select any cards that don't form a pair (or if none do, select all but the highest-value card) and press the Draw button to replace them. If you win, your hand will be scored based on its value and you'll get that many coins, multiplied by your bet.

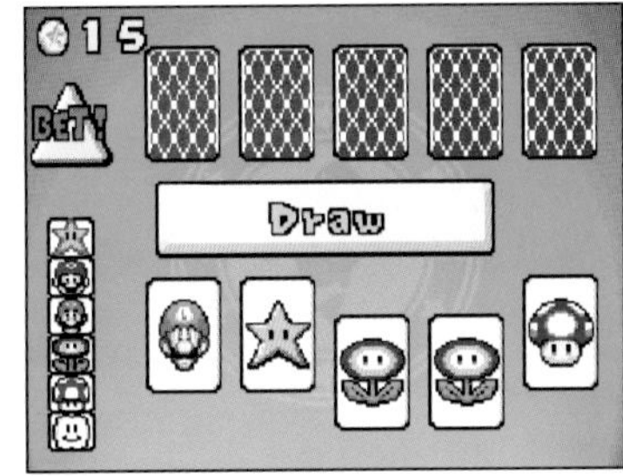

Vs. Battle

In multiplayer, you don't bet against your opponent. Instead, the difference in the values of the hands is tallied and subtracted from the loser's coin total.

Pair-a-Gone Single-Player Only

Match cards vertically, horizontally, or diagonally to remove them from the table, shift everything up two slots, and add two new cards to the bottom. You start out with 10 coins and, if you're stuck with no pairs, lose coins equal to the number of cards left on the board. Early levels have six card patterns, and every consecutive five victories will add a new face card and increase the size of the deck (as well as the potential prize purse). Try to get rid of diagonal and vertical pairs high on the board so you're left with several easy horizontal pairs late in the game.

Bob-omb Reverse Vs. Battle Only

This game is Bob-omb Othello for up to four players. The goal is to steal horizontal, vertical, and diagonal lines of opponents' Bob-ombs by surrounding them with your own Bob-ombs. Players take turn placing one Bob-omb per turn, and the score is tallied when the board is full. Don't worry about taking lots of points early in the game; stake out the outer edges for big points in the final turns.

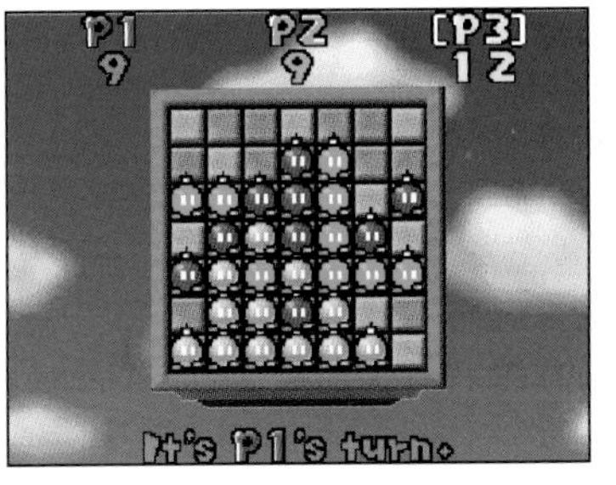

Memory Match

Luigi deals eight cards, and you have three tries to match them all by turning over two matching cards in the same turn. If you win, you'll earn nine coins; if you lose, Luigi will take three coins. After you score five consecutive victories, Luigi will add another row of cards, but he'll flip a few of them briefly to get you started.

Vs. Battle

In Vs. Battle players take turns picking cards, and each player's turn continues until a mistake is made. Pay careful attention to your opponents' turns, since you'll be able to see the cards they reveal. The player who makes the most matches will win the game.

Luigi's Thrilling Cards Vs. Battle Only

This is a multiplayer-only game you may know as "blindman's bluff." Each player is dealt only a single card, which he cannot see, but his opponents can. After a round of betting, the player with the highest card (ace being highest) will win. The strategy comes in bluffing and raising to trick your opponent into folding. If your opponent has a low card or you think you can pull off a successful bluff, tap the Raise button repeatedly to bet an additional five coins. If your opponent is holding a high card, you can fold when he raises the bet.

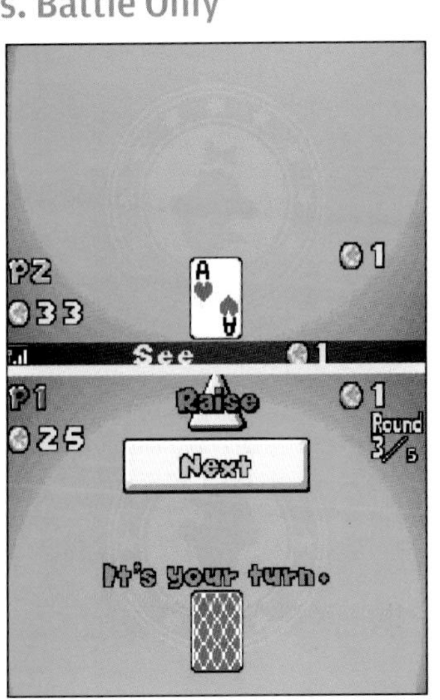

Luigi-Jack Vs. Battle Only

Luigi-Jack is like blackjack, but you don't get to see any of your opponents' starting cards; you see only the cards they gain by hitting. There is no betting—instead the winner wins coins equal to the difference in the value of the players' hands. So a player with a total of 19 will get three coins from a player with a total of 16. The prize is doubled if the winnner has a 21, and tripled if the winner has a "Luigi-Jack" (a 21 with the starting two cards). If you bust by hitting until you have more than 21, the winner will get five of your coins.

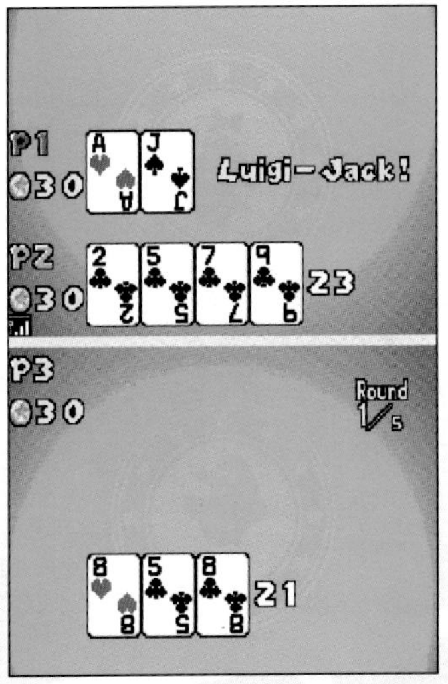

Variety & 1 on 1 This wacky assortment defies classification.

Mario's Slides Single-Player Only (Variety)

In this game, Mario's head slides down the lines, turning to take every connecting path along the way. Try to predict which line he'll come down, and draw the connecting paths necessary to guide him to the star. Draw the lines as high as you can so you'll have room and time for last-minute corrections. When Mario hits the star, he'll return to the top, and you'll have to plan an even more complicated route that takes the previous turn's connecting routes into account. After claiming five stars without hitting any Piranha Plants (Piranha Plants mean game over), you'll move on to a more difficult stage and your previous lines will be cleared. Later stages feature more-complicated routes, faster Mario heads, or even multiple Mario heads!

Vs. Mario's Slides Vs. Battle Only (1 on 1)

When two players battle at Mario Slides, the objective will change. Each screen represents one player's touch screen, and both players can draw lines only on their own sides. After player 1 guides Mario into the star, he'll reverse course and player 2 will have to guide Mario into the star on his own side. To win, you need to keep your Mario alive while doing everything you can to send him down the worst possible line for your opponent. While playing offense is fun, save most of your lines for guiding Mario to the star or your side of the board will become an incomprehensible mess.

Sort or 'Splode Single-Player Only (Variety)

Drag the Bob-ombs into the sections that match their color. Once you have 40 of a color safely corralled, those Bob-ombs will be removed, and the game will continue with more Bob-ombs coming at a progressively faster rate. If you move a Bob-omb into the wrong section or one explodes due to neglect, the game will end. If you don't have time to get a Bob-omb to its section when it begins to explode, tap it to hold off the blast.

Bob-omb Sudden Death Vs. Battle Only (1 on 1)

When there is more than one player, you compete on separate screens. You'll both try to protect your side and to endanger your opponent by sending Bob-ombs to his side of the board. Drag the Bob-ombs into the appropriately colored 10 boxes to add them to your score, and into the 5 boxes to send the little guys after your opponent.

Bounce and Trounce Single-Player Only (Variety)

You're responsible for three Marios floating in space, and they'll die if they fall through the bottom of the lower screen. A lost Mario will be replaced (so you always have three in the air), but the game will end when you lose your third one.

Keep the Marios alive by tapping their legs with your stylus to send them bouncing upward. You can direct the aim of a Mario's jump by hitting slightly to the left or right of his feet, and the goal is to direct the Marios so they stomp on the Shy Guys, which will win you a point. You won't lose a Mario if you bounce him into a Shy Guy headfirst, but the recoil will bounce Mario back down more quickly.

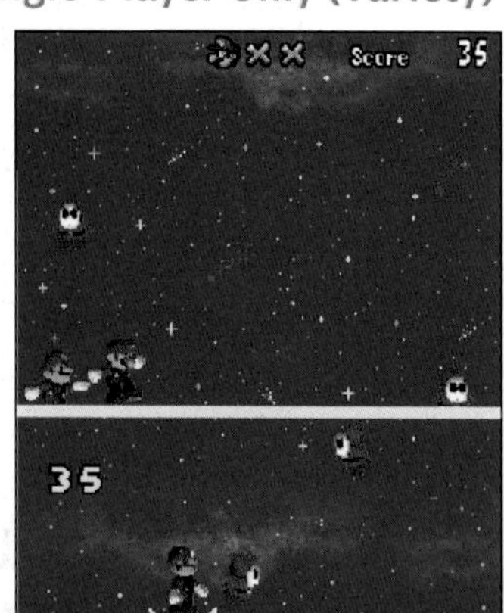

Jumping Brothers Vs. Battle Only (1 on 1)

This one-on-one version of Bounce and Trounce gives each player (Mario or Luigi) two characters to control. As before, you gain one point for landing on a Shy Guy, but you can now score two points for landing on an opponent's character. You have an infinite number of Marios and Luigis, but you'll lose five points each time one falls through the bottom of the screen. The key to success is to master the subtle art of hitting your characters so they bounce in the direction you want; hit them high on the lower screen and target your opponent's characters on the upper screen, where their trajectory is not likely to change. The game ends when the timer runs out.

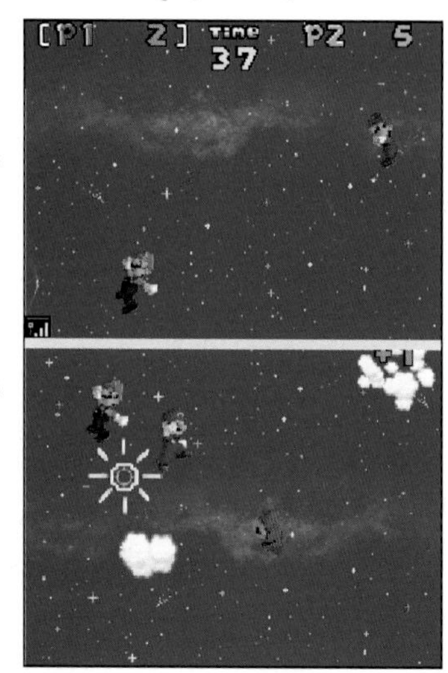

Bob-omb Squad Single-Player Only (Variety)

Use the stylus to drag the slingshot back, and release it to hit the Bob-ombs as they parachute into your garden. If you can hit multiple Bob-ombs with one projectile, the score will double for each successive Bob-omb hit. If you hit a Lakitu, you'll destroy all of the Bob-ombs on both screens, but will score only 100 points per Bob-omb. You'll lose the game if four Bob-ombs slip through to your garden.

When a Bob-omb nears your garden, you can nail it easily by pulling your slingshot bullet behind it and letting go—you can't miss then! Always aim for the lowest Bob-omb, not just to stay alive, but because you'll probably hit all sorts of Bob-ombs behind it for big points.

Lakitu Launch Vs. Battle Only (1 on 1)

In the one-on-one slingshot game, you try to outscore your opponent by shooting down as many Lakitus as you can. As with the Bob-ombs in Bob-omb Squad, the points double if you can shoot down multiple targets in a row. There's a 1,000-point bonus for hitting a Lakitu that's holding a star, but only the player whose screen the star lands on will get the points. If a star-holding Lakitu appears on your side of the screen, drag the slingshot bullet directly behind the Lakitu and release it for a point-blank kill.

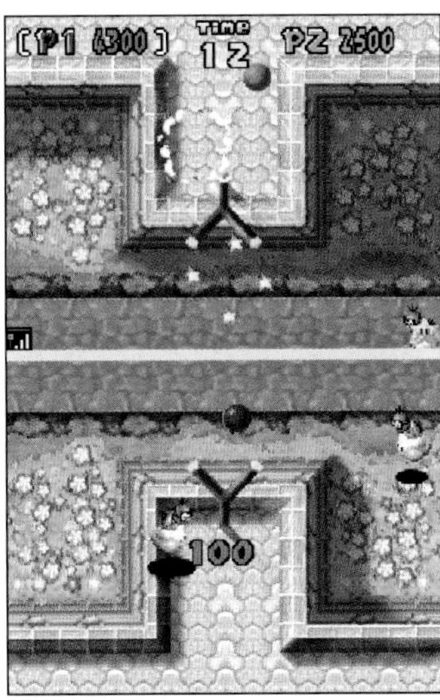

Trampoline Time Single-Player Only (Variety)

Use your stylus to draw lines below Mario, creating a trampoline that will bounce him upward. There's already a big trampoline at the bottom, but it will work only three times and you should save it for emergencies. If you let three Marios fall, you'll lose the game.

The goal is not simply to keep the Marios alive, but to bounce them into the open door on either the upper or lower screen. Angle your lines and draw your trampolines at varying heights to bounce the Marios toward the targeted exit. Smaller trampolines will bounce Mario higher than large ones, but there's a strict one-Mario-per-trampoline limit. If two Marios are together, draw two trampolines; otherwise the second Mario will shoot right through the trampoline!

Jumping Sudden Death Vs. Battle Only (1 on 1)

This game is similar to Jumping Brothers, but the goal is now merely to keep your characters alive. There are no Shy Guys to stomp or points to earn, but you can complicate matters for your opponent by stomping his characters in the head and driving them closer to the spikes. The first player to lose three lives loses the game.

Bob-omb Trampoline Vs. Battle Only (1 on 1)

Use your stylus to move a large orange trampoline under Bob-ombs that are bouncing from screen to screen. A Bob-omb caught in the dead center of the trampoline will bounce higher, but one that hits a corner of the trampoline will bounce off at an angle and may be harder for your opponent to catch. More Bob-ombs will be added as the game progresses, so making them bounce to varying heights and angles will make it harder for your opponent to keep up. The player who misses five Bob-ombs will lose the game.

Vs. Trampoline Time Vs. Battle Only (1 on 1)

The one-on-one version of Trampoline Time doesn't have any destination doors. Instead the goal is to send Mario to his doom . . . but on your opponent's side of the screen. Draw trampolines of varying directions as early as you can to bounce multiple Marios into your opponent's screen at the same time, causing maximum confusion. The game will end when one player lets three Marios fall.

Vs. Pair-a-Gone Vs. Battle Only (1 on 1)

Vs. Pair-a-Gone plays the same as the single-player version, except the game is now timed and the cards you remove are sent straight to your opponent's deck. Forget planning in advance; clear your pairs from bottom to top as quickly as you can spot them to stay a step ahead of your opponent. After 60 seconds, the player with the most cards in his deck will lose.

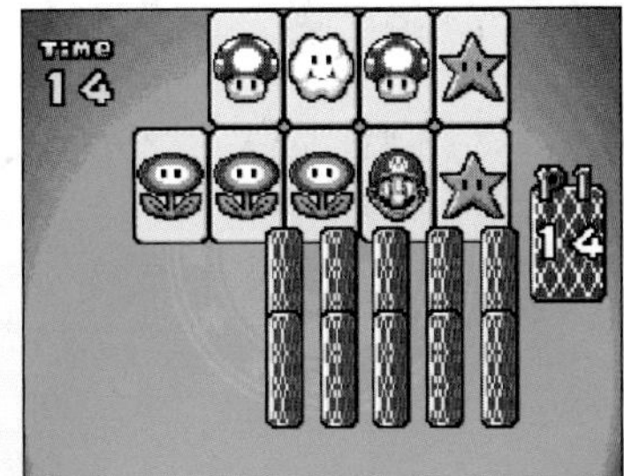

Toad's Secrets & Tricks

There are a few bonuses hidden in New Super Mario Bros. To unlock them all, you'll have to meet the conditions laid out below.

Play as Luigi

After watching the ending, save your game at the prompt. Look carefully at the wallpaper behind "The End" on the lower screen—you'll see the secret code to play as Luigi.

To play as Luigi, select your saved game, hold down the L and R Buttons, and press A to confirm your selection.

Special Background Patterns

When you load a saved file in which you've already beaten the game, you'll discover a new blue Toad house at the beginning of World 1. Inside are four background patterns for the lower screen that you can purchase with extra Star Coins. The fifth and final background will appear for sale when you've cleared every Star Coin sign in the eight worlds.

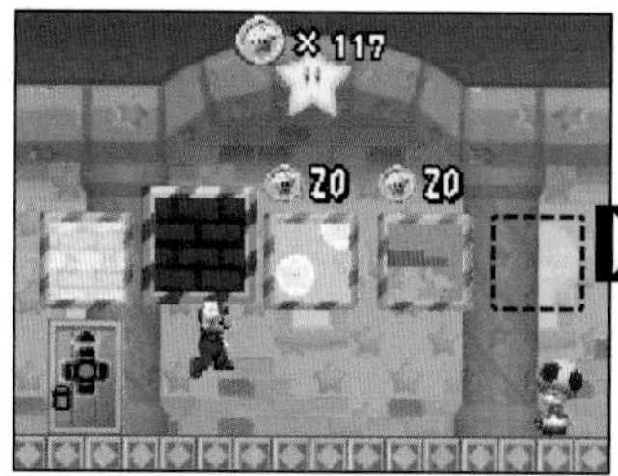

Unlimited Toad-House Items

When you load a saved game in which you've cleared every level in the game, including all of the lettered bonus levels, Toad houses will no longer disappear after you take their items (with the exception of the ones that appear based only on your timer; see below). It's an all-you-can-eat Mega Mushroom buffet!

Extra Lives and Toad Houses

When you've burned through all the Toad houses or run out of lives, here are a few tips to give you a second chance at finding what you need.

Extra Toad Houses!

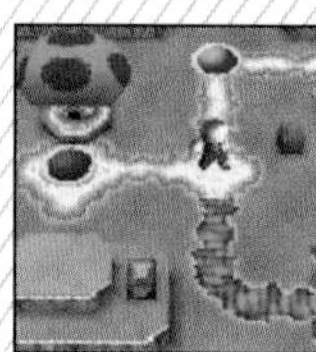

When you jump onto an end-of-level flagpole when the last two digits of your countdown timer are the same (but not zero), a new Toad house will appear! To get the Toad house you want, consult the chart below. However, this will not work if you've already activated a Toad house.

Countdown Timer Ending	
11	Red Toad House
22	Red Toad House
33	Red Toad House
44	Green Toad House
55	Green Toad House
66	Green Toad House
77	Orange Toad House
88	Orange Toad House
99	Orange Toad House

Follow the Red Winged ? Blocks

When you need a power-up boost, return to World 1 and replay the stages where the Red Winged ? Blocks are hovering. You can get great power-ups from the blocks and beat the stages easily.

Collect Infinite 1-Ups

At several spots in the game, some well-timed jumping or a cleverly executed plan can create an infinite 1-Up loop. You can rack up 99 lives in a matter of minutes!

World 1-4	page 22
World 2-2	page 29
World 2-4	page 33
World 4-5	page 58
World 7-5	page 98